IN MEPHISTO WE TRUST

REBORN

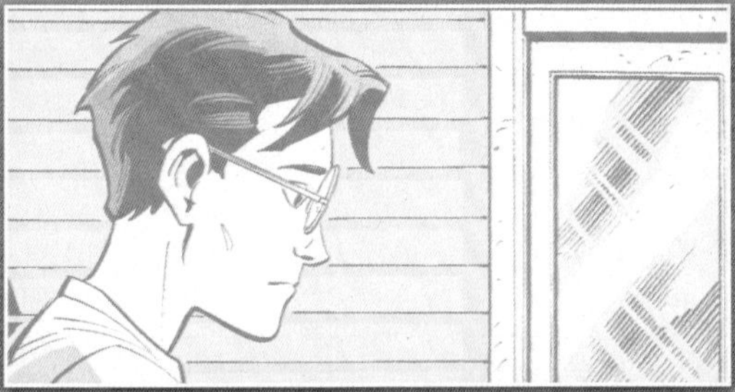

HEROES REBORN: PETER PARKER, THE AMAZING SHUTTERBUG

MARC **BERNARDIN** WRITER
RON **LIM** PENCILER (pp.1-10)
SCOTT **HANNA** INKER (pp.1-10)
RAFAEL **DE LATORRE** ARTIST (pp.11-30)
JIM **CAMPBELL** COLOR ARTIST
VC's ARIANA **MAHER** LETTERER
MIKE **McKONE** & ERICK **ARCINIEGA** COVER ART

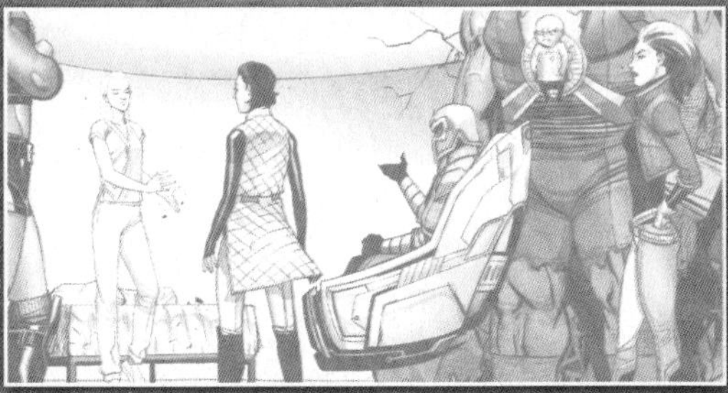

HEROES REBORN: MAGNETO & THE MUTANT FORCE

STEVE **ORLANDO** WRITER
BERNARD **CHANG** ARTIST
DAVID **CURIEL** COLOR ARTIST
VC's CLAYTON **COWLES** LETTERER
NICK **BRADSHAW** & RACHELLE **ROSENBERG** COVER ART

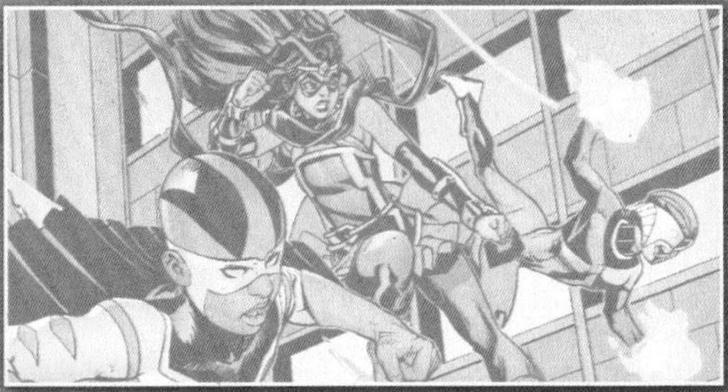

HEROES REBORN: YOUNG SQUADRON

JIM **ZUB** WRITER
STEVEN **CUMMINGS** ARTIST
ERICK **ARCINIEGA** COLOR ARTIST
VC's CLAYTON **COWLES** LETTERER
KARL **KERSCHL** COVER ART

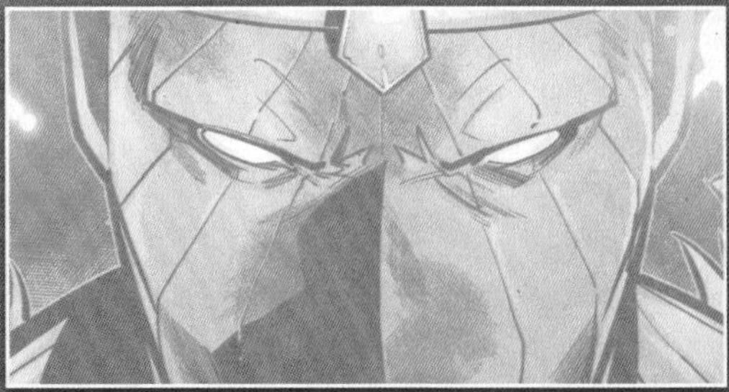

HEROES REBORN: SIEGE SOCIETY

CODY **ZIGLAR** WRITER
PACO **MEDINA** ARTIST
PETE **PANTAZIS** COLOR ARTIST
VC's JOE **SABINO** LETTERER
KEN **LASHLEY** & BRIAN **REBER** COVER ART

DANNY **KHAZEM**, MARTIN **BIRO** & LINDSEY **COHICK** ASSISTANT EDITORS
WIL **MOSS**, DEVIN **LEWIS** & ALANNA **SMITH** EDITORS
RALPH **MACCHIO** CONSULTING EDITOR
TOM **BREVOORT** & **NICK LOWE** EXECUTIVE EDITORS

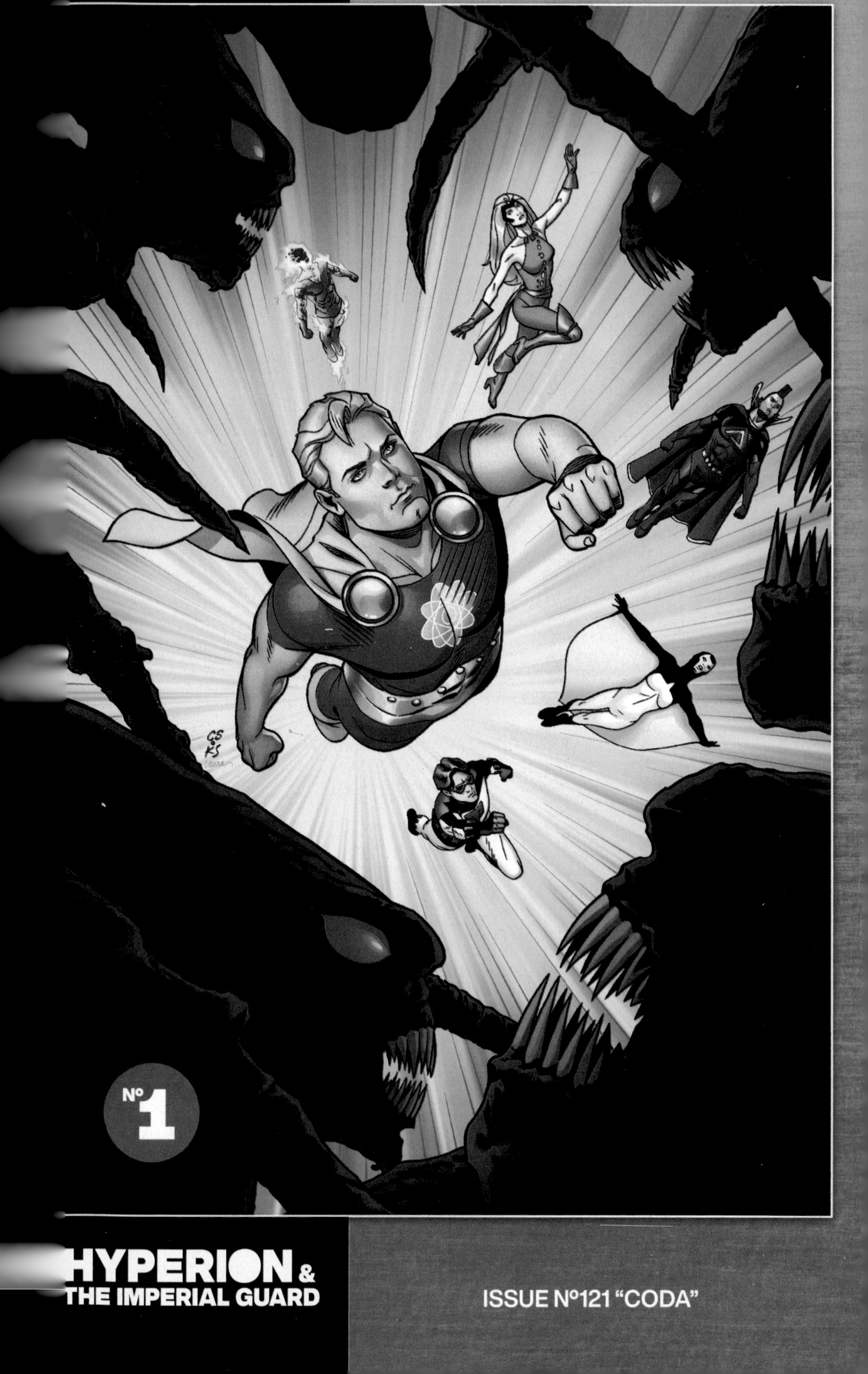
Nº 1

HYPERION & THE IMPERIAL GUARD

ISSUE Nº121 “CODA”

HEROES REBORN

AMERICA'S MIGHTIEST HEROES
COMPANION VOL. 1

HEROES

AMERICA'S MIGHTIEST HEROES COMPANION VOL. 1

HEROES REBORN: HYPERION & THE IMPERIAL GUARD

RYAN **CADY** WRITER

MICHELE **BANDINI** PENCILER

ELISABETTA **D'AMICO** & MICHELE **BANDINI** INKERS

ERICK **ARCINIEGA** COLOR ARTIST

"STARJAMMERS"

RYAN **CADY** WRITER
STEPHEN **BYRNE** ARTIST

VC's CORY **PETIT** LETTERER
CHRIS **SPROUSE**, KARL **STORY** & LAURA **MARTIN** COVER ART

JENNIFER **GRÜNWALD** COLLECTION EDITOR
DANIEL **KIRCHHOFFER** ASSISTANT EDITOR
MAIA **LOY** ASSISTANT MANAGING EDITOR
LISA **MONTALBANO** ASSISTANT MANAGING EDITOR
JEFF **YOUNGQUIST** VP PRODUCTION & SPECIAL PROJECTS
JAY **BOWEN** BOOK DESIGNER
DAVID **GABRIEL** SVP PRINT, SALES & MARKETING
C.B. **CEBULSKI** EDITOR IN CHIEF

HEROES REBORN: AMERICA'S MIGHTIEST HEROES COMPANION VOL. 1. Contains material originally published in magazine form as HEROES REBORN: HYPERION & THE IMPERIAL GUARD (2021) #1, HEROES REBORN: PETER PARKER, THE AMAZING SHUTTERBUG (2021) #1, HEROES REBORN: MAGNETO & THE MUTANT FORCE (2021) #1, HEROES REBORN: YOUNG SQUADRON (2021) #1 and HEROES REBORN: SIEGE SOCIETY (2021) #1. First printing 2021. ISBN 978-1-302-93113-1. Published by MARVEL WORLDWIDE, INC., a subsidiary of MARVEL ENTERTAINMENT, LLC. OFFICE OF PUBLICATION: 1290 Avenue of the Americas, New York, NY 10104. © 2021 MARVEL No similarity between any of the names, characters, persons, and/or institutions in this magazine with those of any living or dead person or institution is intended, and any such similarity which may exist is purely coincidental. **Printed in Canada.** KEVIN FEIGE, Chief Creative Officer; DAN BUCKLEY, President, Marvel Entertainment; JOE QUESADA, EVP & Creative Director; DAVID BOGART, Associate Publisher & SVP of Talent Affairs; TOM BREVOORT, VP, Executive Editor; NICK LOWE, Executive Editor, VP of Content, Digital Publishing; DAVID GABRIEL, VP of Print & Digital Publishing; JEFF YOUNGQUIST, VP of Production & Special Projects; ALEX MORALES, Director of Publishing Operations; DAN EDINGTON, Managing Editor; RICKEY PURDIN, Director of Talent Relations; JENNIFER GRÜNWALD, Senior Editor, Special Projects; SUSAN CRESPI, Production Manager; STAN LEE, Chairman Emeritus. For information regarding advertising in Marvel Comics or on Marvel.com, please contact Vit DeBellis, Custom Solutions & Integrated Advertising Manager, at vdebellis@marvel.com. For Marvel subscription inquiries, please call 888-511-5480. **Manufactured between 7/9/2021 and 8/10/2021 by SOLISCO PRINTERS, SCOTT, QC, CANADA.**

10 9 8 7 6 5 4 3 2 1

In a world in which the Avengers never existed, the Squadron Supreme of America are and have always been Earth's Mightiest Heroes!

But back when Hyperion was a teenager, he belonged to a different team, one far, far away from America. These are the adventures of...

HYPERION & THE IMPERIAL GUARD

Years ago, as part of a good faith agreement with the Shi'ar Empire, Earth's Mightiest Young Hero, Hyperion, was sent to train among the Shi'ar's youngest legion of the Imperial Guard. Under the watchful tutelage of the Imperial Guard's praetor, Gladiator, over months of epic journeys and daring adventures, Hyperion aided the Imperial Guard in protecting the realm and studied the techniques of some of the finest heroes in the cosmos. Along the way, he gained more than mere knowledge or glory.

Hyperion made friends.

Now, having recently triumphed over the Shi'ar Majestor's greatest enemy -- the ruthless Deathbird -- Hyperion finds his journey among the stars at an end. Soon he will return to Earth, rich in experience, but with the greatest friends he's ever known on the other side of the galaxy.

Is it any wonder, then, that our hero would want to hold on a little longer?

ISSUE Nº 121
"CODA"

RYAN **CADY** WRITER

MICHELE **BANDINI** PENCILER

ELISABETTA **D'AMICO**
AND MICHELE **BANDINI** INKERS

ERICK **ARCINIEGA** COLORIST

VC's CORY **PETIT** LETTERER

CHRIS **SPROUSE**, KARL **STORY**
& LAURA **MARTIN** COVER ARTISTS

BEN **CALDWELL** VARIANT COVER ARTIST

JAY **BOWEN** GRAPHIC DESIGN

WIL **MOSS** EDITOR

TOM **BREVOORT** EXECUTIVE EDITOR

C.B. **CEBULSKI** EDITOR IN CHIEF

THIS ISSUE IS DEDICATED TO
DAVE COCKRUM & **CHRIS CLAREMONT**

HEROES
REBORN

KEY MEMBERS OF THE IMPERIAL GUARD

HYPERION

The last son of a powerful race of Celestials, Hyperion crashed on Earth as an infant, raised as Marcus Milton to defend the values of hope and hard-fought liberty. Sent among the Imperial Guard as a diplomatic gesture, Hyperion became fast friends with his extraterrestrial comrades-in-arms, viewing the stalwart Gladiator as a beloved mentor and even nurturing a tender romance with the telepath known as Oracle.

ABILITIES: Superhuman strength, speed and durability. Capable of releasing his body's stored atomic energy in optic blasts and empowered flight.

GLADIATOR

The finest warrior on his home planet of Strontia, the hero known as Kallark was brought to Chandilar, the Shi'ar throneworld, to lead and train a new generation of Imperial Guard. Taking the name Gladiator, he was a different kind of praetor -- always demanding the best of his comrades, leading them with discipline tempered by understanding. While Manta has always been his star pupil, Gladiator has grown to respect the visiting Hyperion as a near-equal, honored to have a hand in his training.

ABILITIES: A naturally talented fighter, the Gladiator-enhancement program gifted Kallark with superior physical abilities, flight and a host of other powers.

ORACLE

While still mastering her psionic abilities, it was foreseen that Lady Sybil would one day grow to be the most powerful telepath in Shi'ar history, earning her the moniker Oracle. During her cadet training, she and teammate Flashfire were nearly betrothed, but even in Hyperion's short time with the team, the Terran hero has won Oracle's heart.

ABILITIES: Capable of telepathy, mental projection and even limited telekinesis, Oracle is invaluable to the Imperial Guard's command structure.

FLASHFIRE

As a cadet on Chandilar, Grannz was considered an exceptionally gifted soldier. Though his cocky demeanor causes frequent clashes with teammates (and ultimately ended his relationship with Oracle), Flashfire backs up his overconfidence with battle acumen and courage. Despite his displays of open hostility toward Oracle and Hyperion's burgeoning relationship, he recently began a fling of his own with teammate Neutron.

ABILITIES: Capable of generating powerful flashes of light and waves of electricity.

NEUTRON

While this mysterious Stygian was once suspected of treachery, his acts of selfless heroism during the Guard's campaign against Deathbird have crystalized his loyalties. Though he possesses powers to rival even Gladiator, Neutron is quietly amiable and never prone to arrogance. Charismatic and impassive, his attraction to the hotheaded Flashfire is something of a mystery to the rest of the team.

ABILITIES: Neutron's body contains a stabilized black hole, allowing him to adjust his density and gravitational pull, endure intense damage and absorb or release energy blasts at will.

MANTA

While one of the physically weaker members of the Imperial Guard, Manta is easily the most intelligent among them. A tactical genius and brilliant polymath, Gladiator regularly relies on her situational analysis and strategies -- while the rest of the team usually receives little more than an eye-roll from this aloof genius.

ABILITIES: In addition to her heightened intellect, Manta can visually process infrared and ultraviolet spectrum, and even project rays of blinding, searing light.

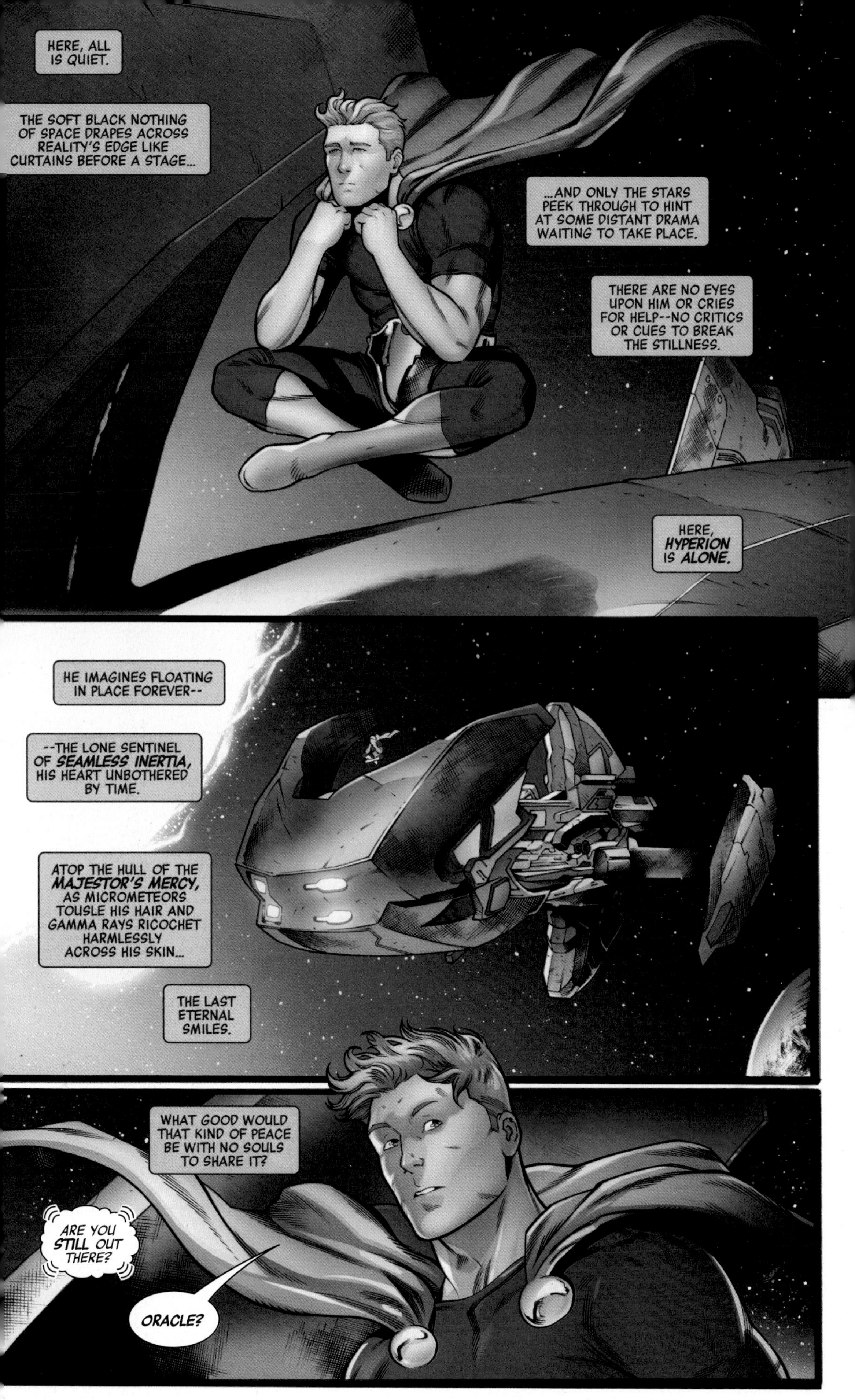
HERE, ALL IS QUIET.
THE SOFT BLACK NOTHING OF SPACE DRAPES ACROSS REALITY'S EDGE LIKE CURTAINS BEFORE A STAGE...
...AND ONLY THE STARS PEEK THROUGH TO HINT AT SOME DISTANT DRAMA WAITING TO TAKE PLACE.
THERE ARE NO EYES UPON HIM OR CRIES FOR HELP--NO CRITICS OR CUES TO BREAK THE STILLNESS.
HERE, HYPERION IS ALONE.
HE IMAGINES FLOATING IN PLACE FOREVER--
--THE LONE SENTINEL OF SEAMLESS INERTIA, HIS HEART UNBOTHERED BY TIME.
ATOP THE HULL OF THE MAJESTOR'S MERCY, AS MICROMETEORS TOUSLE HIS HAIR AND GAMMA RAYS RICOCHET HARMLESSLY ACROSS HIS SKIN...
THE LAST ETERNAL SMILES.
WHAT GOOD WOULD THAT KIND OF PEACE BE WITH NO SOULS TO SHARE IT?
ARE YOU STILL OUT THERE?
ORACLE?

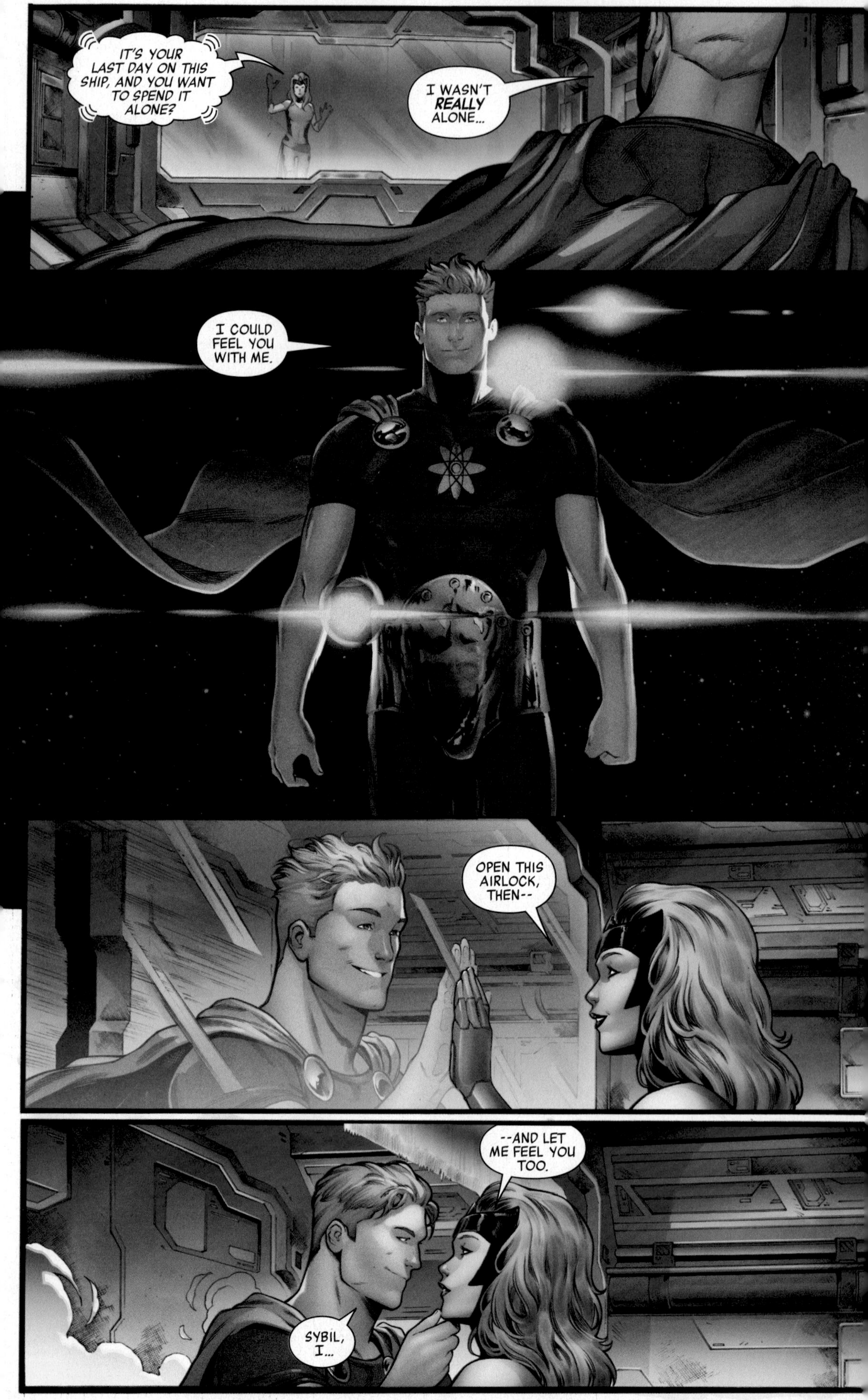
IT'S YOUR LAST DAY ON THIS SHIP, AND YOU WANT TO SPEND IT ALONE?
I WASN'T REALLY ALONE...
I COULD FEEL YOU WITH ME.
OPEN THIS AIRLOCK, THEN--
--AND LET ME FEEL YOU TOO.
SYBIL, I...

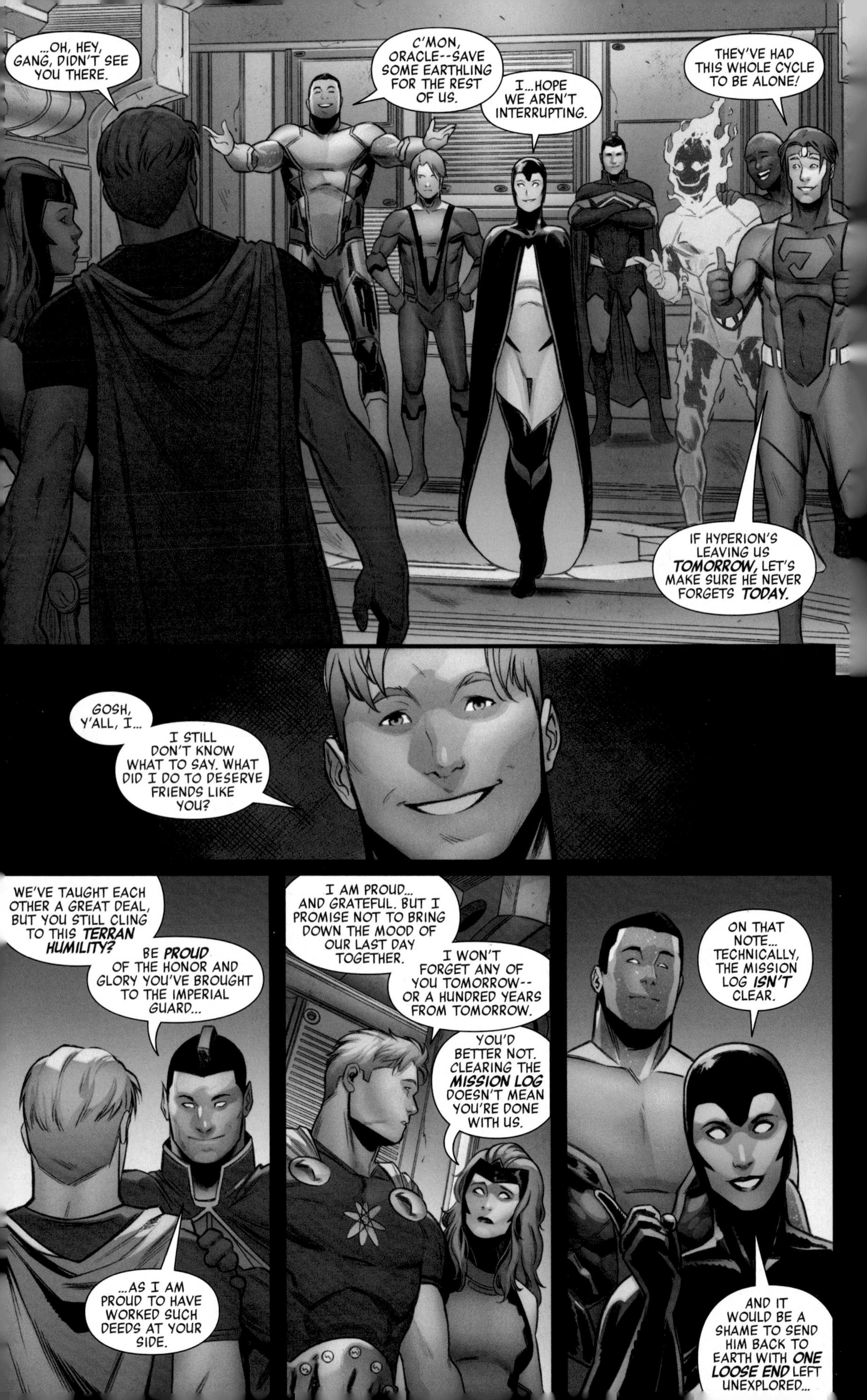

...OH, HEY, GANG, DIDN'T SEE YOU THERE.
C'MON, ORACLE--SAVE SOME EARTHLING FOR THE REST OF US.
I...HOPE WE AREN'T INTERRUPTING.
THEY'VE HAD THIS WHOLE CYCLE TO BE ALONE!
IF HYPERION'S LEAVING US TOMORROW, LET'S MAKE SURE HE NEVER FORGETS TODAY.
GOSH, Y'ALL, I...
I STILL DON'T KNOW WHAT TO SAY. WHAT DID I DO TO DESERVE FRIENDS LIKE YOU?
WE'VE TAUGHT EACH OTHER A GREAT DEAL, BUT YOU STILL CLING TO THIS TERRAN HUMILITY?
BE PROUD OF THE HONOR AND GLORY YOU'VE BROUGHT TO THE IMPERIAL GUARD...
...AS I AM PROUD TO HAVE WORKED SUCH DEEDS AT YOUR SIDE.
I AM PROUD... AND GRATEFUL. BUT I PROMISE NOT TO BRING DOWN THE MOOD OF OUR LAST DAY TOGETHER.
I WON'T FORGET ANY OF YOU TOMORROW-- OR A HUNDRED YEARS FROM TOMORROW.
YOU'D BETTER NOT. CLEARING THE MISSION LOG DOESN'T MEAN YOU'RE DONE WITH US.
ON THAT NOTE... TECHNICALLY, THE MISSION LOG ISN'T CLEAR.
AND IT WOULD BE A SHAME TO SEND HIM BACK TO EARTH WITH ONE LOOSE END LEFT UNEXPLORED...

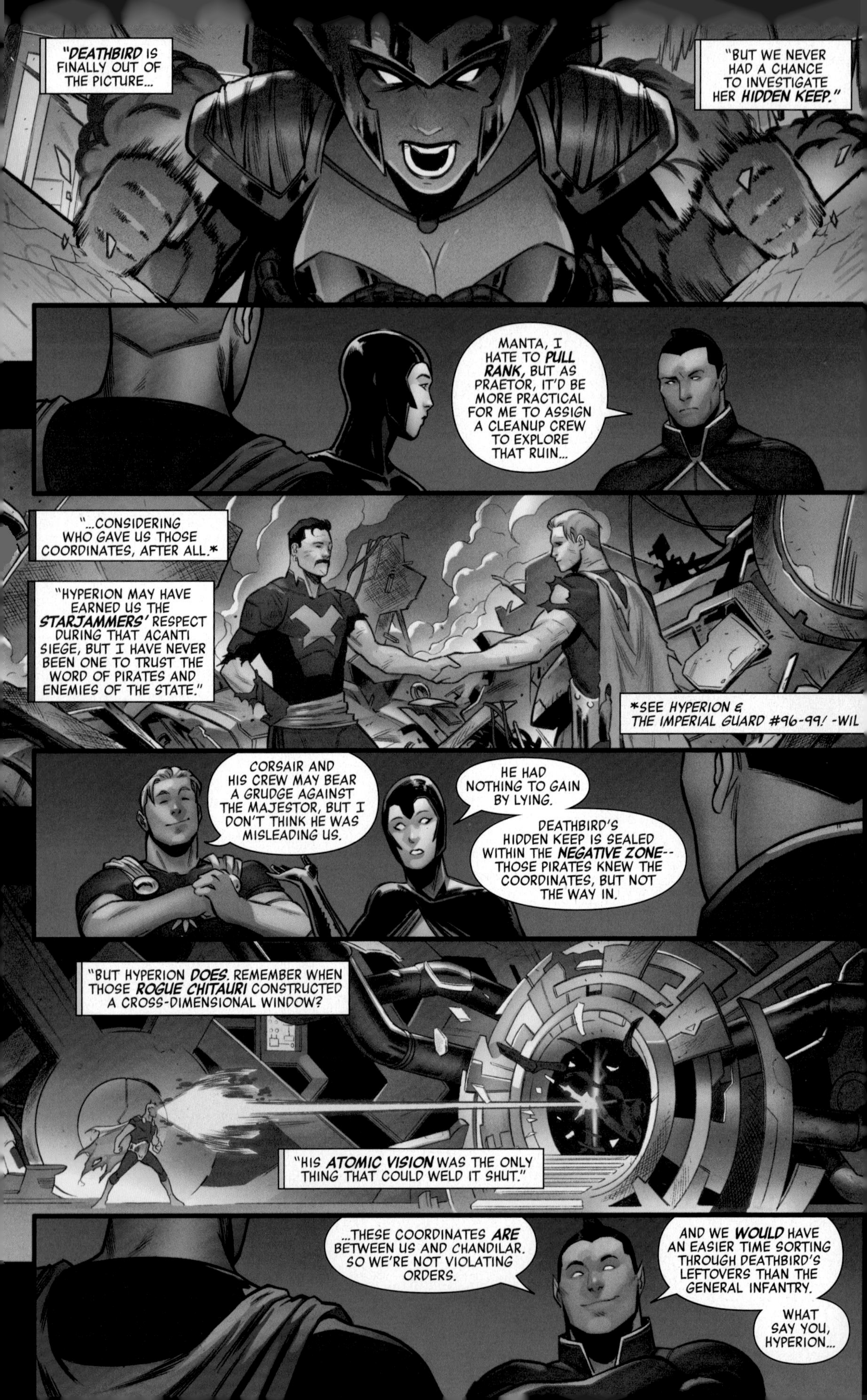

"DEATHBIRD IS FINALLY OUT OF THE PICTURE...
"BUT WE NEVER HAD A CHANCE TO INVESTIGATE HER HIDDEN KEEP."
MANTA, I HATE TO PULL RANK, BUT AS PRAETOR, IT'D BE MORE PRACTICAL FOR ME TO ASSIGN A CLEANUP CREW TO EXPLORE THAT RUIN...
"...CONSIDERING WHO GAVE US THOSE COORDINATES, AFTER ALL.*
"HYPERION MAY HAVE EARNED US THE STARJAMMERS' RESPECT DURING THAT ACANTI SIEGE, BUT I HAVE NEVER BEEN ONE TO TRUST THE WORD OF PIRATES AND ENEMIES OF THE STATE."
*SEE HYPERION & THE IMPERIAL GUARD #96-99! -WIL
CORSAIR AND HIS CREW MAY BEAR A GRUDGE AGAINST THE MAJESTOR, BUT I DON'T THINK HE WAS MISLEADING US.
HE HAD NOTHING TO GAIN BY LYING.
DEATHBIRD'S HIDDEN KEEP IS SEALED WITHIN THE NEGATIVE ZONE-- THOSE PIRATES KNEW THE COORDINATES, BUT NOT THE WAY IN.
"BUT HYPERION DOES. REMEMBER WHEN THOSE ROGUE CHITAURI CONSTRUCTED A CROSS-DIMENSIONAL WINDOW?
"HIS ATOMIC VISION WAS THE ONLY THING THAT COULD WELD IT SHUT."
...THESE COORDINATES ARE BETWEEN US AND CHANDILAR. SO WE'RE NOT VIOLATING ORDERS.
AND WE WOULD HAVE AN EASIER TIME SORTING THROUGH DEATHBIRD'S LEFTOVERS THAN THE GENERAL INFANTRY.
WHAT SAY YOU, HYPERION...

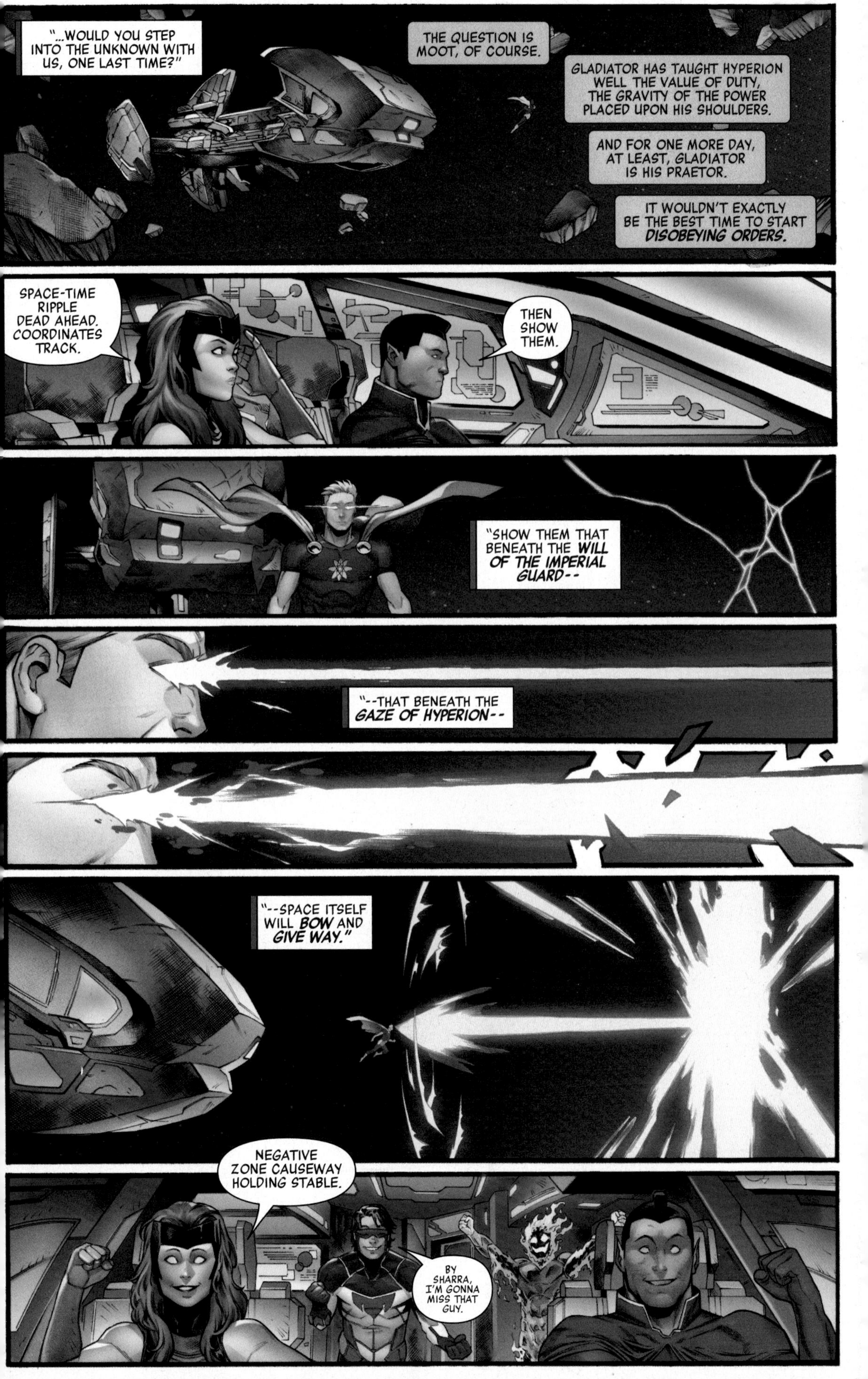
"...WOULD YOU STEP INTO THE UNKNOWN WITH US, ONE LAST TIME?"
THE QUESTION IS MOOT, OF COURSE.
GLADIATOR HAS TAUGHT HYPERION WELL THE VALUE OF DUTY, THE GRAVITY OF THE POWER PLACED UPON HIS SHOULDERS.
AND FOR ONE MORE DAY, AT LEAST, GLADIATOR IS HIS PRAETOR.
IT WOULDN'T EXACTLY BE THE BEST TIME TO START DISOBEYING ORDERS.
SPACE-TIME RIPPLE DEAD AHEAD. COORDINATES TRACK.
THEN SHOW THEM.
"SHOW THEM THAT BENEATH THE WILL OF THE IMPERIAL GUARD--
"--THAT BENEATH THE GAZE OF HYPERION--
"--SPACE ITSELF WILL BOW AND GIVE WAY."
NEGATIVE ZONE CAUSEWAY HOLDING STABLE.
BY SHARRA, I'M GONNA MISS THAT GUY.

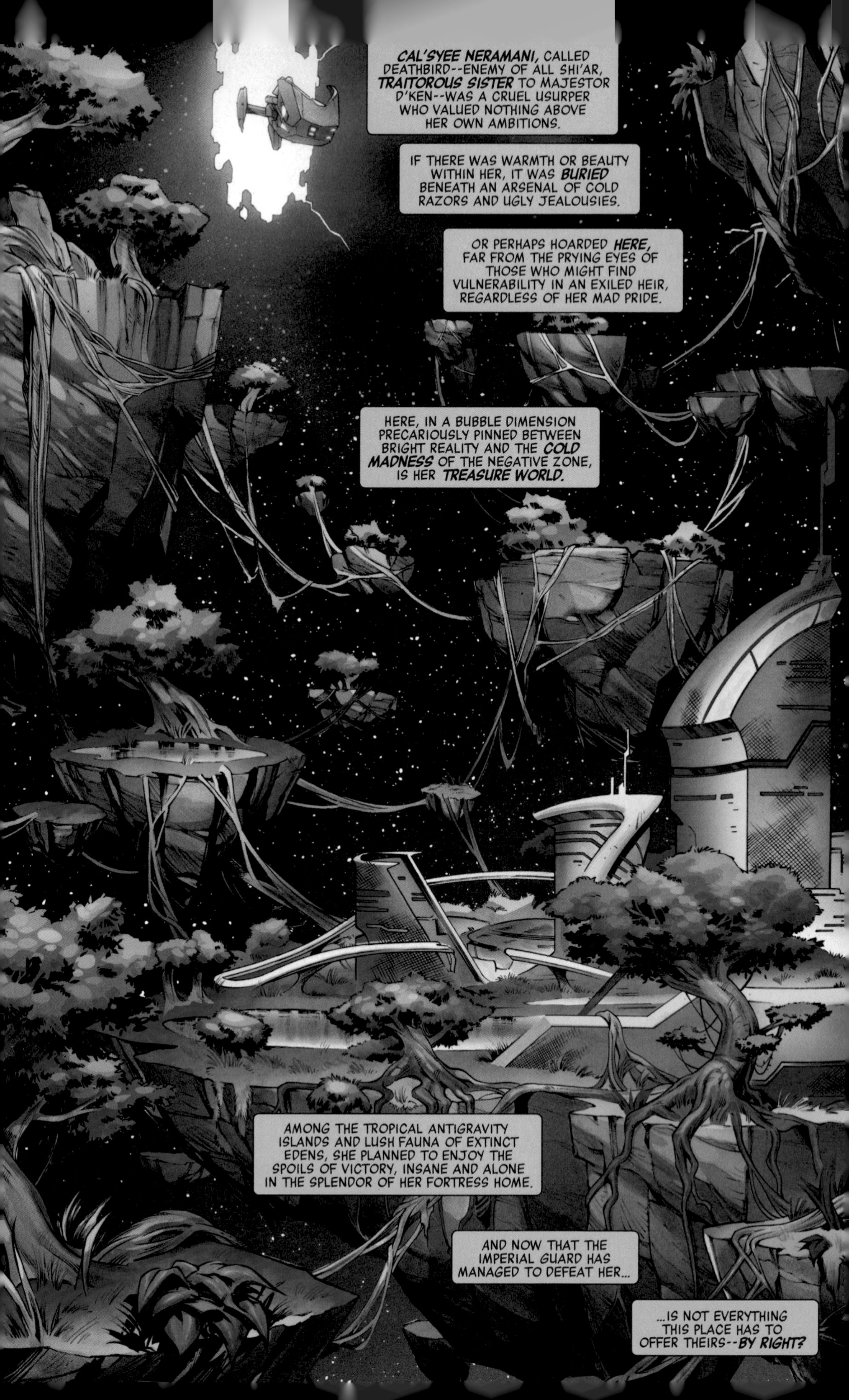
CAL'SYEE NERAMANI, CALLED DEATHBIRD--ENEMY OF ALL SHI'AR, TRAITOROUS SISTER TO MAJESTOR D'KEN--WAS A CRUEL USURPER WHO VALUED NOTHING ABOVE HER OWN AMBITIONS.
IF THERE WAS WARMTH OR BEAUTY WITHIN HER, IT WAS BURIED BENEATH AN ARSENAL OF COLD RAZORS AND UGLY JEALOUSIES.
OR PERHAPS HOARDED HERE, FAR FROM THE PRYING EYES OF THOSE WHO MIGHT FIND VULNERABILITY IN AN EXILED HEIR, REGARDLESS OF HER MAD PRIDE.
HERE, IN A BUBBLE DIMENSION PRECARIOUSLY PINNED BETWEEN BRIGHT REALITY AND THE COLD MADNESS OF THE NEGATIVE ZONE, IS HER TREASURE WORLD.
AMONG THE TROPICAL ANTIGRAVITY ISLANDS AND LUSH FAUNA OF EXTINCT EDENS, SHE PLANNED TO ENJOY THE SPOILS OF VICTORY, INSANE AND ALONE IN THE SPLENDOR OF HER FORTRESS HOME.
AND NOW THAT THE IMPERIAL GUARD HAS MANAGED TO DEFEAT HER...
...IS NOT EVERYTHING THIS PLACE HAS TO OFFER THEIRS--BY RIGHT?

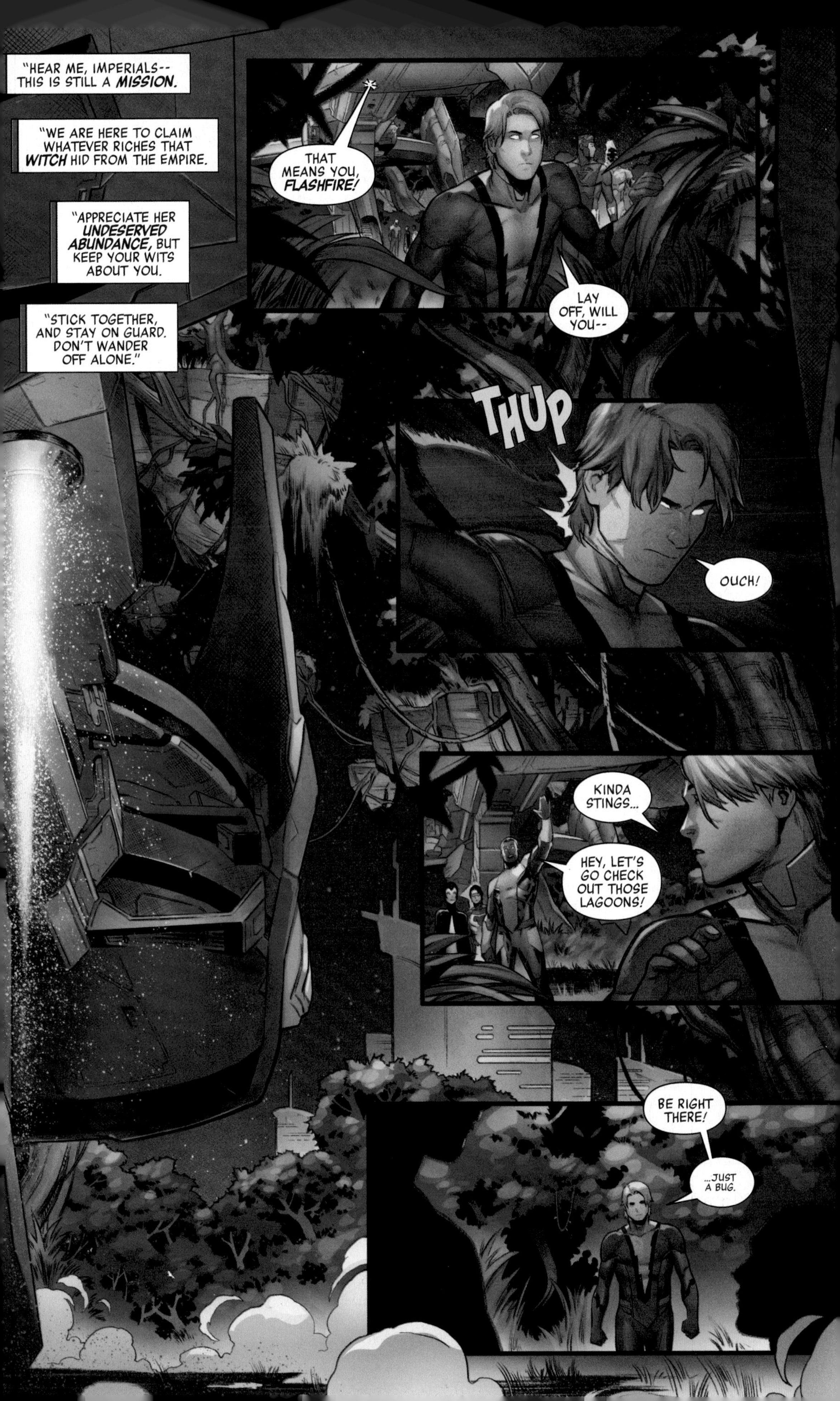
"HEAR ME, IMPERIALS-- THIS IS STILL A MISSION.
"WE ARE HERE TO CLAIM WHATEVER RICHES THAT WITCH HID FROM THE EMPIRE.
THAT MEANS YOU, FLASHFIRE!
"APPRECIATE HER UNDESERVED ABUNDANCE, BUT KEEP YOUR WITS ABOUT YOU.
LAY OFF, WILL YOU--
"STICK TOGETHER, AND STAY ON GUARD. DON'T WANDER OFF ALONE."
THUP
OUCH!
KINDA STINGS...
HEY, LET'S GO CHECK OUT THOSE LAGOONS!
BE RIGHT THERE!
...JUST A BUG.

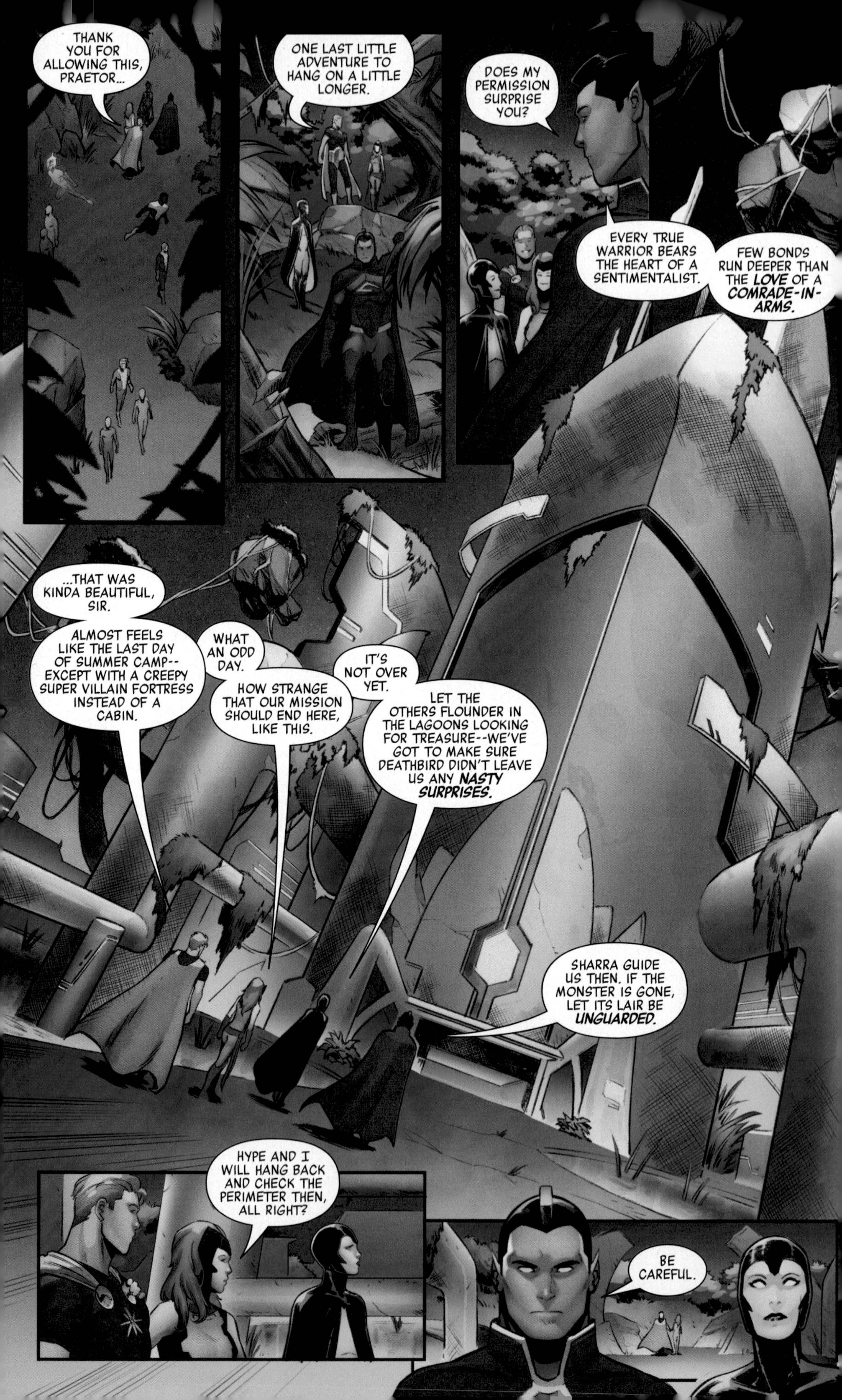
THANK YOU FOR ALLOWING THIS, PRAETOR...
ONE LAST LITTLE ADVENTURE TO HANG ON A LITTLE LONGER.
DOES MY PERMISSION SURPRISE YOU?
EVERY TRUE WARRIOR BEARS THE HEART OF A SENTIMENTALIST.
FEW BONDS RUN DEEPER THAN THE LOVE OF A COMRADE-IN-ARMS.
...THAT WAS KINDA BEAUTIFUL, SIR.
ALMOST FEELS LIKE THE LAST DAY OF SUMMER CAMP--EXCEPT WITH A CREEPY SUPER VILLAIN FORTRESS INSTEAD OF A CABIN.
WHAT AN ODD DAY.
HOW STRANGE THAT OUR MISSION SHOULD END HERE, LIKE THIS.
IT'S NOT OVER YET.
LET THE OTHERS FLOUNDER IN THE LAGOONS LOOKING FOR TREASURE--WE'VE GOT TO MAKE SURE DEATHBIRD DIDN'T LEAVE US ANY NASTY SURPRISES.
SHARRA GUIDE US THEN. IF THE MONSTER IS GONE, LET ITS LAIR BE UNGUARDED.
HYPE AND I WILL HANG BACK AND CHECK THE PERIMETER THEN, ALL RIGHT?
BE CAREFUL.

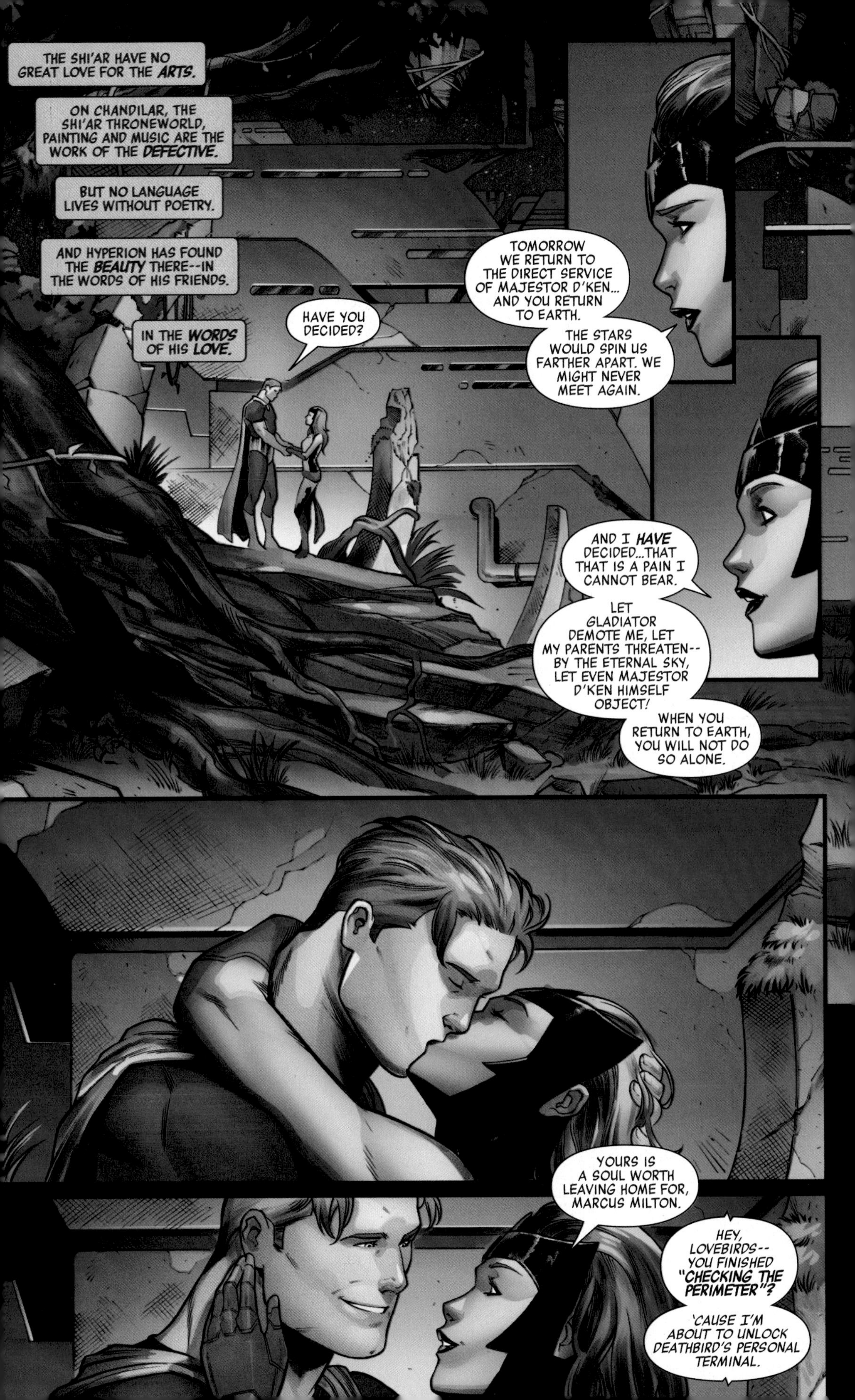

THE SHI'AR HAVE NO GREAT LOVE FOR THE ARTS.
ON CHANDILAR, THE SHI'AR THRONEWORLD, PAINTING AND MUSIC ARE THE WORK OF THE DEFECTIVE.
BUT NO LANGUAGE LIVES WITHOUT POETRY.
AND HYPERION HAS FOUND THE BEAUTY THERE--IN THE WORDS OF HIS FRIENDS.
IN THE WORDS OF HIS LOVE.
HAVE YOU DECIDED?
TOMORROW WE RETURN TO THE DIRECT SERVICE OF MAJESTOR D'KEN... AND YOU RETURN TO EARTH.
THE STARS WOULD SPIN US FARTHER APART. WE MIGHT NEVER MEET AGAIN.
AND I HAVE DECIDED...THAT THAT IS A PAIN I CANNOT BEAR.
LET GLADIATOR DEMOTE ME, LET MY PARENTS THREATEN-- BY THE ETERNAL SKY, LET EVEN MAJESTOR D'KEN HIMSELF OBJECT!
WHEN YOU RETURN TO EARTH, YOU WILL NOT DO SO ALONE.
YOURS IS A SOUL WORTH LEAVING HOME FOR, MARCUS MILTON.
HEY, LOVEBIRDS-- YOU FINISHED "CHECKING THE PERIMETER"?
'CAUSE I'M ABOUT TO UNLOCK DEATHBIRD'S PERSONAL TERMINAL.

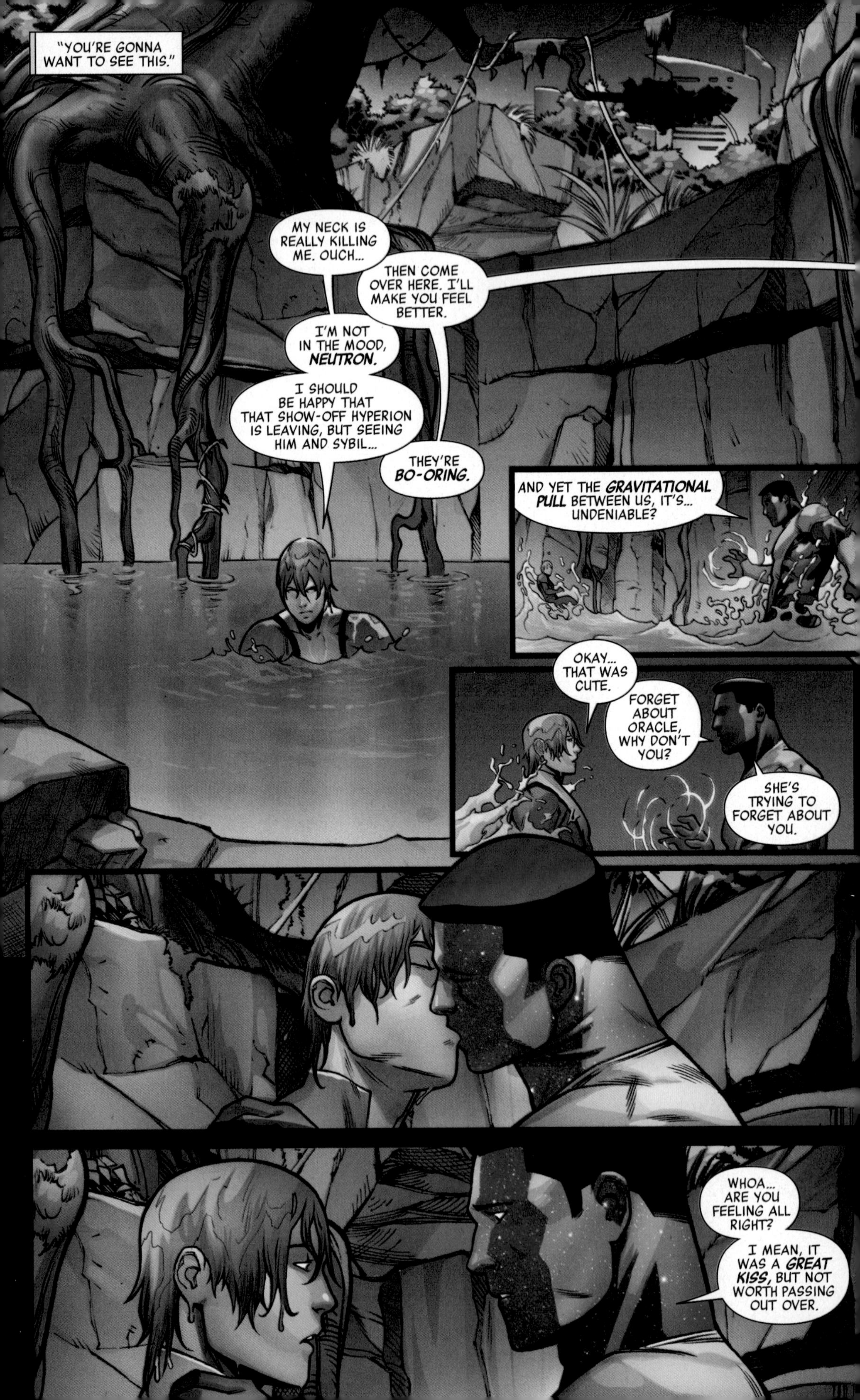
"YOU'RE GONNA WANT TO SEE THIS."
MY NECK IS REALLY KILLING ME. OUCH...
THEN COME OVER HERE. I'LL MAKE YOU FEEL BETTER.
I'M NOT IN THE MOOD, NEUTRON.
I SHOULD BE HAPPY THAT THAT SHOW-OFF HYPERION IS LEAVING, BUT SEEING HIM AND SYBIL...
THEY'RE BO-ORING.
AND YET THE GRAVITATIONAL PULL BETWEEN US, IT'S... UNDENIABLE?
OKAY... THAT WAS CUTE.
FORGET ABOUT ORACLE, WHY DON'T YOU?
SHE'S TRYING TO FORGET ABOUT YOU.
WHOA... ARE YOU FEELING ALL RIGHT?
I MEAN, IT WAS A GREAT KISS, BUT NOT WORTH PASSING OUT OVER.

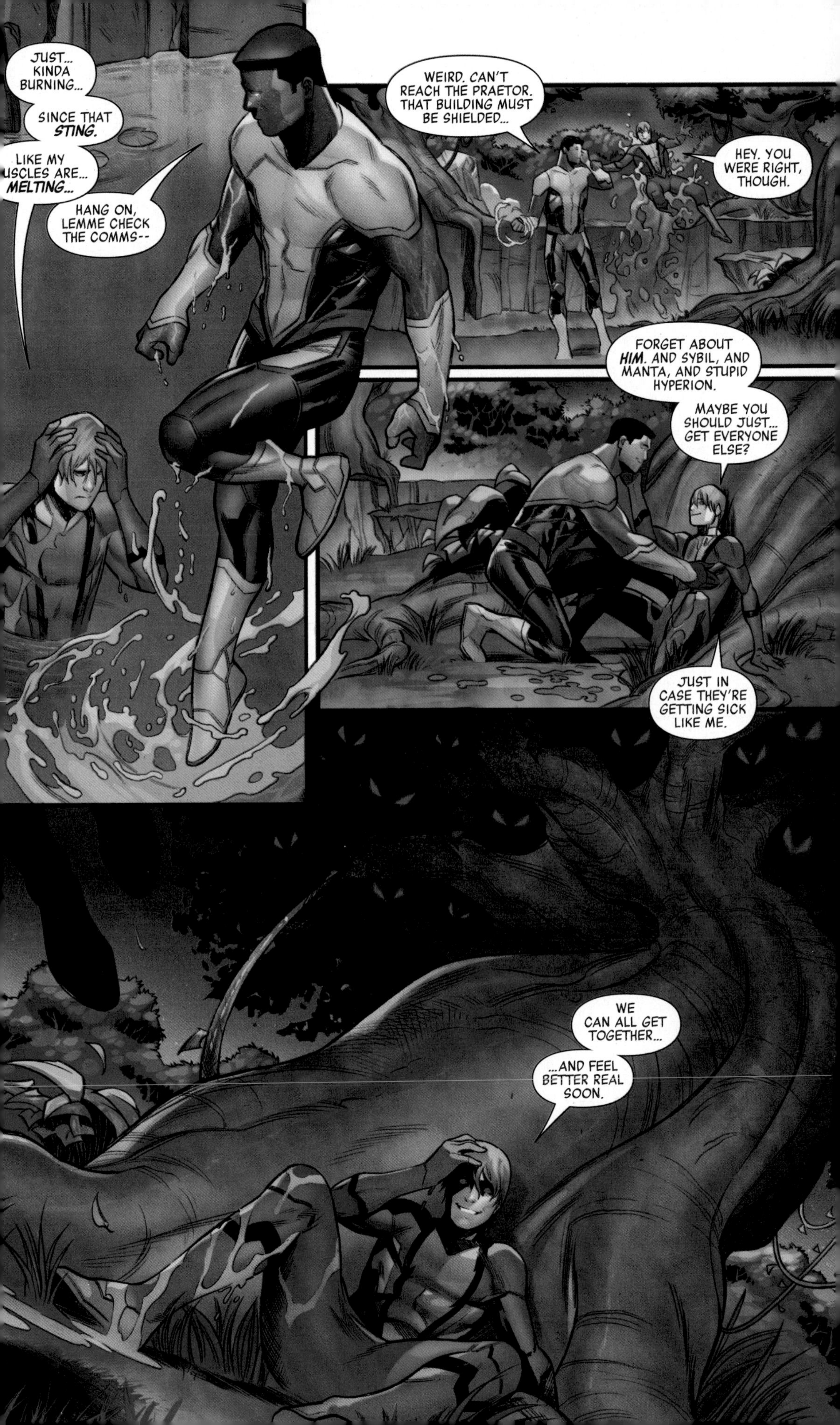
JUST... KINDA BURNING...
SINCE THAT STING.
LIKE MY USCLES ARE... MELTING...
HANG ON, LEMME CHECK THE COMMS--
WEIRD. CAN'T REACH THE PRAETOR. THAT BUILDING MUST BE SHIELDED...
HEY. YOU WERE RIGHT, THOUGH.
FORGET ABOUT HIM. AND SYBIL, AND MANTA, AND STUPID HYPERION.
MAYBE YOU SHOULD JUST... GET EVERYONE ELSE?
JUST IN CASE THEY'RE GETTING SICK LIKE ME.
WE CAN ALL GET TOGETHER...
...AND FEEL BETTER REAL SOON.

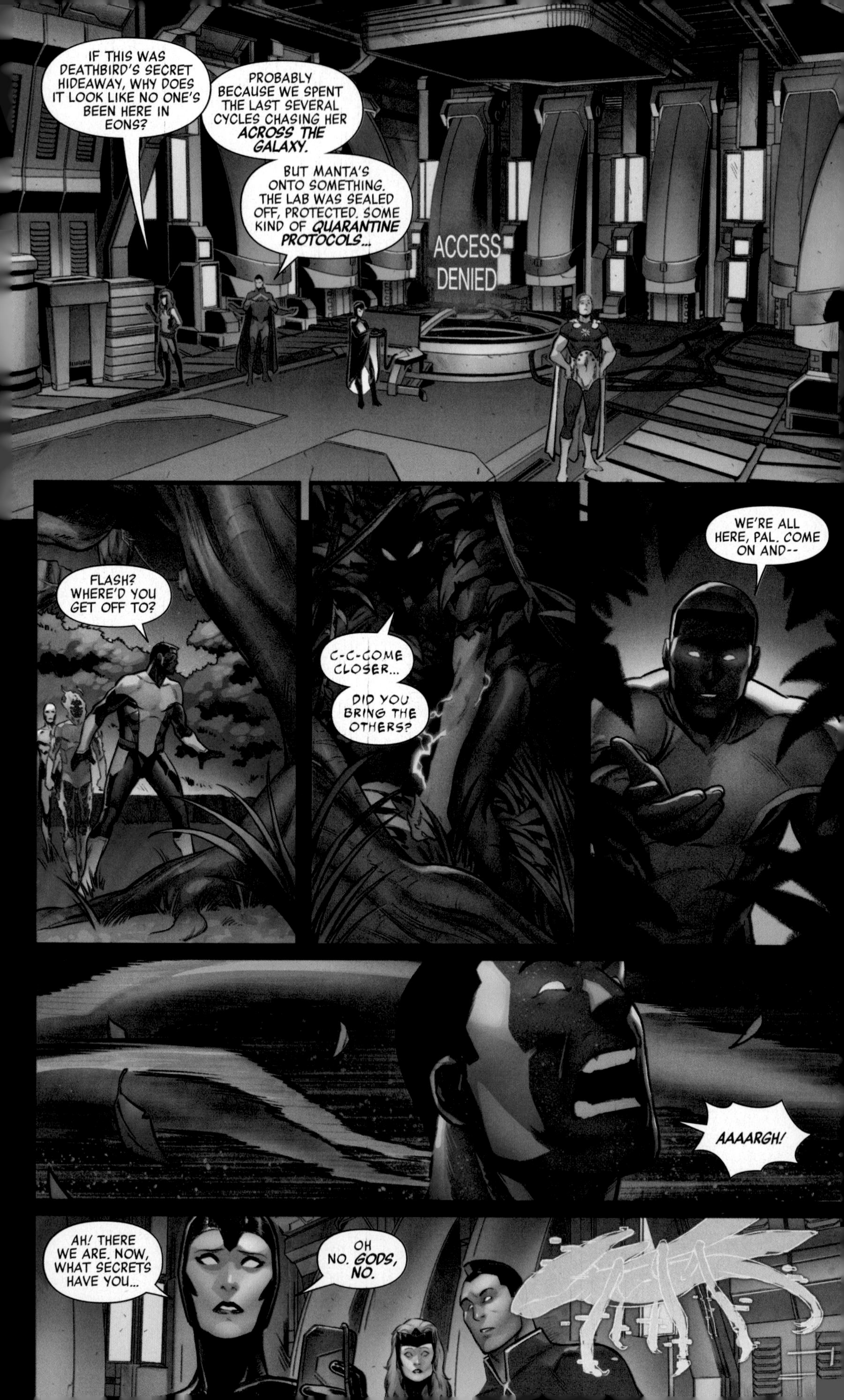
IF THIS WAS DEATHBIRD'S SECRET HIDEAWAY, WHY DOES IT LOOK LIKE NO ONE'S BEEN HERE IN EONS?
PROBABLY BECAUSE WE SPENT THE LAST SEVERAL CYCLES CHASING HER ACROSS THE GALAXY.
BUT MANTA'S ONTO SOMETHING. THE LAB WAS SEALED OFF, PROTECTED. SOME KIND OF QUARANTINE PROTOCOLS...
ACCESS DENIED
FLASH? WHERE'D YOU GET OFF TO?
C-C-COME CLOSER...
DID YOU BRING THE OTHERS?
WE'RE ALL HERE, PAL. COME ON AND--
AAAARGH!
AH! THERE WE ARE. NOW, WHAT SECRETS HAVE YOU...
OH NO. GODS, NO.

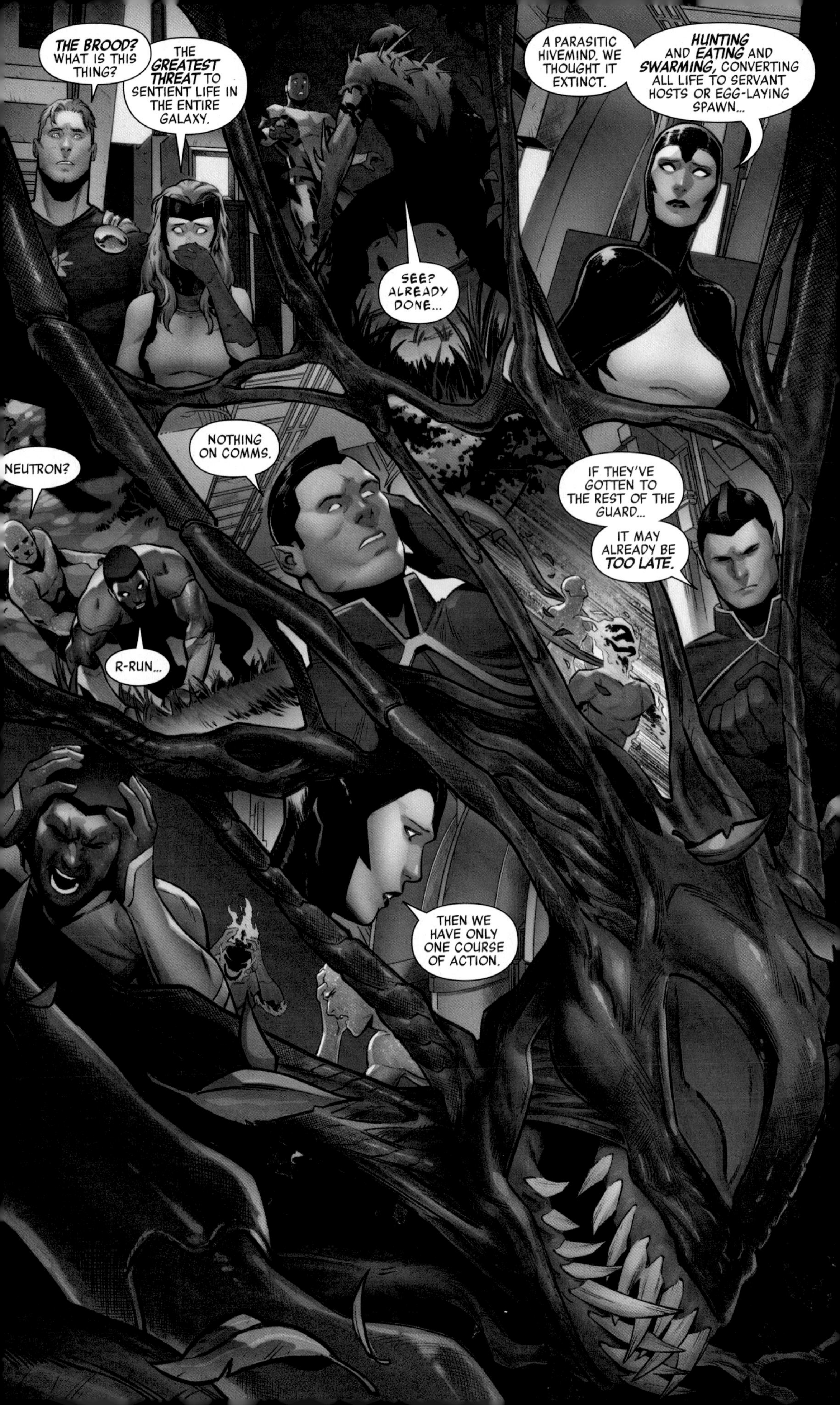
THE BROOD? WHAT IS THIS THING?
THE GREATEST THREAT TO SENTIENT LIFE IN THE ENTIRE GALAXY.
A PARASITIC HIVEMIND. WE THOUGHT IT EXTINCT.
HUNTING AND EATING AND SWARMING, CONVERTING ALL LIFE TO SERVANT HOSTS OR EGG-LAYING SPAWN...
SEE? ALREADY DONE...
NEUTRON?
NOTHING ON COMMS.
IF THEY'VE GOTTEN TO THE REST OF THE GUARD...
IT MAY ALREADY BE TOO LATE.
R-RUN...
THEN WE HAVE ONLY ONE COURSE OF ACTION.

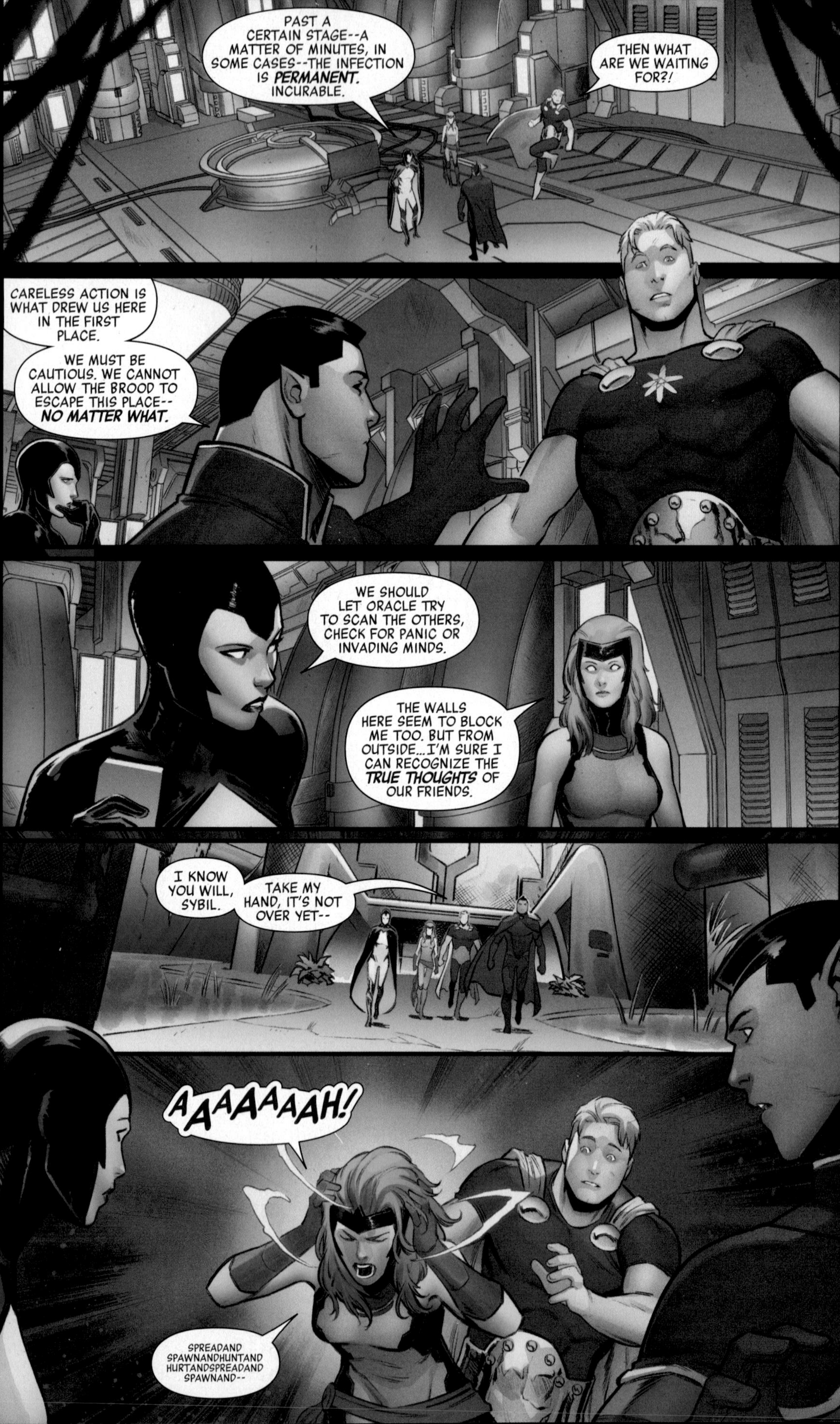
PAST A CERTAIN STAGE--A MATTER OF MINUTES, IN SOME CASES--THE INFECTION IS PERMANENT. INCURABLE.
THEN WHAT ARE WE WAITING FOR?!
CARELESS ACTION IS WHAT DREW US HERE IN THE FIRST PLACE.
WE MUST BE CAUTIOUS. WE CANNOT ALLOW THE BROOD TO ESCAPE THIS PLACE-- NO MATTER WHAT.
WE SHOULD LET ORACLE TRY TO SCAN THE OTHERS, CHECK FOR PANIC OR INVADING MINDS.
THE WALLS HERE SEEM TO BLOCK ME TOO. BUT FROM OUTSIDE...I'M SURE I CAN RECOGNIZE THE TRUE THOUGHTS OF OUR FRIENDS.
I KNOW YOU WILL, SYBIL.
TAKE MY HAND, IT'S NOT OVER YET--
AAAAAAAH!
SPREADAND SPAWNANDHUNTAND HURTANDSPREADAND SPAWNAND--

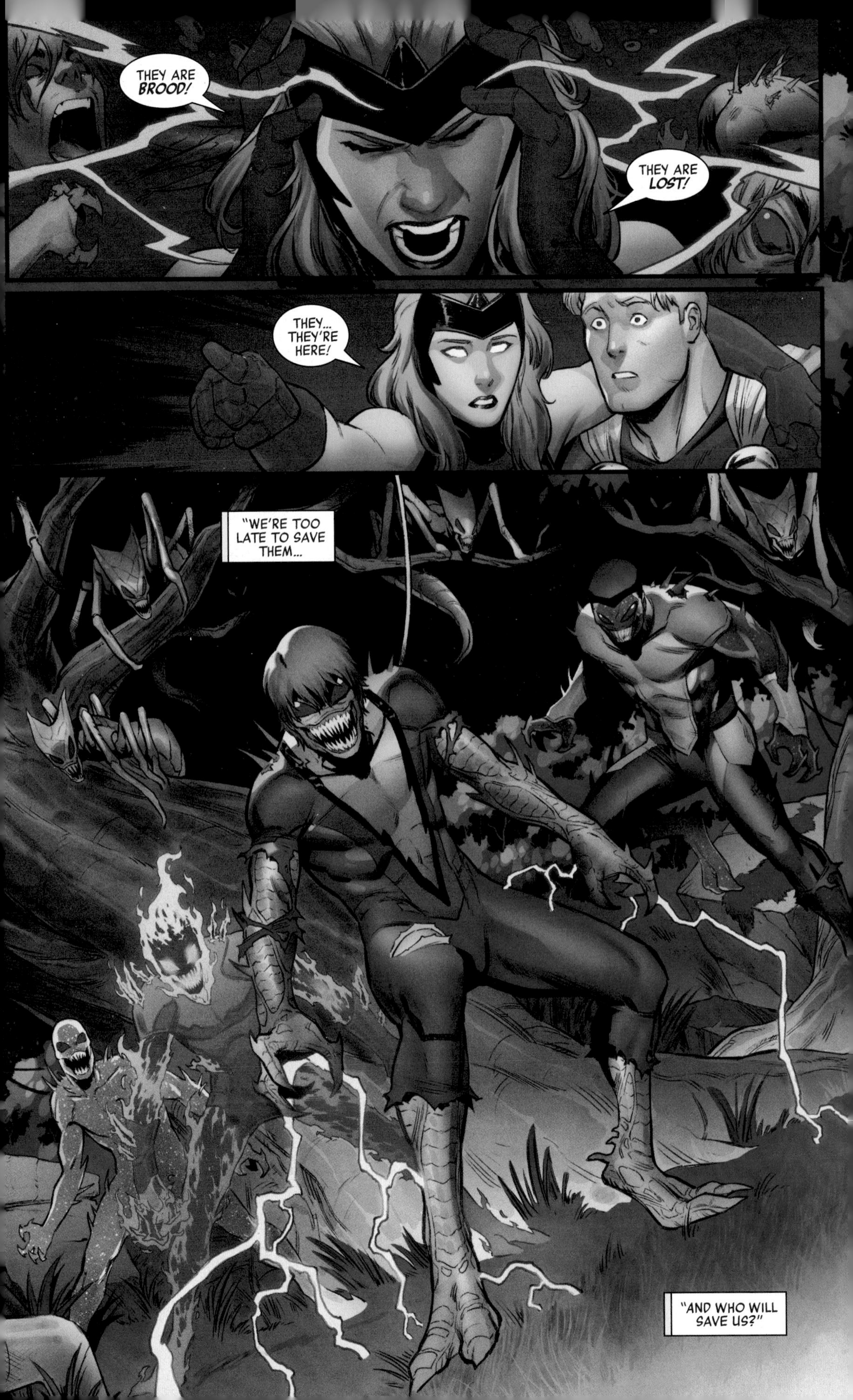
THEY ARE BROOD!
THEY ARE LOST!
THEY... THEY'RE HERE!
"WE'RE TOO LATE TO SAVE THEM...
"AND WHO WILL SAVE US?"

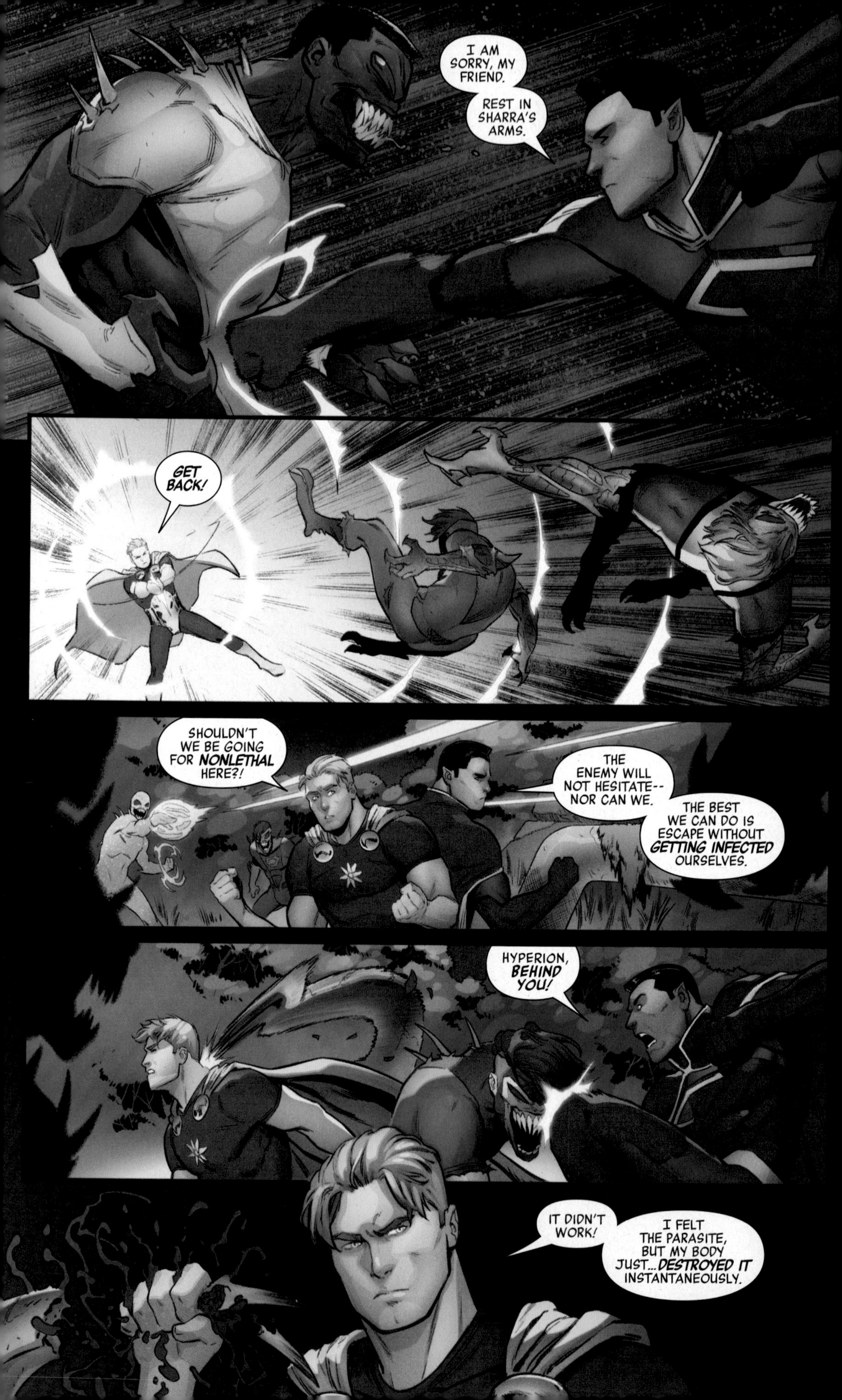
I AM SORRY, MY FRIEND.
REST IN SHARRA'S ARMS.
GET BACK!
SHOULDN'T WE BE GOING FOR **NONLETHAL** HERE?!
THE ENEMY WILL NOT HESITATE-- NOR CAN WE.
THE BEST WE CAN DO IS ESCAPE WITHOUT ***GETTING INFECTED*** OURSELVES.
HYPERION, ***BEHIND YOU!***
IT DIDN'T WORK!
I FELT THE PARASITE, BUT MY BODY JUST... ***DESTROYED IT*** INSTANTANEOUSLY.

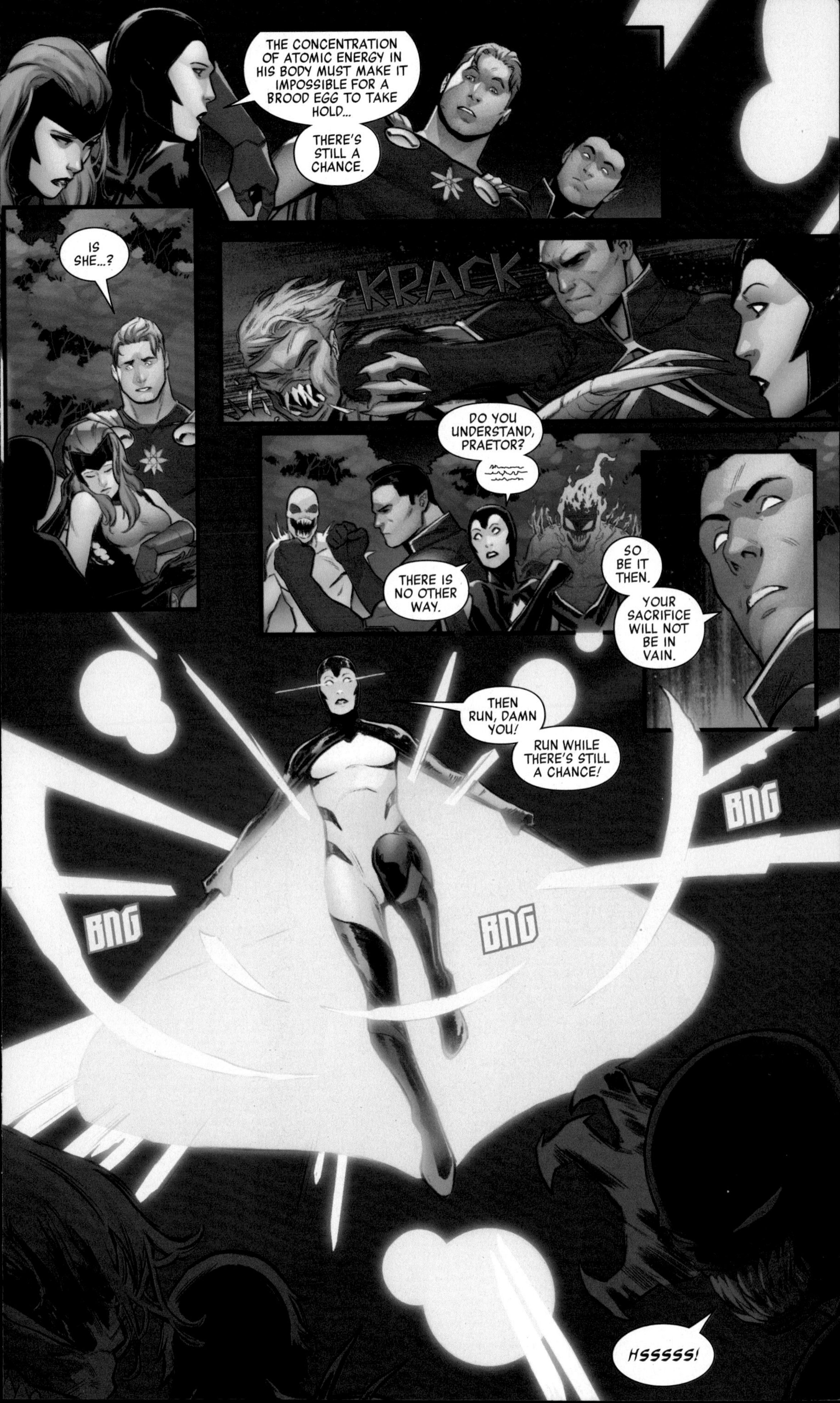
THE CONCENTRATION OF ATOMIC ENERGY IN HIS BODY MUST MAKE IT IMPOSSIBLE FOR A BROOD EGG TO TAKE HOLD...
THERE'S STILL A CHANCE.
IS SHE...?
KRACK
DO YOU UNDERSTAND, PRAETOR?
THERE IS NO OTHER WAY.
SO BE IT THEN.
YOUR SACRIFICE WILL NOT BE IN VAIN.
THEN RUN, DAMN YOU!
RUN WHILE THERE'S STILL A CHANCE!
BNG
BNG
BNG
HSSSSS!

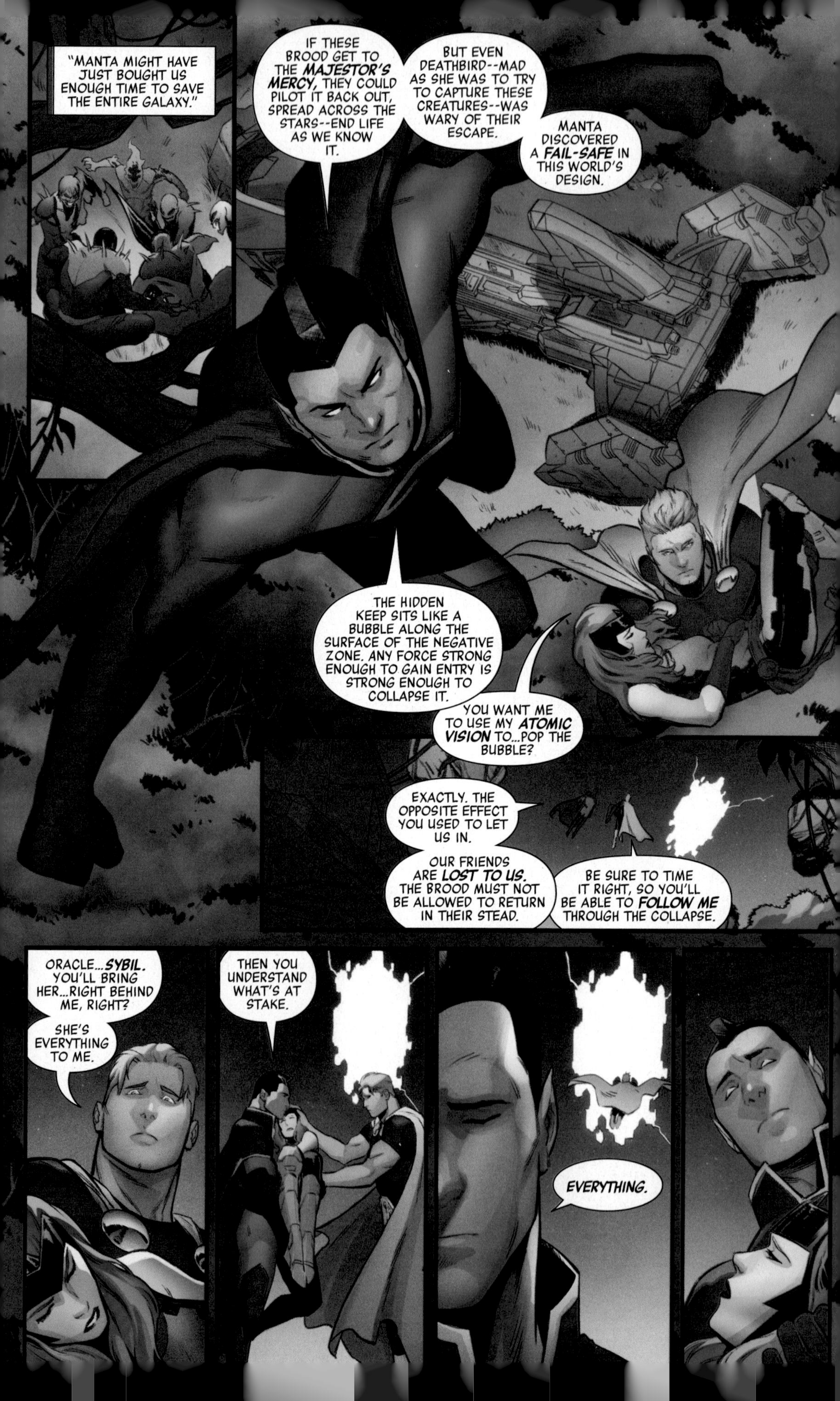
"MANTA MIGHT HAVE JUST BOUGHT US ENOUGH TIME TO SAVE THE ENTIRE GALAXY."
IF THESE BROOD GET TO THE MAJESTOR'S MERCY, THEY COULD PILOT IT BACK OUT, SPREAD ACROSS THE STARS--END LIFE AS WE KNOW IT.
BUT EVEN DEATHBIRD--MAD AS SHE WAS TO TRY TO CAPTURE THESE CREATURES--WAS WARY OF THEIR ESCAPE.
MANTA DISCOVERED A FAIL-SAFE IN THIS WORLD'S DESIGN.
THE HIDDEN KEEP SITS LIKE A BUBBLE ALONG THE SURFACE OF THE NEGATIVE ZONE. ANY FORCE STRONG ENOUGH TO GAIN ENTRY IS STRONG ENOUGH TO COLLAPSE IT.
YOU WANT ME TO USE MY ATOMIC VISION TO...POP THE BUBBLE?
EXACTLY. THE OPPOSITE EFFECT YOU USED TO LET US IN.
OUR FRIENDS ARE LOST TO US. THE BROOD MUST NOT BE ALLOWED TO RETURN IN THEIR STEAD.
BE SURE TO TIME IT RIGHT, SO YOU'LL BE ABLE TO FOLLOW ME THROUGH THE COLLAPSE.
ORACLE...SYBIL. YOU'LL BRING HER...RIGHT BEHIND ME, RIGHT?
SHE'S EVERYTHING TO ME.
THEN YOU UNDERSTAND WHAT'S AT STAKE.
EVERYTHING.

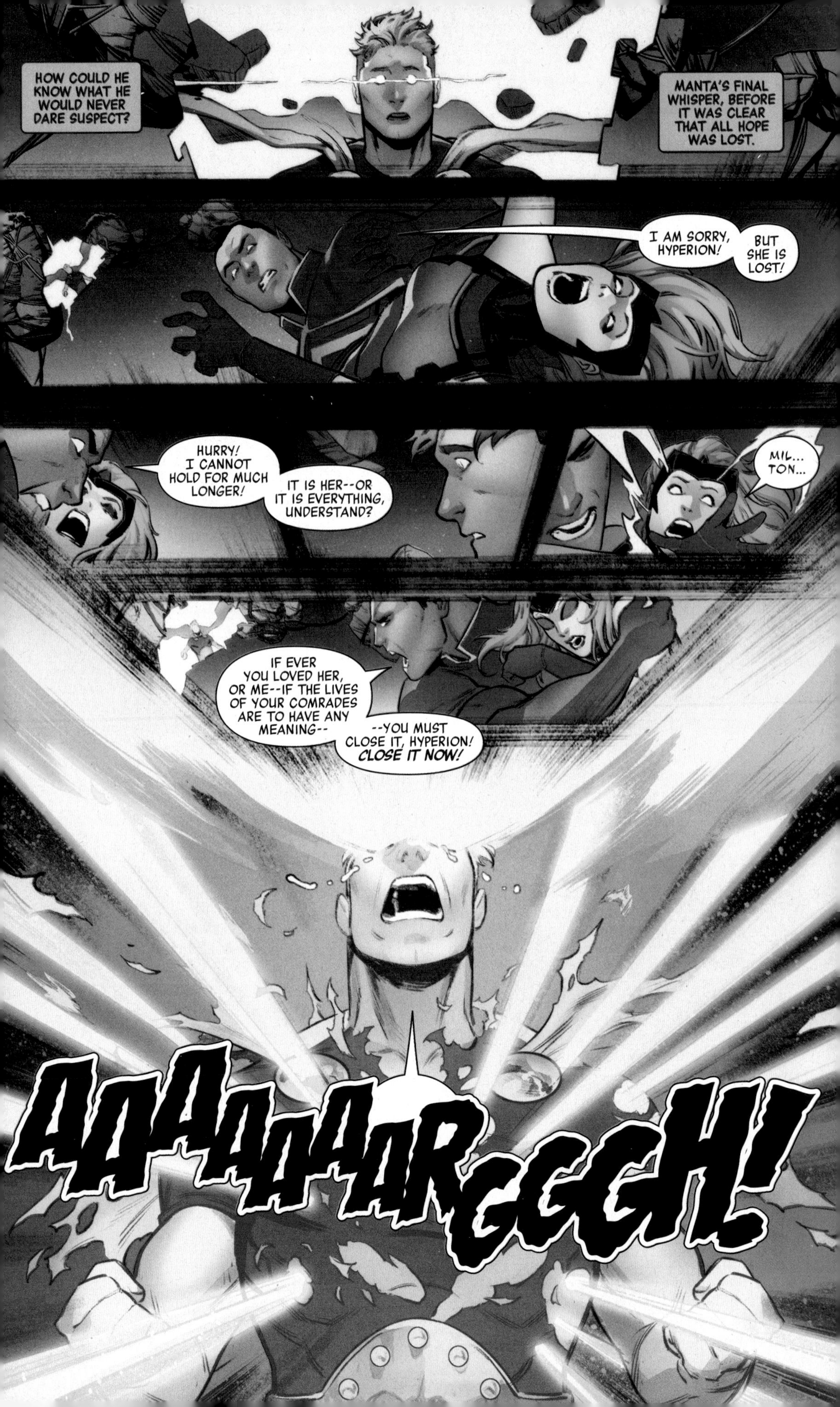

HOW COULD HE KNOW WHAT HE WOULD NEVER DARE SUSPECT?
MANTA'S FINAL WHISPER, BEFORE IT WAS CLEAR THAT ALL HOPE WAS LOST.
I AM SORRY, HYPERION!
BUT SHE IS LOST!
HURRY! I CANNOT HOLD FOR MUCH LONGER!
IT IS HER--OR IT IS EVERYTHING, UNDERSTAND?
MIL... TON...
IF EVER YOU LOVED HER, OR ME--IF THE LIVES OF YOUR COMRADES ARE TO HAVE ANY MEANING--
--YOU MUST CLOSE IT, HYPERION! *CLOSE IT NOW!*
AAAAAARGGGH!

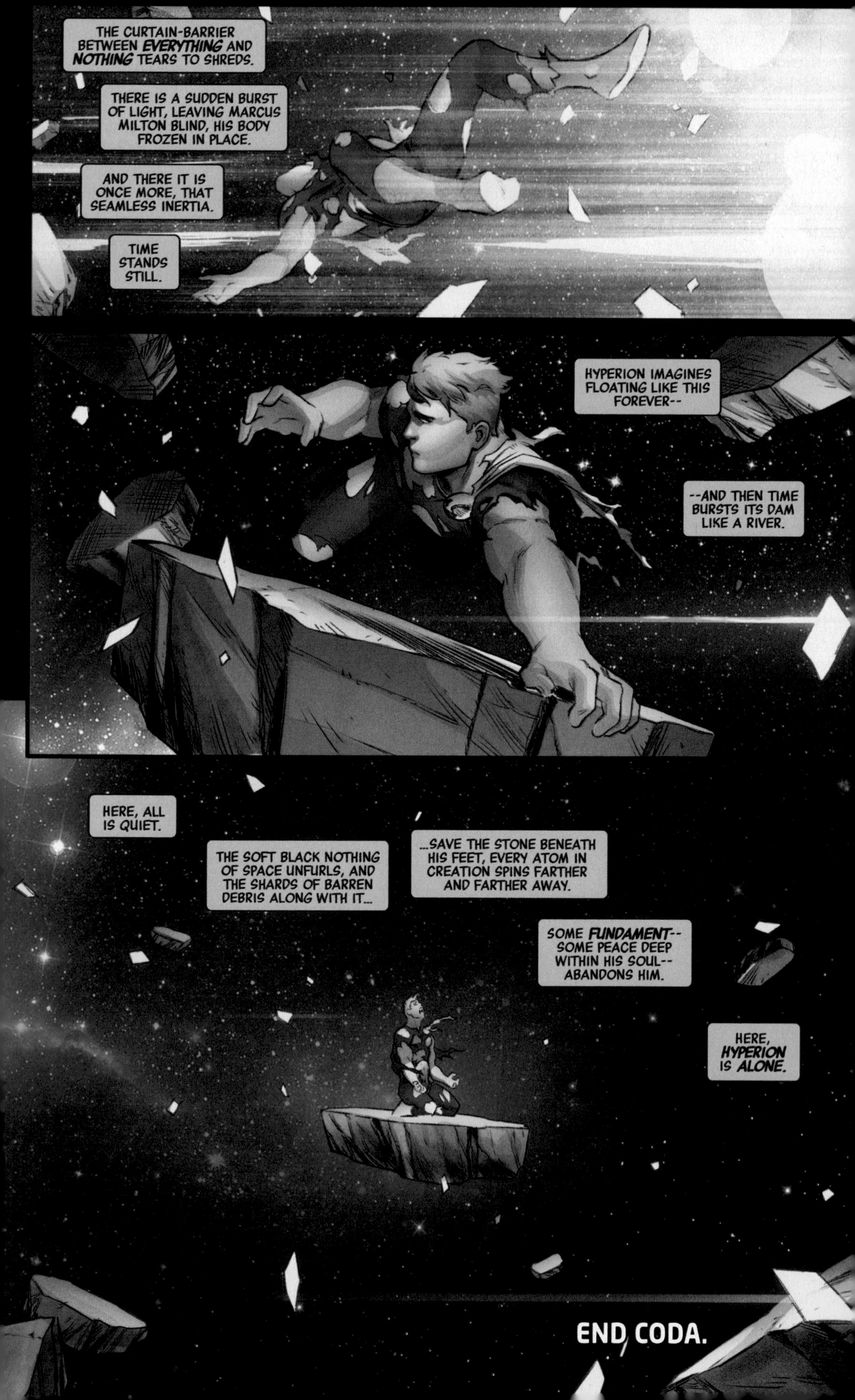
THE CURTAIN-BARRIER BETWEEN EVERYTHING AND NOTHING TEARS TO SHREDS.
THERE IS A SUDDEN BURST OF LIGHT, LEAVING MARCUS MILTON BLIND, HIS BODY FROZEN IN PLACE.
AND THERE IT IS ONCE MORE, THAT SEAMLESS INERTIA.
TIME STANDS STILL.
HYPERION IMAGINES FLOATING LIKE THIS FOREVER--
--AND THEN TIME BURSTS ITS DAM LIKE A RIVER.
HERE, ALL IS QUIET.
THE SOFT BLACK NOTHING OF SPACE UNFURLS, AND THE SHARDS OF BARREN DEBRIS ALONG WITH IT...
...SAVE THE STONE BENEATH HIS FEET, EVERY ATOM IN CREATION SPINS FARTHER AND FARTHER AWAY.
SOME FUNDAMENT-- SOME PEACE DEEP WITHIN HIS SOUL-- ABANDONS HIM.
HERE, HYPERION IS ALONE.
END CODA.

THE IMPERIAL MAILBAG

To whom it may concern,

I must admit I am not certain why HYPERION & THE IMPERIAL GUARD is getting an additional issue after #120 -- it's a fine series, but the lighthearted tone has always struck me as outdated. And now I hear that this STARJAMMERS book is taking its place? What about the rumors in last year's *Wizard* magazine that the House of Ideas was bringing back WWII characters, like Captain America? I'd take that over another "teens in space" adventure.

Maybe it was a fine fit for Marvel's lineup a few years ago, but comics are heading in a more mature direction these days. If it were up to me, we'd have a lot more grit and realism and less pandering.

> Resignedly,
> **Jim Zazzle**
> King of Prussia, PA

Well, Jim, I hope this issue was "gritty" and "realistic" enough for you. I would've been content to leave Hyperion and his friends where the last issue left off, with Deathbird defeated and the future looking bright, but sometimes the story has to go on.

Oh, and as for those rumors--come on. Captain America? Next you'll wanna see them bring back the Human Torch.

Dear Imperial Mailbag,

I have been a faithful reader of this comic since issue #1, but this is my first letter. While I have always loved this series, the recent trend toward realism is testing my faith. It feels like you're trying to write to today's readers without respecting all of us who've been supporting the book since the '80s!

Back in issue #45, Hyperion CLEARLY states that "he feels the power of a thousand dying suns coursing through his veins," but in issue #114, he tells Gladiator that "my body collects cosmic radiation and creates fission to power my abilities." Why are you throwing away years of continuity to sound "cool" and "real"? If I wanted the real world, I would turn on the news.

Please keep comics exciting and fun. I'm seriously considering canceling my subscription.

> **Curt Waidz**
> Salt Lake City, UT

I...don't think you'll like this issue very much, Curt, but as Jim Zazzle pointed out above--maybe some comics DO need to be grittier and more realistic! Should Hyperion just always have a great, fun day?

But if you're in the mood for classic cosmic swashbuckling action, hopefully STARJAMMERS will fill the void in your heart!

Dear team,

I've never written a letter like this simply because I've never had the opportunity, but I can't tell you how much it means to me to see Flashfire and Neutron together. Even if no one else on the team gets it, I get it.

> Thank you,
> **Ellie Moon**
> Brooklyn, NY

P.S. I don't care about the world, I care about Hyperion and Oracle staying together! Tell us there's a way!

Ellie, thank you for writing, and let me say, very genuinely, that I'm glad Flashfire and Neutron's romance had so many earnest fans. It was a joy to show their budding relationship alongside--or in contrast to--Hyperion and Oracle's, and it certainly pained me to kill them all off horribly in this issue.

Maybe in the future another writer will find a way to bring them back! Hope springs...

Dear Editor,

I was walking out of a screening of the brilliant new film *Alien³* (you would be wise to consider publishing some ALIEN comics right away) when I came upon a brand-new storefront dedicated to the sale of special edition single-issue comic books that are guaranteed to go up in value over time--I believe the clerk called them "variants"? Seeing an investment opportunity, I bought two of everything--one to read now and one to flip in the new millennium -- including an edition of the "Death of Hyperion" issue with chromium blood on the cover.

Having been out of the loop in the last few years, where did Hyperion's living costume go? I wish there were compiled editions of all the issues I missed, like a paperback book of comics. Who knows what kind of market there is for that kind of thing.

Until the top creators form their own rival publisher, Make Mine Marvel!

> Your loyal reader,
> **Reese Chobbinson**
> Queens, NY

I only have one quibble with your letter, Reese, and that's this "variant" business. I don't dislike them, but "investment opportunity"? Come on. You think anybody's gonna be printing or collecting special covers in 2002? But I'd love to see Marvel keep up the licensed comics game. Imagine Hyperion and Ripley teaming up to fight the Brood and Xenomorphs together? Fans will be lining up and down the block.

And we did away with the living costume after Howard's run. Check out issues #56-57 to learn why!

Dear Marvel Bullpen,

I'm writing in support of the upcoming STARJAMMERS series. It's a GREAT idea, and I think it really is going to be Marvel's next big hit! I'd love to see more adventures of Scott and Alex Summers. I'd love a whole series about them stowing away on missions, solving mysteries and more! Go Team Summers!

> Signed,
> **Hepzibah's Chew Toy**
> Pasadena, CA

P.S. Are there any plans to bring Captain Britain into the book? She's my favorite.

Thanks so much! I think it's going to have something for everyone -- whether you appreciate the Summers Brothers' boy-adventurer hijinks or prefer Hepzibah's...well, your word choice sort of covers that. Ahem. I've been trying to pitch the Bullpen on more space stories for all kinds of readers--and this is why!

And I'm a big fan of Betsy, but she might have her hands full in Otherworld. But maybe if the Starjammers had a way to enter other dimensions...

Okay, thanks for reading HYPERION & THE IMPERIAL GUARD. It's been an honor to contribute to--and close out--this wonderful series! I hope you'll follow me over to STARJAMMERS when that launches next month-- check out the following preview of #1!

--Ryan

Even though the series is over, we still want to hear from you! Write us at mheroes@marvel.com and mark it "okay to print"--your letter may see print in an upcoming issue of STARJAMMERS!

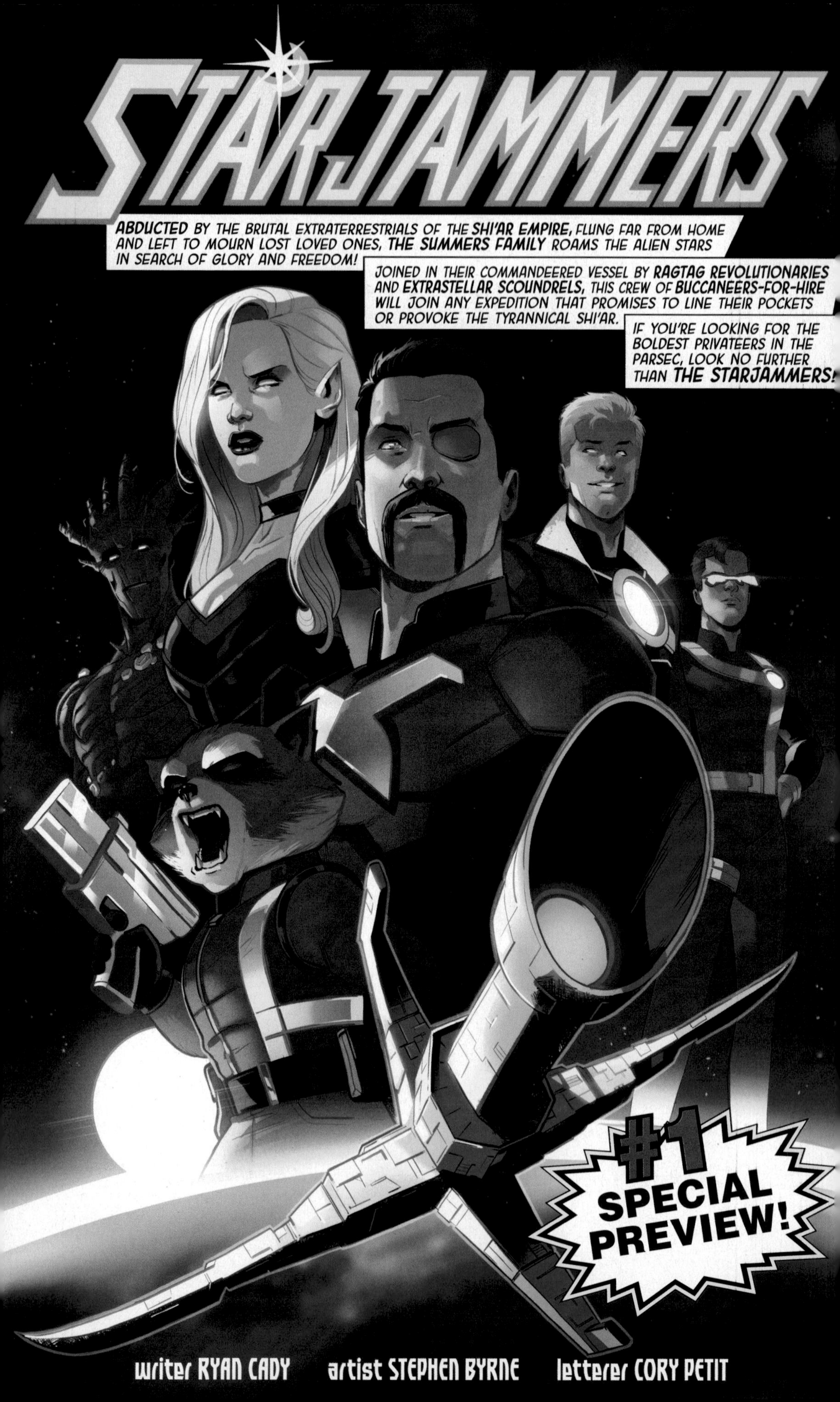
STARJAMMERS
ABDUCTED BY THE BRUTAL EXTRATERRESTRIALS OF THE SHI'AR EMPIRE, FLUNG FAR FROM HOME AND LEFT TO MOURN LOST LOVED ONES, THE SUMMERS FAMILY ROAMS THE ALIEN STARS IN SEARCH OF GLORY AND FREEDOM!
JOINED IN THEIR COMMANDEERED VESSEL BY RAGTAG REVOLUTIONARIES AND EXTRASTELLAR SCOUNDRELS, THIS CREW OF BUCCANEERS-FOR-HIRE WILL JOIN ANY EXPEDITION THAT PROMISES TO LINE THEIR POCKETS OR PROVOKE THE TYRANNICAL SHI'AR.
IF YOU'RE LOOKING FOR THE BOLDEST PRIVATEERS IN THE PARSEC, LOOK NO FURTHER THAN THE STARJAMMERS!
#1 SPECIAL PREVIEW!
writer RYAN CADY
artist STEPHEN BYRNE
letterer CORY PETIT

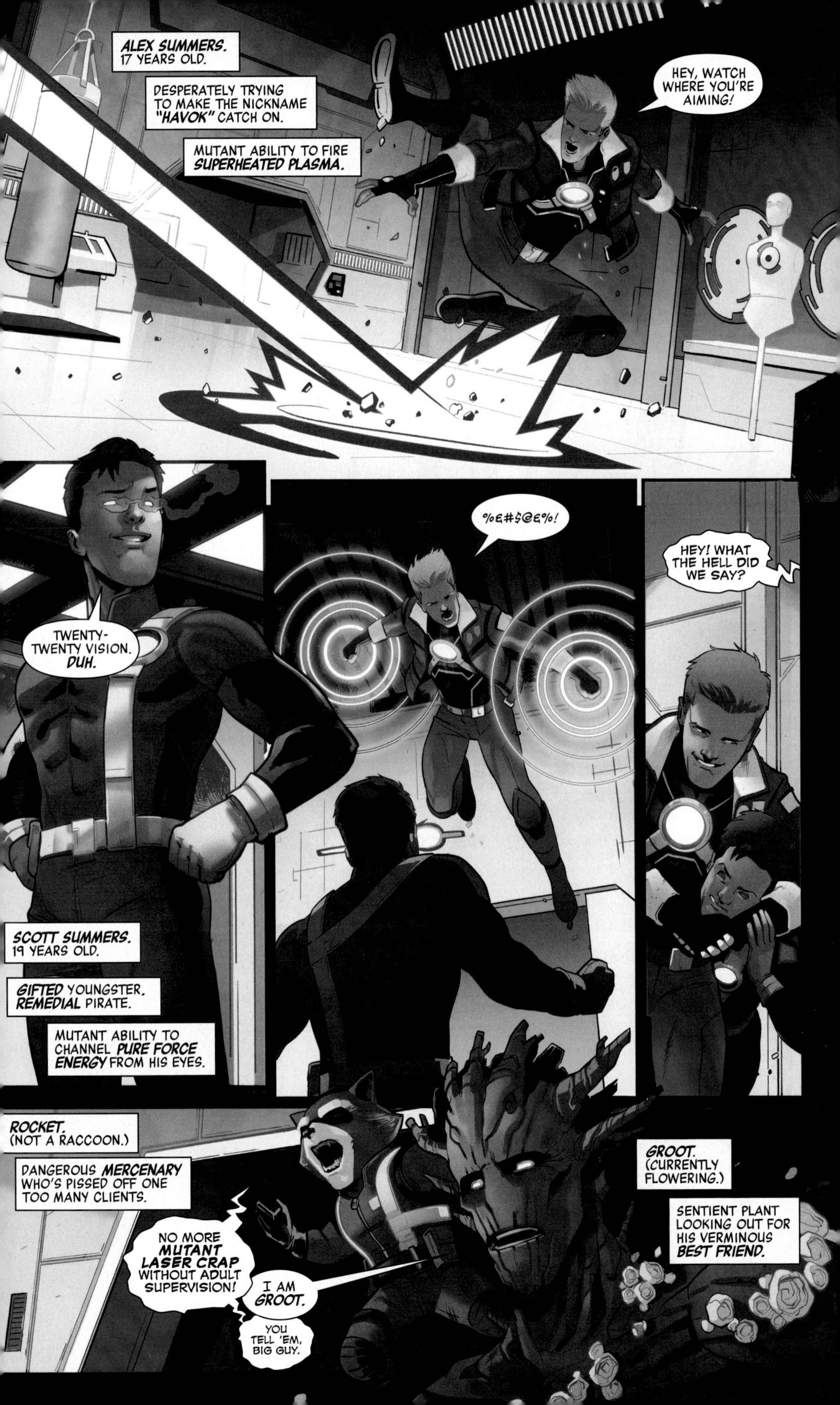

ALEX SUMMERS. 17 YEARS OLD.
DESPERATELY TRYING TO MAKE THE NICKNAME "HAVOK" CATCH ON.
MUTANT ABILITY TO FIRE SUPERHEATED PLASMA.
HEY, WATCH WHERE YOU'RE AIMING!
TWENTY-TWENTY VISION. DUH.
SCOTT SUMMERS. 19 YEARS OLD.
GIFTED YOUNGSTER. REMEDIAL PIRATE.
MUTANT ABILITY TO CHANNEL PURE FORCE ENERGY FROM HIS EYES.
%€#$@€%!
HEY! WHAT THE HELL DID WE SAY?
ROCKET. (NOT A RACCOON.)
DANGEROUS MERCENARY WHO'S PISSED OFF ONE TOO MANY CLIENTS.
NO MORE MUTANT LASER CRAP WITHOUT ADULT SUPERVISION!
I AM GROOT.
YOU TELL 'EM, BIG GUY.
GROOT. (CURRENTLY FLOWERING.)
SENTIENT PLANT LOOKING OUT FOR HIS VERMINOUS BEST FRIEND.

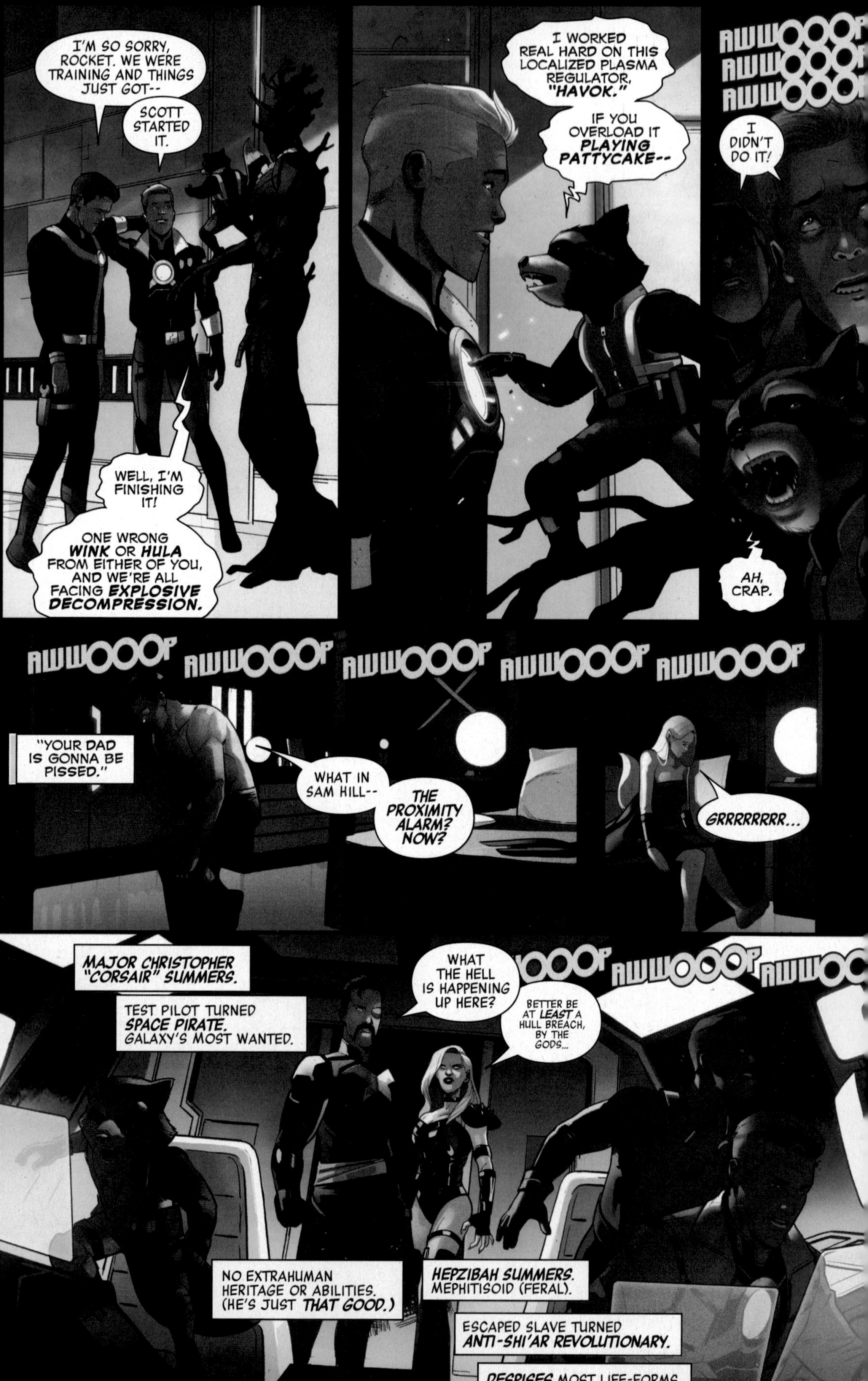

I'M SO SORRY, ROCKET. WE WERE TRAINING AND THINGS JUST GOT--
SCOTT STARTED IT.
WELL, I'M FINISHING IT!
ONE WRONG WINK OR HULA FROM EITHER OF YOU, AND WE'RE ALL FACING EXPLOSIVE DECOMPRESSION.
I WORKED REAL HARD ON THIS LOCALIZED PLASMA REGULATOR, "HAVOK."
IF YOU OVERLOAD IT PLAYING PATTYCAKE--
AWWOOOF AWWOOOF AWWOOOF
I DIDN'T DO IT!
AH, CRAP.
AWWOOOP AWWOOOP AWWOOOP AWWOOOP AWWOOOP
"YOUR DAD IS GONNA BE PISSED."
WHAT IN SAM HILL--
THE PROXIMITY ALARM? NOW?
GRRRRRRRR...
MAJOR CHRISTOPHER "CORSAIR" SUMMERS.
TEST PILOT TURNED SPACE PIRATE. GALAXY'S MOST WANTED.
WHAT THE HELL IS HAPPENING UP HERE?
BETTER BE AT LEAST A HULL BREACH, BY THE GODS...
OOOP AWWOOOP AWWO
NO EXTRAHUMAN HERITAGE OR ABILITIES. (HE'S JUST THAT GOOD.)
HEPZIBAH SUMMERS. MEPHITISOID (FERAL).
ESCAPED SLAVE TURNED ANTI-SHI'AR REVOLUTIONARY.
DESPISES MOST LIFE-FORMS. (HER STUDLY SOULMATE IS A RARE EXCEPTION.)

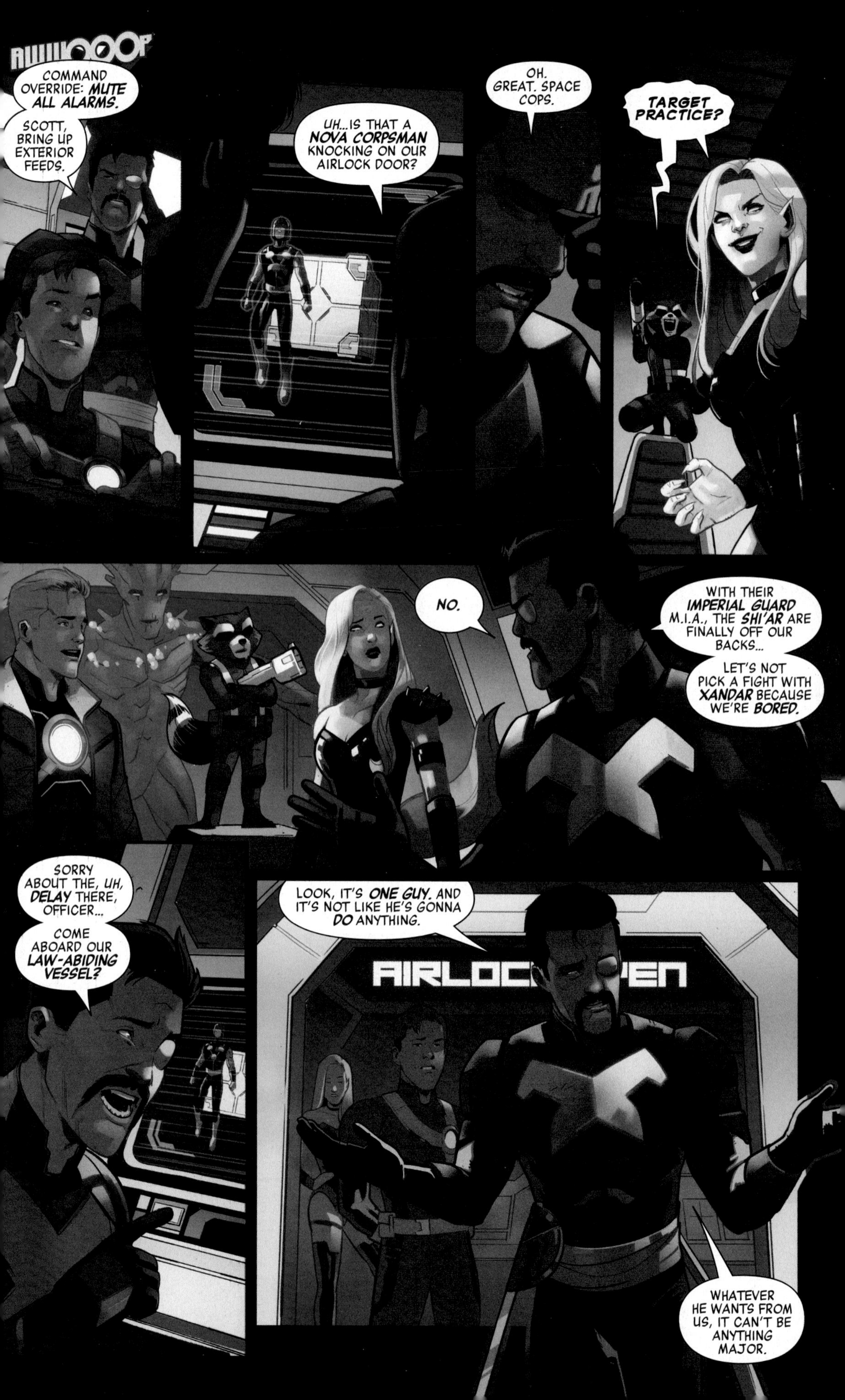
AWWOOOP
COMMAND OVERRIDE: MUTE ALL ALARMS.
SCOTT, BRING UP EXTERIOR FEEDS.
UH...IS THAT A NOVA CORPSMAN KNOCKING ON OUR AIRLOCK DOOR?
OH. GREAT. SPACE COPS.
TARGET PRACTICE?
NO.
WITH THEIR IMPERIAL GUARD M.I.A., THE SHI'AR ARE FINALLY OFF OUR BACKS...
LET'S NOT PICK A FIGHT WITH XANDAR BECAUSE WE'RE BORED.
SORRY ABOUT THE, UH, DELAY THERE, OFFICER...
COME ABOARD OUR LAW-ABIDING VESSEL?
LOOK, IT'S ONE GUY. AND IT'S NOT LIKE HE'S GONNA DO ANYTHING.
WHATEVER HE WANTS FROM US, IT CAN'T BE ANYTHING MAJOR.

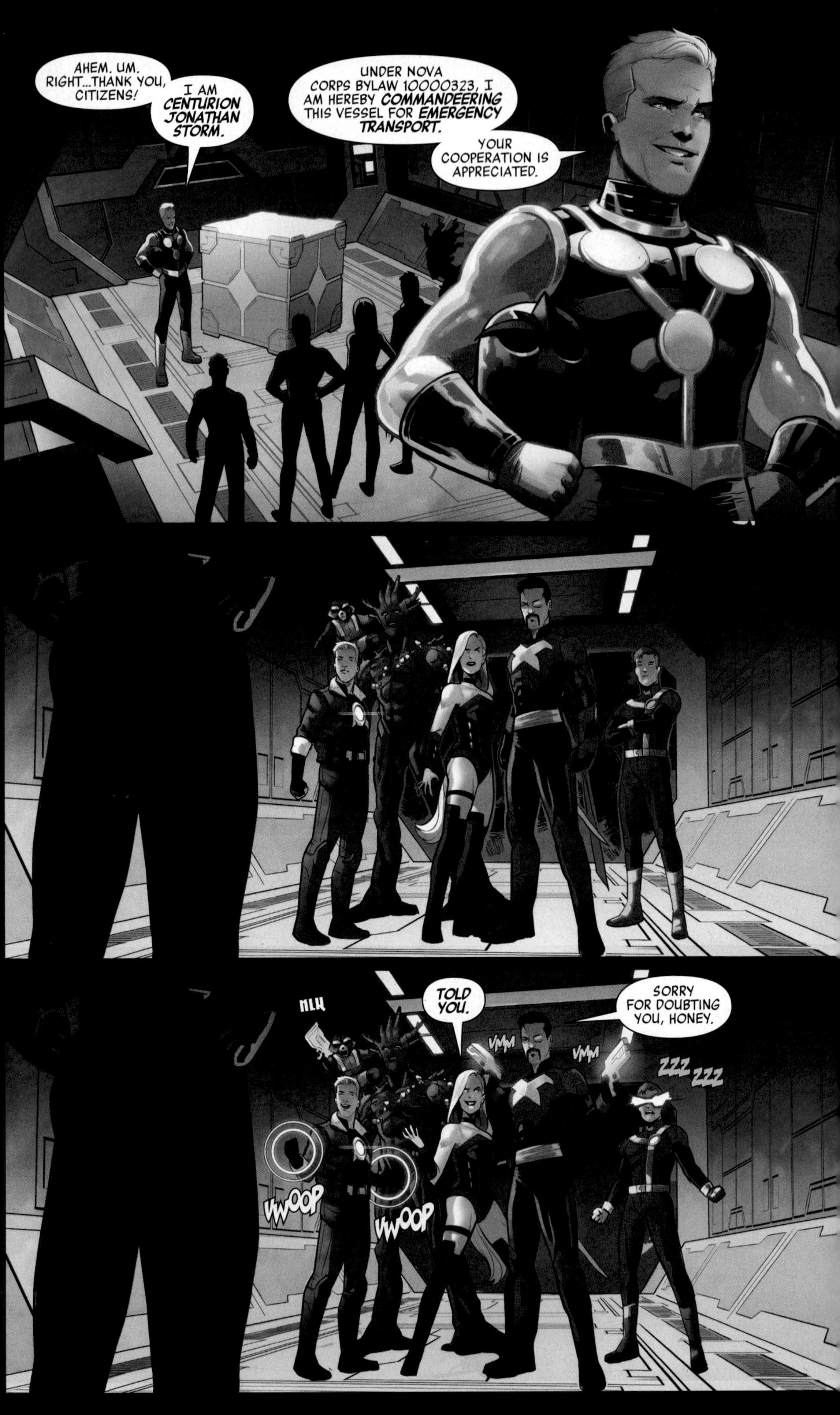
AHEM. UM. RIGHT...THANK YOU, CITIZENS!
I AM CENTURION JONATHAN STORM.
UNDER NOVA CORPS BYLAW 10000323, I AM HEREBY COMMANDEERING THIS VESSEL FOR EMERGENCY TRANSPORT.
YOUR COOPERATION IS APPRECIATED.
KLIK
TOLD YOU.
SORRY FOR DOUBTING YOU, HONEY.
VMM
VMM
ZZZ ZZZ
VWOOP
VWOOP

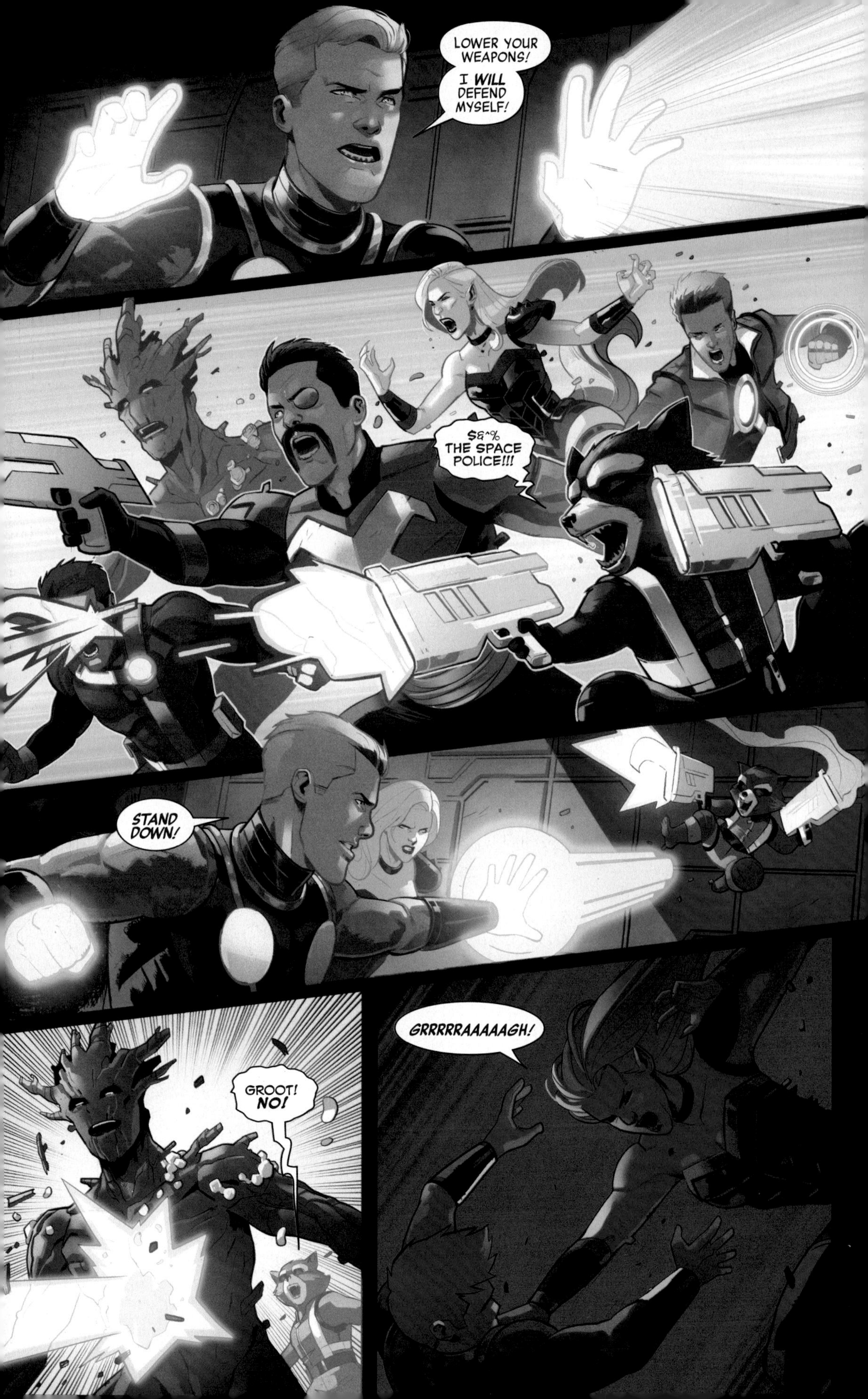

LOWER YOUR WEAPONS!
I WILL DEFEND MYSELF!
$&^% THE SPACE POLICE!!!
STAND DOWN!
GROOT! NO!
GRRRRRAAAAAGH!

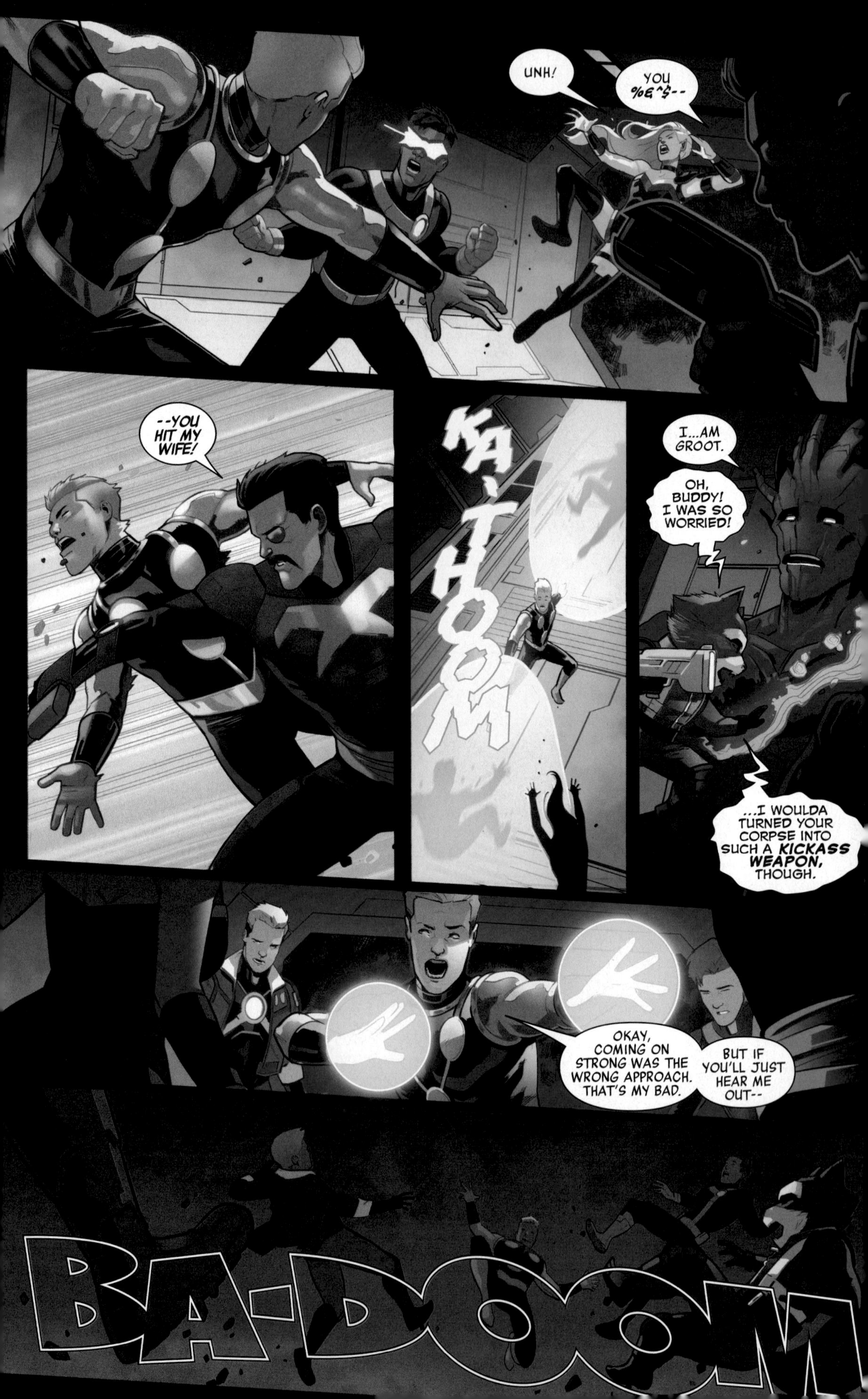
UNH!
YOU %£^$--
--YOU HIT MY WIFE!
KA-THOOM
I...AM GROOT.
OH, BUDDY! I WAS SO WORRIED!
...I WOULDA TURNED YOUR CORPSE INTO SUCH A KICKASS WEAPON, THOUGH.
OKAY, COMING ON STRONG WAS THE WRONG APPROACH. THAT'S MY BAD.
BUT IF YOU'LL JUST HEAR ME OUT--
BA-DOOM

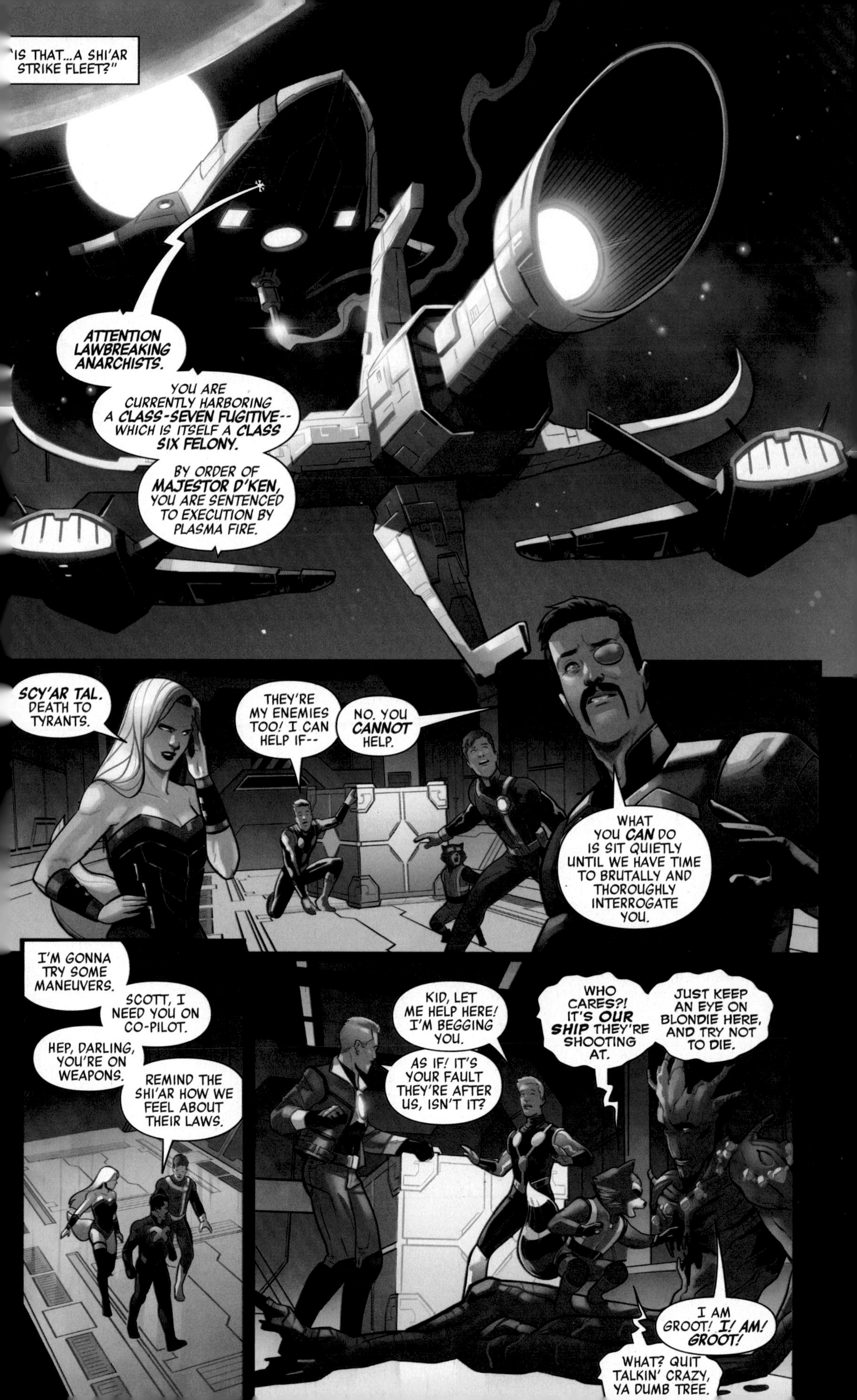

"IS THAT...A SHI'AR STRIKE FLEET?"
ATTENTION LAWBREAKING ANARCHISTS.
YOU ARE CURRENTLY HARBORING A CLASS-SEVEN FUGITIVE-- WHICH IS ITSELF A CLASS SIX FELONY.
BY ORDER OF MAJESTOR D'KEN, YOU ARE SENTENCED TO EXECUTION BY PLASMA FIRE.
SCY'AR TAL. DEATH TO TYRANTS.
THEY'RE MY ENEMIES TOO! I CAN HELP IF--
NO. YOU CANNOT HELP.
WHAT YOU CAN DO IS SIT QUIETLY UNTIL WE HAVE TIME TO BRUTALLY AND THOROUGHLY INTERROGATE YOU.
I'M GONNA TRY SOME MANEUVERS.
SCOTT, I NEED YOU ON CO-PILOT.
HEP, DARLING, YOU'RE ON WEAPONS.
REMIND THE SHI'AR HOW WE FEEL ABOUT THEIR LAWS.
KID, LET ME HELP HERE! I'M BEGGING YOU.
AS IF! IT'S YOUR FAULT THEY'RE AFTER US, ISN'T IT?
WHO CARES?! IT'S OUR SHIP THEY'RE SHOOTING AT.
JUST KEEP AN EYE ON BLONDIE HERE, AND TRY NOT TO DIE.
I AM GROOT! I! AM! GROOT!
WHAT? QUIT TALKIN' CRAZY, YA DUMB TREE.

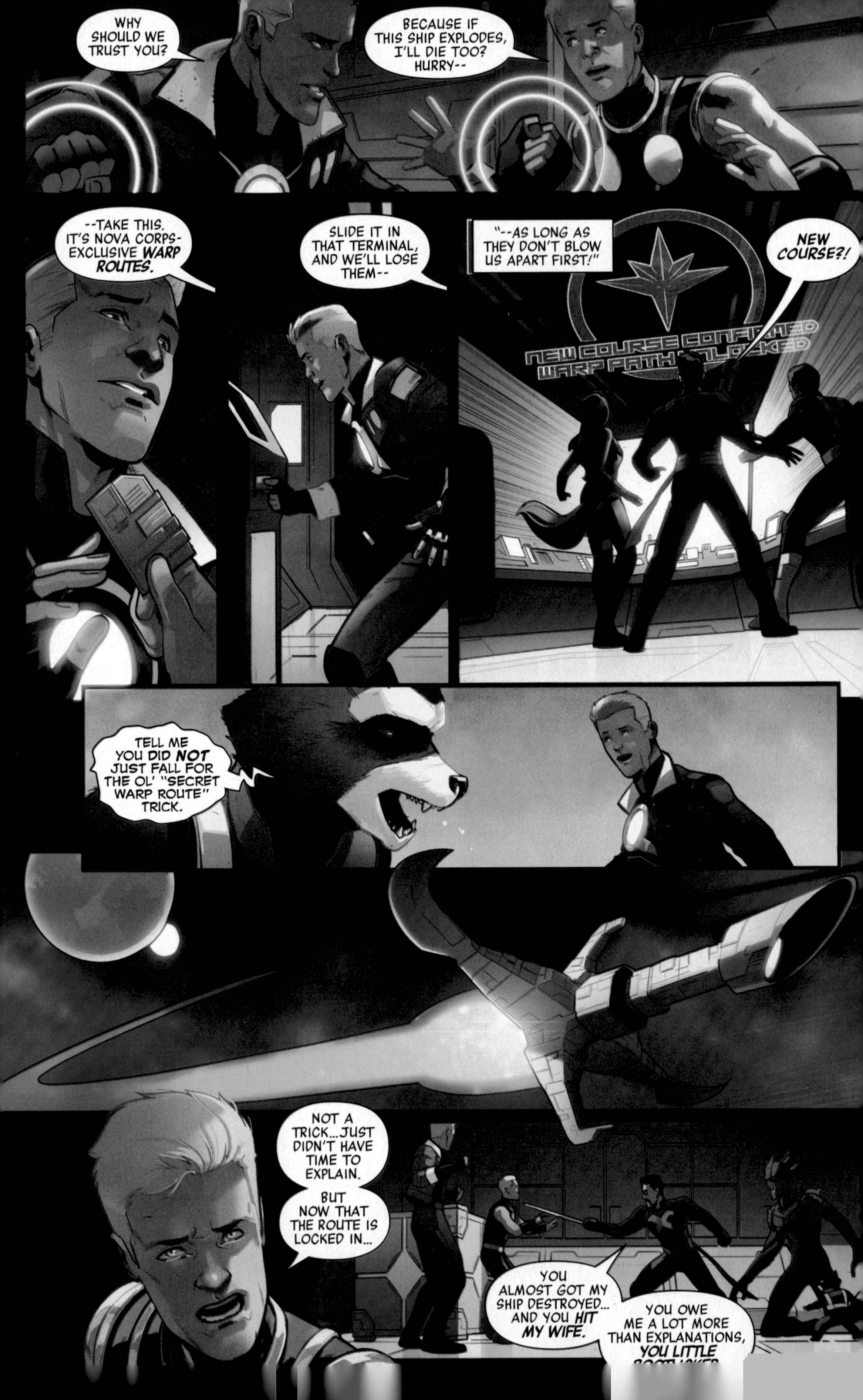
WHY SHOULD WE TRUST YOU?
BECAUSE IF THIS SHIP EXPLODES, I'LL DIE TOO? HURRY--
--TAKE THIS. IT'S NOVA CORPS-EXCLUSIVE *WARP ROUTES.*
SLIDE IT IN THAT TERMINAL, AND WE'LL LOSE THEM--
"--AS LONG AS THEY DON'T BLOW US APART FIRST!"
NEW COURSE?!
NEW COURSE CONFIRMED
WARP PATH
TELL ME YOU DID *NOT* JUST FALL FOR THE OL' "SECRET WARP ROUTE" TRICK.
NOT A TRICK...JUST DIDN'T HAVE TIME TO EXPLAIN.
BUT NOW THAT THE ROUTE IS LOCKED IN...
YOU ALMOST GOT MY SHIP DESTROYED... AND YOU *HIT MY WIFE.*
YOU OWE ME A LOT MORE THAN EXPLANATIONS, *YOU LITTLE*

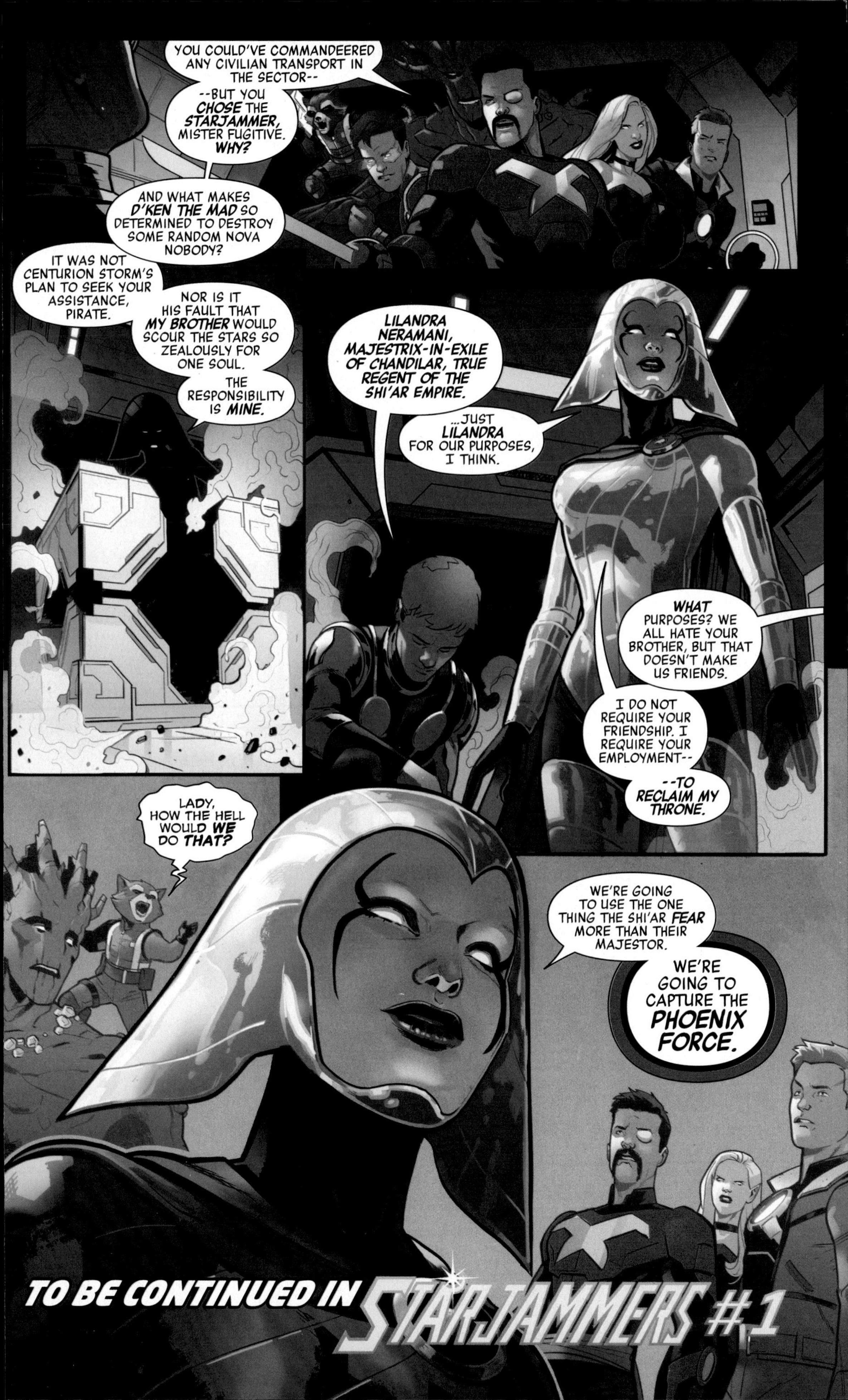
YOU COULD'VE COMMANDEERED ANY CIVILIAN TRANSPORT IN THE SECTOR--
--BUT YOU CHOSE THE STARJAMMER, MISTER FUGITIVE. WHY?
AND WHAT MAKES D'KEN THE MAD SO DETERMINED TO DESTROY SOME RANDOM NOVA NOBODY?
IT WAS NOT CENTURION STORM'S PLAN TO SEEK YOUR ASSISTANCE, PIRATE.
NOR IS IT HIS FAULT THAT MY BROTHER WOULD SCOUR THE STARS SO ZEALOUSLY FOR ONE SOUL.
THE RESPONSIBILITY IS MINE.
LILANDRA NERAMANI, MAJESTRIX-IN-EXILE OF CHANDILAR, TRUE REGENT OF THE SHI'AR EMPIRE.
...JUST LILANDRA FOR OUR PURPOSES, I THINK.
WHAT PURPOSES? WE ALL HATE YOUR BROTHER, BUT THAT DOESN'T MAKE US FRIENDS.
I DO NOT REQUIRE YOUR FRIENDSHIP. I REQUIRE YOUR EMPLOYMENT--
--TO RECLAIM MY THRONE.
LADY, HOW THE HELL WOULD WE DO THAT?
WE'RE GOING TO USE THE ONE THING THE SHI'AR FEAR MORE THAN THEIR MAJESTOR.
WE'RE GOING TO CAPTURE THE PHOENIX FORCE.
TO BE CONTINUED IN STARJAMMERS #1

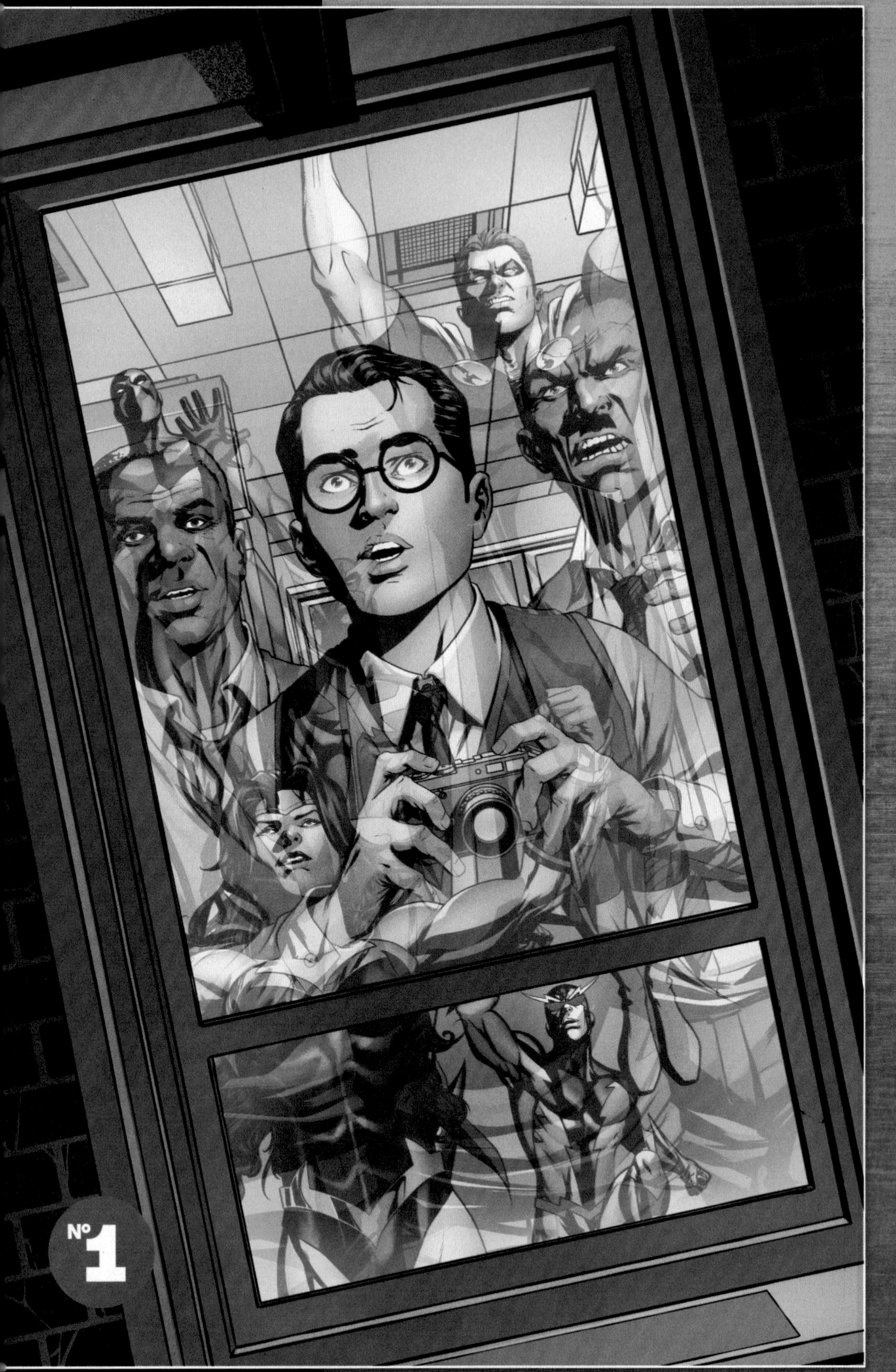

Nº 1

PETER PARKER
THE AMAZING SHUTTERBUG

"DESTINY CALLS"

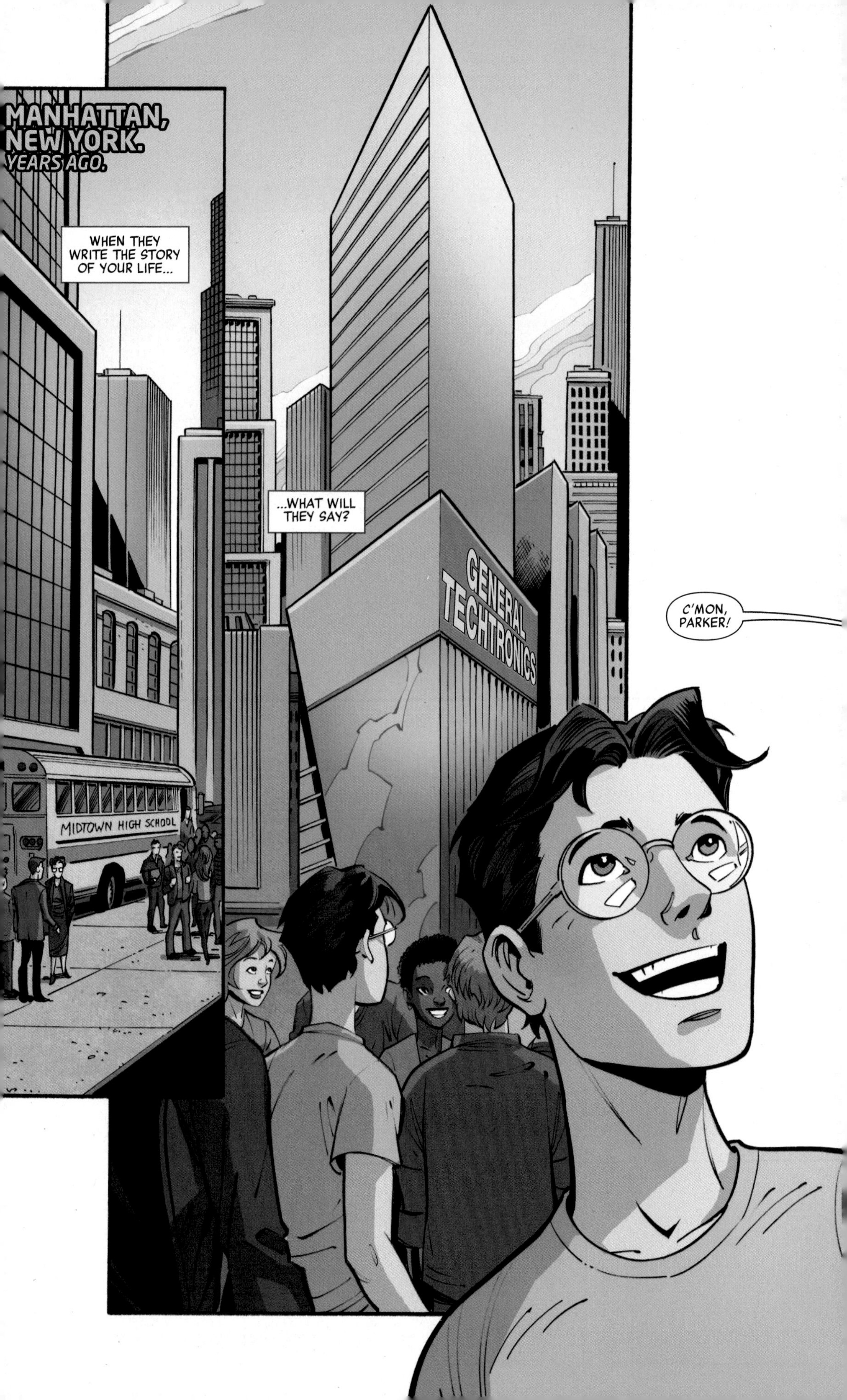
MANHATTAN, NEW YORK.
YEARS AGO.
WHEN THEY WRITE THE STORY OF YOUR LIFE...
...WHAT WILL THEY SAY?
GENERAL TECHTRONICS
MIDTOWN HIGH SCHOOL
C'MON, PARKER!

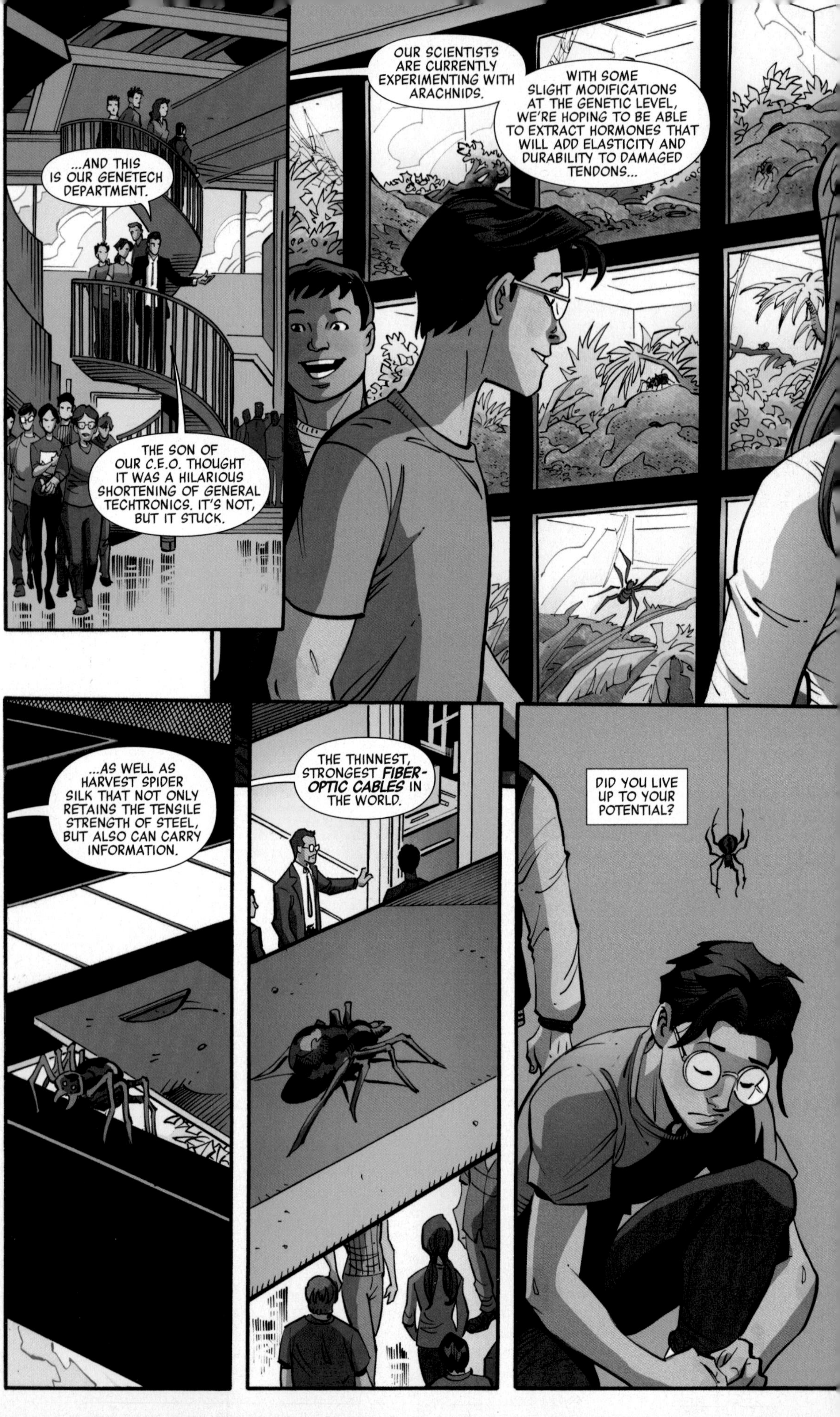
...AND THIS IS OUR GENETECH DEPARTMENT.
THE SON OF OUR C.E.O. THOUGHT IT WAS A HILARIOUS SHORTENING OF GENERAL TECHTRONICS. IT'S NOT, BUT IT STUCK.
OUR SCIENTISTS ARE CURRENTLY EXPERIMENTING WITH ARACHNIDS.
WITH SOME SLIGHT MODIFICATIONS AT THE GENETIC LEVEL, WE'RE HOPING TO BE ABLE TO EXTRACT HORMONES THAT WILL ADD ELASTICITY AND DURABILITY TO DAMAGED TENDONS...
...AS WELL AS HARVEST SPIDER SILK THAT NOT ONLY RETAINS THE TENSILE STRENGTH OF STEEL, BUT ALSO CAN CARRY INFORMATION.
THE THINNEST, STRONGEST FIBER-OPTIC CABLES IN THE WORLD.
DID YOU LIVE UP TO YOUR POTENTIAL?

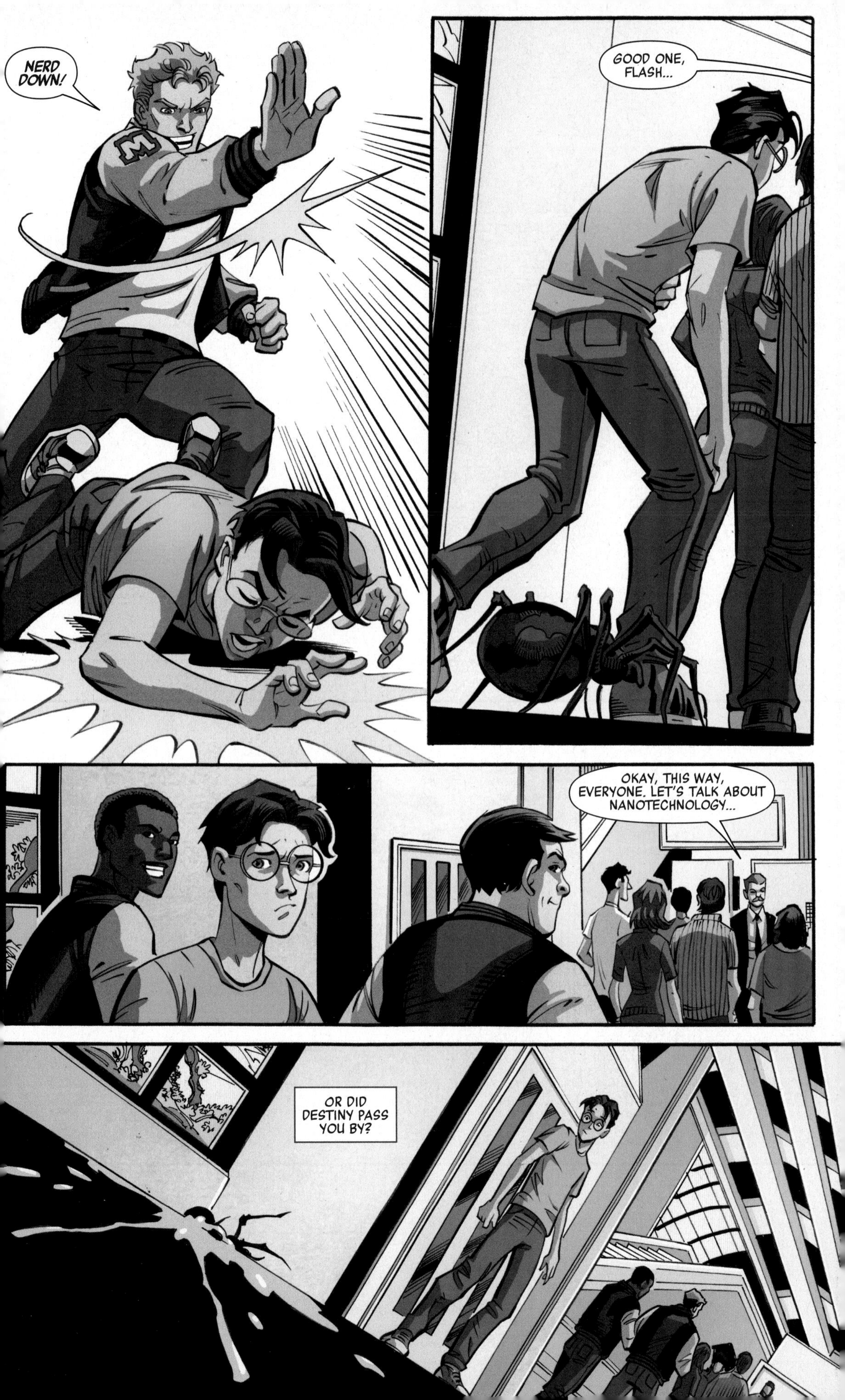
NERD DOWN!
GOOD ONE, FLASH...
OKAY, THIS WAY, EVERYONE. LET'S TALK ABOUT NANOTECHNOLOGY...
OR DID DESTINY PASS YOU BY?

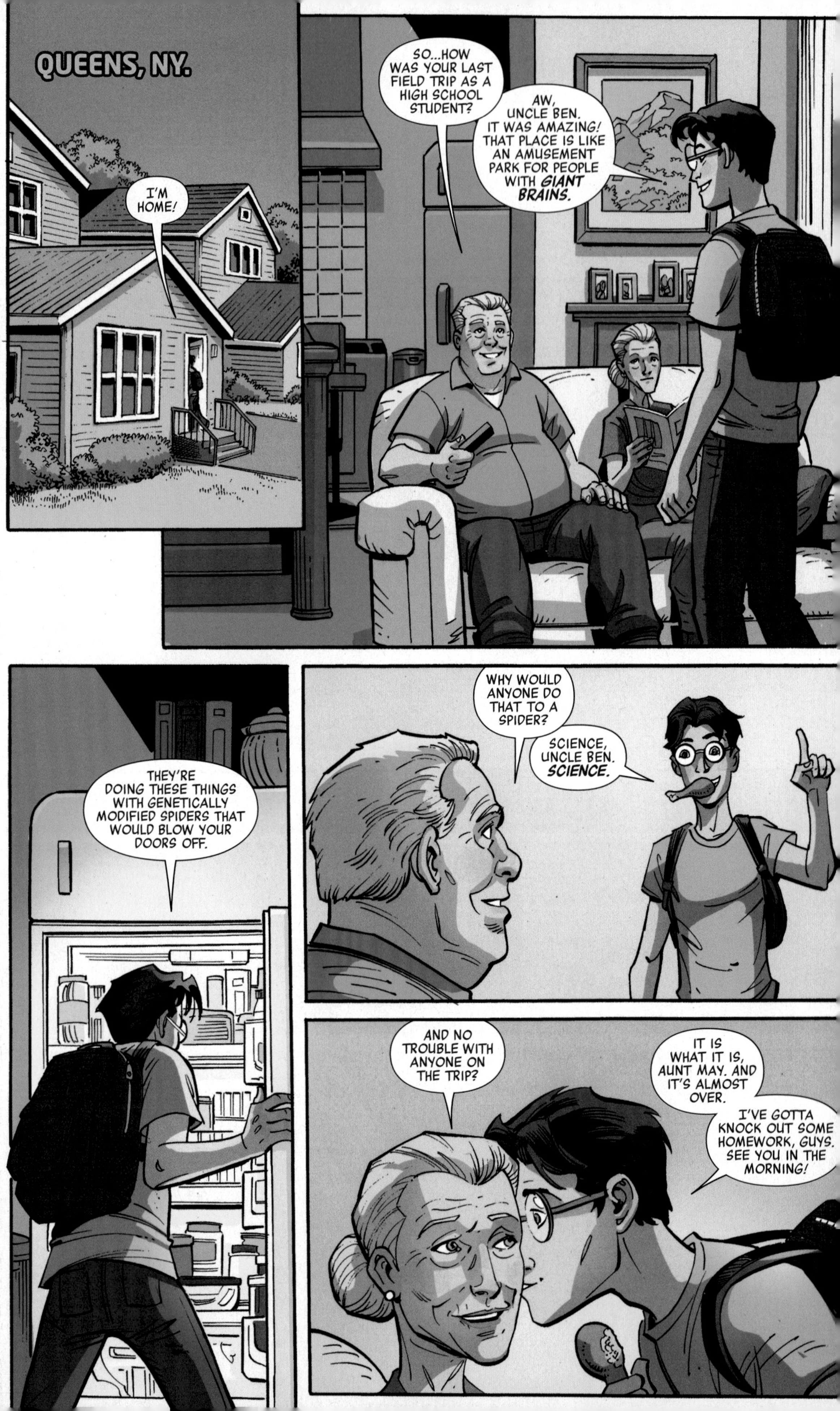
QUEENS, NY.
I'M HOME!
SO...HOW WAS YOUR LAST FIELD TRIP AS A HIGH SCHOOL STUDENT?
AW, UNCLE BEN. IT WAS AMAZING! THAT PLACE IS LIKE AN AMUSEMENT PARK FOR PEOPLE WITH GIANT BRAINS.
THEY'RE DOING THESE THINGS WITH GENETICALLY MODIFIED SPIDERS THAT WOULD BLOW YOUR DOORS OFF.
WHY WOULD ANYONE DO THAT TO A SPIDER?
SCIENCE, UNCLE BEN. SCIENCE.
AND NO TROUBLE WITH ANYONE ON THE TRIP?
IT IS WHAT IT IS, AUNT MAY. AND IT'S ALMOST OVER.
I'VE GOTTA KNOCK OUT SOME HOMEWORK, GUYS. SEE YOU IN THE MORNING!

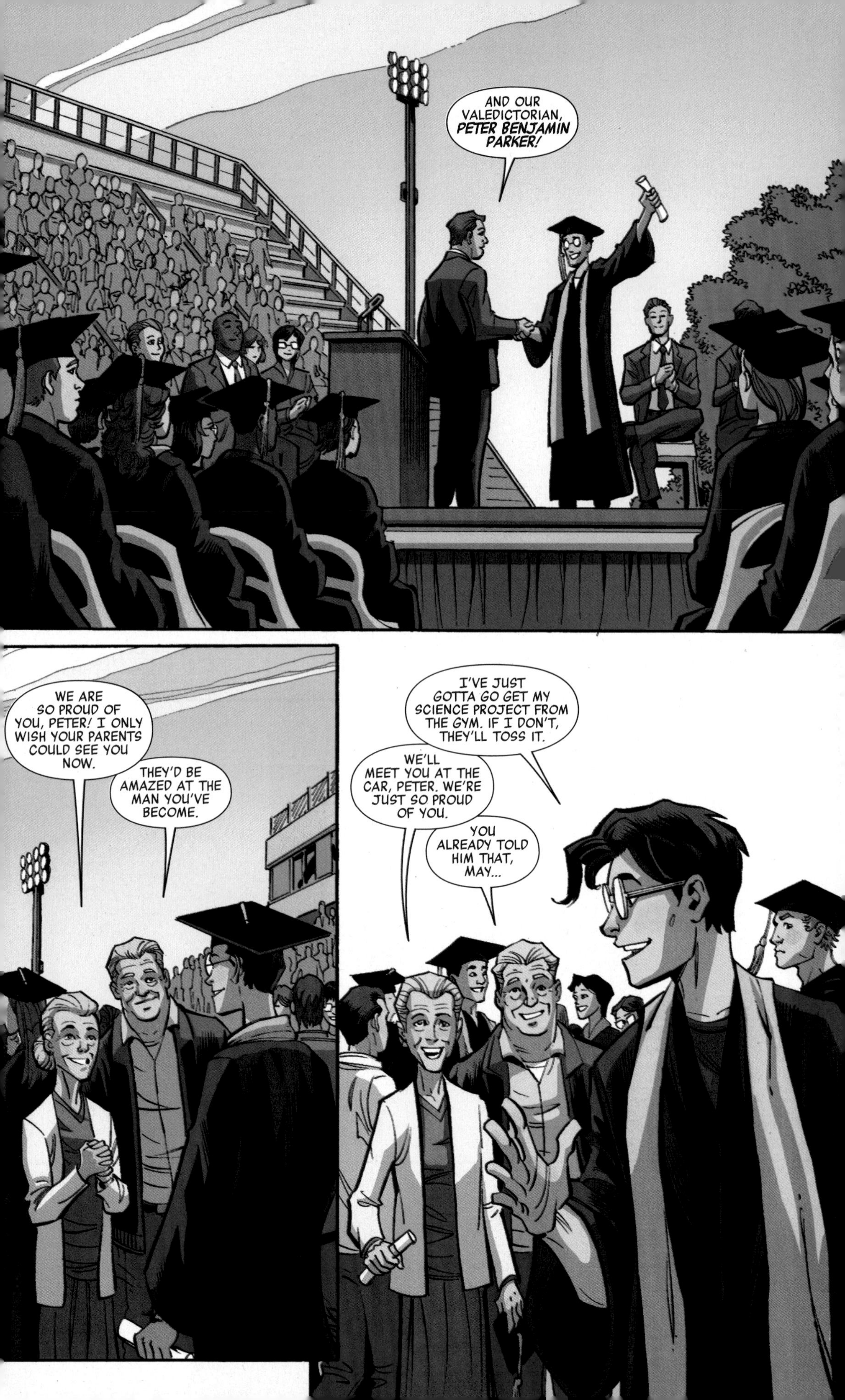
AND OUR VALEDICTORIAN, PETER BENJAMIN PARKER!
WE ARE SO PROUD OF YOU, PETER! I ONLY WISH YOUR PARENTS COULD SEE YOU NOW.
THEY'D BE AMAZED AT THE MAN YOU'VE BECOME.
I'VE JUST GOTTA GO GET MY SCIENCE PROJECT FROM THE GYM. IF I DON'T, THEY'LL TOSS IT.
WE'LL MEET YOU AT THE CAR, PETER. WE'RE JUST SO PROUD OF YOU.
YOU ALREADY TOLD HIM THAT, MAY...

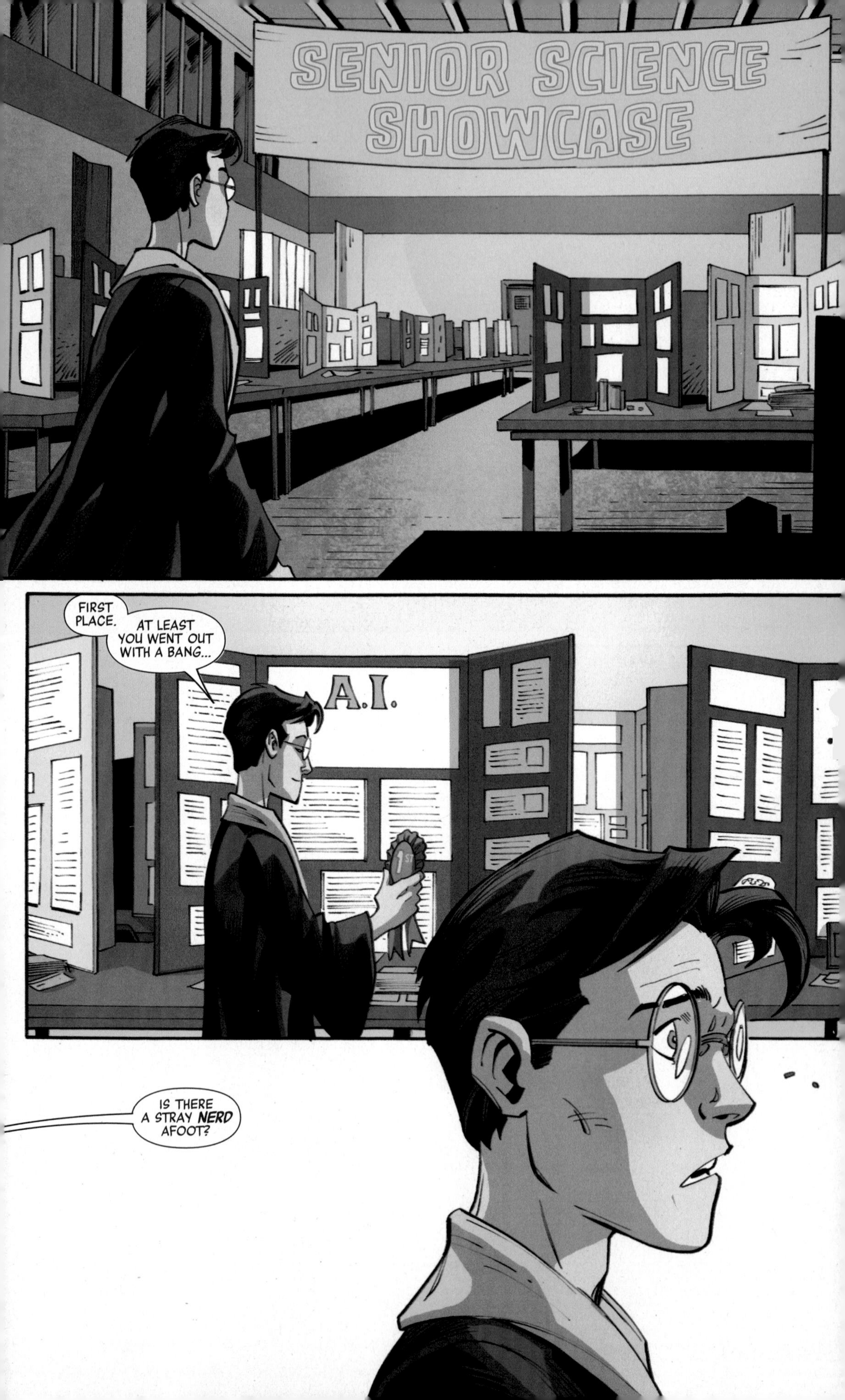
SENIOR SCIENCE SHOWCASE
FIRST PLACE.
AT LEAST YOU WENT OUT WITH A BANG...
A.I.
1ST
IS THERE A STRAY NERD AFOOT?

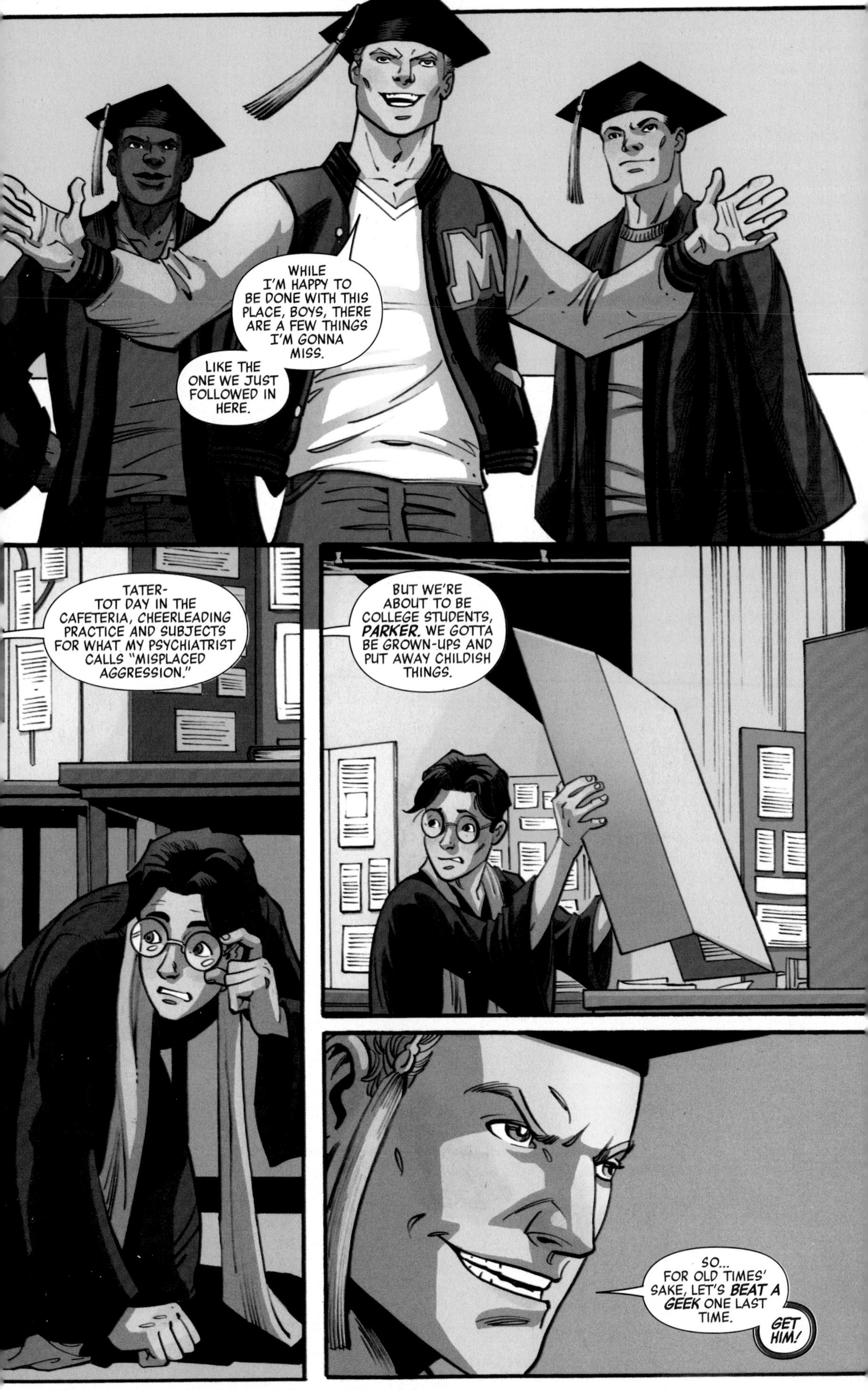
WHILE I'M HAPPY TO BE DONE WITH THIS PLACE, BOYS, THERE ARE A FEW THINGS I'M GONNA MISS.
LIKE THE ONE WE JUST FOLLOWED IN HERE.
TATER-TOT DAY IN THE CAFETERIA, CHEERLEADING PRACTICE AND SUBJECTS FOR WHAT MY PSYCHIATRIST CALLS "MISPLACED AGGRESSION."
BUT WE'RE ABOUT TO BE COLLEGE STUDENTS, PARKER. WE GOTTA BE GROWN-UPS AND PUT AWAY CHILDISH THINGS.
SO... FOR OLD TIMES' SAKE, LET'S BEAT A GEEK ONE LAST TIME.
GET HIM!

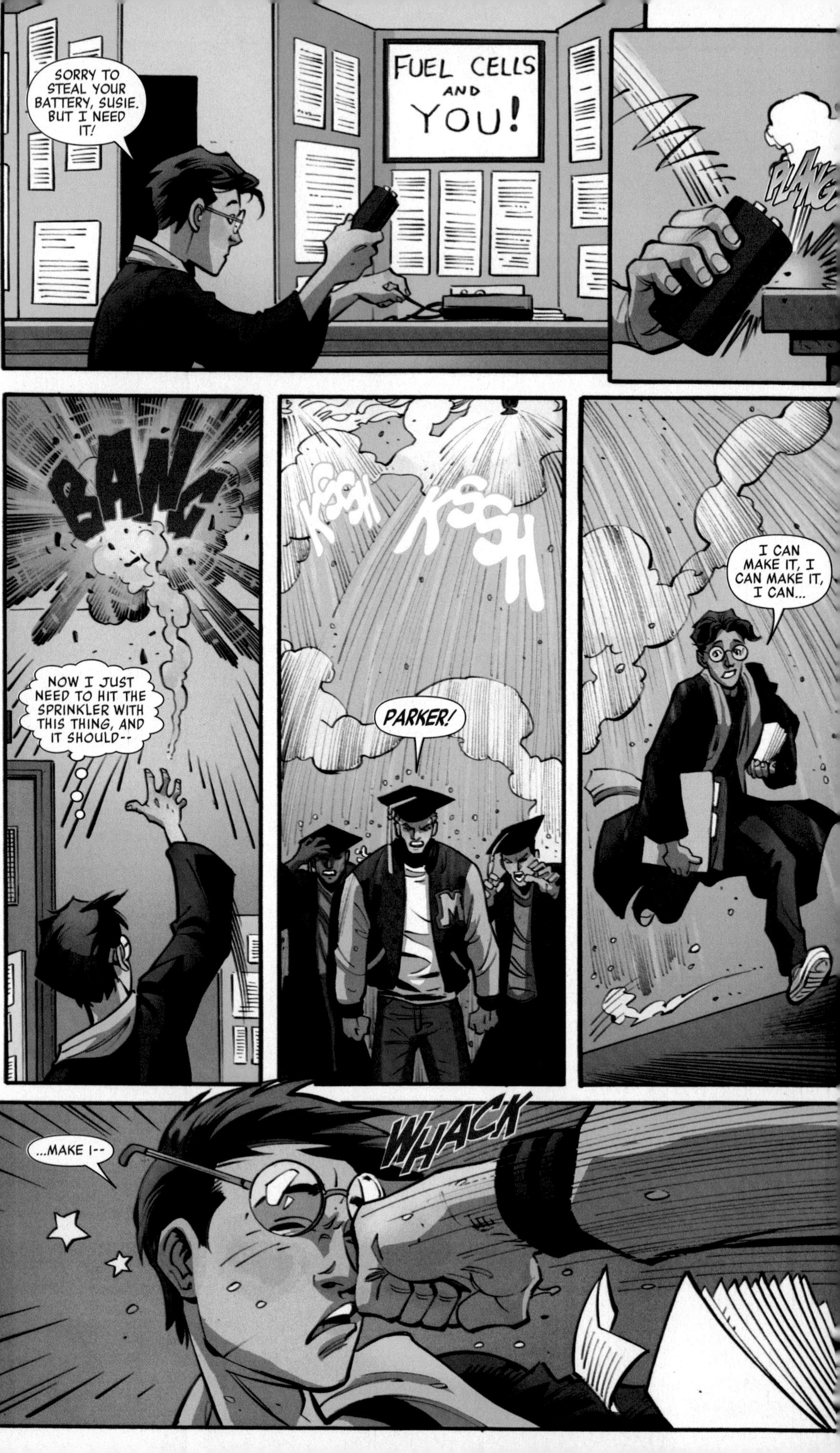
SORRY TO STEAL YOUR BATTERY, SUSIE. BUT I NEED IT!
FUEL CELLS AND YOU!
PLANG
BANG
NOW I JUST NEED TO HIT THE SPRINKLER WITH THIS THING, AND IT SHOULD--
KSSH KSSH
PARKER!
I CAN MAKE IT, I CAN MAKE IT, I CAN...
...MAKE I--
WHACK

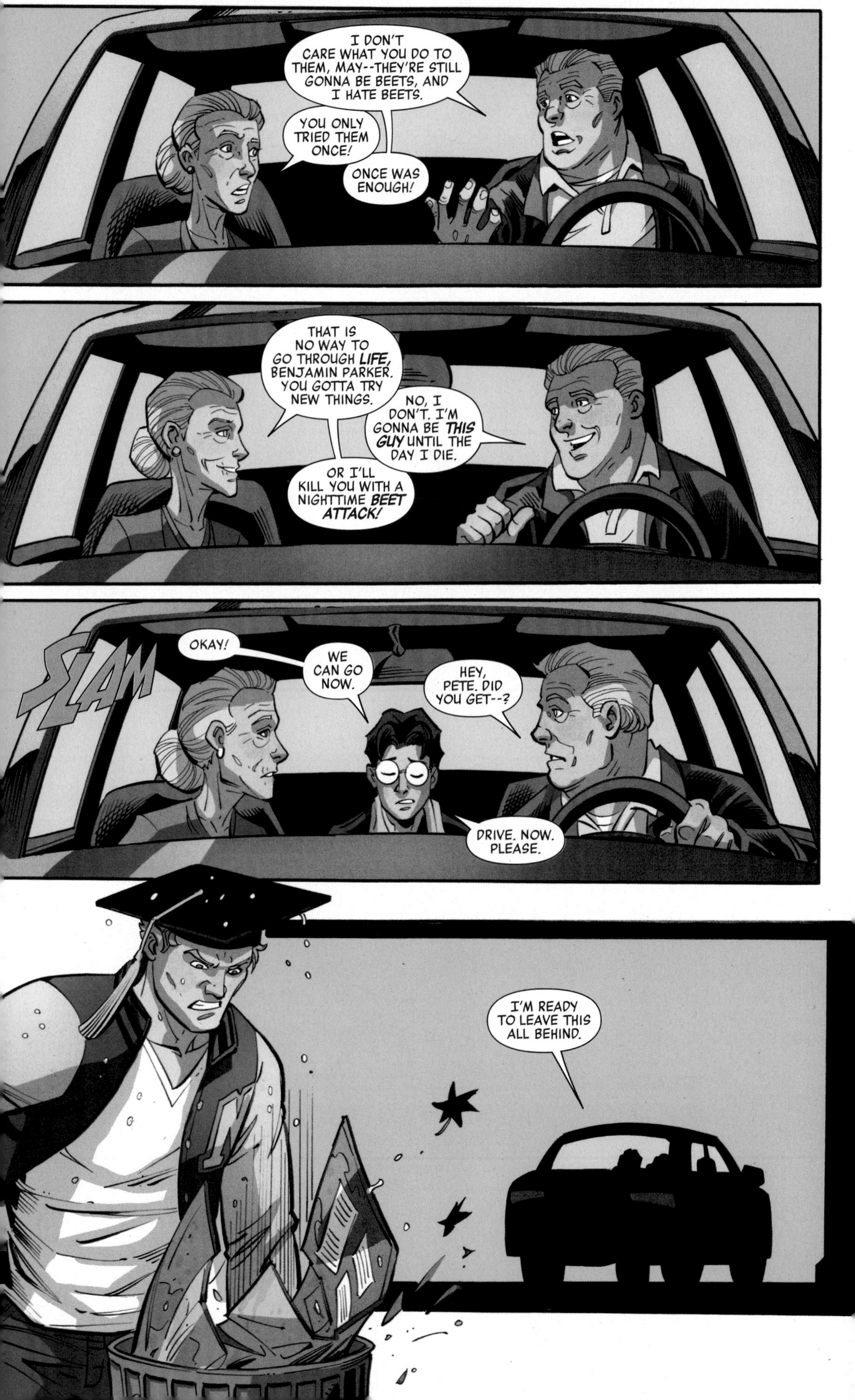

I DON'T CARE WHAT YOU DO TO THEM, MAY--THEY'RE STILL GONNA BE BEETS, AND I HATE BEETS.
YOU ONLY TRIED THEM ONCE!
ONCE WAS ENOUGH!
THAT IS NO WAY TO GO THROUGH LIFE, BENJAMIN PARKER. YOU GOTTA TRY NEW THINGS.
NO, I DON'T. I'M GONNA BE THIS GUY UNTIL THE DAY I DIE.
OR I'LL KILL YOU WITH A NIGHTTIME BEET ATTACK!
SLAM
OKAY!
WE CAN GO NOW.
HEY, PETE. DID YOU GET--?
DRIVE. NOW. PLEASE.
I'M READY TO LEAVE THIS ALL BEHIND.

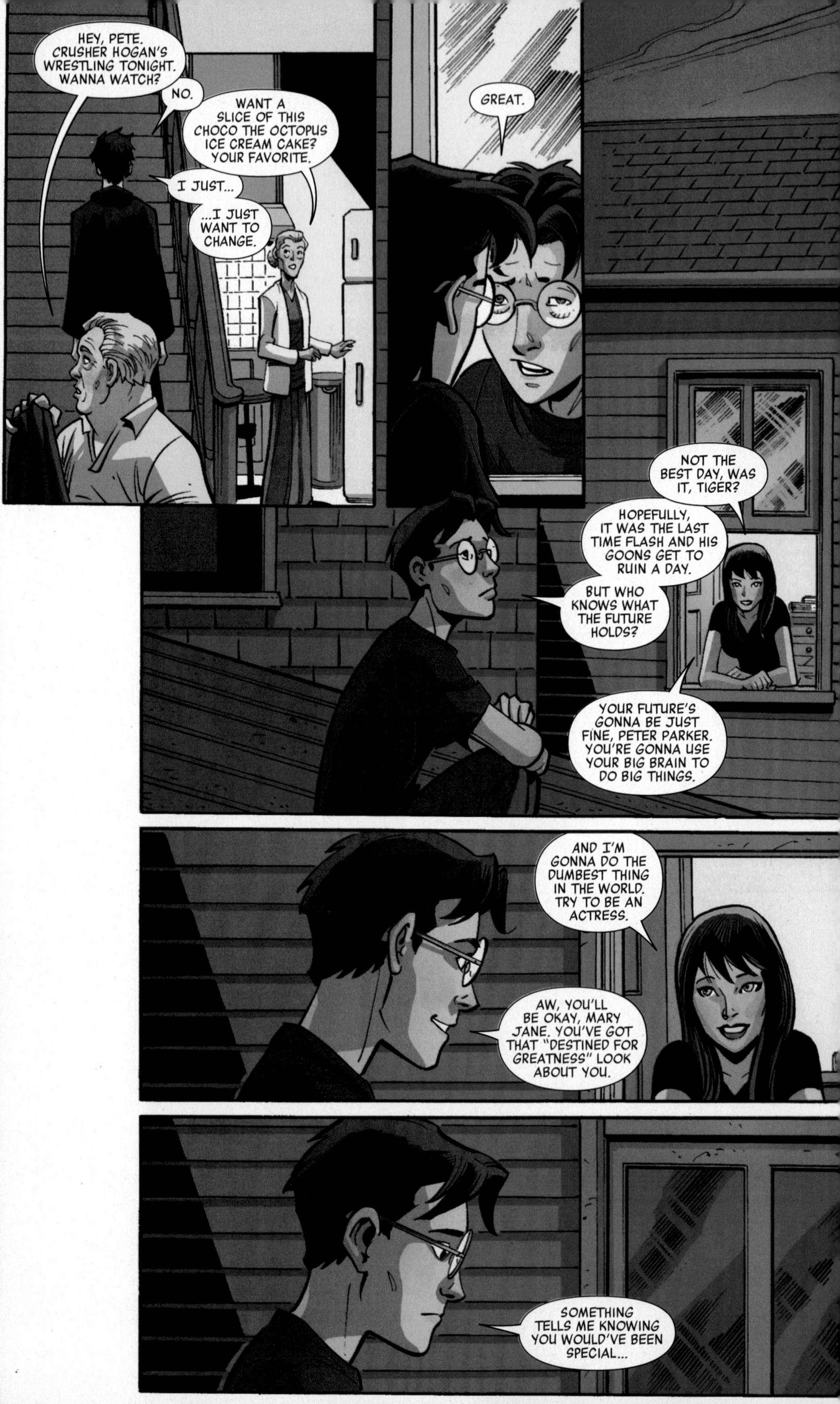
HEY, PETE. CRUSHER HOGAN'S WRESTLING TONIGHT. WANNA WATCH?
NO.
WANT A SLICE OF THIS CHOCO THE OCTOPUS ICE CREAM CAKE? YOUR FAVORITE.
I JUST...
...I JUST WANT TO CHANGE.
GREAT.
NOT THE BEST DAY, WAS IT, TIGER?
HOPEFULLY, IT WAS THE LAST TIME FLASH AND HIS GOONS GET TO RUIN A DAY.
BUT WHO KNOWS WHAT THE FUTURE HOLDS?
YOUR FUTURE'S GONNA BE JUST FINE, PETER PARKER. YOU'RE GONNA USE YOUR BIG BRAIN TO DO BIG THINGS.
AND I'M GONNA DO THE DUMBEST THING IN THE WORLD. TRY TO BE AN ACTRESS.
AW, YOU'LL BE OKAY, MARY JANE. YOU'VE GOT THAT "DESTINED FOR GREATNESS" LOOK ABOUT YOU.
SOMETHING TELLS ME KNOWING YOU WOULD'VE BEEN SPECIAL...

In a world in which the Avengers never existed, the Squadron Supreme
of America are and have always been Earth's Mightiest Heroes!

In this world, the absence of the Avengers has had myriad
unforeseen and unexpected ramifications, including on one
unsuspecting teenager and family in Queens...

PETER PARKER
THE AMAZING SHUTTERBUG

"DESTINY CALLS"

MARC BERNARDIN WRITER

RAFAEL DE LATORRE ARTIST (PAGES 11–30)

RON LIM PENCILER (PAGES 1–10)

SCOTT HANNA INKER (PAGES 1–10)

JIM CAMPBELL COLORIST

VC's **ARIANA MAHER** LETTERER

MIKE **McKONE** & ERICK **ARCINIEGA** COVER ARTISTS

GREG **LAND** & FRANK **D'ARMATA** VARIANT COVER ARTISTS

JAY **BOWEN** GRAPHIC DESIGN

DANNY **KHAZEM** ASSISTANT EDITOR

DEVIN **LEWIS** EDITOR

TOM **BREVOORT** EXECUTIVE EDITOR

C.B. **CEBULSKI** EDITOR IN CHIEF

HEROES REBORN

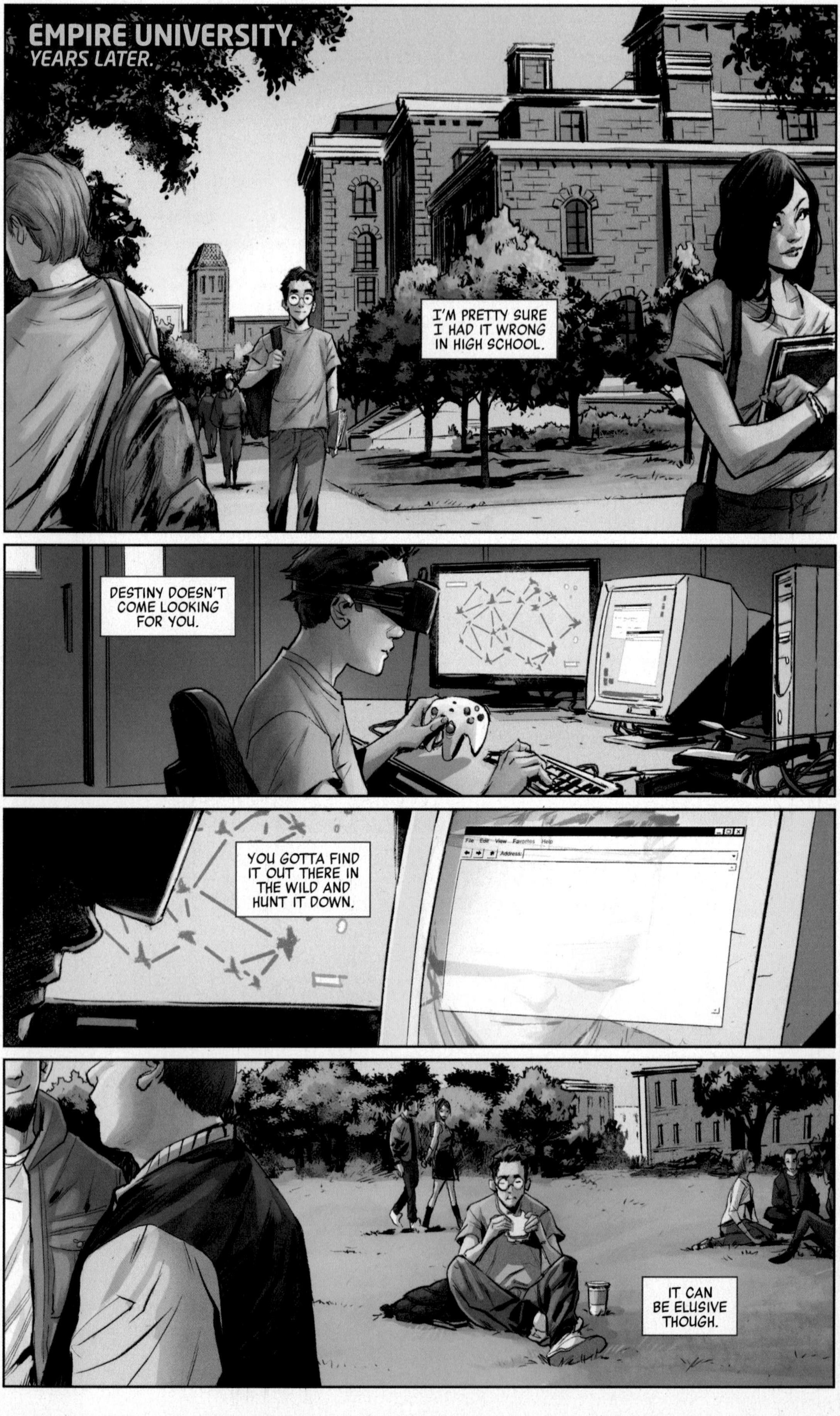
EMPIRE UNIVERSITY.
YEARS LATER.
I'M PRETTY SURE I HAD IT WRONG IN HIGH SCHOOL.
DESTINY DOESN'T COME LOOKING FOR YOU.
YOU GOTTA FIND IT OUT THERE IN THE WILD AND HUNT IT DOWN.
IT CAN BE ELUSIVE THOUGH.

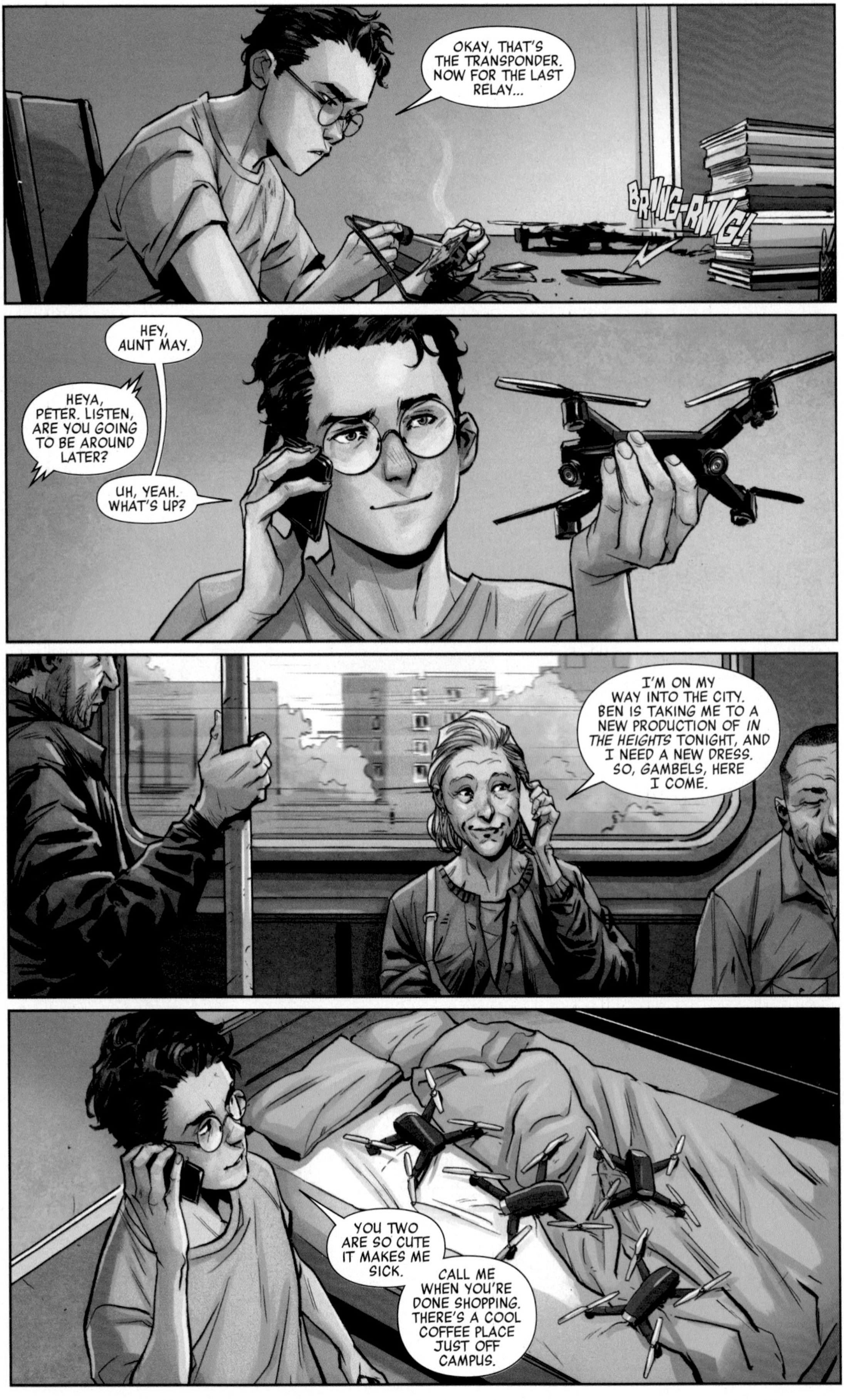
OKAY, THAT'S THE TRANSPONDER. NOW FOR THE LAST RELAY...
BRNNG-RNNG!
HEY, AUNT MAY.
HEYA, PETER. LISTEN, ARE YOU GOING TO BE AROUND LATER?
UH, YEAH. WHAT'S UP?
I'M ON MY WAY INTO THE CITY. BEN IS TAKING ME TO A NEW PRODUCTION OF *IN THE HEIGHTS* TONIGHT, AND I NEED A NEW DRESS. SO, GAMBELS, HERE I COME.
YOU TWO ARE SO CUTE IT MAKES ME SICK.
CALL ME WHEN YOU'RE DONE SHOPPING. THERE'S A COOL COFFEE PLACE JUST OFF CAMPUS.

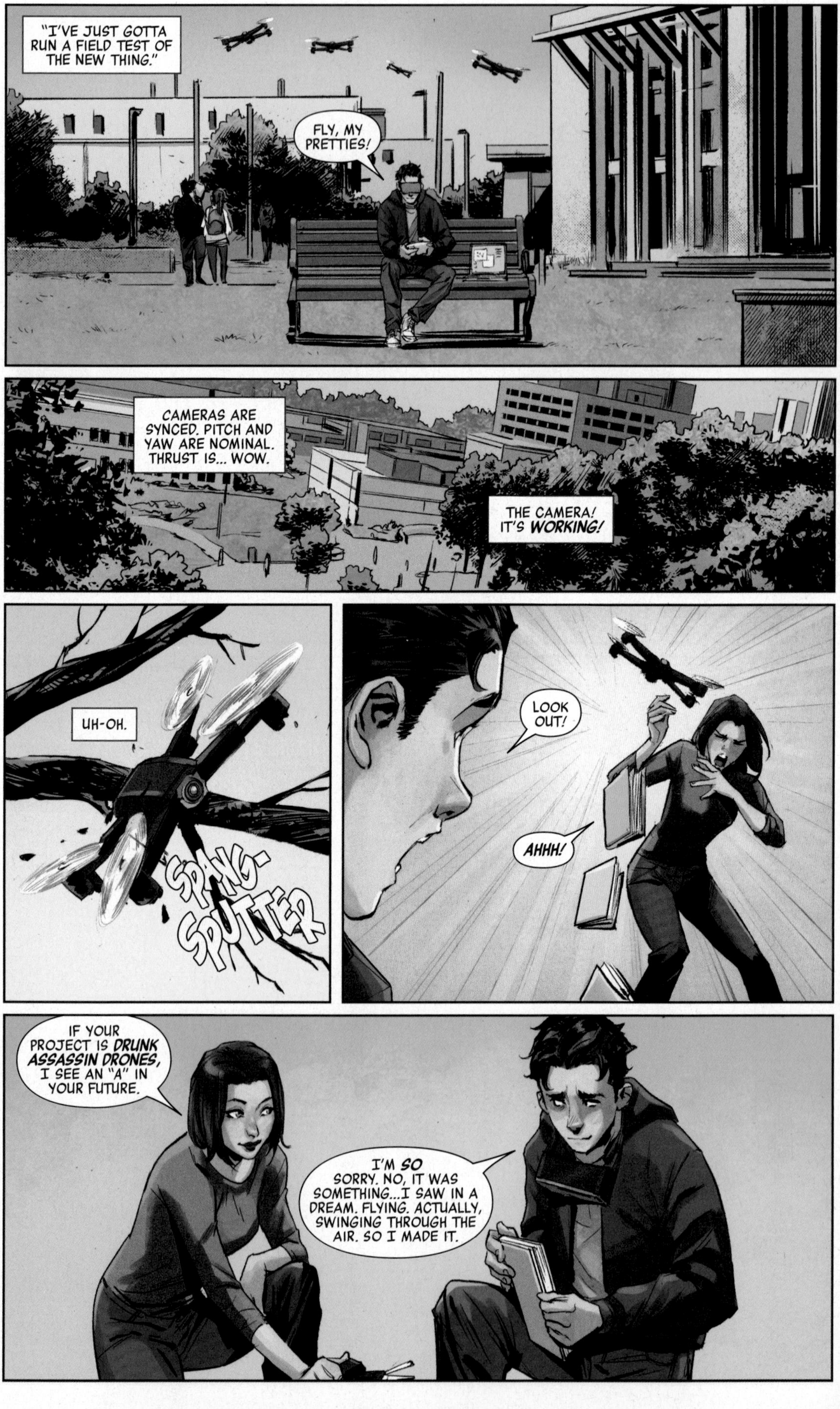
"I'VE JUST GOTTA RUN A FIELD TEST OF THE NEW THING."
FLY, MY PRETTIES!
CAMERAS ARE SYNCED. PITCH AND YAW ARE NOMINAL. THRUST IS... WOW.
THE CAMERA! IT'S WORKING!
UH-OH.
SPANG-
SPUTTER
LOOK OUT!
AHHH!
IF YOUR PROJECT IS DRUNK ASSASSIN DRONES, I SEE AN "A" IN YOUR FUTURE.
I'M SO SORRY. NO, IT WAS SOMETHING...I SAW IN A DREAM. FLYING. ACTUALLY, SWINGING THROUGH THE AIR. SO I MADE IT.

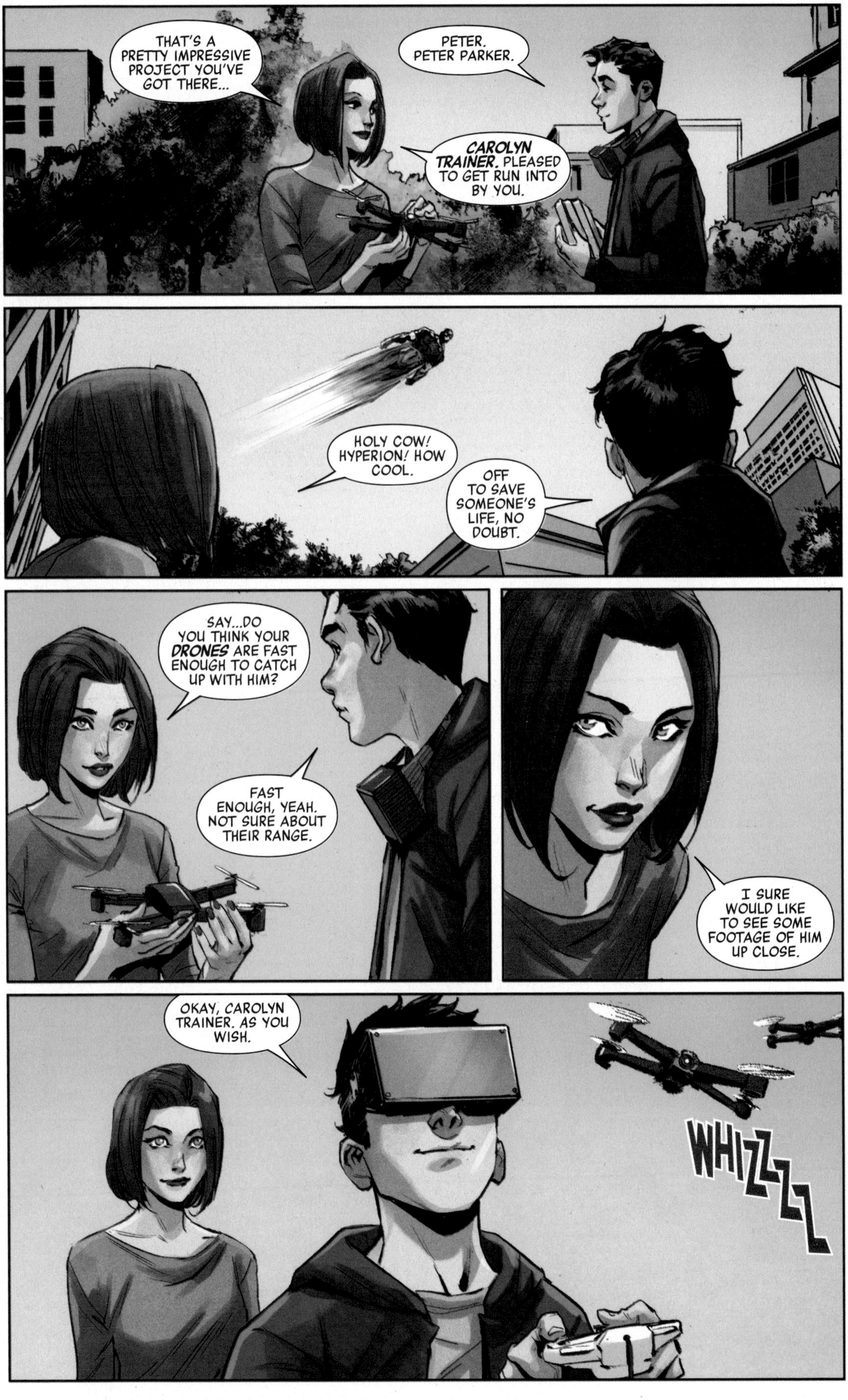
THAT'S A PRETTY IMPRESSIVE PROJECT YOU'VE GOT THERE...
PETER. PETER PARKER.
CAROLYN TRAINER. PLEASED TO GET RUN INTO BY YOU.
HOLY COW! HYPERION! HOW COOL.
OFF TO SAVE SOMEONE'S LIFE, NO DOUBT.
SAY...DO YOU THINK YOUR DRONES ARE FAST ENOUGH TO CATCH UP WITH HIM?
FAST ENOUGH, YEAH. NOT SURE ABOUT THEIR RANGE.
I SURE WOULD LIKE TO SEE SOME FOOTAGE OF HIM UP CLOSE.
OKAY, CAROLYN TRAINER. AS YOU WISH.
WHIZZZZ

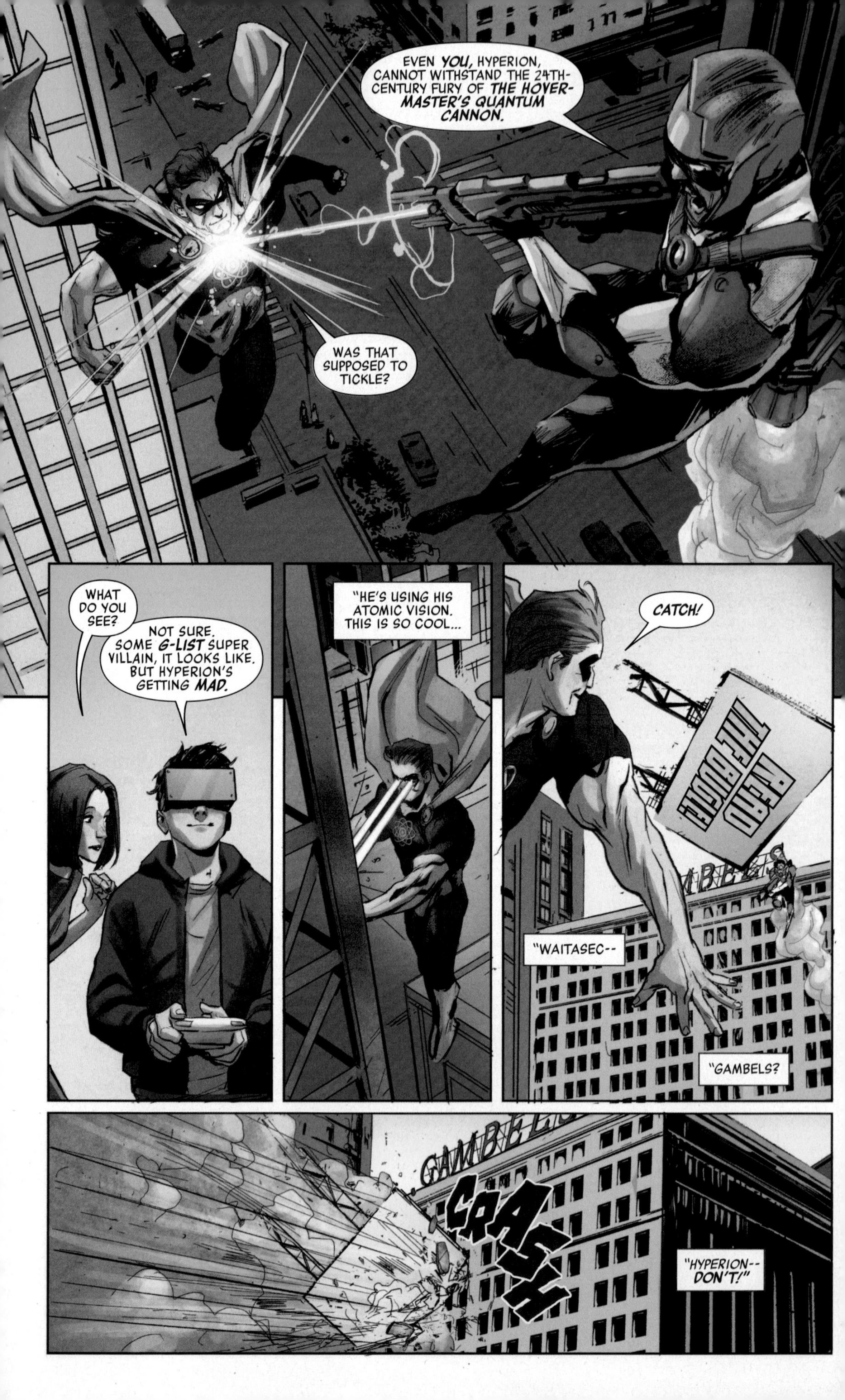
EVEN YOU, HYPERION, CANNOT WITHSTAND THE 24TH-CENTURY FURY OF THE HOVER-MASTER'S QUANTUM CANNON.
WAS THAT SUPPOSED TO TICKLE?
WHAT DO YOU SEE?
NOT SURE. SOME G-LIST SUPER VILLAIN, IT LOOKS LIKE. BUT HYPERION'S GETTING MAD.
"HE'S USING HIS ATOMIC VISION. THIS IS SO COOL...
CATCH!
"WAITASEC--
"GAMBELS?
CRASH
"HYPERION--DON'T!"

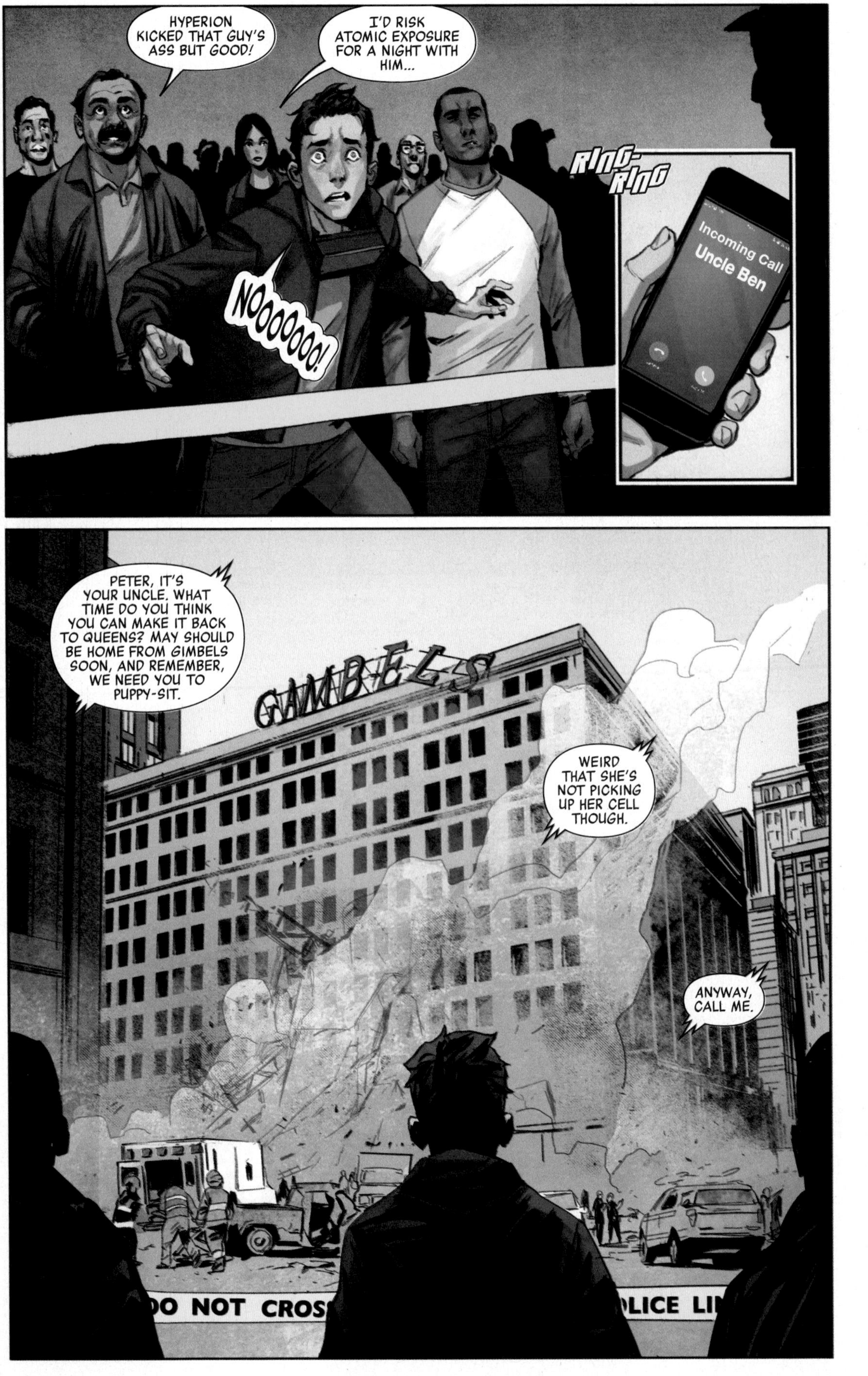
HYPERION KICKED THAT GUY'S ASS BUT GOOD!
I'D RISK ATOMIC EXPOSURE FOR A NIGHT WITH HIM...
RING-RING
Incoming Call
Uncle Ben
NOOOOOOO!
PETER, IT'S YOUR UNCLE. WHAT TIME DO YOU THINK YOU CAN MAKE IT BACK TO QUEENS? MAY SHOULD BE HOME FROM GIMBELS SOON, AND REMEMBER, WE NEED YOU TO PUPPY-SIT.
GIMBELS
WEIRD THAT SHE'S NOT PICKING UP HER CELL THOUGH.
ANYWAY, CALL ME.
DO NOT CROSS
OLICE LI

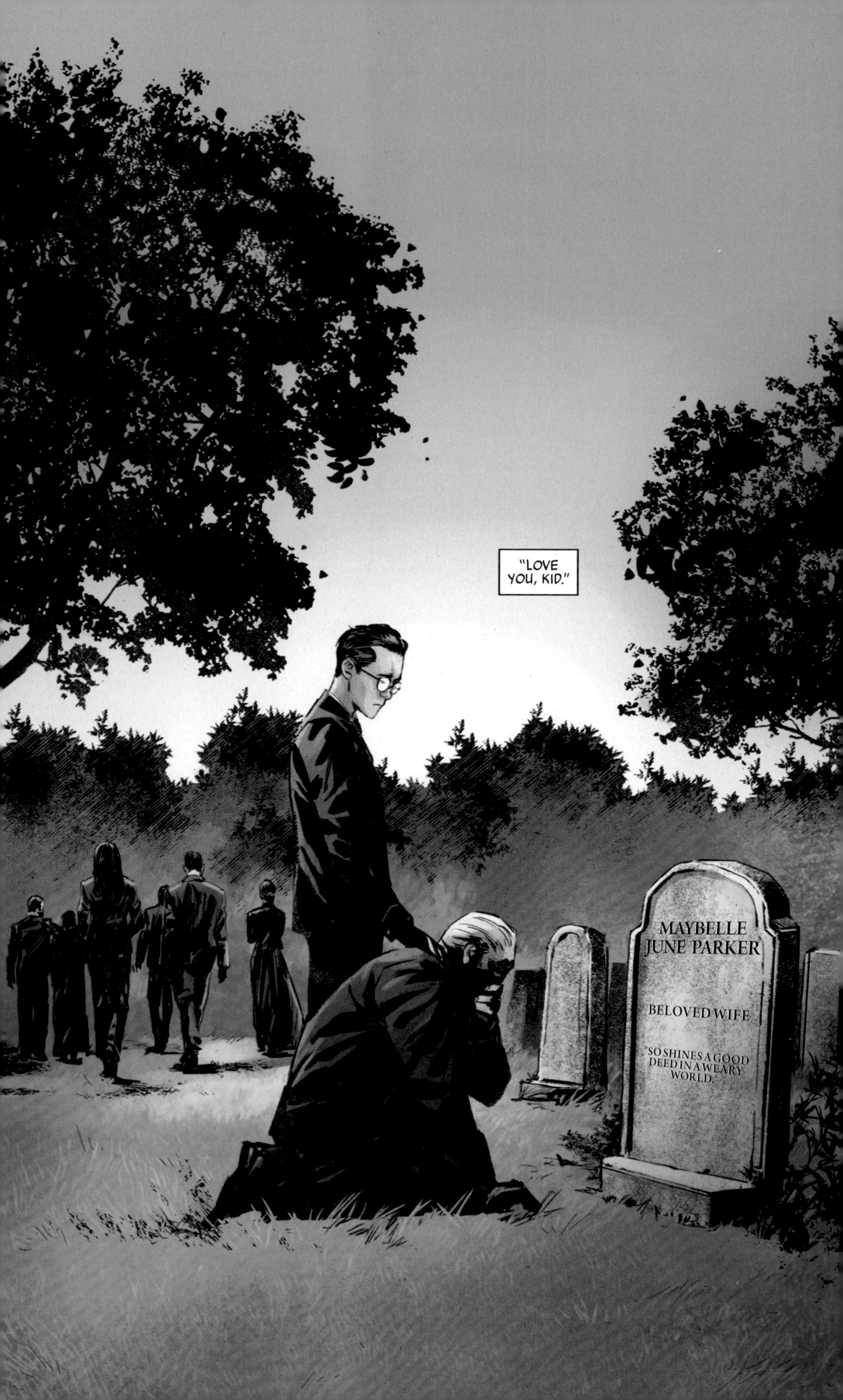
"LOVE YOU, KID."
MAYBELLE JUNE PARKER
BELOVED WIFE
"SO SHINES A GOOD DEED IN A WEARY WORLD."

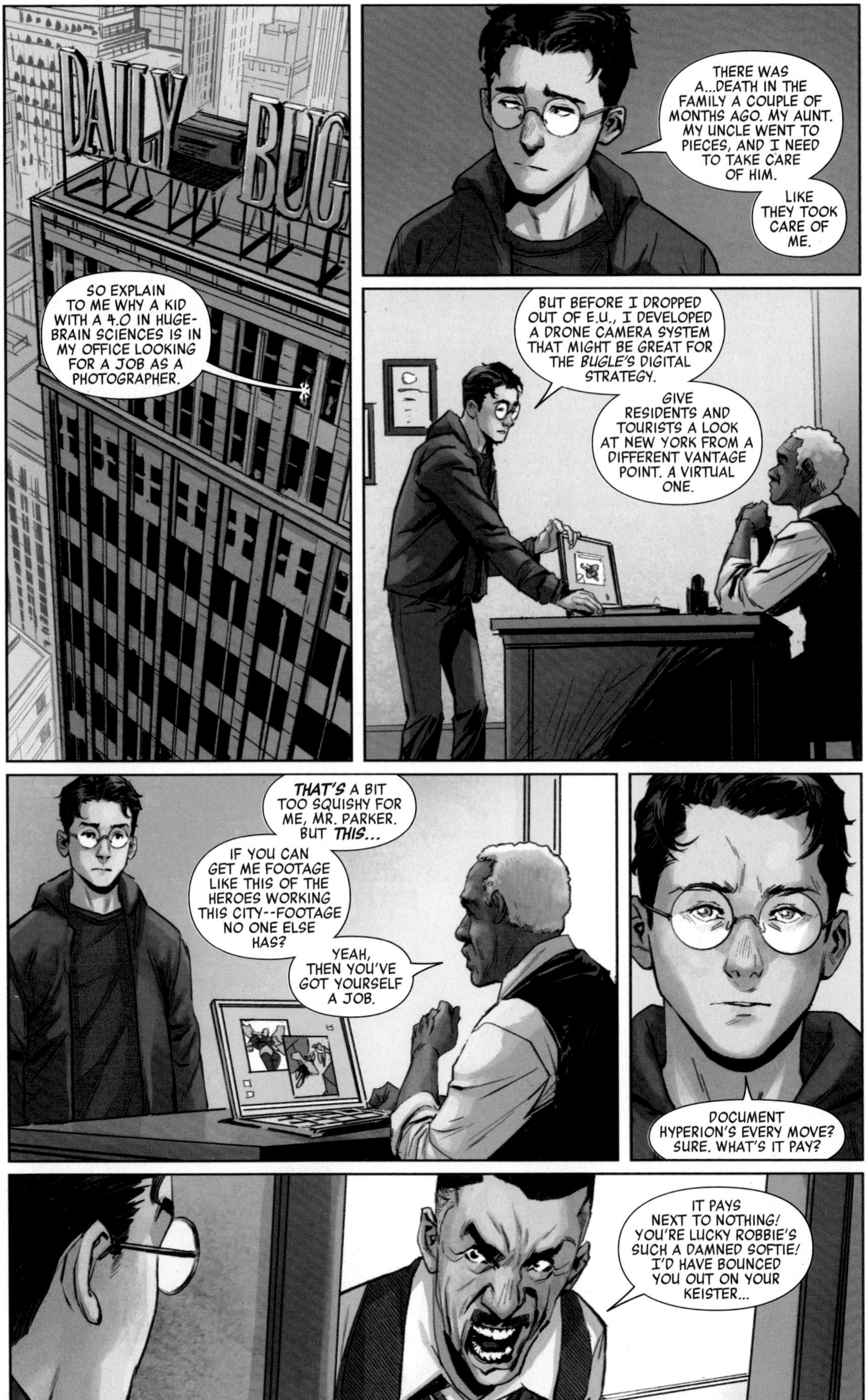
DAILY BUG
SO EXPLAIN TO ME WHY A KID WITH A 4.0 IN HUGE-BRAIN SCIENCES IS IN MY OFFICE LOOKING FOR A JOB AS A PHOTOGRAPHER.
THERE WAS A...DEATH IN THE FAMILY A COUPLE OF MONTHS AGO. MY AUNT. MY UNCLE WENT TO PIECES, AND I NEED TO TAKE CARE OF HIM.
LIKE THEY TOOK CARE OF ME.
BUT BEFORE I DROPPED OUT OF E.U., I DEVELOPED A DRONE CAMERA SYSTEM THAT MIGHT BE GREAT FOR THE *BUGLE*'S DIGITAL STRATEGY.
GIVE RESIDENTS AND TOURISTS A LOOK AT NEW YORK FROM A DIFFERENT VANTAGE POINT. A VIRTUAL ONE.
THAT'S A BIT TOO SQUISHY FOR ME, MR. PARKER. BUT ***THIS...***
IF YOU CAN GET ME FOOTAGE LIKE THIS OF THE HEROES WORKING THIS CITY--FOOTAGE NO ONE ELSE HAS?
YEAH, THEN YOU'VE GOT YOURSELF A JOB.
DOCUMENT HYPERION'S EVERY MOVE? SURE. WHAT'S IT PAY?
IT PAYS NEXT TO NOTHING! YOU'RE LUCKY ROBBIE'S SUCH A DAMNED SOFTIE! I'D HAVE BOUNCED YOU OUT ON YOUR KEISTER...

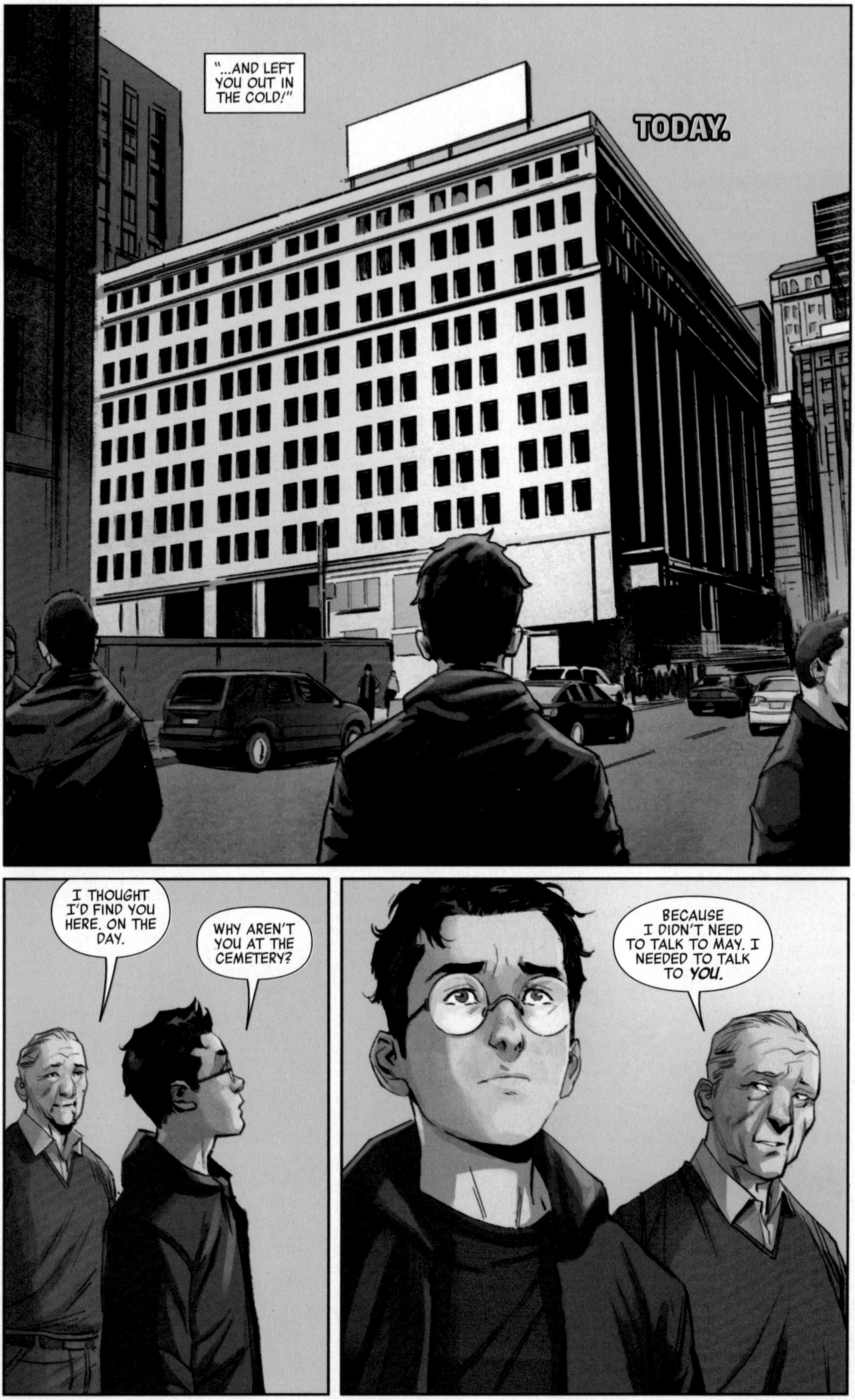
"...AND LEFT YOU OUT IN THE COLD!"
TODAY.
I THOUGHT I'D FIND YOU HERE. ON THE DAY.
WHY AREN'T YOU AT THE CEMETERY?
BECAUSE I DIDN'T NEED TO TALK TO MAY. I NEEDED TO TALK TO YOU.

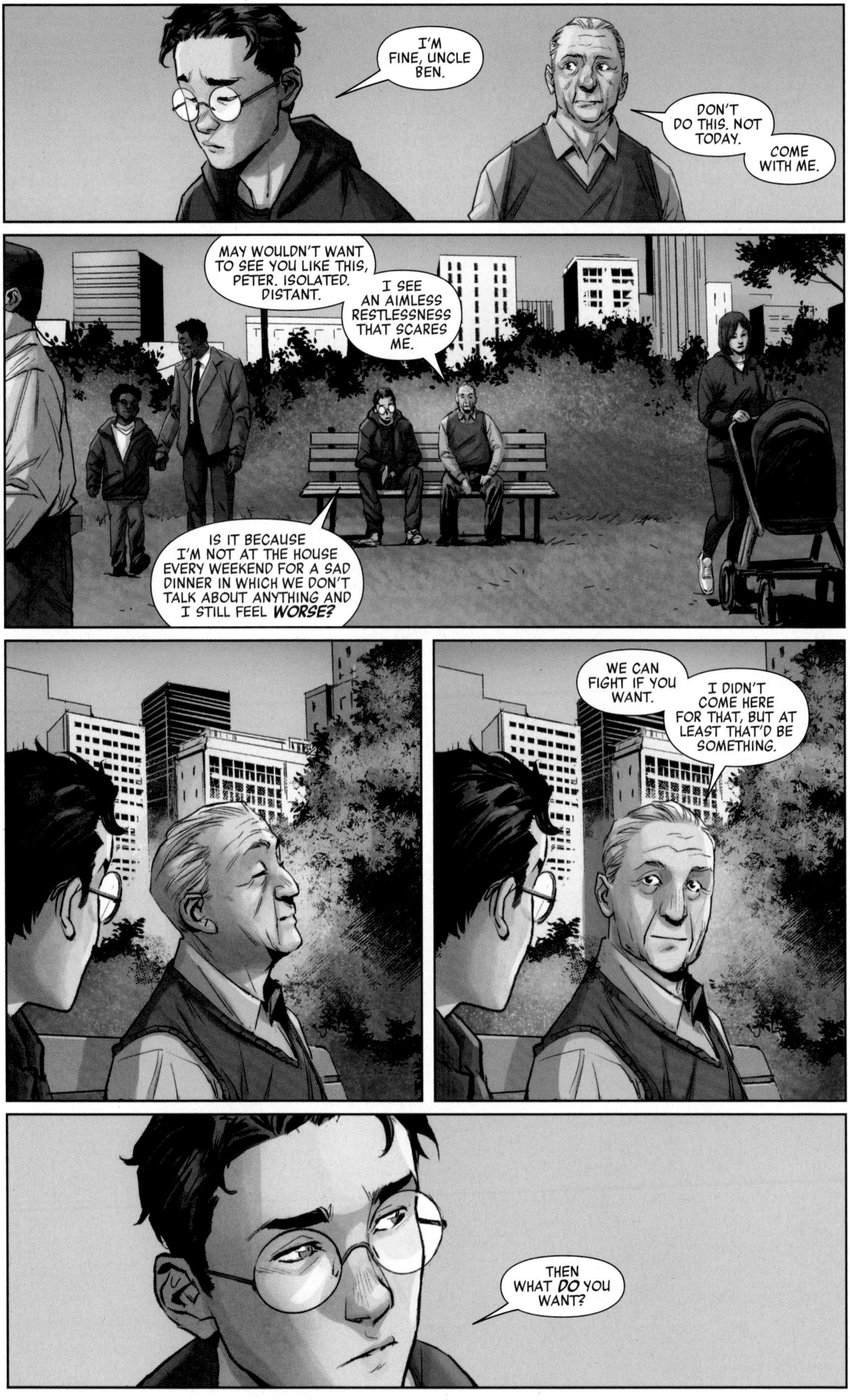
I'M FINE, UNCLE BEN.
DON'T DO THIS. NOT TODAY.
COME WITH ME.
MAY WOULDN'T WANT TO SEE YOU LIKE THIS, PETER. ISOLATED. DISTANT.
I SEE AN AIMLESS RESTLESSNESS THAT SCARES ME.
IS IT BECAUSE I'M NOT AT THE HOUSE EVERY WEEKEND FOR A SAD DINNER IN WHICH WE DON'T TALK ABOUT ANYTHING AND I STILL FEEL WORSE?
WE CAN FIGHT IF YOU WANT.
I DIDN'T COME HERE FOR THAT, BUT AT LEAST THAT'D BE SOMETHING.
THEN WHAT DO YOU WANT?

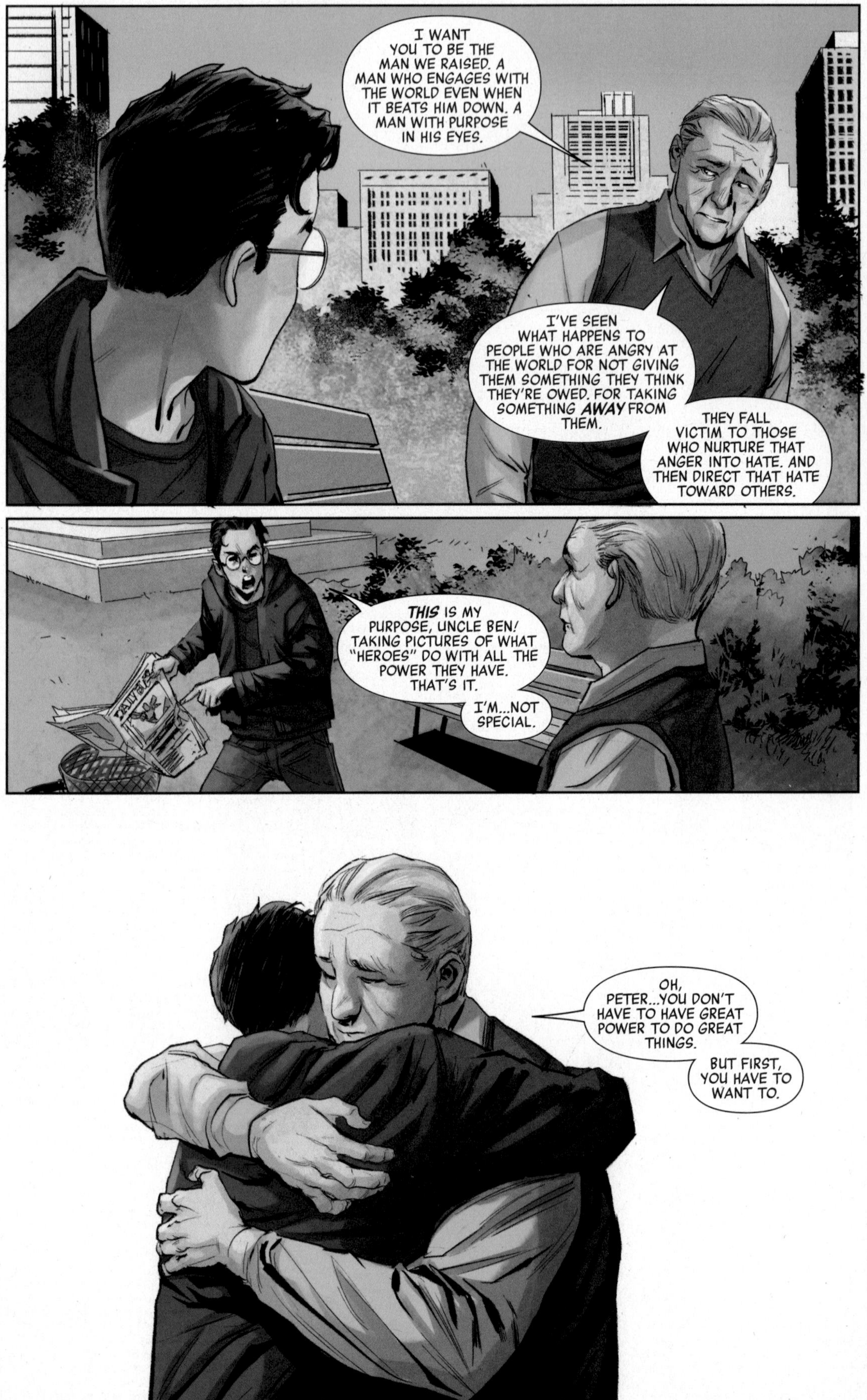
I WANT YOU TO BE THE MAN WE RAISED. A MAN WHO ENGAGES WITH THE WORLD EVEN WHEN IT BEATS HIM DOWN. A MAN WITH PURPOSE IN HIS EYES.
I'VE SEEN WHAT HAPPENS TO PEOPLE WHO ARE ANGRY AT THE WORLD FOR NOT GIVING THEM SOMETHING THEY THINK THEY'RE OWED. FOR TAKING SOMETHING ***AWAY*** FROM THEM.
THEY FALL VICTIM TO THOSE WHO NURTURE THAT ANGER INTO HATE. AND THEN DIRECT THAT HATE TOWARD OTHERS.
THIS IS MY PURPOSE, UNCLE BEN! TAKING PICTURES OF WHAT "HEROES" DO WITH ALL THE POWER THEY HAVE. THAT'S IT.
I'M...NOT SPECIAL.
OH, PETER...YOU DON'T HAVE TO HAVE GREAT POWER TO DO GREAT THINGS.
BUT FIRST, YOU HAVE TO WANT TO.

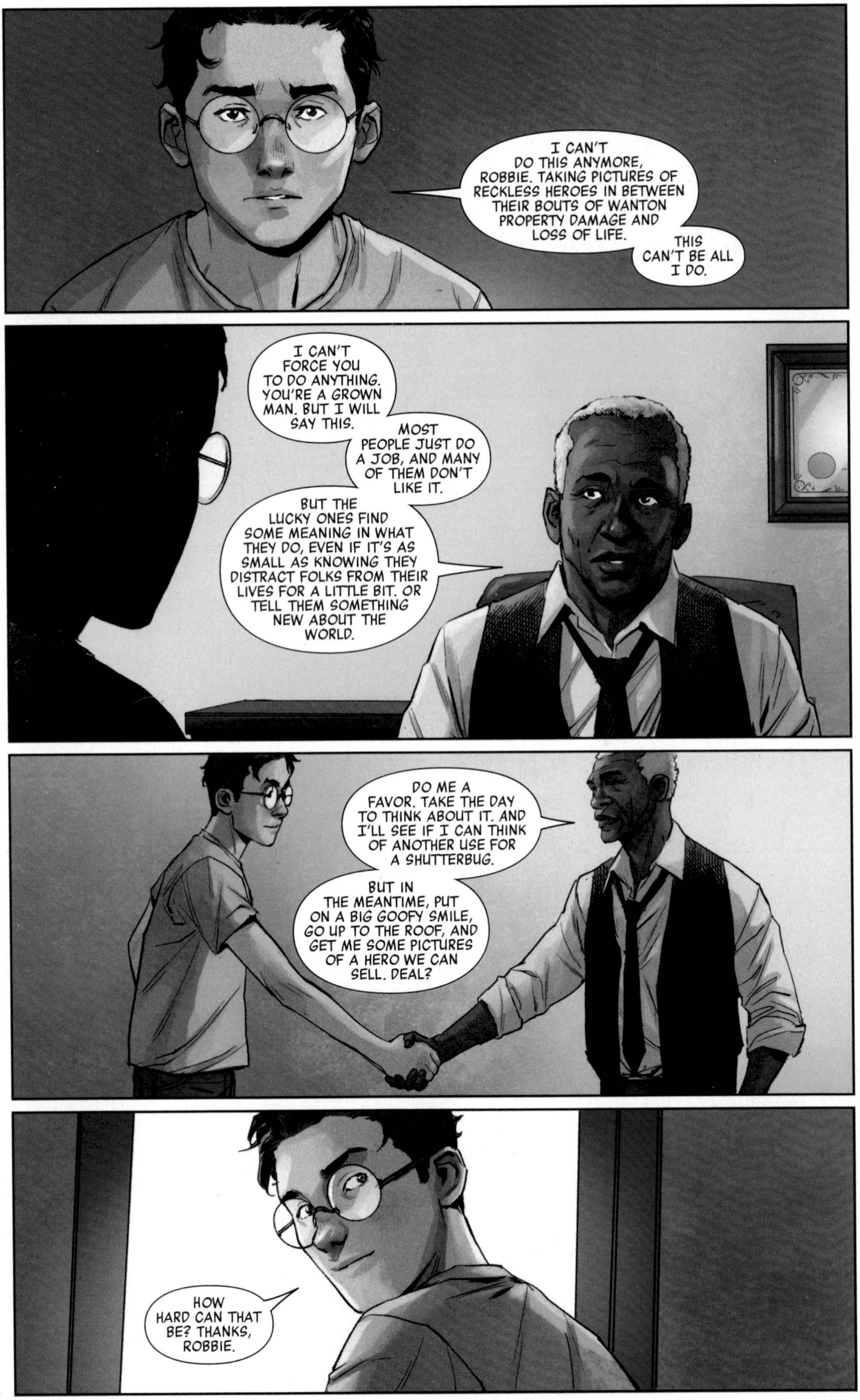
I CAN'T DO THIS ANYMORE, ROBBIE. TAKING PICTURES OF RECKLESS HEROES IN BETWEEN THEIR BOUTS OF WANTON PROPERTY DAMAGE AND LOSS OF LIFE.
THIS CAN'T BE ALL I DO.
I CAN'T FORCE YOU TO DO ANYTHING. YOU'RE A GROWN MAN. BUT I WILL SAY THIS.
MOST PEOPLE JUST DO A JOB, AND MANY OF THEM DON'T LIKE IT.
BUT THE LUCKY ONES FIND SOME MEANING IN WHAT THEY DO, EVEN IF IT'S AS SMALL AS KNOWING THEY DISTRACT FOLKS FROM THEIR LIVES FOR A LITTLE BIT. OR TELL THEM SOMETHING NEW ABOUT THE WORLD.
DO ME A FAVOR. TAKE THE DAY TO THINK ABOUT IT. AND I'LL SEE IF I CAN THINK OF ANOTHER USE FOR A SHUTTERBUG.
BUT IN THE MEANTIME, PUT ON A BIG GOOFY SMILE, GO UP TO THE ROOF, AND GET ME SOME PICTURES OF A HERO WE CAN SELL. DEAL?
HOW HARD CAN THAT BE? THANKS, ROBBIE.

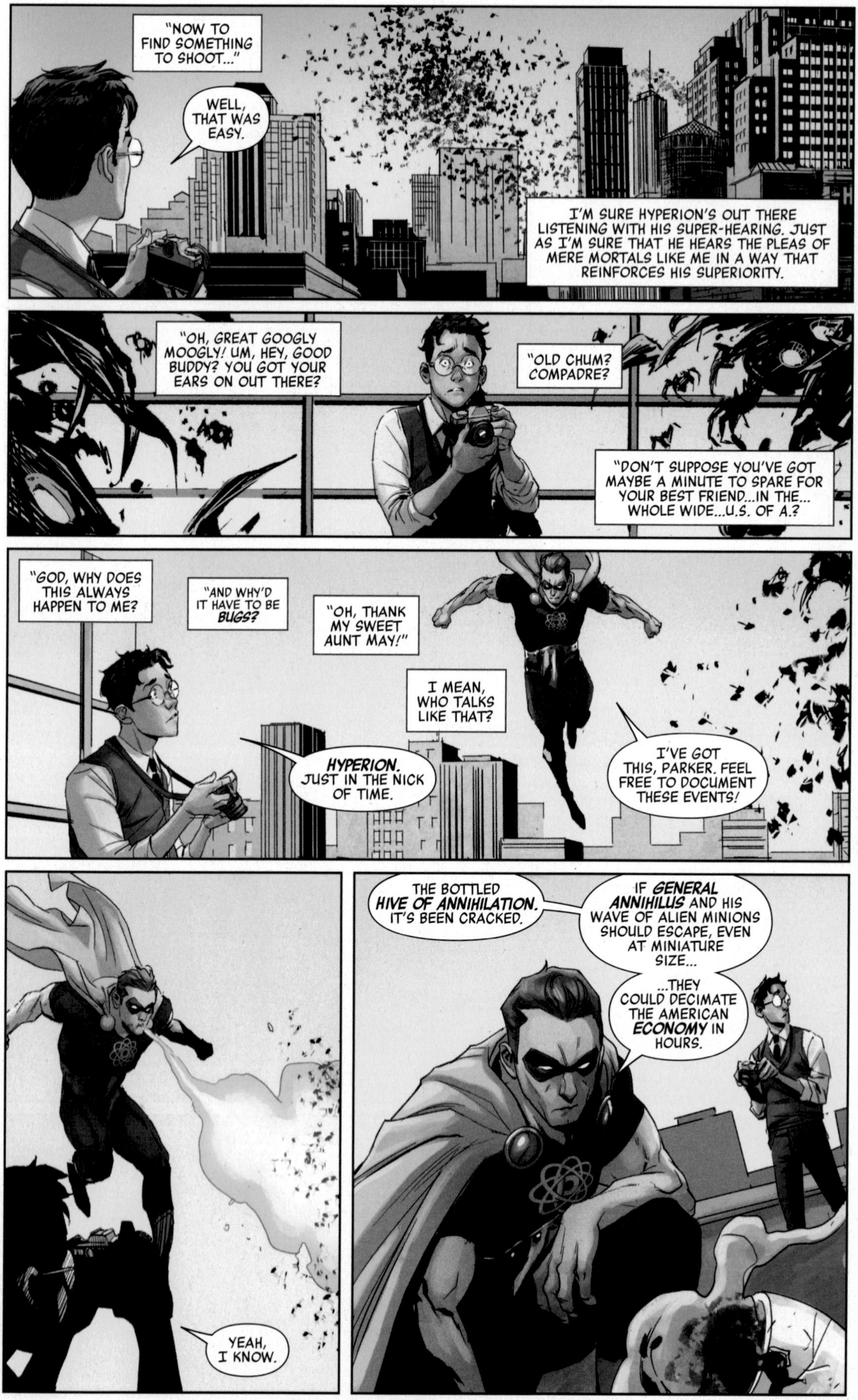
"NOW TO FIND SOMETHING TO SHOOT..."
WELL, THAT WAS EASY.
I'M SURE HYPERION'S OUT THERE LISTENING WITH HIS SUPER-HEARING. JUST AS I'M SURE THAT HE HEARS THE PLEAS OF MERE MORTALS LIKE ME IN A WAY THAT REINFORCES HIS SUPERIORITY.
"OH, GREAT GOOGLY MOOGLY! UM, HEY, GOOD BUDDY? YOU GOT YOUR EARS ON OUT THERE?
"OLD CHUM? COMPADRE?
"DON'T SUPPOSE YOU'VE GOT MAYBE A MINUTE TO SPARE FOR YOUR BEST FRIEND...IN THE... WHOLE WIDE...U.S. OF A.?
"GOD, WHY DOES THIS ALWAYS HAPPEN TO ME?
"AND WHY'D IT HAVE TO BE *BUGS?*
"OH, THANK MY SWEET AUNT MAY!"
I MEAN, WHO TALKS LIKE THAT?
HYPERION. JUST IN THE NICK OF TIME.
I'VE GOT THIS, PARKER. FEEL FREE TO DOCUMENT THESE EVENTS!
YEAH, I KNOW.
THE BOTTLED *HIVE OF ANNIHILATION.* IT'S BEEN CRACKED.
IF *GENERAL ANNIHILUS* AND HIS WAVE OF ALIEN MINIONS SHOULD ESCAPE, EVEN AT MINIATURE SIZE...
...THEY COULD DECIMATE THE AMERICAN *ECONOMY* IN HOURS.

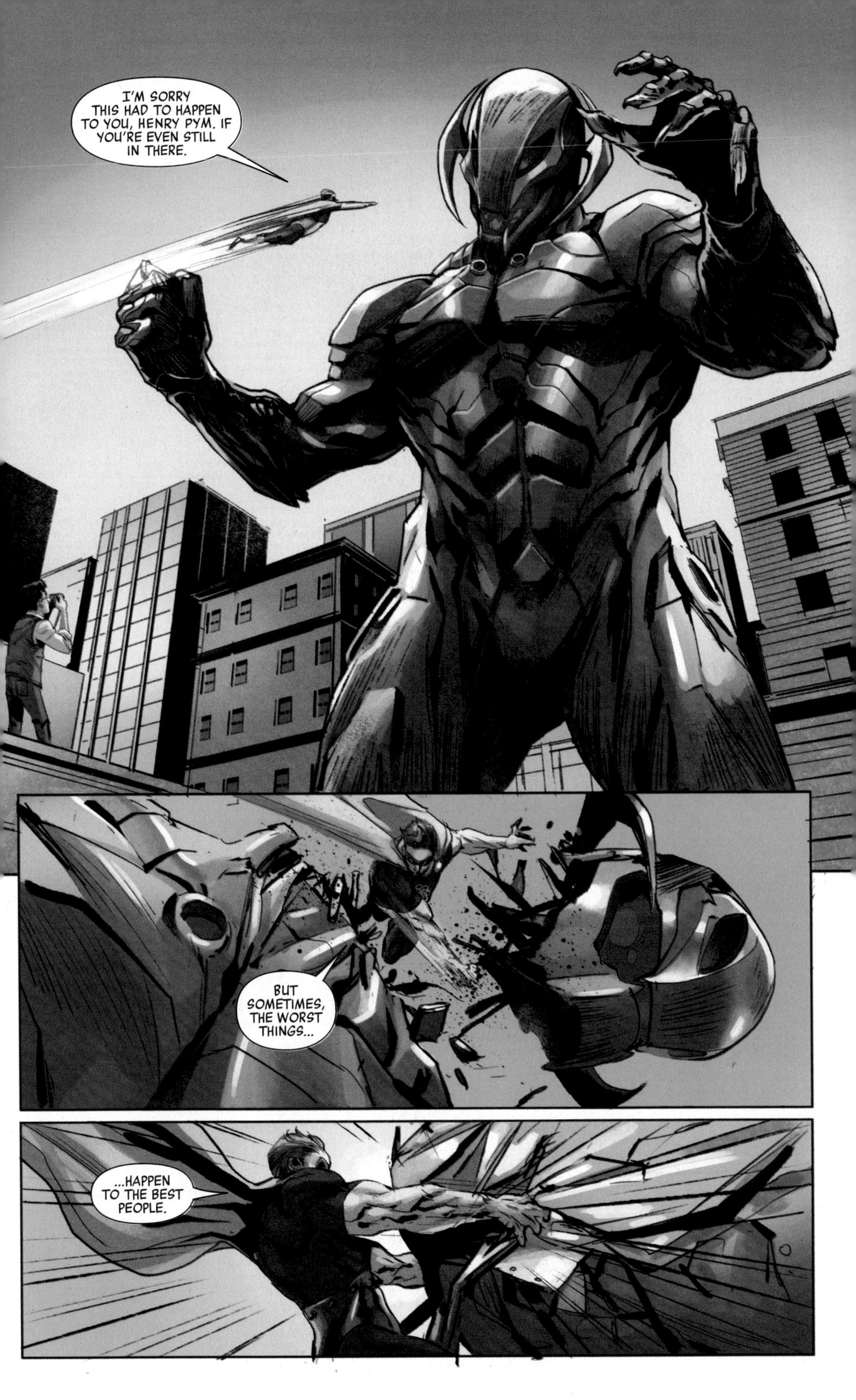

I'M SORRY THIS HAD TO HAPPEN TO YOU, HENRY PYM. IF YOU'RE EVEN STILL IN THERE.
BUT SOMETIMES, THE WORST THINGS...
...HAPPEN TO THE BEST PEOPLE.

THE TECHS FROM *S.H.I.E.L.D.* LABS WILL BE HERE SOON.

TELL THEM THIS IS ALMOST THE LAST OF THE NEGATIVE ZONE VILLAINS.

WINTER SOLDIER AND HIS COMMIE *WIDOW GUARD.*

THE UNDERSEA TERROR-KING, *NAMOR.* THE FREAK SHOW *MUTANT FORCE.*

I'VE DETAINED THEM ALL.

UM, OKAY.

THERE'S JUST ONE MORE LEFT.

KEEP YOUR HEAD ON A SWIVEL, PETER. SOMETHING TELLS ME THERE'S STILL MORE TO BE DONE.

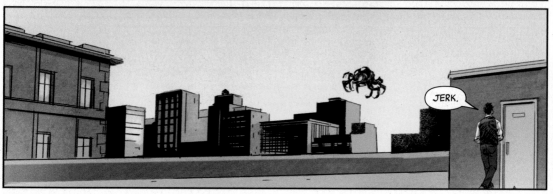

JERK.

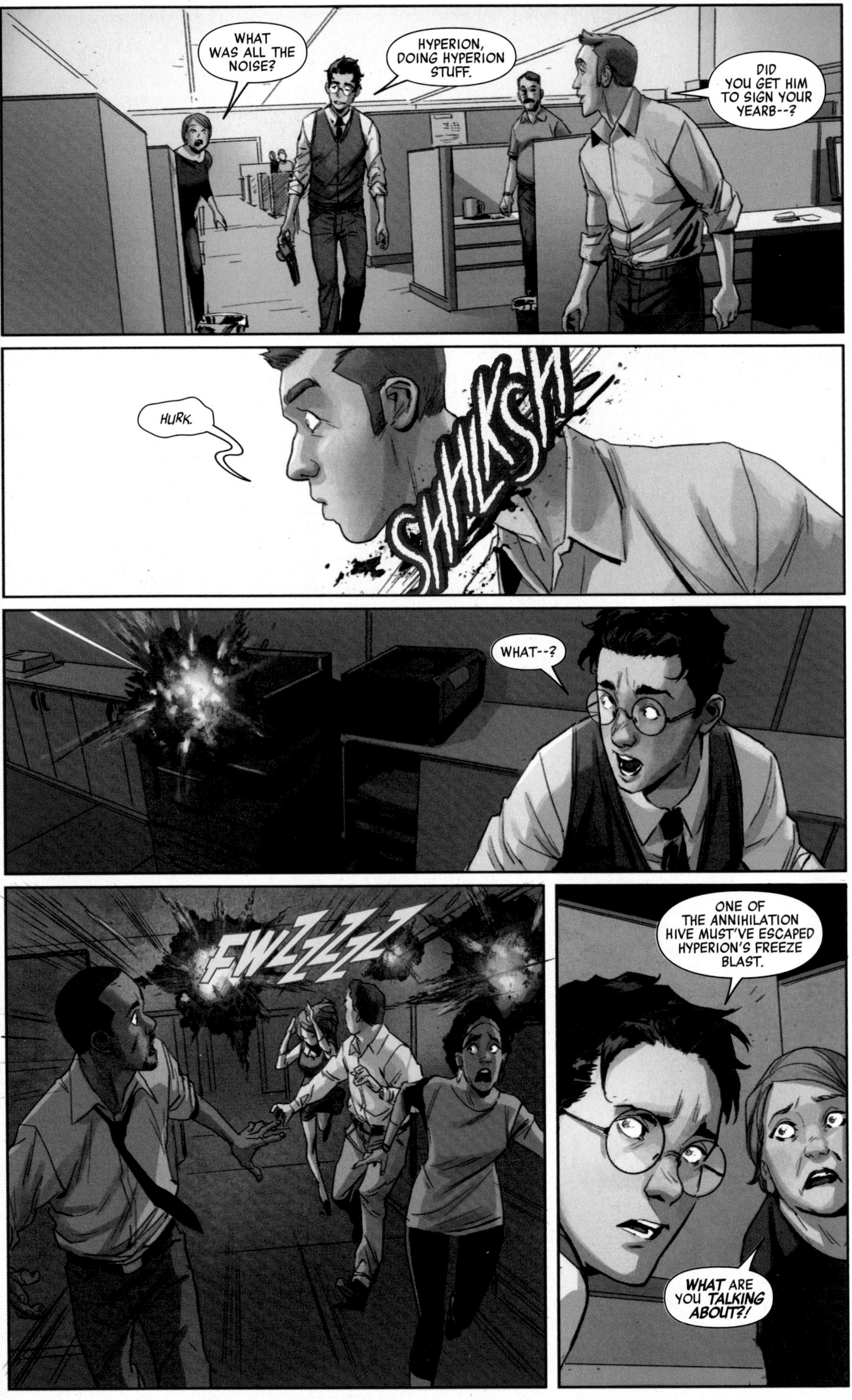
WHAT WAS ALL THE NOISE?
HYPERION, DOING HYPERION STUFF.
DID YOU GET HIM TO SIGN YOUR YEARB--?
HURK.
SHHLKSH
WHAT--?
FWZZZZZ
ONE OF THE ANNIHILATION HIVE MUST'VE ESCAPED HYPERION'S FREEZE BLAST.
WHAT ARE YOU TALKING ABOUT?!

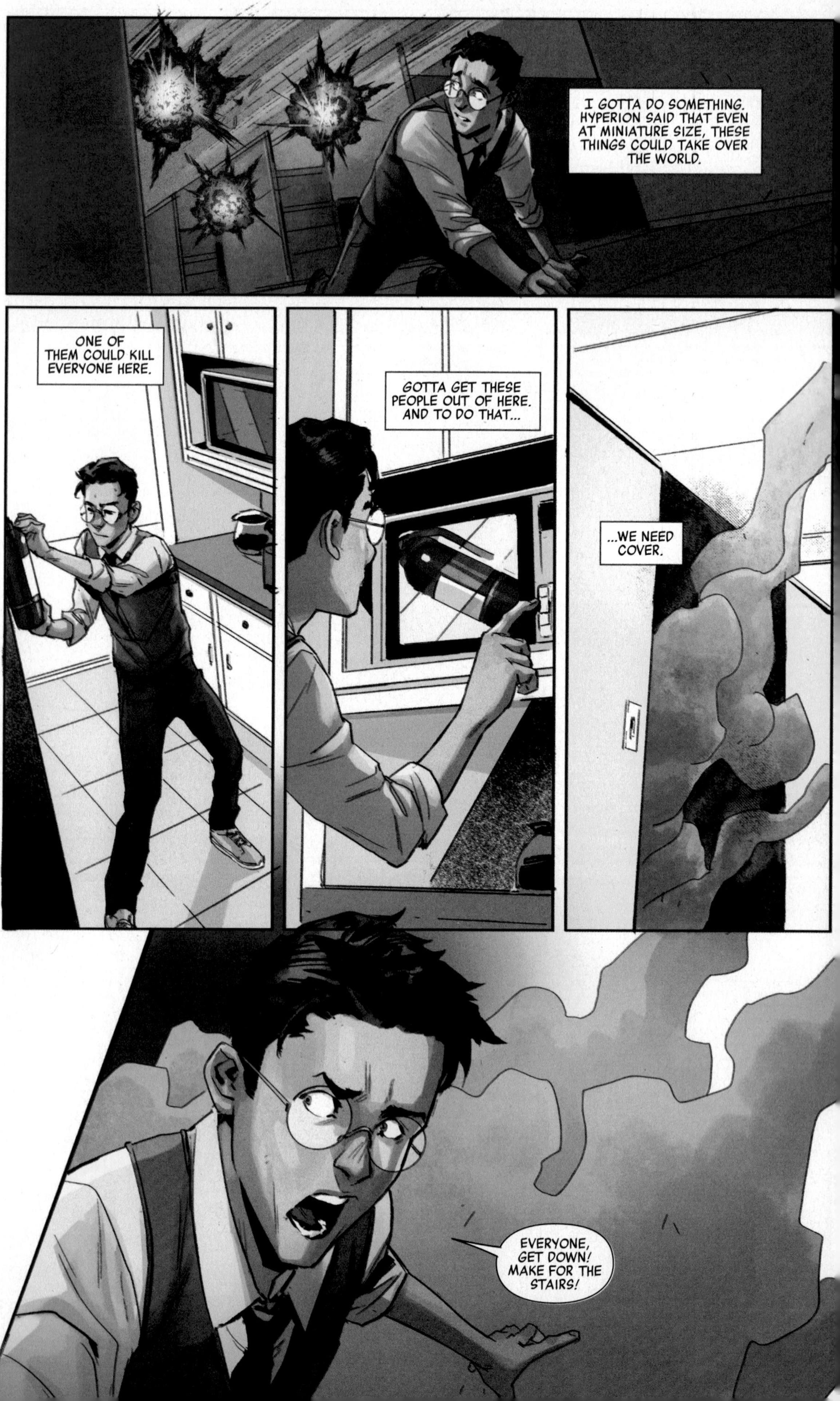
I GOTTA DO SOMETHING. HYPERION SAID THAT EVEN AT MINIATURE SIZE, THESE THINGS COULD TAKE OVER THE WORLD.
ONE OF THEM COULD KILL EVERYONE HERE.
GOTTA GET THESE PEOPLE OUT OF HERE. AND TO DO THAT...
...WE NEED COVER.
EVERYONE, GET DOWN! MAKE FOR THE STAIRS!

OKAY, EVERYONE'S GONE. NOW WHAT?

THAT THING'S GOTTA HAVE A POWER SOURCE, RIGHT?

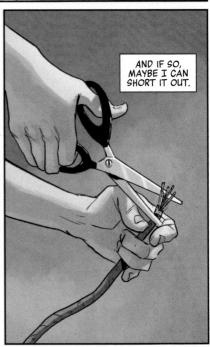

AND IF SO, MAYBE I CAN SHORT IT OUT.

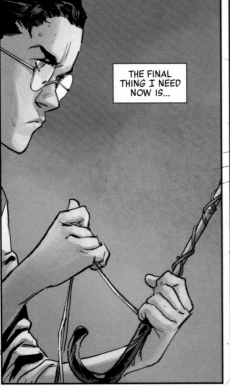

THE FINAL THING I NEED NOW IS...

...BAIT!

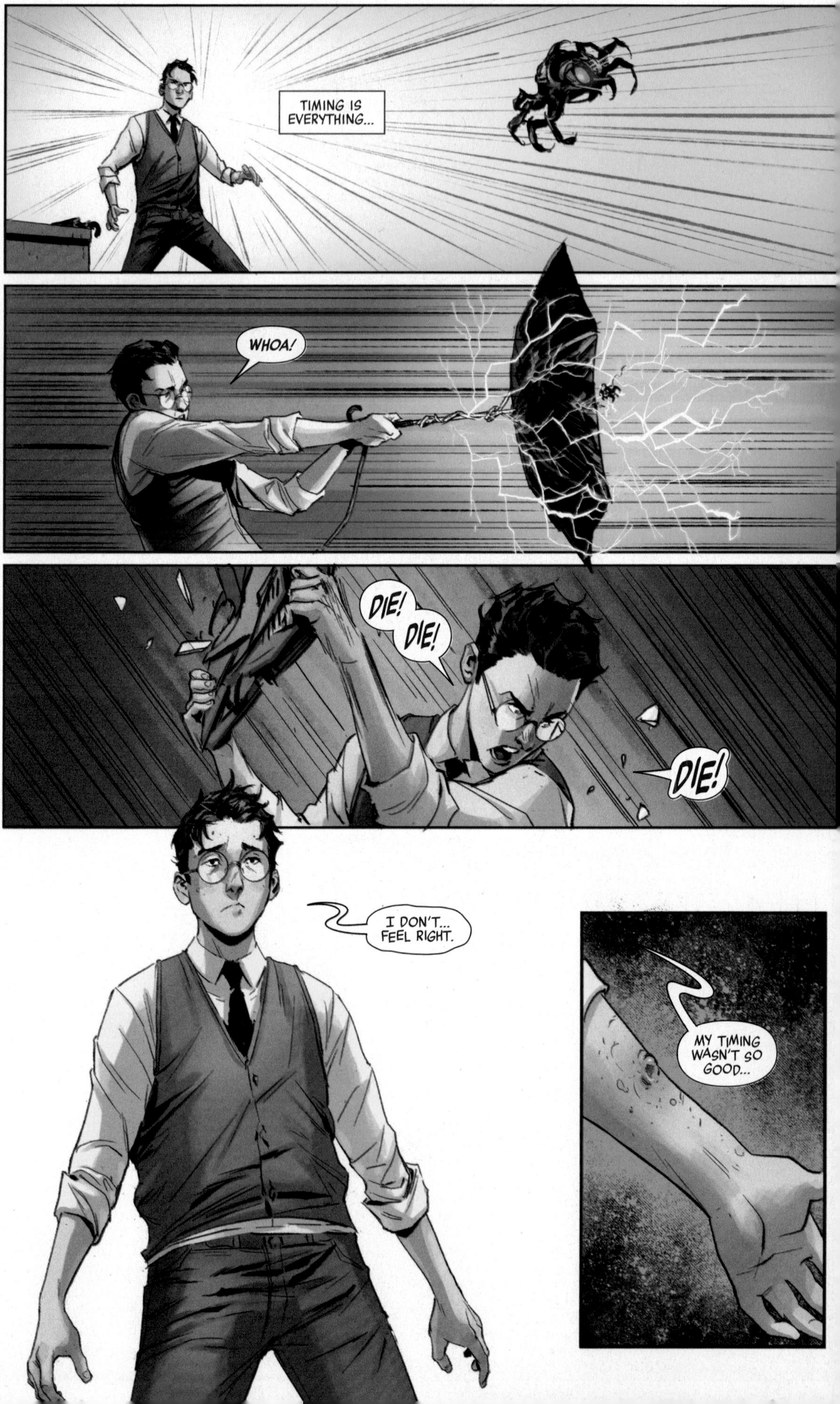
TIMING IS EVERYTHING...
WHOA!
DIE!
DIE!
DIE!
I DON'T... FEEL RIGHT.
MY TIMING WASN'T SO GOOD...

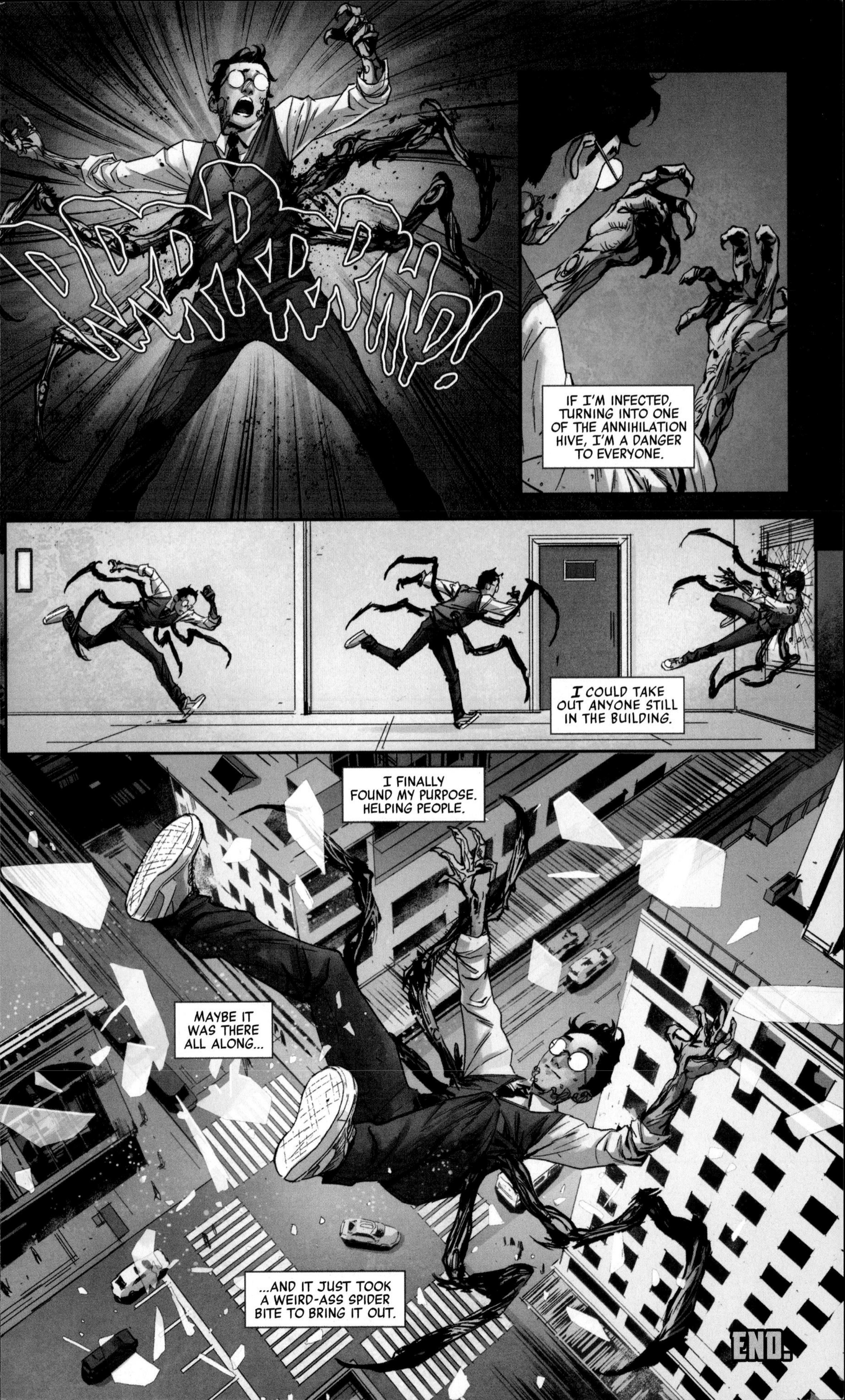
IF I'M INFECTED, TURNING INTO ONE OF THE ANNIHILATION HIVE, I'M A DANGER TO EVERYONE.
I COULD TAKE OUT ANYONE STILL IN THE BUILDING.
I FINALLY FOUND MY PURPOSE. HELPING PEOPLE.
MAYBE IT WAS THERE ALL ALONG...
...AND IT JUST TOOK A WEIRD-ASS SPIDER BITE TO BRING IT OUT.
END.

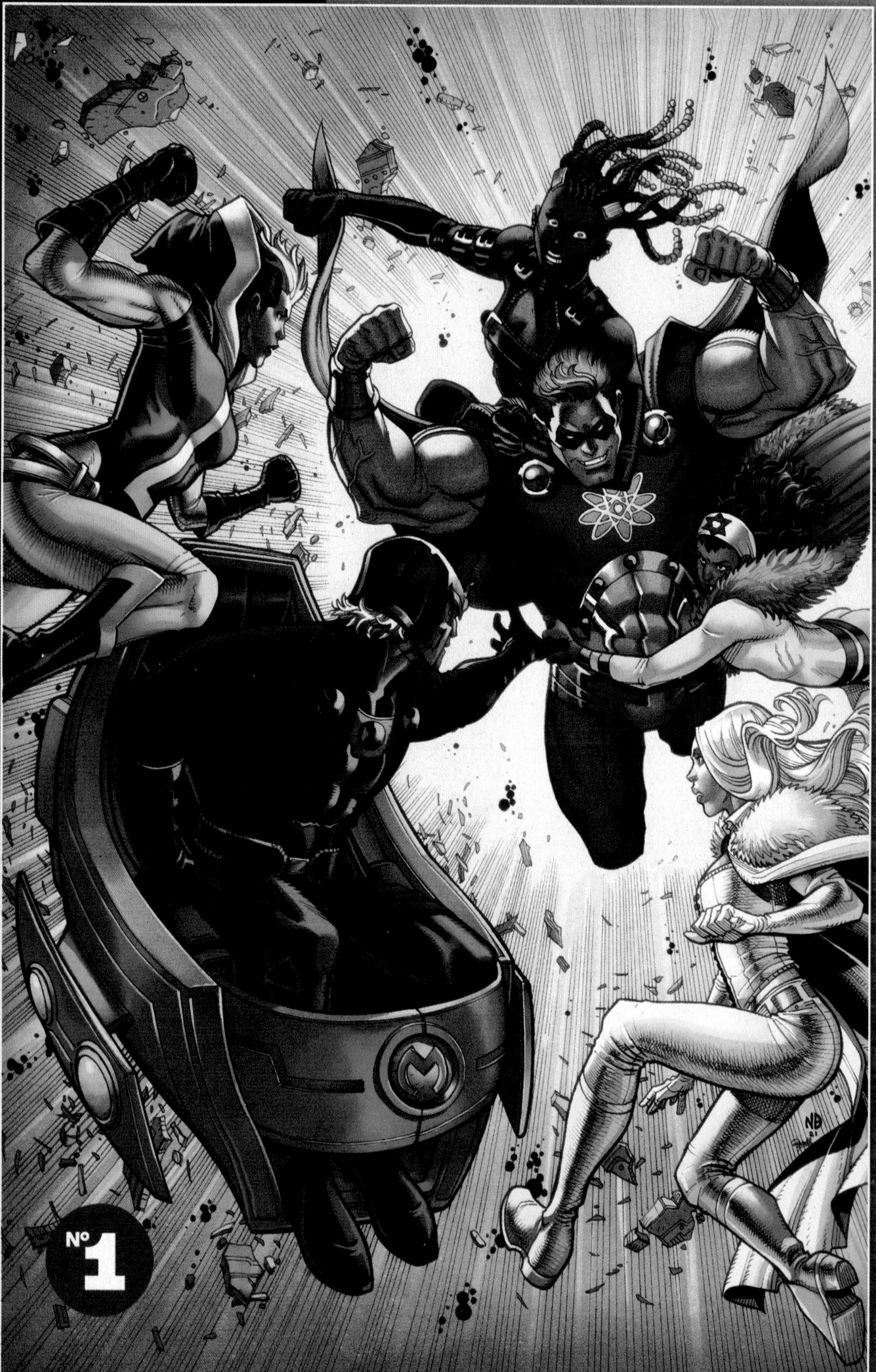

Nº 1

MAGNETO
& THE MUTANT FORCE

"BEWARE! PSYCHIC RESCUE IN PROGRESS!"

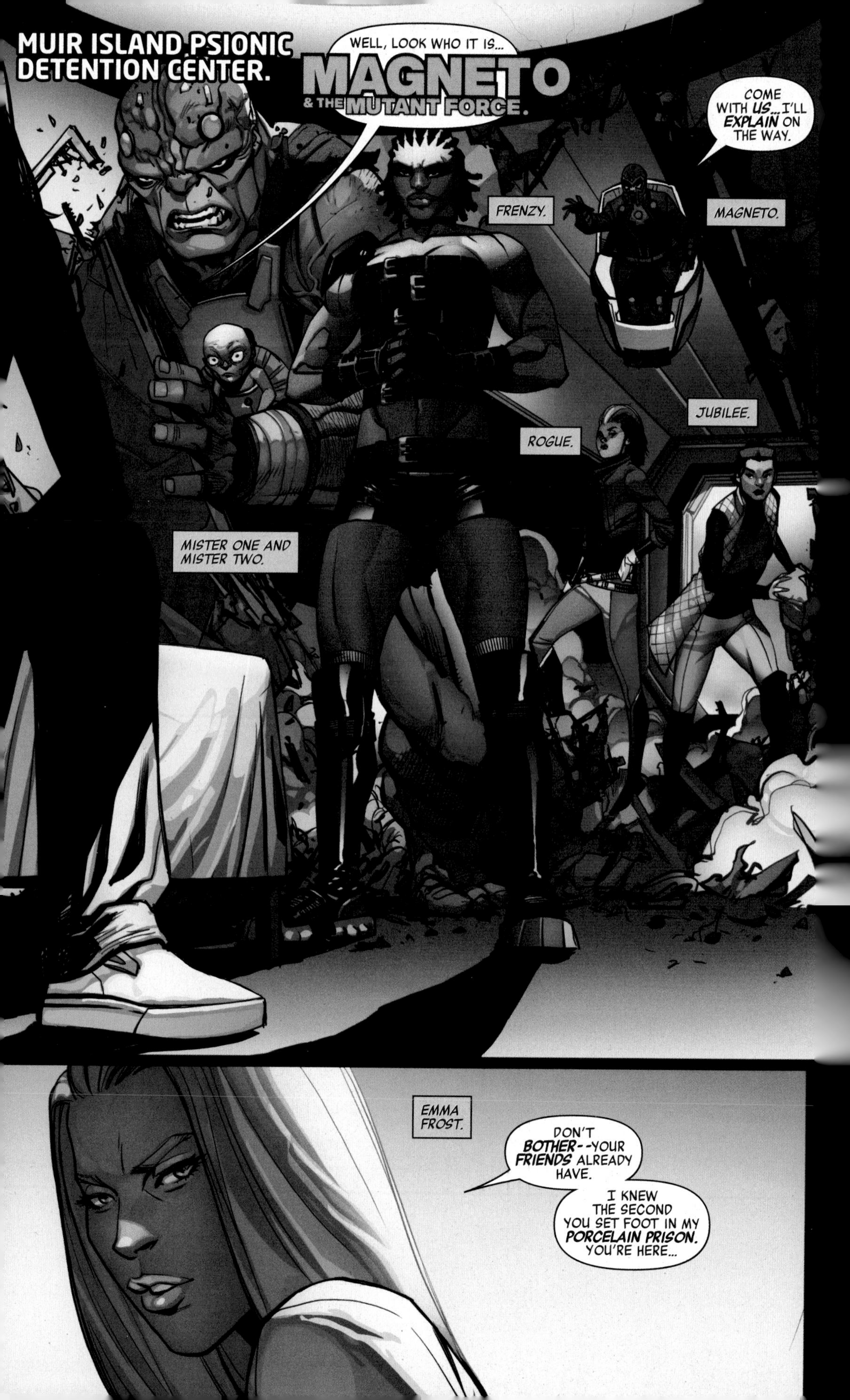

MUIR ISLAND PSIONIC DETENTION CENTER.
WELL, LOOK WHO IT IS...
MAGNETO & THE MUTANT FORCE.
COME WITH US... I'LL EXPLAIN ON THE WAY.
FRENZY.
MAGNETO.
JUBILEE.
ROGUE.
MISTER ONE AND MISTER TWO.
EMMA FROST.
DON'T BOTHER--YOUR FRIENDS ALREADY HAVE.
I KNEW THE SECOND YOU SET FOOT IN MY PORCELAIN PRISON. YOU'RE HERE...

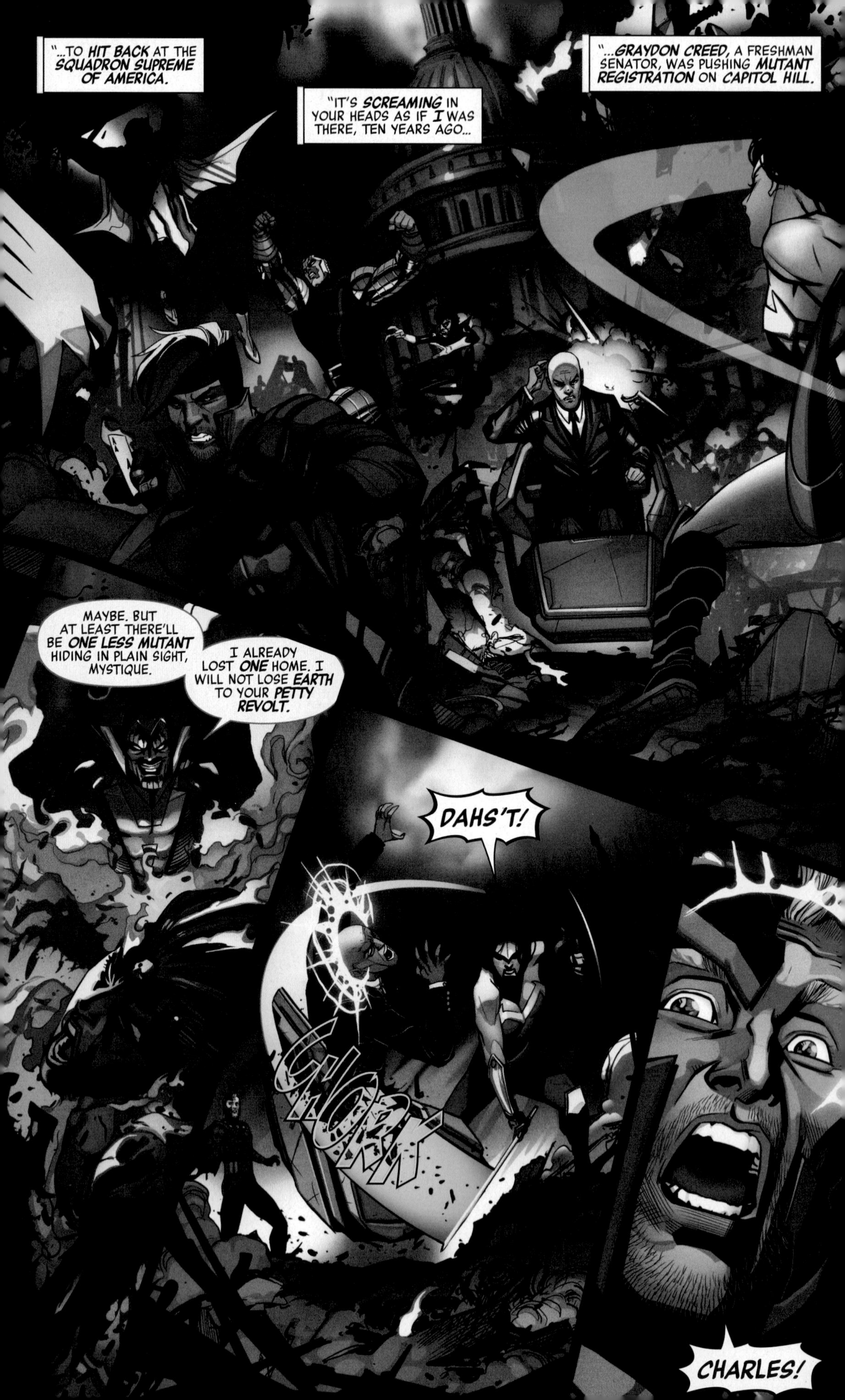
"...TO HIT BACK AT THE SQUADRON SUPREME OF AMERICA.
"IT'S SCREAMING IN YOUR HEADS AS IF I WAS THERE, TEN YEARS AGO...
"...GRAYDON CREED, A FRESHMAN SENATOR, WAS PUSHING MUTANT REGISTRATION ON CAPITOL HILL.
MAYBE. BUT AT LEAST THERE'LL BE ONE LESS MUTANT HIDING IN PLAIN SIGHT, MYSTIQUE.
I ALREADY LOST ONE HOME. I WILL NOT LOSE EARTH TO YOUR PETTY REVOLT.
DAHS'T!
CHOKK
CHARLES!

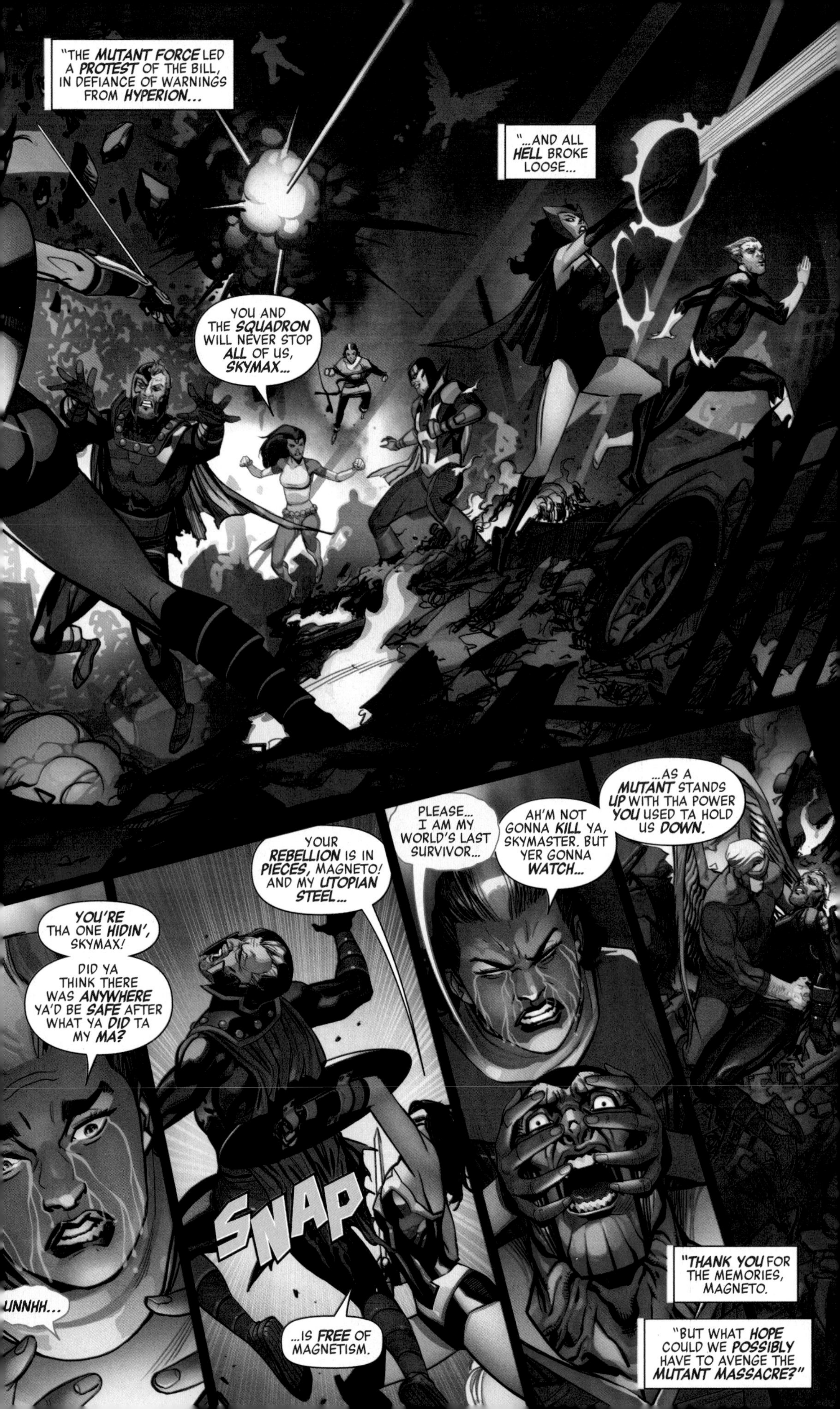

"THE MUTANT FORCE LED A PROTEST OF THE BILL, IN DEFIANCE OF WARNINGS FROM HYPERION...
"...AND ALL HELL BROKE LOOSE...
YOU AND THE SQUADRON WILL NEVER STOP ALL OF US, SKYMAX...
YOU'RE THA ONE HIDIN', SKYMAX!
DID YA THINK THERE WAS ANYWHERE YA'D BE SAFE AFTER WHAT YA DID TA MY MA?
UNNHH...
YOUR REBELLION IS IN PIECES, MAGNETO! AND MY UTOPIAN STEEL...
SNAP
...IS FREE OF MAGNETISM.
PLEASE... I AM MY WORLD'S LAST SURVIVOR...
AH'M NOT GONNA KILL YA, SKYMASTER. BUT YER GONNA WATCH...
...AS A MUTANT STANDS UP WITH THA POWER YOU USED TA HOLD US DOWN.
"THANK YOU FOR THE MEMORIES, MAGNETO.
"BUT WHAT HOPE COULD WE POSSIBLY HAVE TO AVENGE THE MUTANT MASSACRE?"

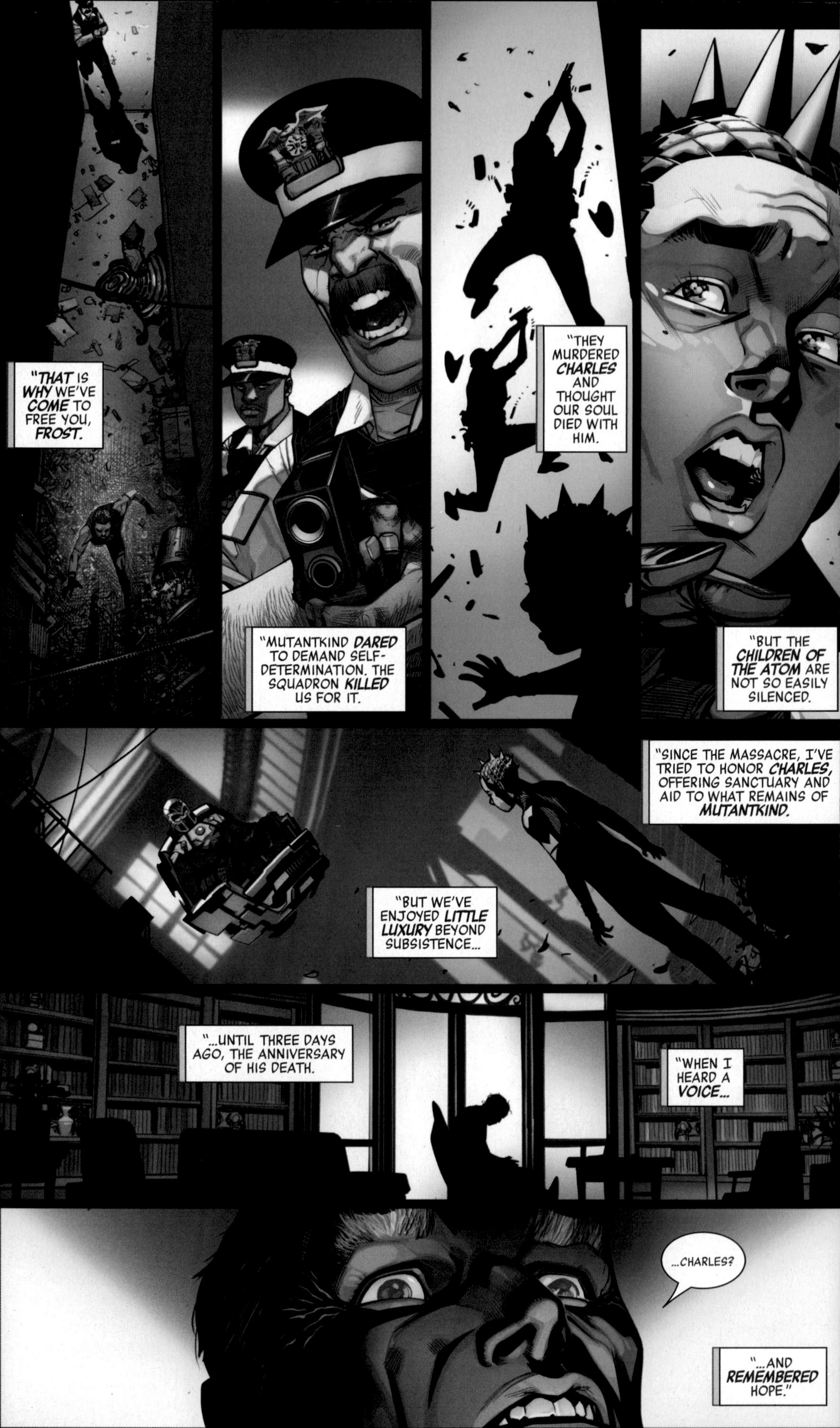
"THAT IS WHY WE'VE COME TO FREE YOU, FROST.
"MUTANTKIND DARED TO DEMAND SELF-DETERMINATION. THE SQUADRON KILLED US FOR IT.
"THEY MURDERED CHARLES AND THOUGHT OUR SOUL DIED WITH HIM.
"BUT THE CHILDREN OF THE ATOM ARE NOT SO EASILY SILENCED.
"SINCE THE MASSACRE, I'VE TRIED TO HONOR CHARLES, OFFERING SANCTUARY AND AID TO WHAT REMAINS OF MUTANTKIND.
"BUT WE'VE ENJOYED LITTLE LUXURY BEYOND SUBSISTENCE...
"...UNTIL THREE DAYS AGO, THE ANNIVERSARY OF HIS DEATH.
"WHEN I HEARD A VOICE...
...CHARLES?
"...AND REMEMBERED HOPE."

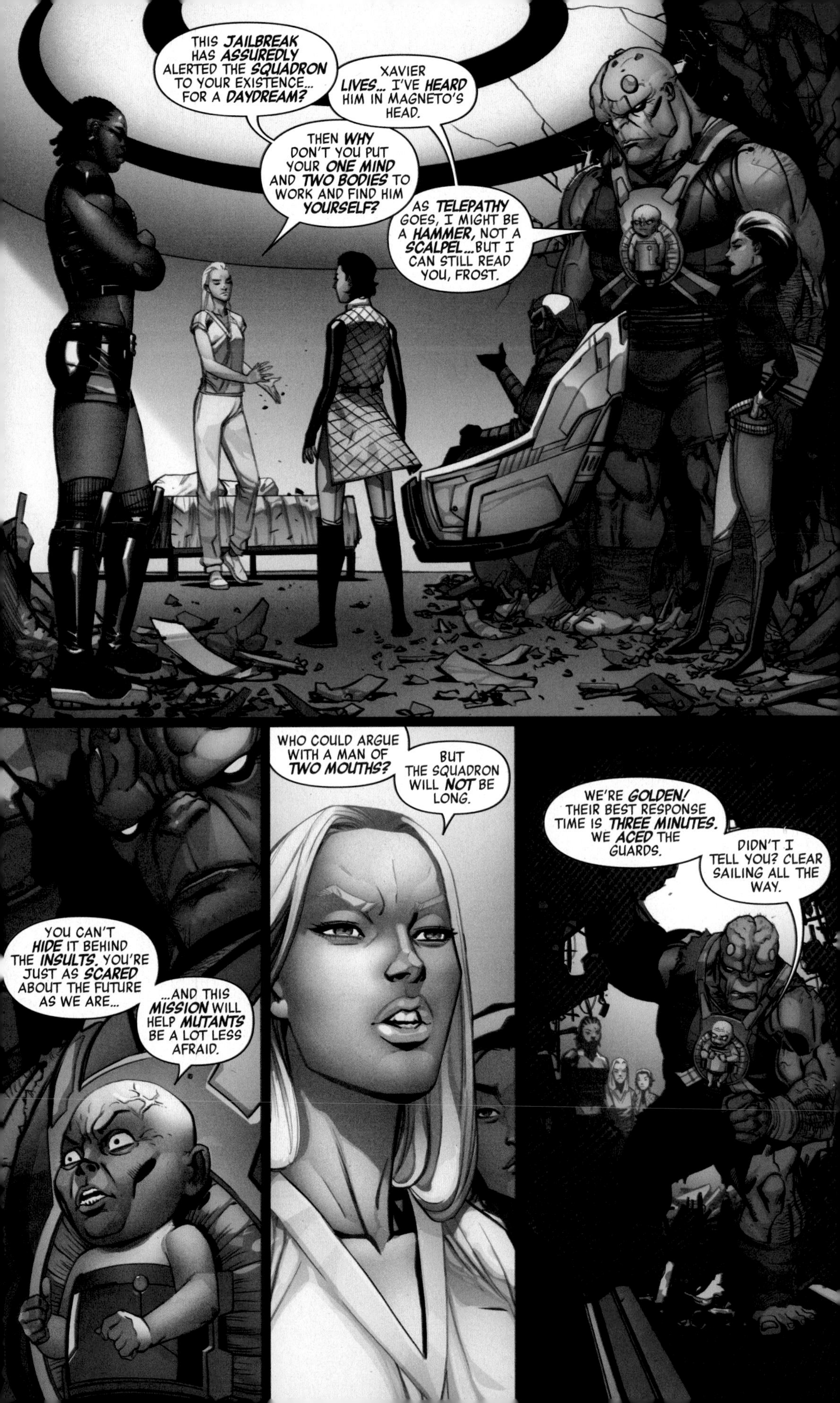
THIS JAILBREAK HAS ASSUREDLY ALERTED THE SQUADRON TO YOUR EXISTENCE... FOR A DAYDREAM?
XAVIER LIVES... I'VE HEARD HIM IN MAGNETO'S HEAD.
THEN WHY DON'T YOU PUT YOUR ONE MIND AND TWO BODIES TO WORK AND FIND HIM YOURSELF?
AS TELEPATHY GOES, I MIGHT BE A HAMMER, NOT A SCALPEL...BUT I CAN STILL READ YOU, FROST.
YOU CAN'T HIDE IT BEHIND THE INSULTS. YOU'RE JUST AS SCARED ABOUT THE FUTURE AS WE ARE...
...AND THIS MISSION WILL HELP MUTANTS BE A LOT LESS AFRAID.
WHO COULD ARGUE WITH A MAN OF TWO MOUTHS?
BUT THE SQUADRON WILL NOT BE LONG.
WE'RE GOLDEN! THEIR BEST RESPONSE TIME IS THREE MINUTES. WE ACED THE GUARDS.
DIDN'T I TELL YOU? CLEAR SAILING ALL THE WAY.

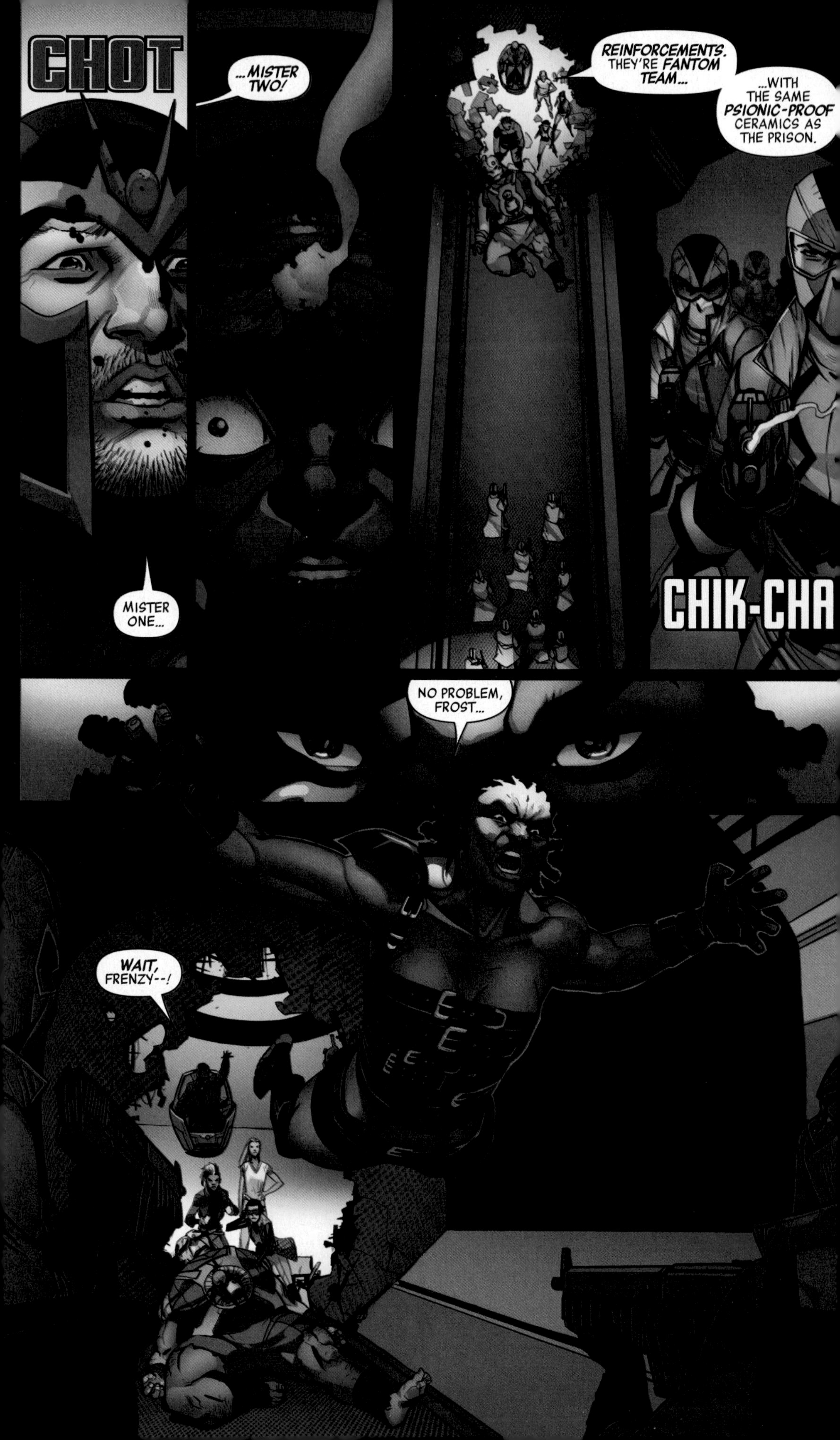

CHOT
MISTER ONE...
...MISTER TWO!
REINFORCEMENTS. THEY'RE FANTOM TEAM...
...WITH THE SAME PSIONIC-PROOF CERAMICS AS THE PRISON.
CHIK-CHA
NO PROBLEM, FROST...
WAIT, FRENZY--!

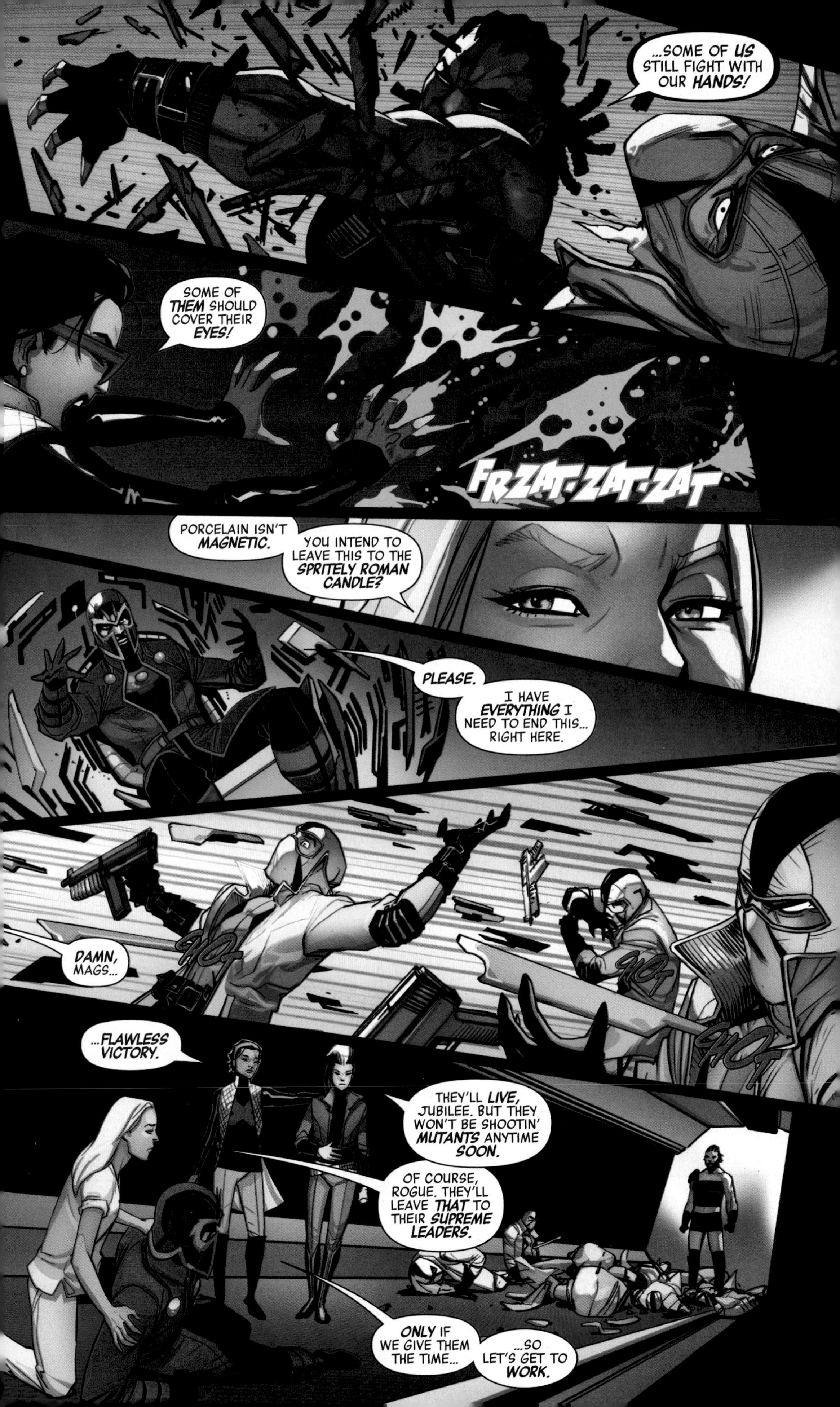

...SOME OF US STILL FIGHT WITH OUR HANDS!
SOME OF THEM SHOULD COVER THEIR EYES!
FRZAT-ZAT-ZAT
PORCELAIN ISN'T MAGNETIC.
YOU INTEND TO LEAVE THIS TO THE SPRITELY ROMAN CANDLE?
PLEASE.
I HAVE EVERYTHING I NEED TO END THIS... RIGHT HERE.
DAMN, MAGS...
...FLAWLESS VICTORY.
THEY'LL LIVE, JUBILEE. BUT THEY WON'T BE SHOOTIN' MUTANTS ANYTIME SOON.
OF COURSE, ROGUE. THEY'LL LEAVE THAT TO THEIR SUPREME LEADERS.
ONLY IF WE GIVE THEM THE TIME...
...SO LET'S GET TO WORK.

In a world in which the Avengers never existed, the Squadron Supreme of America are and have always been Earth's Mightiest Heroes!

But there are those who do not see them as heroes at all. Those who are feared and hated by the Squadron. Those such as....

MAGNETO
& THE MUTANT FORCE

Years ago, Magneto and Professor X led Earth's mutants in a final push for independence against the Squadron Supreme. What followed became known as the Mutant Massacre, a violent rebuttal that left mutantkind forever wounded and Xavier dead. Now the Master of Magnetism offers sanctuary to the world's remaining mutants on his island fortress and offers hope for mutantkind's future in the form of his team, the Mutant Force.

HEROES REBORN

"BEWARE! PSYCHIC RESCUE IN PROGRESS!"

STEVE **ORLANDO** WRITER

BERNARD **CHANG** ARTIST

DAVID **CURIEL** COLOR ARTIST

VC's CLAYTON **COWLES** LETTERER & PRODUCTION

NICK **BRADSHAW** & RACHELLE **ROSENBERG** COVER ARTISTS

RYAN **BENJAMIN** & RAIN **BEREDO**;
BERNARD **CHANG** & MARCELO **MAIOLO** VARIANT COVER ARTISTS

JAY **BOWEN** GRAPHIC DESIGN

WIL **MOSS** EDITOR

TOM **BREVOORT** EXECUTIVE EDITOR

C.B. **CEBULSKI** EDITOR IN CHIEF

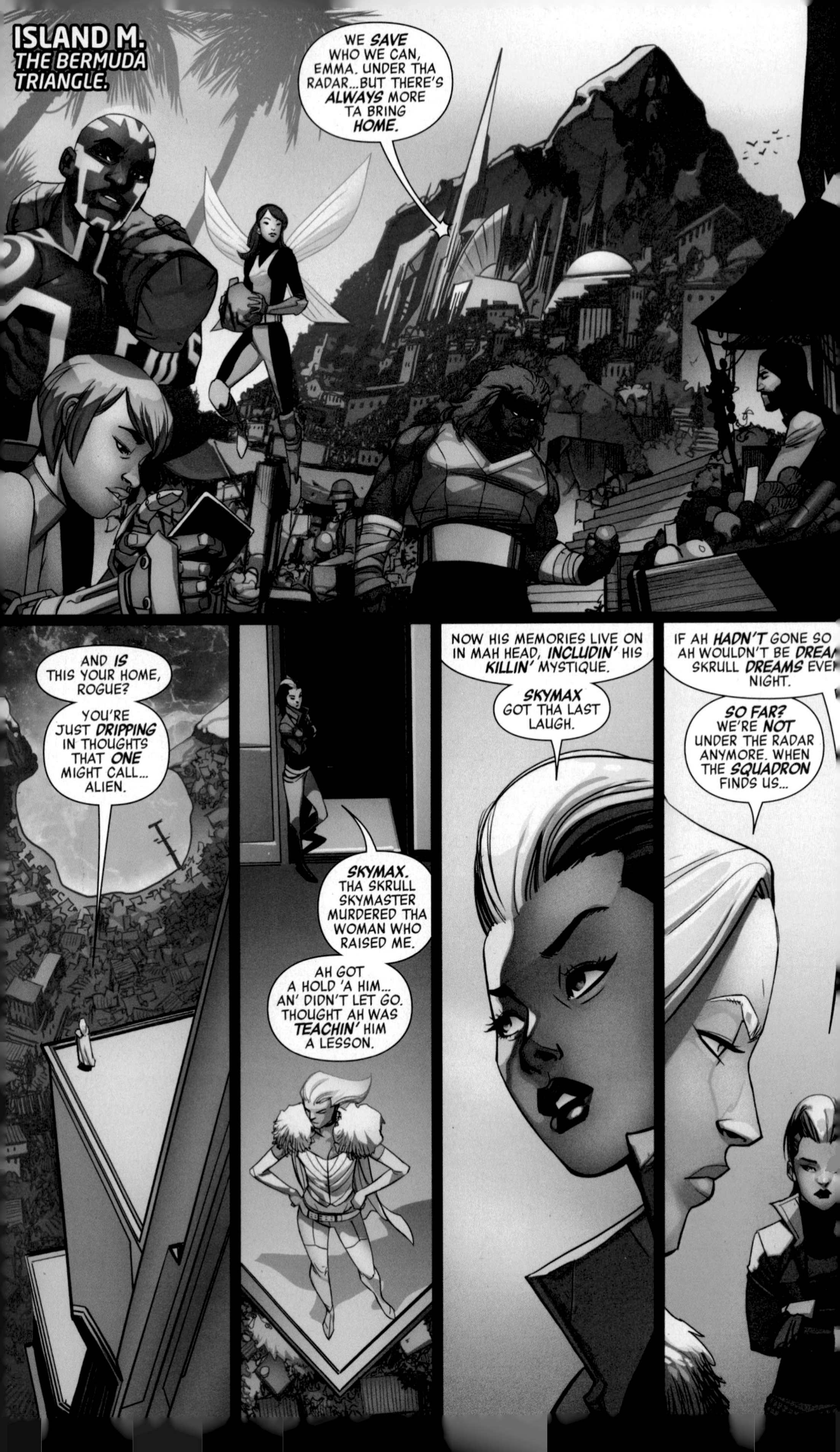
ISLAND M.
THE BERMUDA TRIANGLE.
WE SAVE WHO WE CAN, EMMA. UNDER THA RADAR...BUT THERE'S ALWAYS MORE TA BRING HOME.
AND IS THIS YOUR HOME, ROGUE?
YOU'RE JUST DRIPPING IN THOUGHTS THAT ONE MIGHT CALL... ALIEN.
SKYMAX. THA SKRULL SKYMASTER MURDERED THA WOMAN WHO RAISED ME.
AH GOT A HOLD 'A HIM... AN' DIDN'T LET GO. THOUGHT AH WAS TEACHIN' HIM A LESSON.
NOW HIS MEMORIES LIVE ON IN MAH HEAD, INCLUDIN' HIS KILLIN' MYSTIQUE.
SKYMAX GOT THA LAST LAUGH.
SO FAR? WE'RE NOT UNDER THE RADAR ANYMORE. WHEN THE SQUADRON FINDS US...

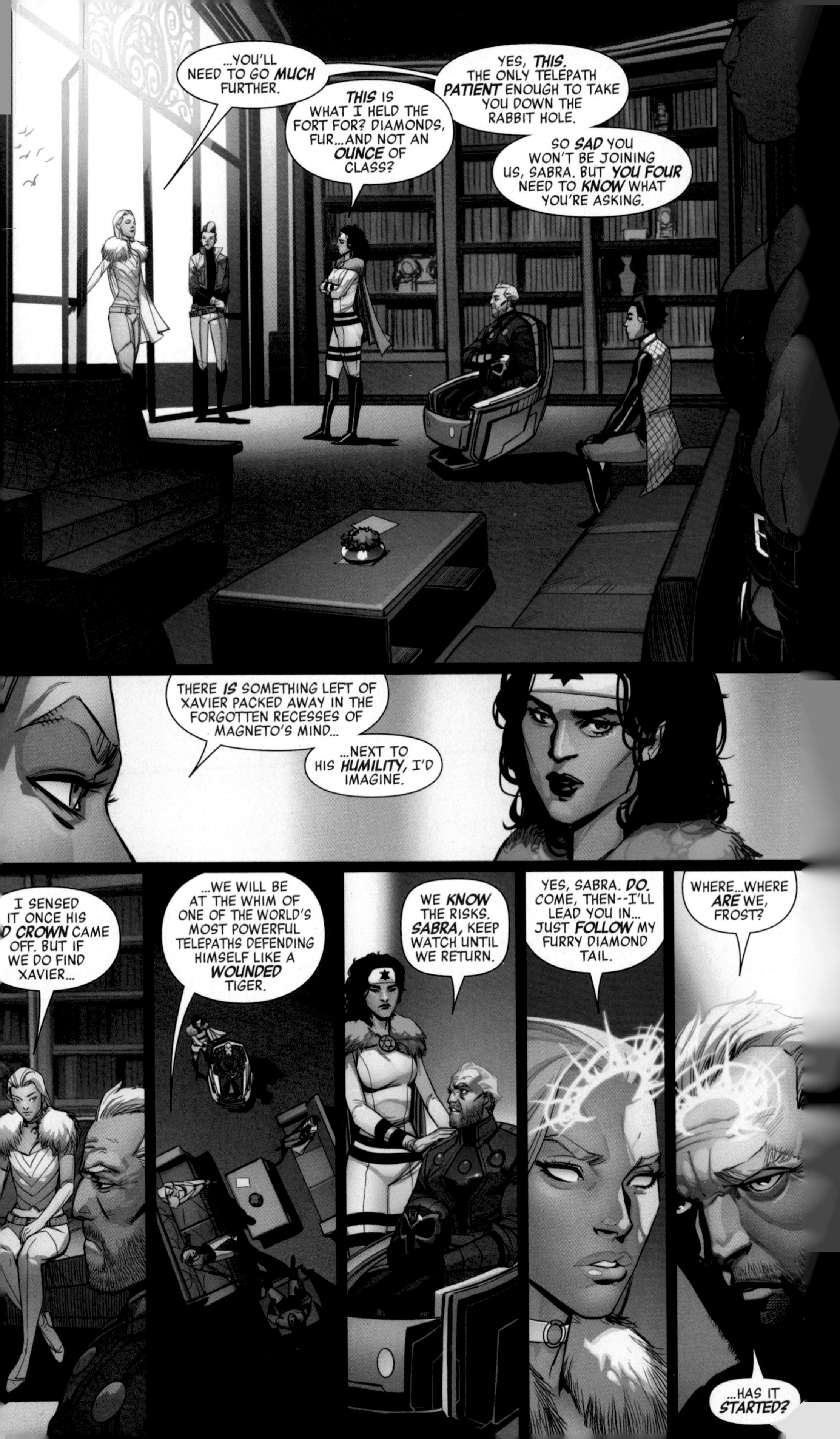
...YOU'LL NEED TO GO MUCH FURTHER.
THIS IS WHAT I HELD THE FORT FOR? DIAMONDS, FUR...AND NOT AN OUNCE OF CLASS?
YES, THIS. THE ONLY TELEPATH PATIENT ENOUGH TO TAKE YOU DOWN THE RABBIT HOLE.
SO SAD YOU WON'T BE JOINING US, SABRA. BUT YOU FOUR NEED TO KNOW WHAT YOU'RE ASKING.
THERE IS SOMETHING LEFT OF XAVIER PACKED AWAY IN THE FORGOTTEN RECESSES OF MAGNETO'S MIND...
...NEXT TO HIS HUMILITY, I'D IMAGINE.
I SENSED IT ONCE HIS D CROWN CAME OFF. BUT IF WE DO FIND XAVIER...
...WE WILL BE AT THE WHIM OF ONE OF THE WORLD'S MOST POWERFUL TELEPATHS DEFENDING HIMSELF LIKE A WOUNDED TIGER.
WE KNOW THE RISKS. SABRA, KEEP WATCH UNTIL WE RETURN.
YES, SABRA. DO. COME, THEN--I'LL LEAD YOU IN... JUST FOLLOW MY FURRY DIAMOND TAIL.
WHERE...WHERE ARE WE, FROST?
...HAS IT STARTED?

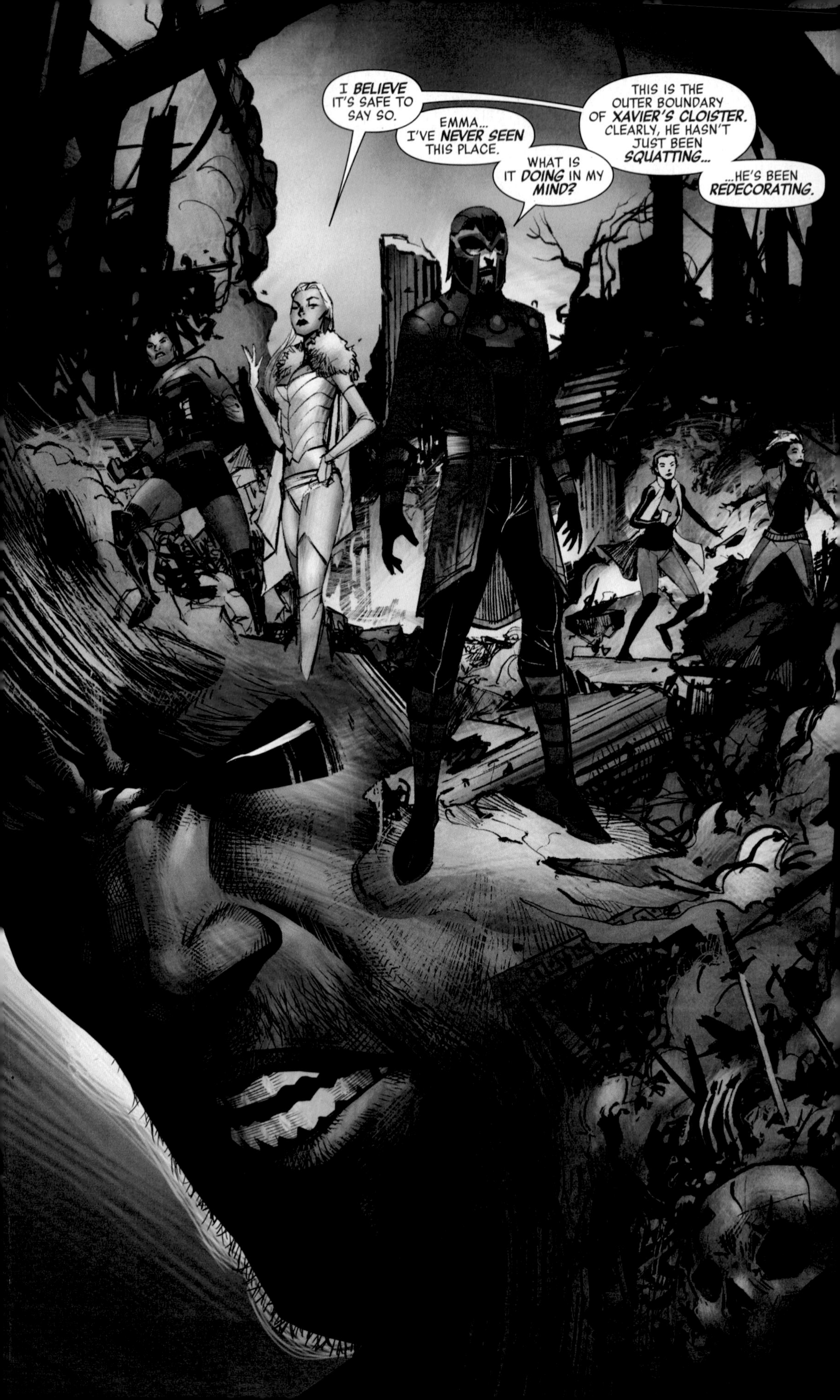
I BELIEVE IT'S SAFE TO SAY SO.
EMMA... I'VE NEVER SEEN THIS PLACE.
WHAT IS IT DOING IN MY MIND?
THIS IS THE OUTER BOUNDARY OF XAVIER'S CLOISTER. CLEARLY, HE HASN'T JUST BEEN SQUATTING...
...HE'S BEEN REDECORATING.

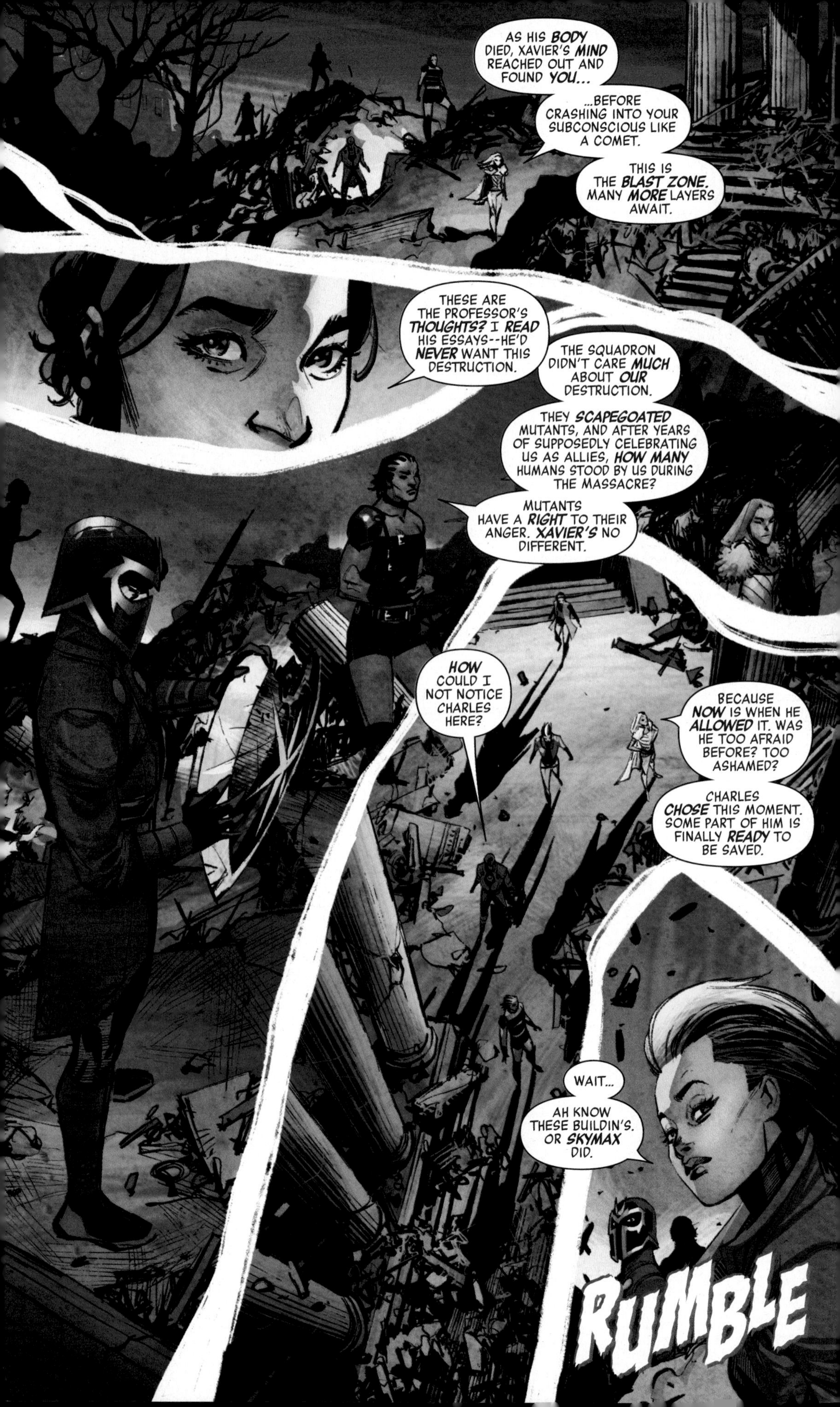

AS HIS BODY DIED, XAVIER'S MIND REACHED OUT AND FOUND YOU...
...BEFORE CRASHING INTO YOUR SUBCONSCIOUS LIKE A COMET.
THIS IS THE BLAST ZONE. MANY MORE LAYERS AWAIT.
THESE ARE THE PROFESSOR'S THOUGHTS? I READ HIS ESSAYS--HE'D NEVER WANT THIS DESTRUCTION.
THE SQUADRON DIDN'T CARE MUCH ABOUT OUR DESTRUCTION.
THEY SCAPEGOATED MUTANTS, AND AFTER YEARS OF SUPPOSEDLY CELEBRATING US AS ALLIES, HOW MANY HUMANS STOOD BY US DURING THE MASSACRE?
MUTANTS HAVE A RIGHT TO THEIR ANGER. XAVIER'S NO DIFFERENT.
HOW COULD I NOT NOTICE CHARLES HERE?
BECAUSE NOW IS WHEN HE ALLOWED IT. WAS HE TOO AFRAID BEFORE? TOO ASHAMED?
CHARLES CHOSE THIS MOMENT. SOME PART OF HIM IS FINALLY READY TO BE SAVED.
WAIT...
AH KNOW THESE BUILDIN'S. OR SKYMAX DID.
RUMBLE

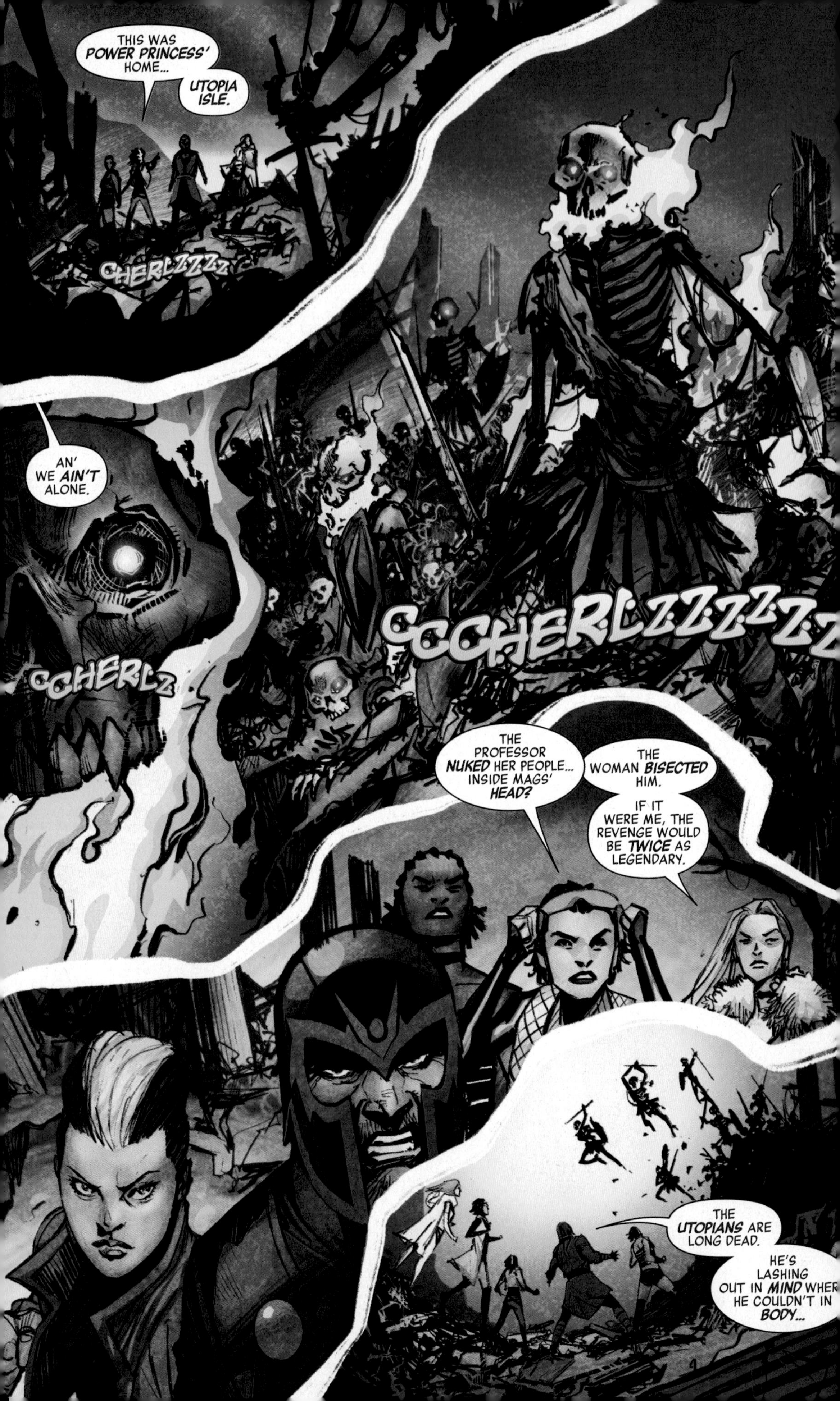
THIS WAS POWER PRINCESS' HOME...
UTOPIA ISLE.
CHERLZZZZ
AN' WE AIN'T ALONE.
CCHERLZ
CCCHERLZZZZZZ
THE PROFESSOR NUKED HER PEOPLE... INSIDE MAGS' HEAD?
THE WOMAN BISECTED HIM.
IF IT WERE ME, THE REVENGE WOULD BE TWICE AS LEGENDARY.
THE UTOPIANS ARE LONG DEAD.
HE'S LASHING OUT IN MIND WHERE HE COULDN'T IN BODY...

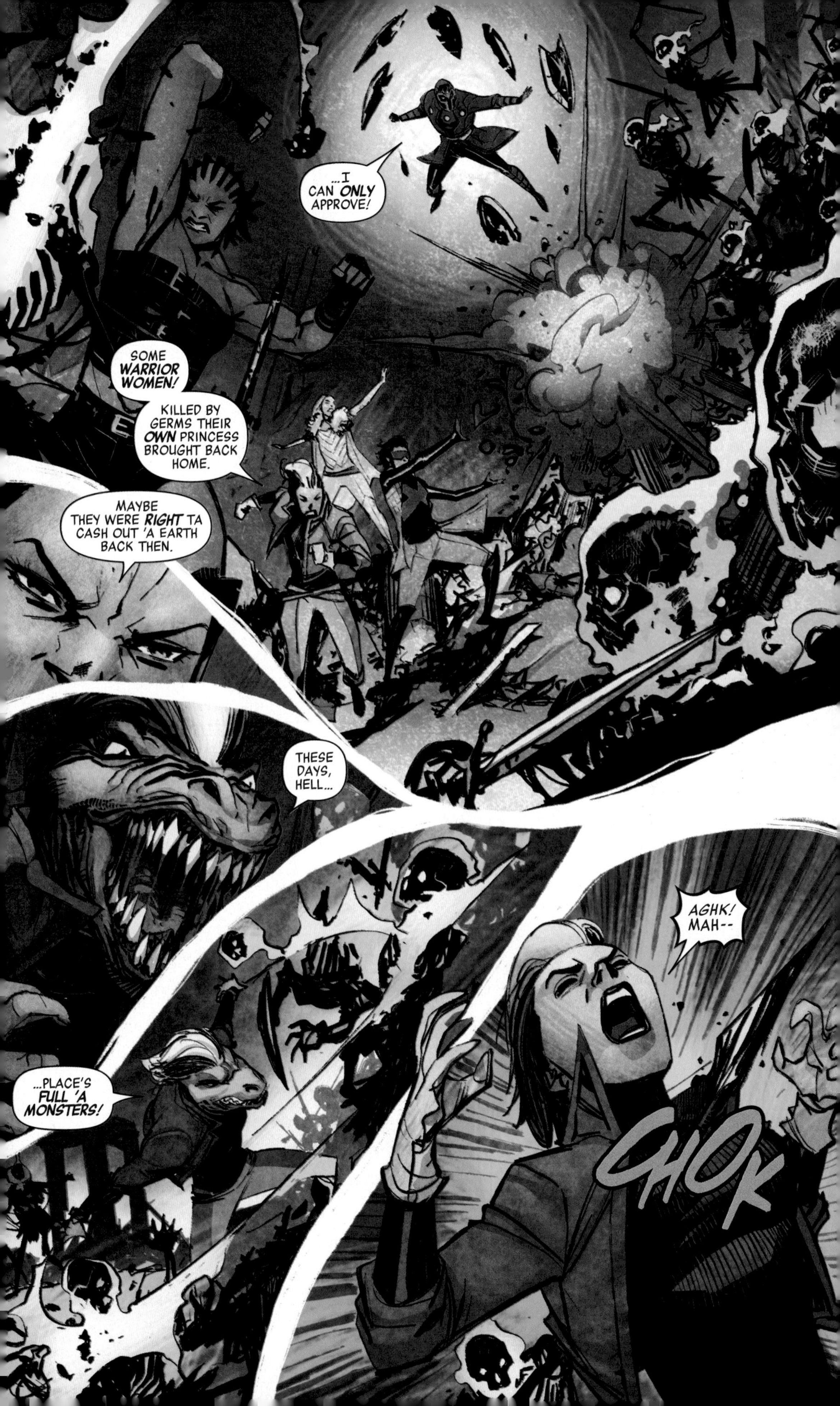
...I CAN ONLY APPROVE!
SOME WARRIOR WOMEN!
KILLED BY GERMS THEIR OWN PRINCESS BROUGHT BACK HOME.
MAYBE THEY WERE RIGHT TA CASH OUT 'A EARTH BACK THEN.
THESE DAYS, HELL...
...PLACE'S FULL 'A MONSTERS!
AGHK! MAH--
CHOK

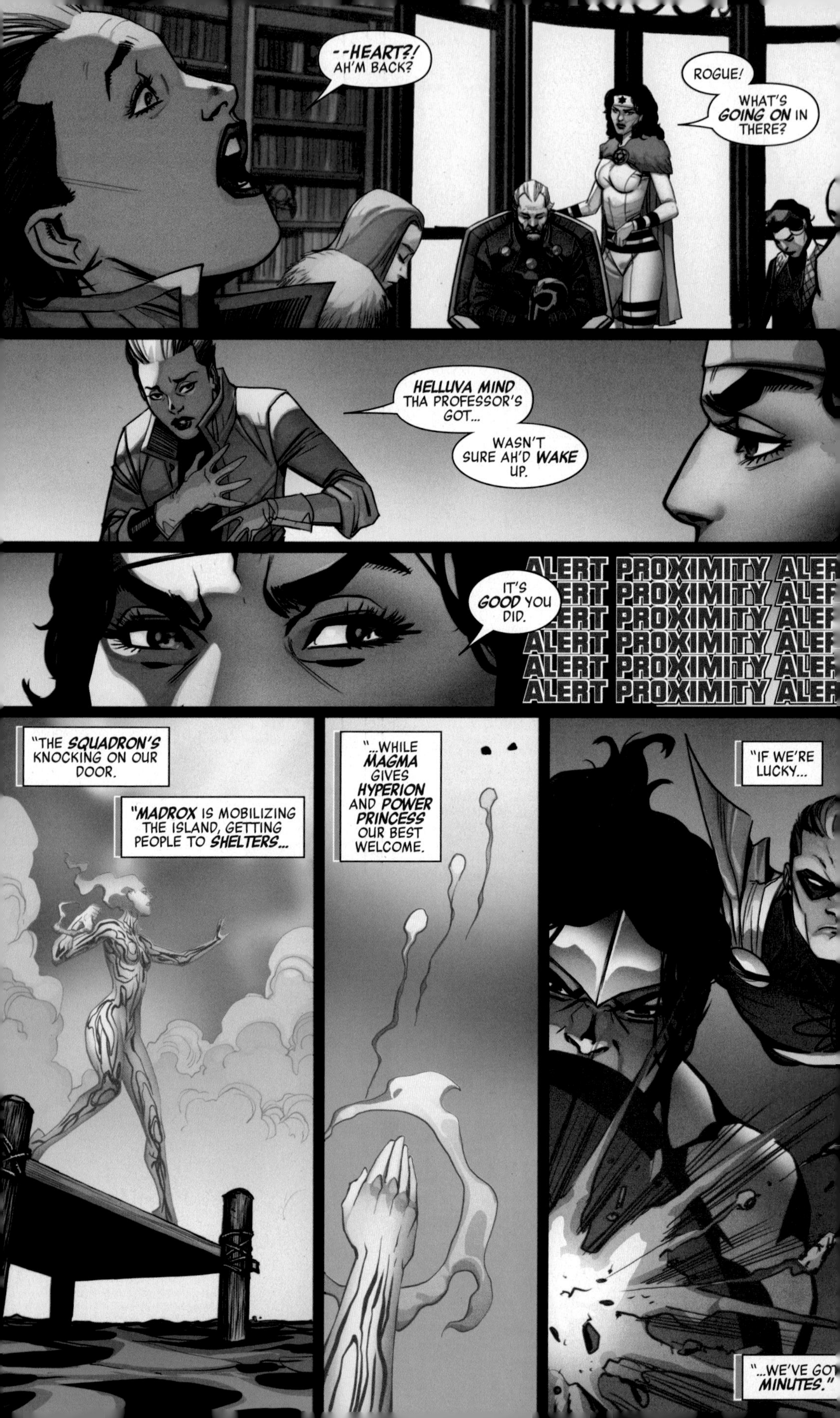
--HEART?! AH'M BACK?
ROGUE!
WHAT'S GOING ON IN THERE?
HELLUVA MIND THA PROFESSOR'S GOT...
WASN'T SURE AH'D WAKE UP.
IT'S GOOD YOU DID.
ALERT PROXIMITY ALER
ALERT PROXIMITY ALER
ALERT PROXIMITY ALER
ALERT PROXIMITY ALER
ALERT PROXIMITY ALER
ALERT PROXIMITY ALER
"THE SQUADRON'S KNOCKING ON OUR DOOR.
"MADROX IS MOBILIZING THE ISLAND, GETTING PEOPLE TO SHELTERS...
"...WHILE MAGMA GIVES HYPERION AND POWER PRINCESS OUR BEST WELCOME.
"IF WE'RE LUCKY...
"...WE'VE GOT MINUTES."

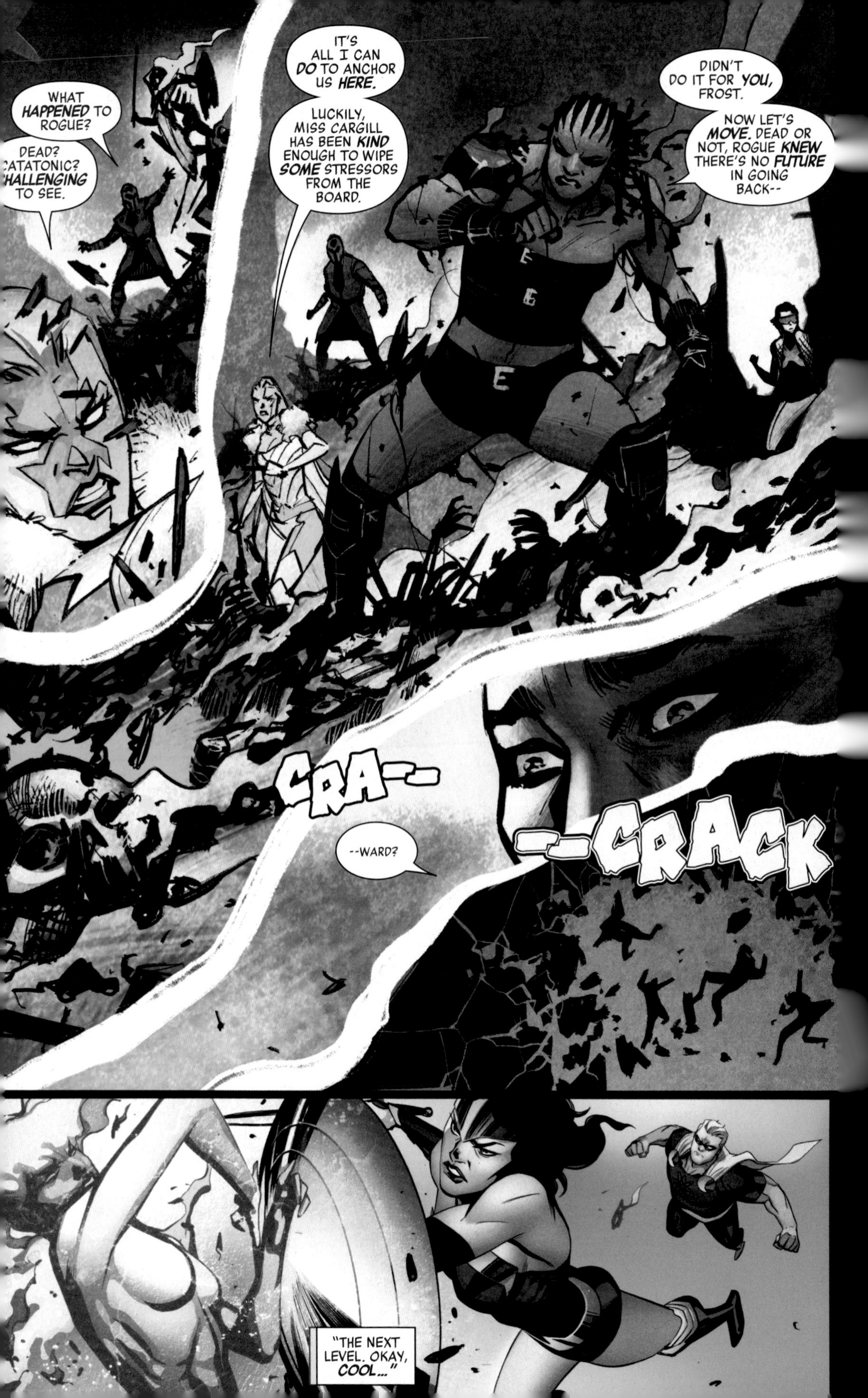

WHAT HAPPENED TO ROGUE?
DEAD? CATATONIC? CHALLENGING TO SEE.
IT'S ALL I CAN DO TO ANCHOR US HERE.
LUCKILY, MISS CARGILL HAS BEEN KIND ENOUGH TO WIPE SOME STRESSORS FROM THE BOARD.
DIDN'T DO IT FOR YOU, FROST.
NOW LET'S MOVE. DEAD OR NOT, ROGUE KNEW THERE'S NO FUTURE IN GOING BACK--
CRA--
--WARD?
--CRACK
"THE NEXT LEVEL. OKAY, COOL..."

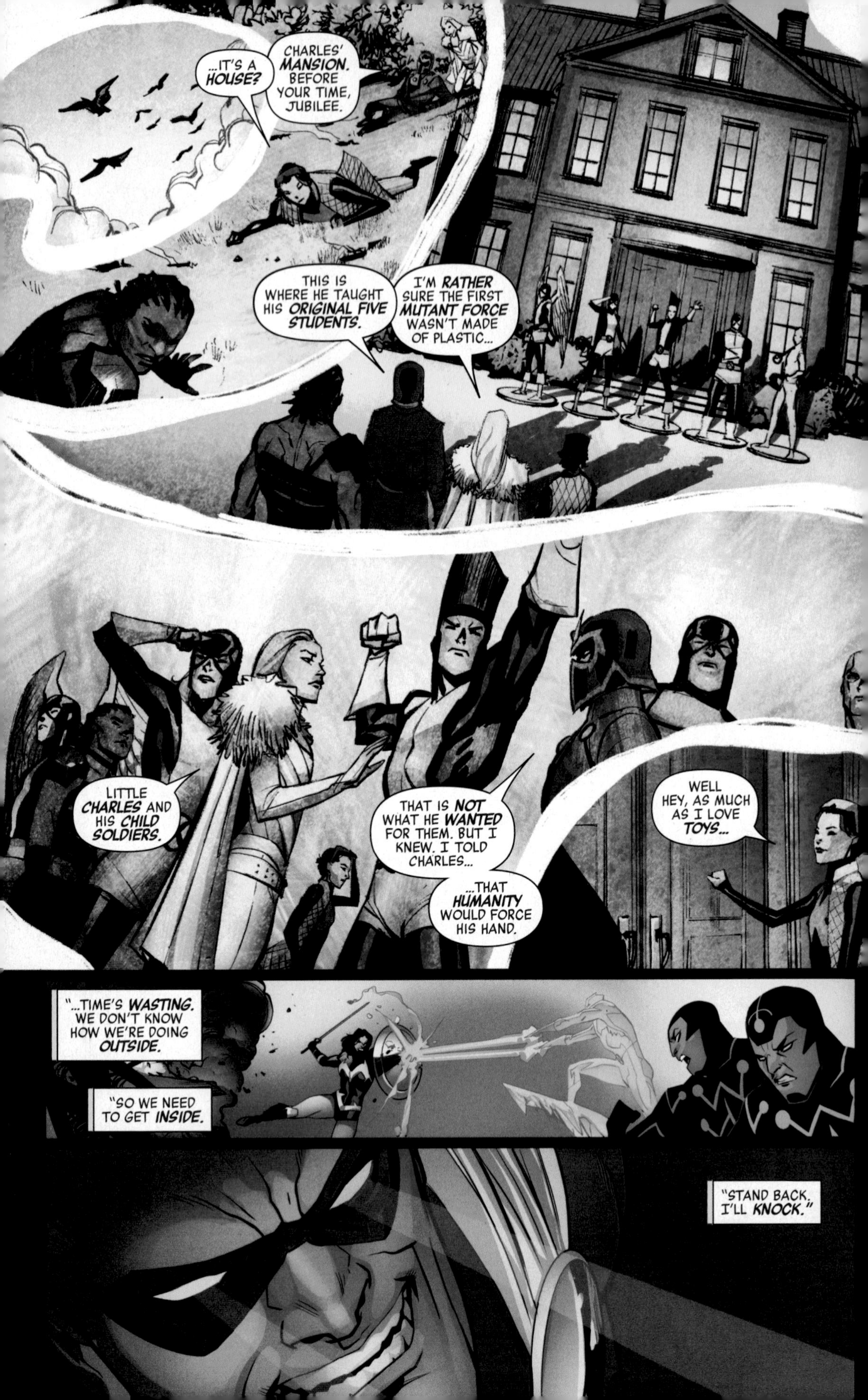
...IT'S A HOUSE?
CHARLES' MANSION. BEFORE YOUR TIME, JUBILEE.
THIS IS WHERE HE TAUGHT HIS ORIGINAL FIVE STUDENTS.
I'M RATHER SURE THE FIRST MUTANT FORCE WASN'T MADE OF PLASTIC...
LITTLE CHARLES AND HIS CHILD SOLDIERS.
THAT IS NOT WHAT HE WANTED FOR THEM. BUT I KNEW. I TOLD CHARLES...
...THAT HUMANITY WOULD FORCE HIS HAND.
WELL HEY, AS MUCH AS I LOVE TOYS...
"...TIME'S WASTING. WE DON'T KNOW HOW WE'RE DOING OUTSIDE.
"SO WE NEED TO GET INSIDE.
"STAND BACK. I'LL KNOCK."

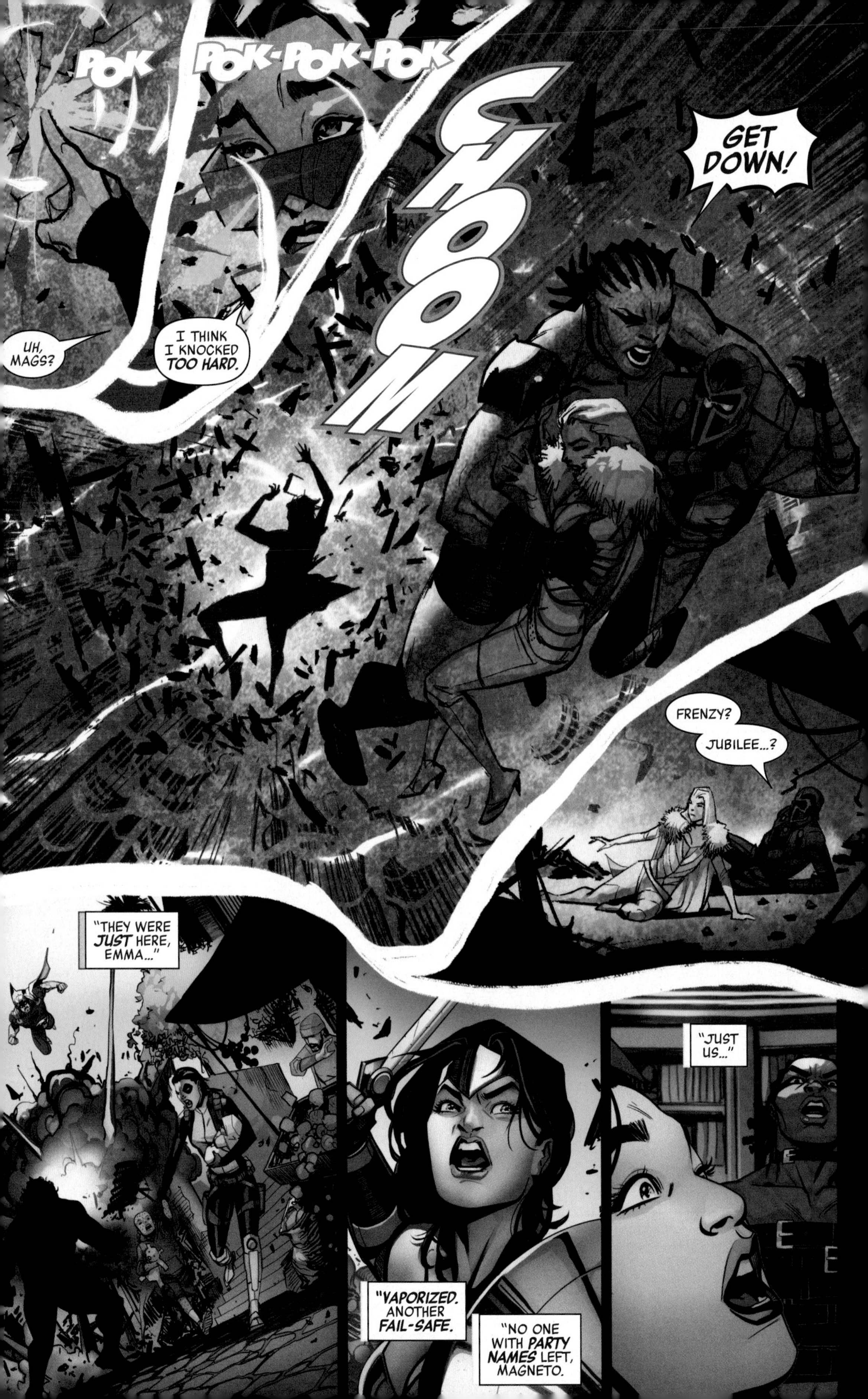
POK POK-POK-POK
CHOOM
GET DOWN!
UH, MAGS?
I THINK I KNOCKED TOO HARD.
FRENZY?
JUBILEE...?
"THEY WERE JUST HERE, EMMA..."
"VAPORIZED. ANOTHER FAIL-SAFE.
"JUST US..."
"NO ONE WITH PARTY NAMES LEFT, MAGNETO.

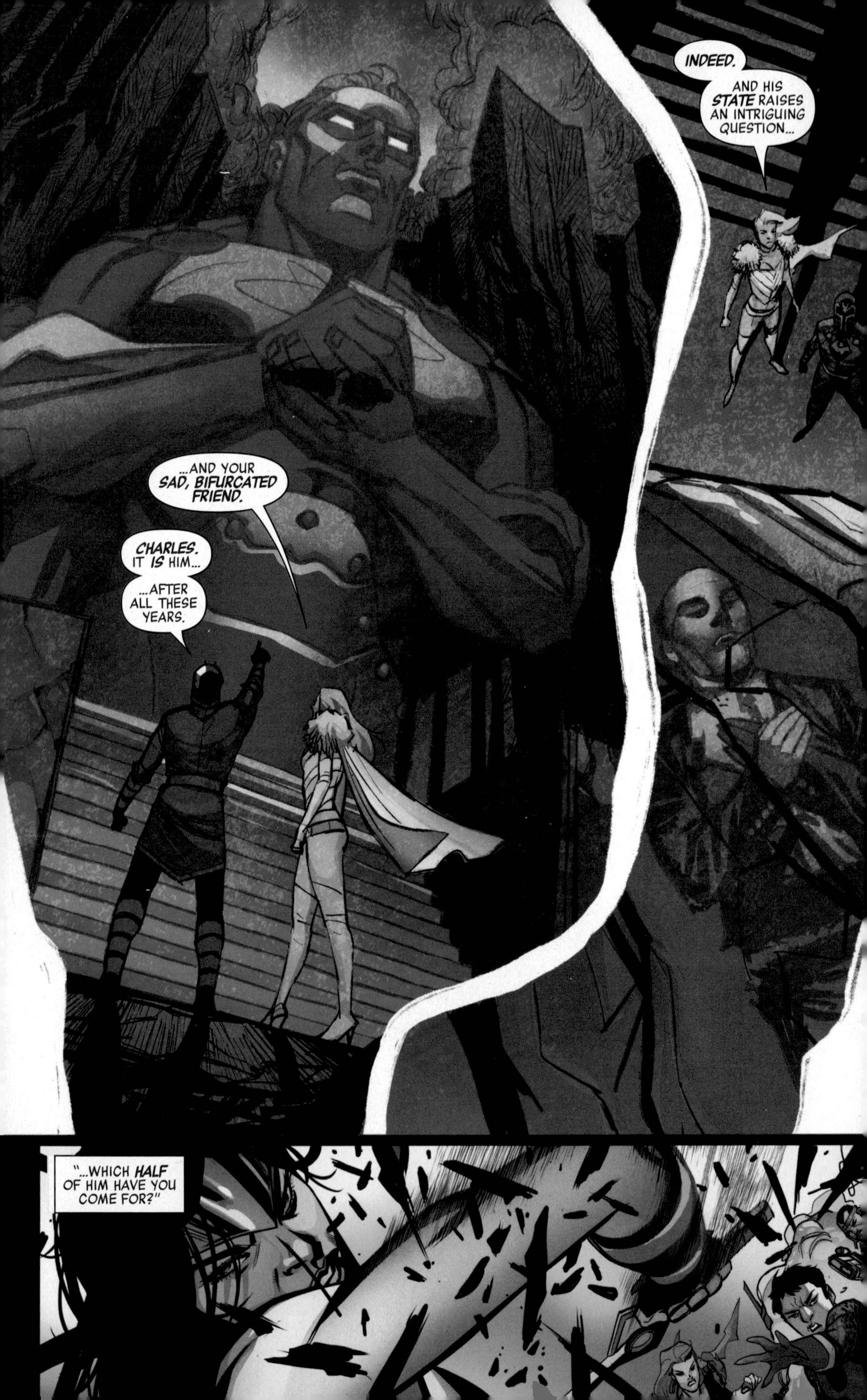
...AND YOUR SAD, BIFURCATED FRIEND.
CHARLES. IT IS HIM...
...AFTER ALL THESE YEARS.
INDEED.
AND HIS STATE RAISES AN INTRIGUING QUESTION...
"...WHICH HALF OF HIM HAVE YOU COME FOR?"

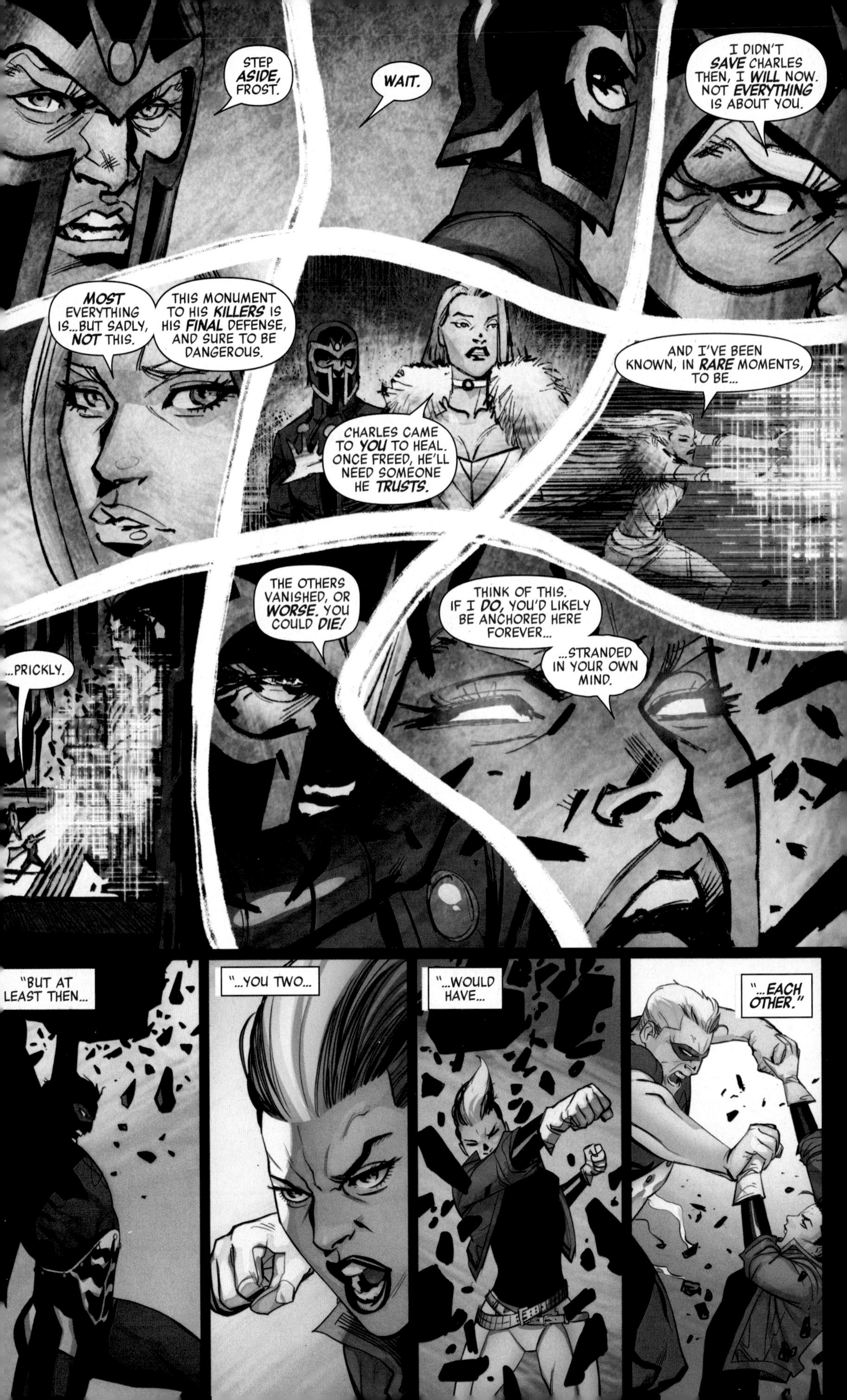
STEP ASIDE, FROST.
WAIT.
I DIDN'T SAVE CHARLES THEN, I WILL NOW. NOT EVERYTHING IS ABOUT YOU.
MOST EVERYTHING IS...BUT SADLY, NOT THIS.
THIS MONUMENT TO HIS KILLERS IS HIS FINAL DEFENSE, AND SURE TO BE DANGEROUS.
CHARLES CAME TO YOU TO HEAL. ONCE FREED, HE'LL NEED SOMEONE HE TRUSTS.
AND I'VE BEEN KNOWN, IN RARE MOMENTS, TO BE...
...PRICKLY.
THE OTHERS VANISHED, OR WORSE. YOU COULD DIE!
THINK OF THIS. IF I DO, YOU'D LIKELY BE ANCHORED HERE FOREVER...
...STRANDED IN YOUR OWN MIND.
"BUT AT LEAST THEN...
"...YOU TWO...
"...WOULD HAVE...
"...EACH OTHER."

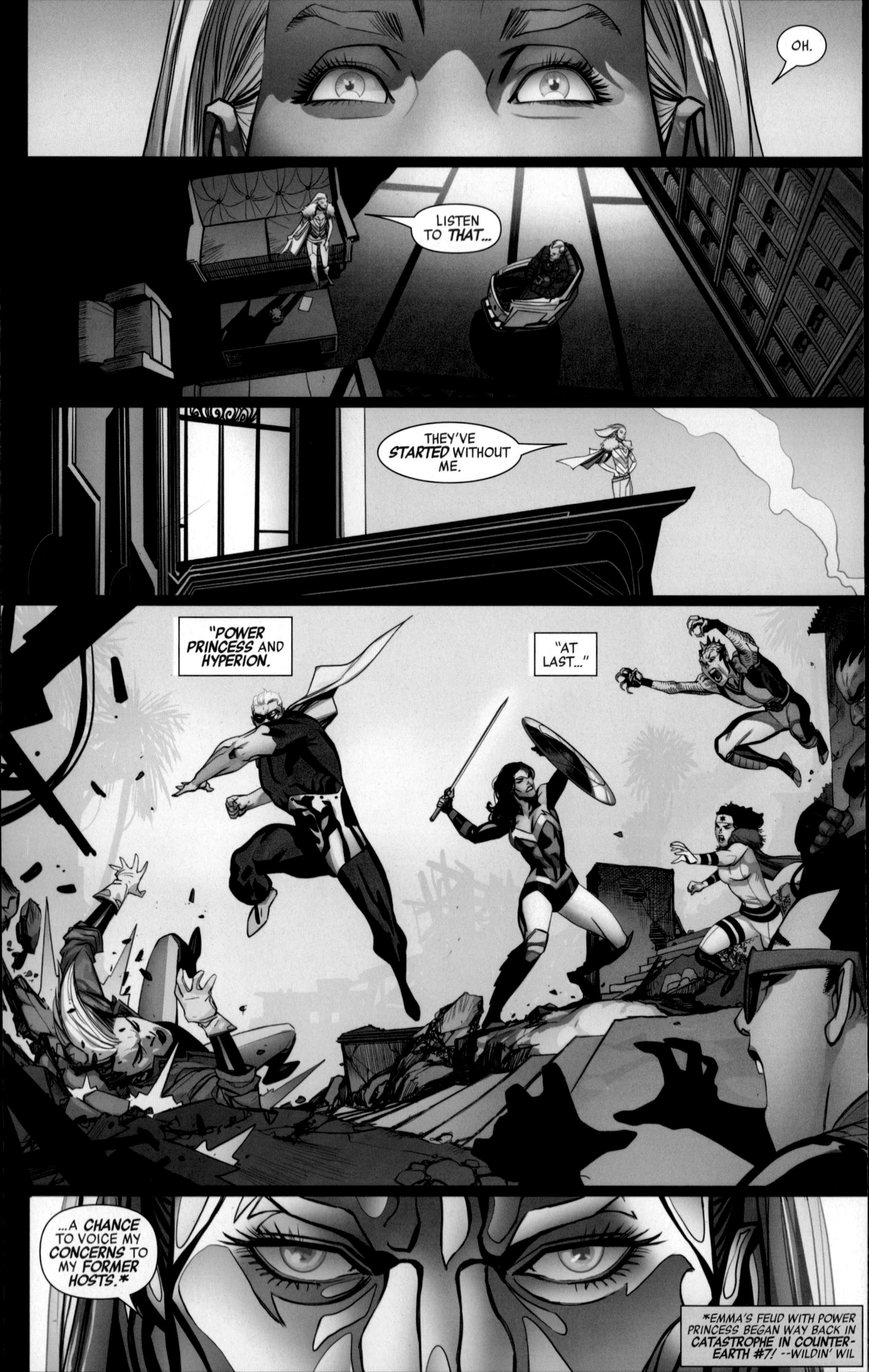
OH.
LISTEN TO THAT...
THEY'VE STARTED WITHOUT ME.
"POWER PRINCESS AND HYPERION.
"AT LAST..."
...A CHANCE TO VOICE MY CONCERNS TO MY FORMER HOSTS.*
*EMMA'S FEUD WITH POWER PRINCESS BEGAN WAY BACK IN CATASTROPHE IN COUNTER-EARTH #7! --WILDIN' WIL

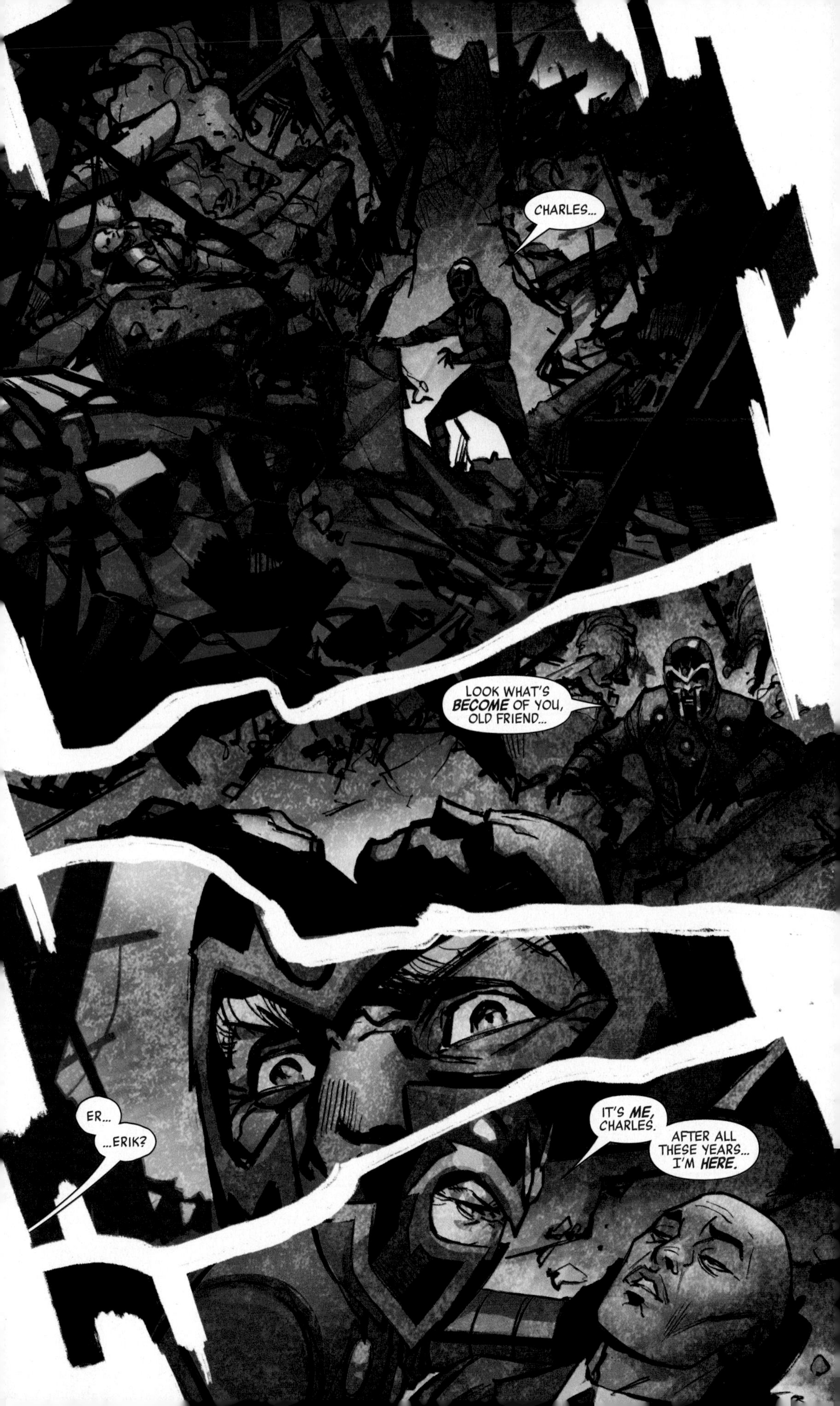
CHARLES...
LOOK WHAT'S BECOME OF YOU, OLD FRIEND...
ER...
...ERIK?
IT'S ME, CHARLES.
AFTER ALL THESE YEARS... I'M HERE.

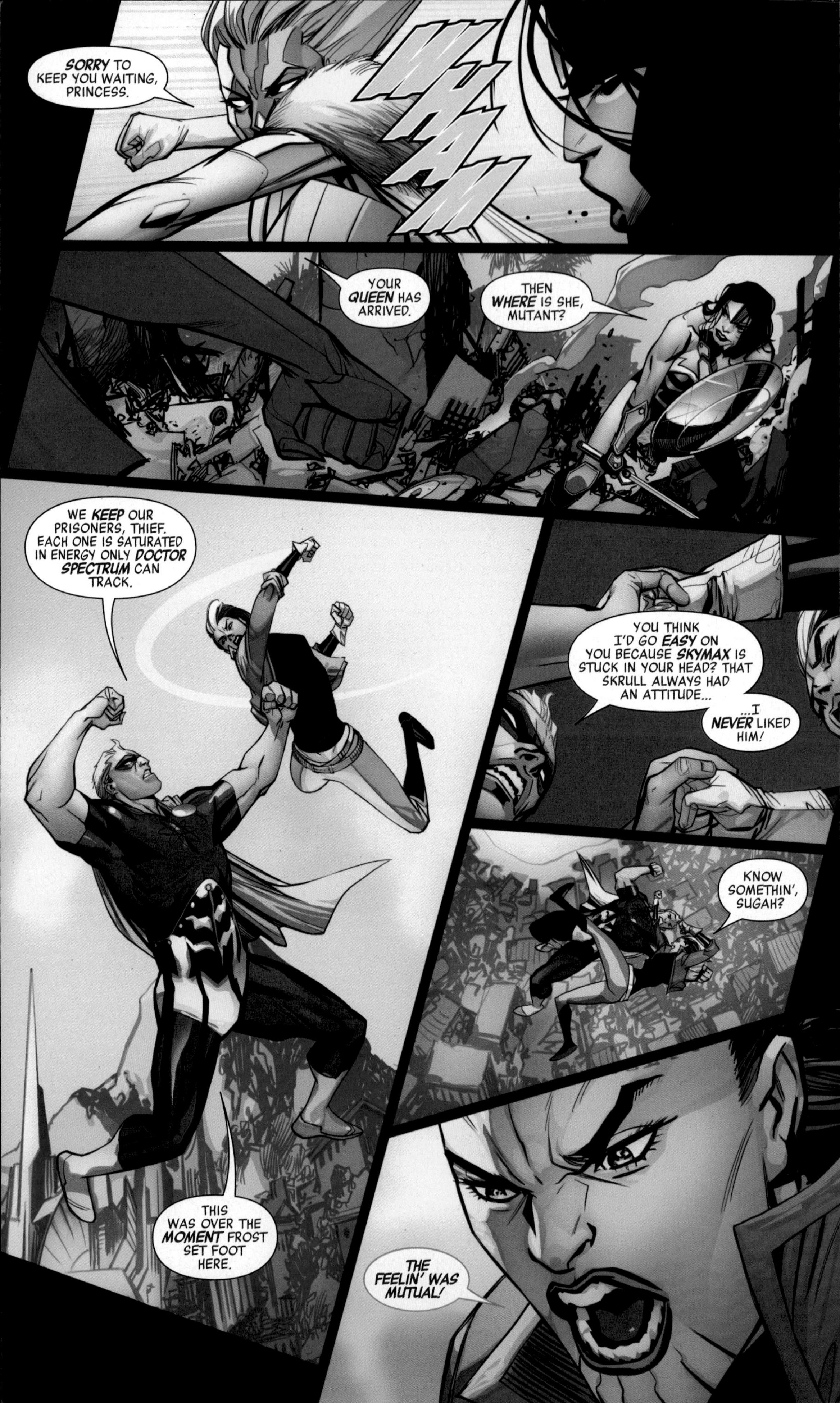
SORRY TO KEEP YOU WAITING, PRINCESS.
WHAM
YOUR QUEEN HAS ARRIVED.
THEN WHERE IS SHE, MUTANT?
WE KEEP OUR PRISONERS, THIEF. EACH ONE IS SATURATED IN ENERGY ONLY DOCTOR SPECTRUM CAN TRACK.
THIS WAS OVER THE MOMENT FROST SET FOOT HERE.
YOU THINK I'D GO EASY ON YOU BECAUSE SKYMAX IS STUCK IN YOUR HEAD? THAT SKRULL ALWAYS HAD AN ATTITUDE...
...I NEVER LIKED HIM!
KNOW SOMETHIN', SUGAH?
THE FEELIN' WAS MUTUAL!

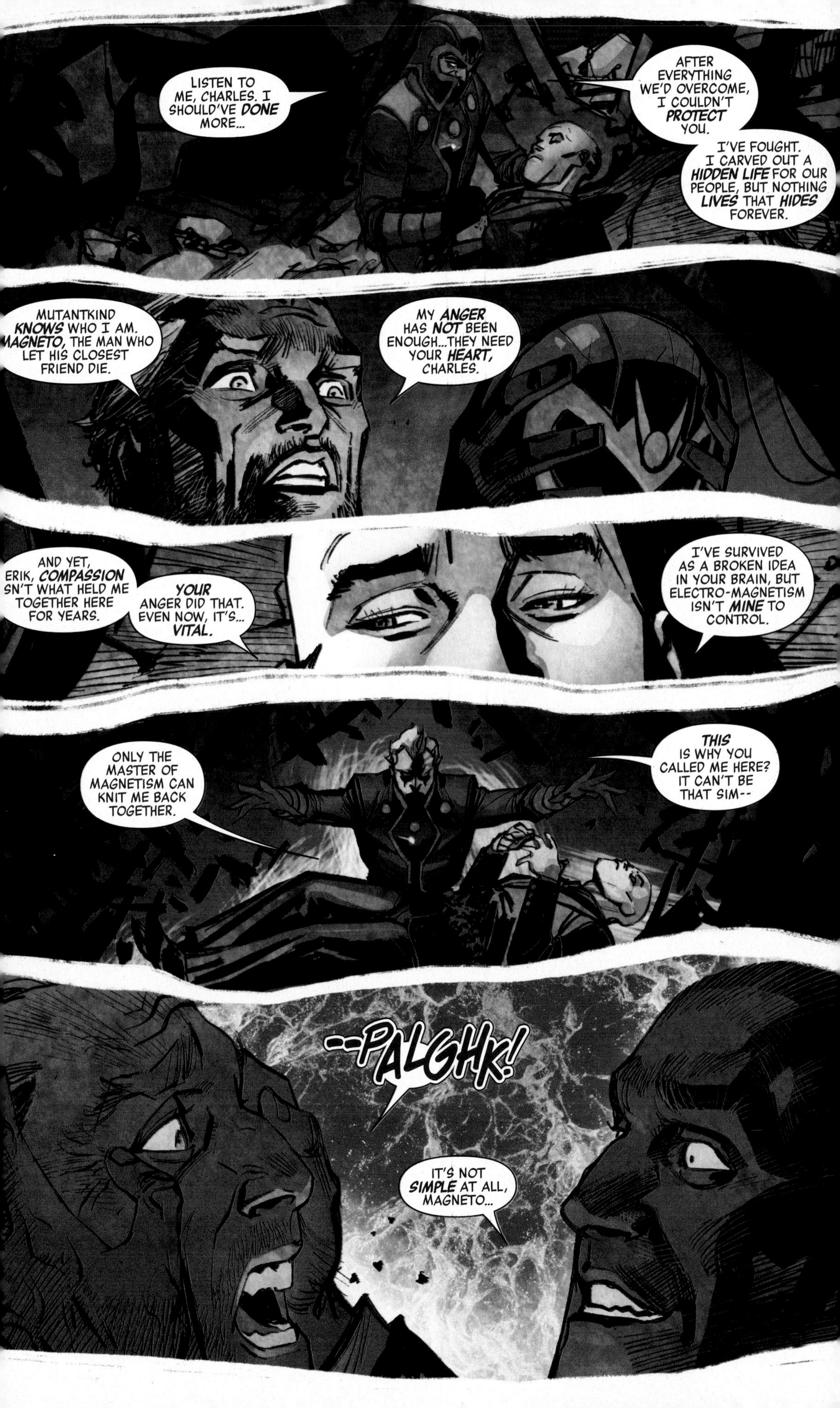

LISTEN TO ME, CHARLES. I SHOULD'VE DONE MORE...
AFTER EVERYTHING WE'D OVERCOME, I COULDN'T PROTECT YOU.
I'VE FOUGHT. I CARVED OUT A HIDDEN LIFE FOR OUR PEOPLE, BUT NOTHING LIVES THAT HIDES FOREVER.
MUTANTKIND KNOWS WHO I AM. MAGNETO, THE MAN WHO LET HIS CLOSEST FRIEND DIE.
MY ANGER HAS NOT BEEN ENOUGH...THEY NEED YOUR HEART, CHARLES.
AND YET, ERIK, COMPASSION ISN'T WHAT HELD ME TOGETHER HERE FOR YEARS.
YOUR ANGER DID THAT. EVEN NOW, IT'S... VITAL.
I'VE SURVIVED AS A BROKEN IDEA IN YOUR BRAIN, BUT ELECTRO-MAGNETISM ISN'T MINE TO CONTROL.
ONLY THE MASTER OF MAGNETISM CAN KNIT ME BACK TOGETHER.
THIS IS WHY YOU CALLED ME HERE? IT CAN'T BE THAT SIM--
--PALGHK!
IT'S NOT SIMPLE AT ALL, MAGNETO...

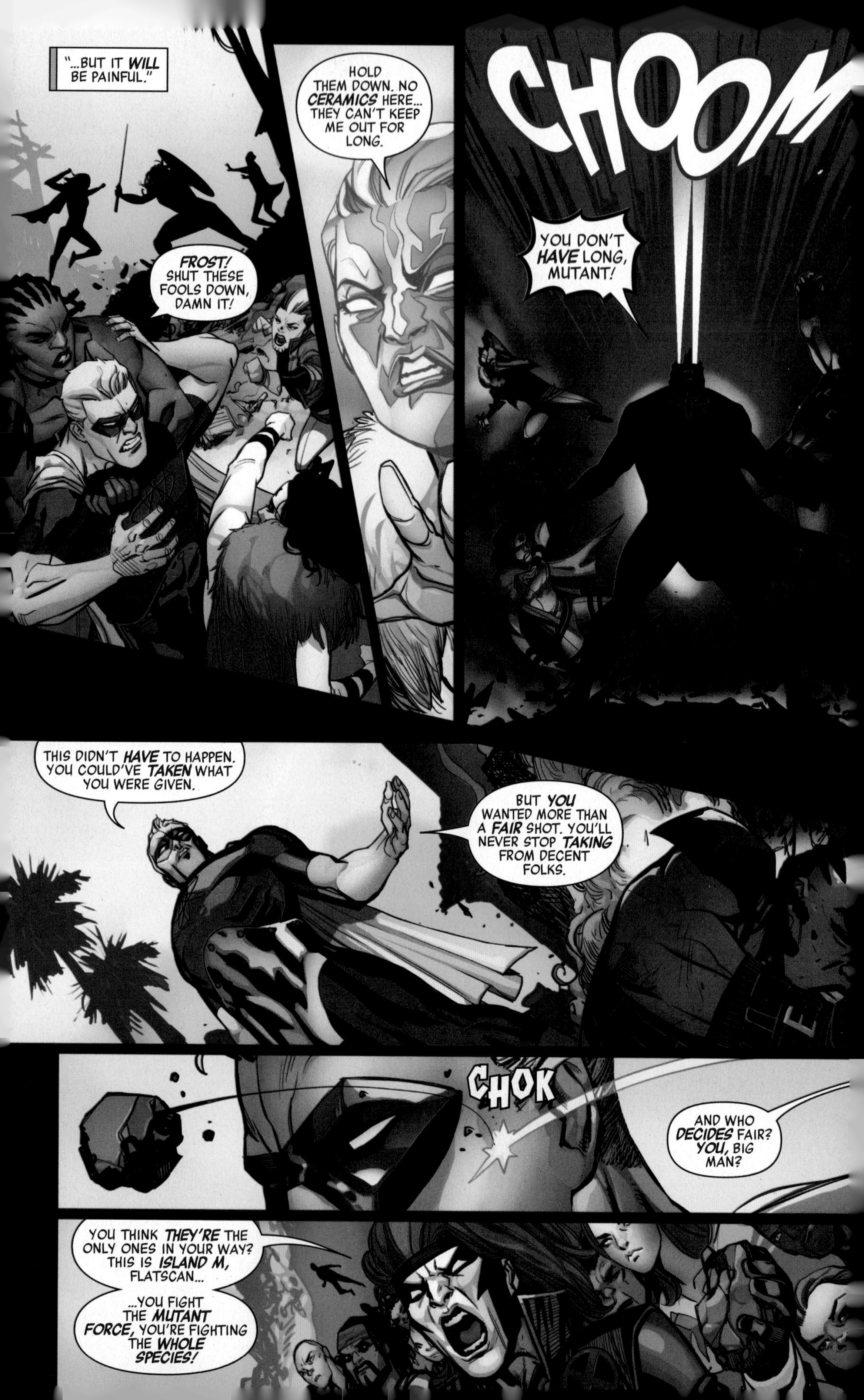
"...BUT IT WILL BE PAINFUL."
HOLD THEM DOWN. NO CERAMICS HERE... THEY CAN'T KEEP ME OUT FOR LONG.
FROST! SHUT THESE FOOLS DOWN, DAMN IT!
CHOOM
YOU DON'T HAVE LONG, MUTANT!
THIS DIDN'T HAVE TO HAPPEN. YOU COULD'VE TAKEN WHAT YOU WERE GIVEN.
BUT YOU WANTED MORE THAN A FAIR SHOT. YOU'LL NEVER STOP TAKING FROM DECENT FOLKS.
CHOK
AND WHO DECIDES FAIR? YOU, BIG MAN?
YOU THINK THEY'RE THE ONLY ONES IN YOUR WAY? THIS IS ISLAND M, FLATSCAN...
...YOU FIGHT THE MUTANT FORCE, YOU'RE FIGHTING THE WHOLE SPECIES!

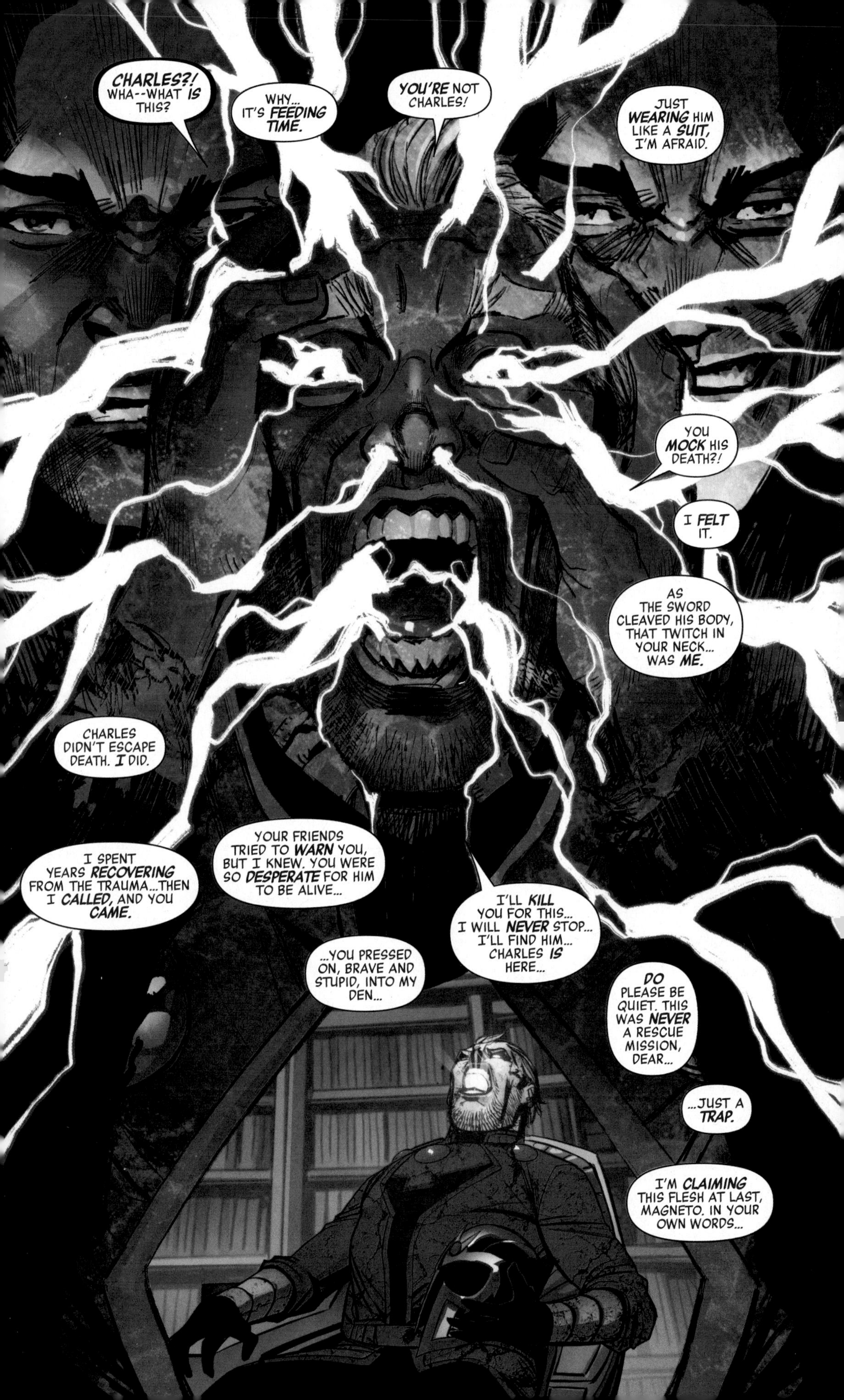
CHARLES?! WHA--WHAT IS THIS?
WHY... IT'S FEEDING TIME.
YOU'RE NOT CHARLES!
JUST WEARING HIM LIKE A SUIT, I'M AFRAID.
YOU MOCK HIS DEATH?!
I FELT IT.
AS THE SWORD CLEAVED HIS BODY, THAT TWITCH IN YOUR NECK... WAS ME.
CHARLES DIDN'T ESCAPE DEATH. I DID.
I SPENT YEARS RECOVERING FROM THE TRAUMA...THEN I CALLED, AND YOU CAME.
YOUR FRIENDS TRIED TO WARN YOU, BUT I KNEW. YOU WERE SO DESPERATE FOR HIM TO BE ALIVE...
...YOU PRESSED ON, BRAVE AND STUPID, INTO MY DEN...
I'LL KILL YOU FOR THIS... I WILL NEVER STOP... I'LL FIND HIM... CHARLES IS HERE...
DO PLEASE BE QUIET. THIS WAS NEVER A RESCUE MISSION, DEAR...
...JUST A TRAP.
I'M CLAIMING THIS FLESH AT LAST, MAGNETO. IN YOUR OWN WORDS...

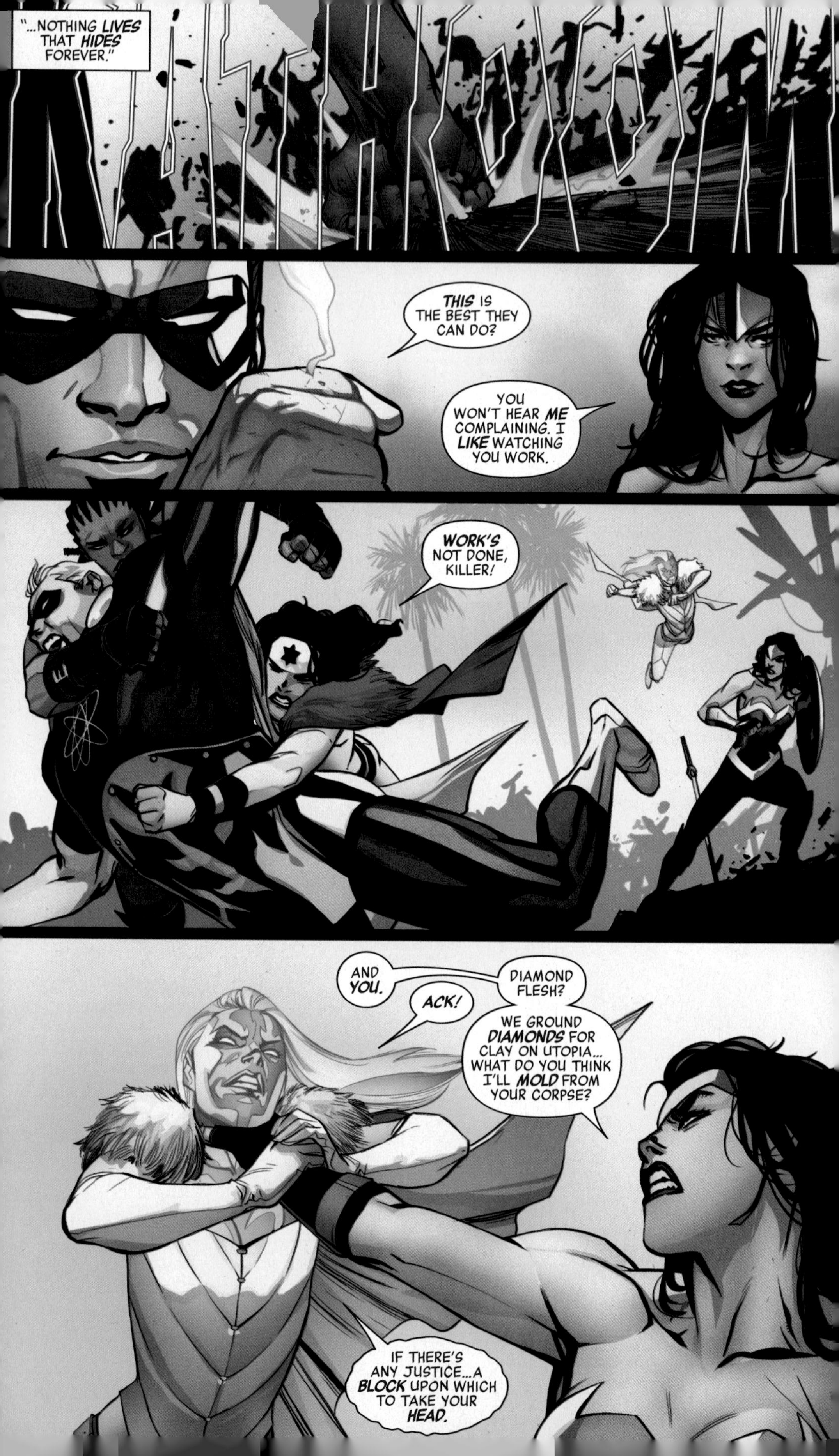
"...NOTHING LIVES THAT HIDES FOREVER."
THIS IS THE BEST THEY CAN DO?
YOU WON'T HEAR ME COMPLAINING. I LIKE WATCHING YOU WORK.
WORK'S NOT DONE, KILLER!
AND YOU.
ACK!
DIAMOND FLESH?
WE GROUND DIAMONDS FOR CLAY ON UTOPIA... WHAT DO YOU THINK I'LL MOLD FROM YOUR CORPSE?
IF THERE'S ANY JUSTICE...A BLOCK UPON WHICH TO TAKE YOUR HEAD.

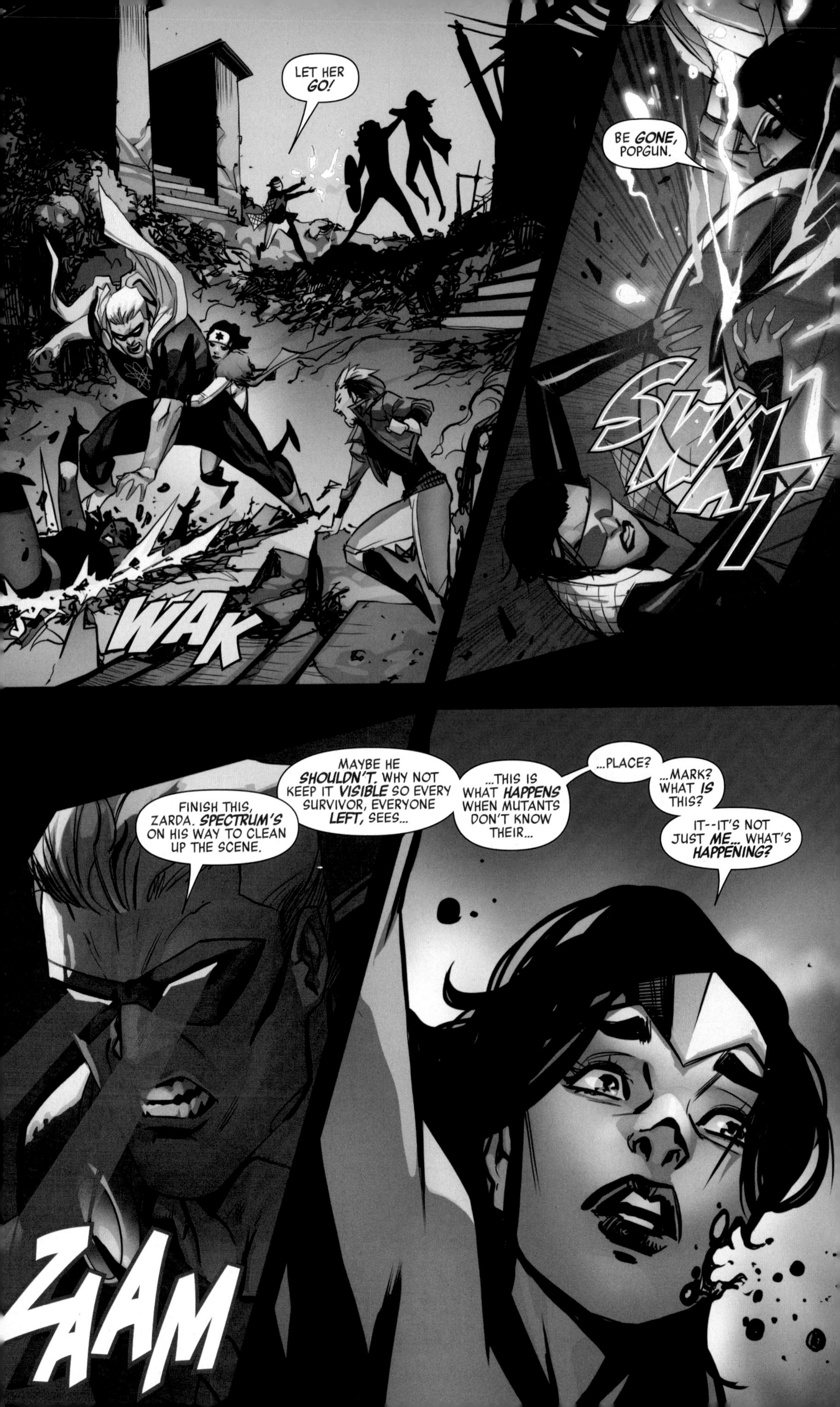
LET HER GO!
BE GONE, POPGUN.
SWAT
WAK
FINISH THIS, ZARDA. SPECTRUM'S ON HIS WAY TO CLEAN UP THE SCENE.
MAYBE HE SHOULDN'T. WHY NOT KEEP IT VISIBLE SO EVERY SURVIVOR, EVERYONE LEFT, SEES...
...THIS IS WHAT HAPPENS WHEN MUTANTS DON'T KNOW THEIR...
...PLACE?
...MARK? WHAT IS THIS?
IT--IT'S NOT JUST ME... WHAT'S HAPPENING?
ZAAM

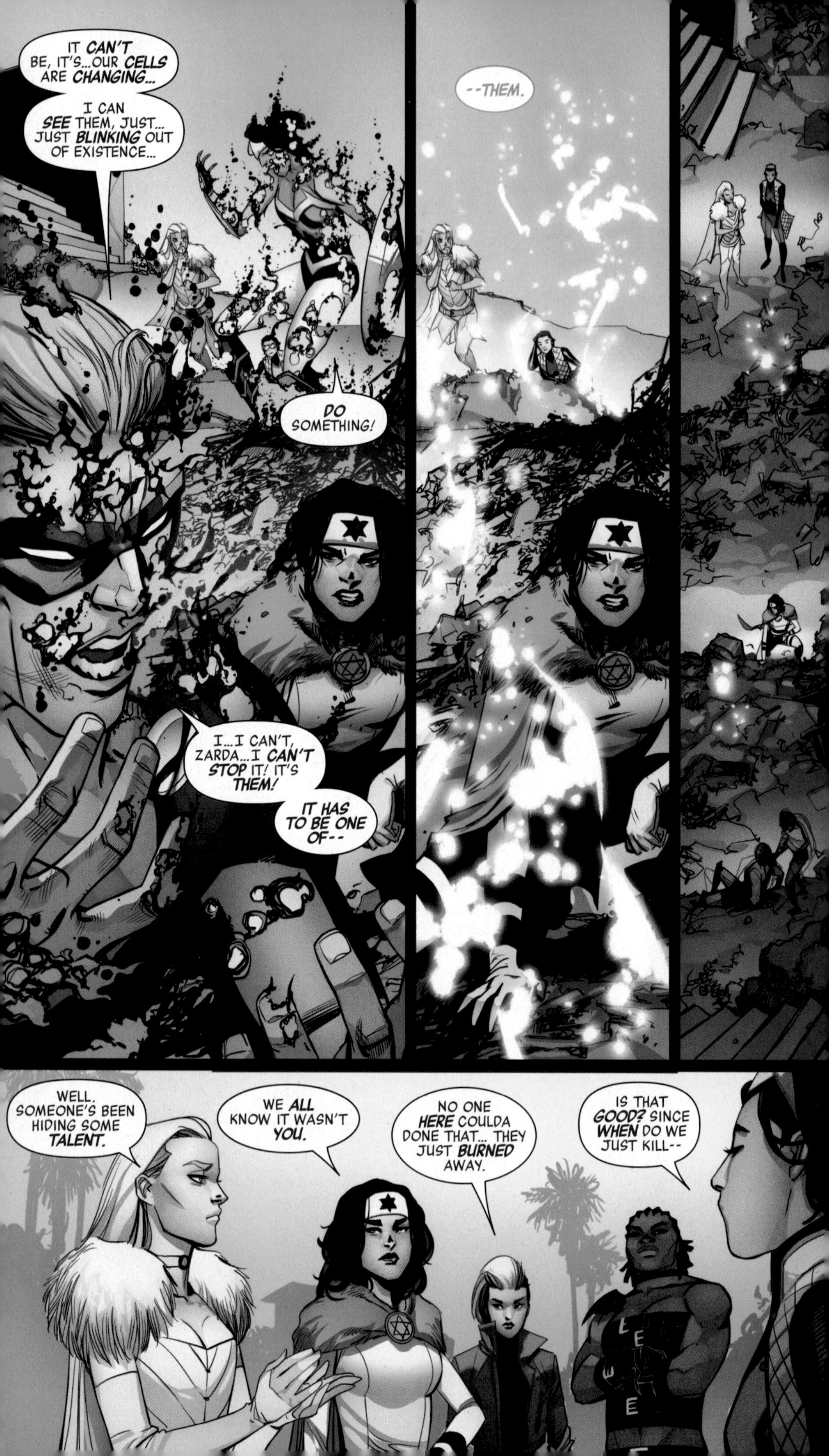
IT CAN'T BE, IT'S...OUR CELLS ARE CHANGING...
I CAN SEE THEM, JUST... JUST BLINKING OUT OF EXISTENCE...
DO SOMETHING!
I...I CAN'T, ZARDA...I CAN'T STOP IT! IT'S THEM!
IT HAS TO BE ONE OF--
--THEM.
WELL. SOMEONE'S BEEN HIDING SOME TALENT.
WE ALL KNOW IT WASN'T YOU.
NO ONE HERE COULDA DONE THAT... THEY JUST BURNED AWAY.
IS THAT GOOD? SINCE WHEN DO WE JUST KILL--

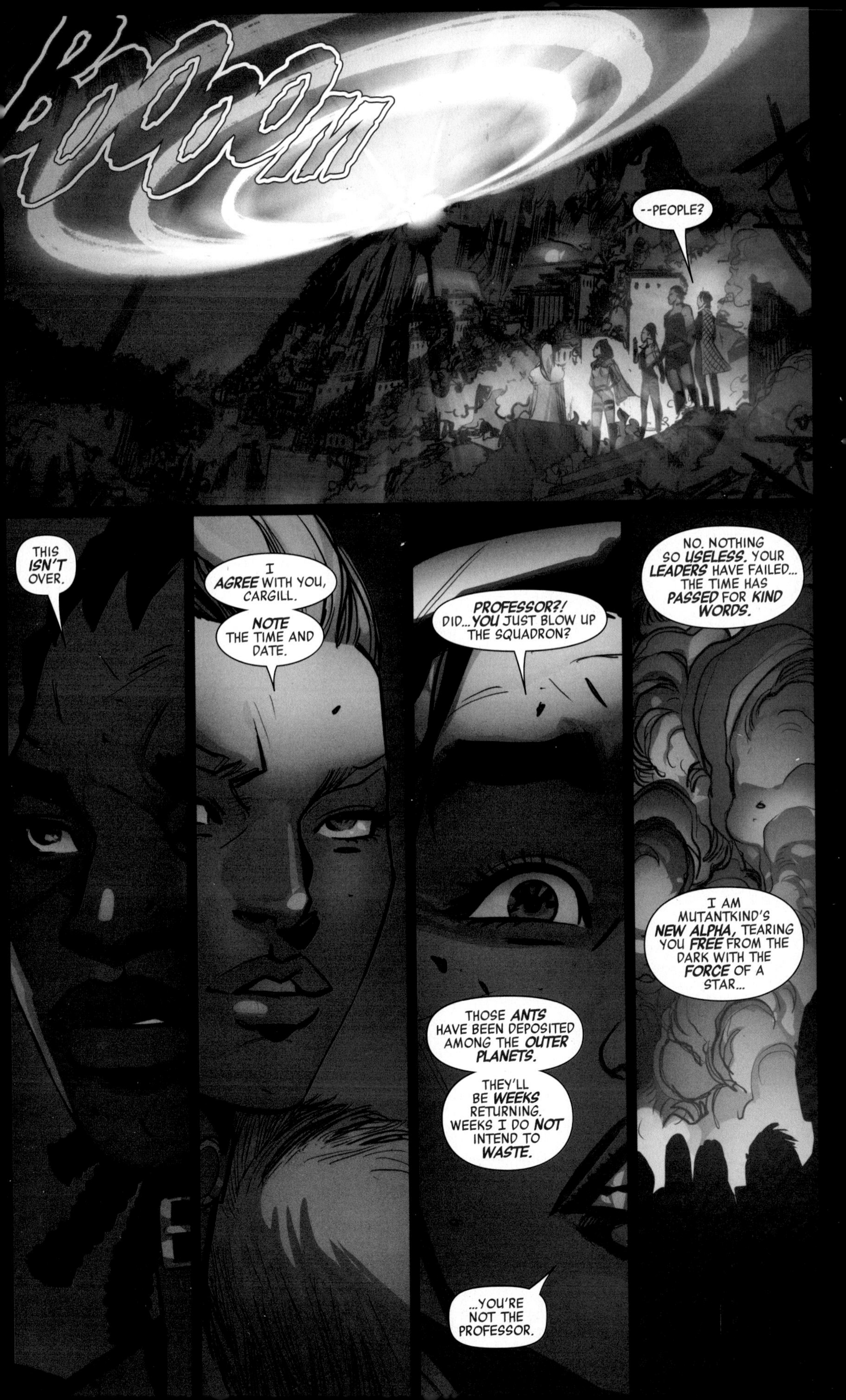

KRAKOOOM
--PEOPLE?
THIS ISN'T OVER.
I AGREE WITH YOU, CARGILL.
NOTE THE TIME AND DATE.
PROFESSOR?! DID...YOU JUST BLOW UP THE SQUADRON?
NO. NOTHING SO USELESS. YOUR LEADERS HAVE FAILED... THE TIME HAS PASSED FOR KIND WORDS.
I AM MUTANTKIND'S NEW ALPHA, TEARING YOU FREE FROM THE DARK WITH THE FORCE OF A STAR...
THOSE ANTS HAVE BEEN DEPOSITED AMONG THE OUTER PLANETS.
THEY'LL BE WEEKS RETURNING. WEEKS I DO NOT INTEND TO WASTE.
...YOU'RE NOT THE PROFESSOR.

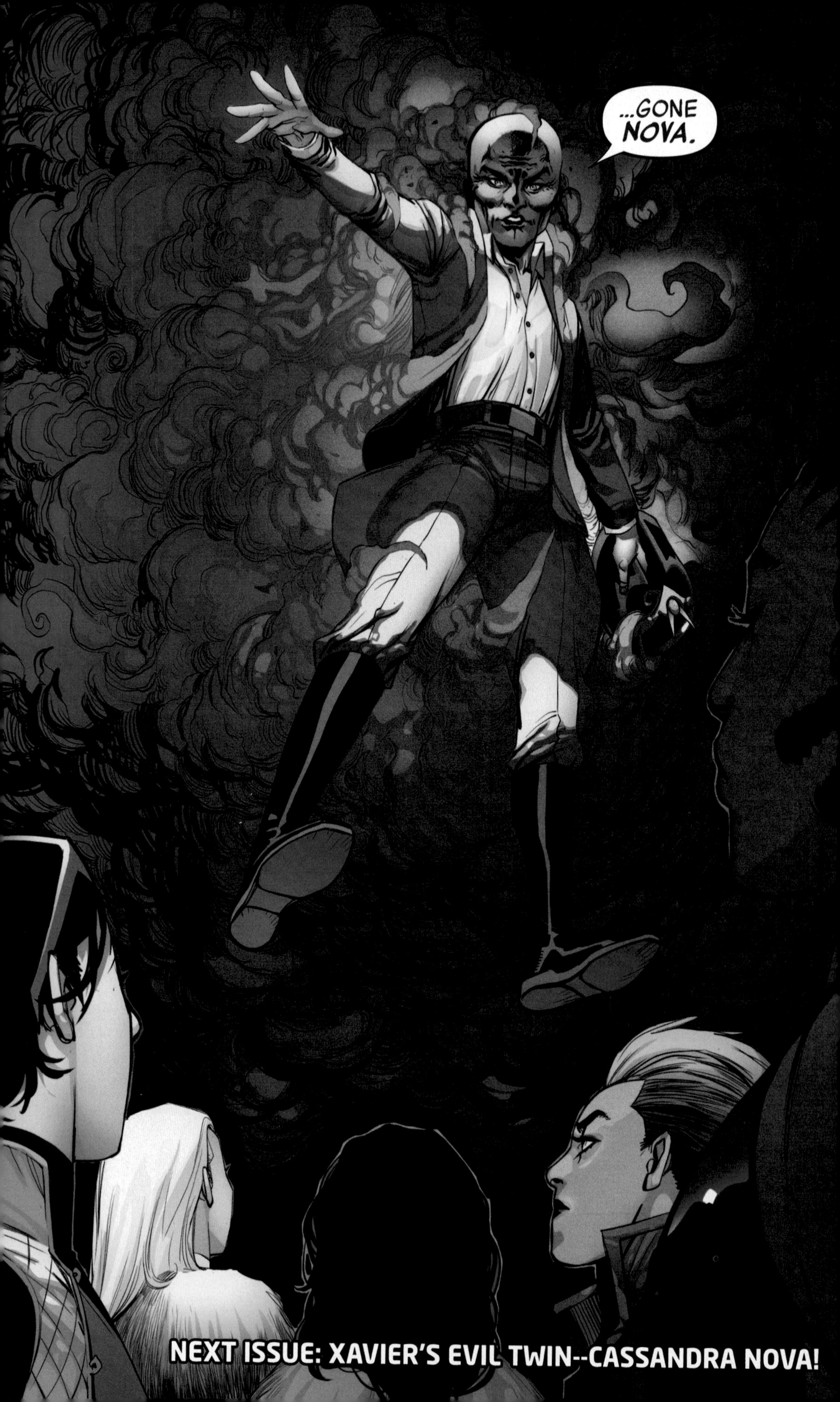
...GONE NOVA.
NEXT ISSUE: XAVIER'S EVIL TWIN--CASSANDRA NOVA!

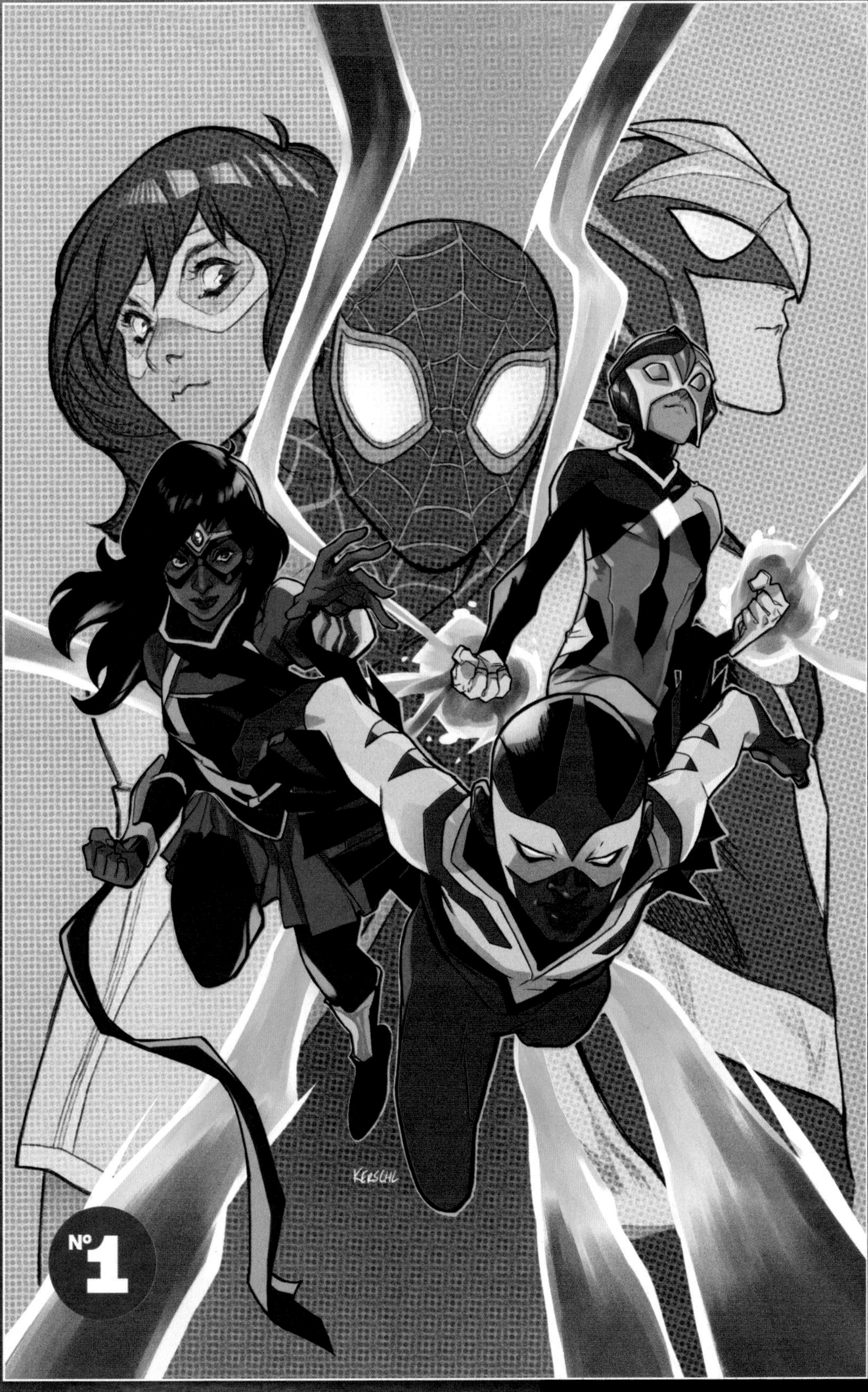
KERSCHL
Nº 1

“TRUTH AT ALL COSTS”

YOUNG SQUADRON

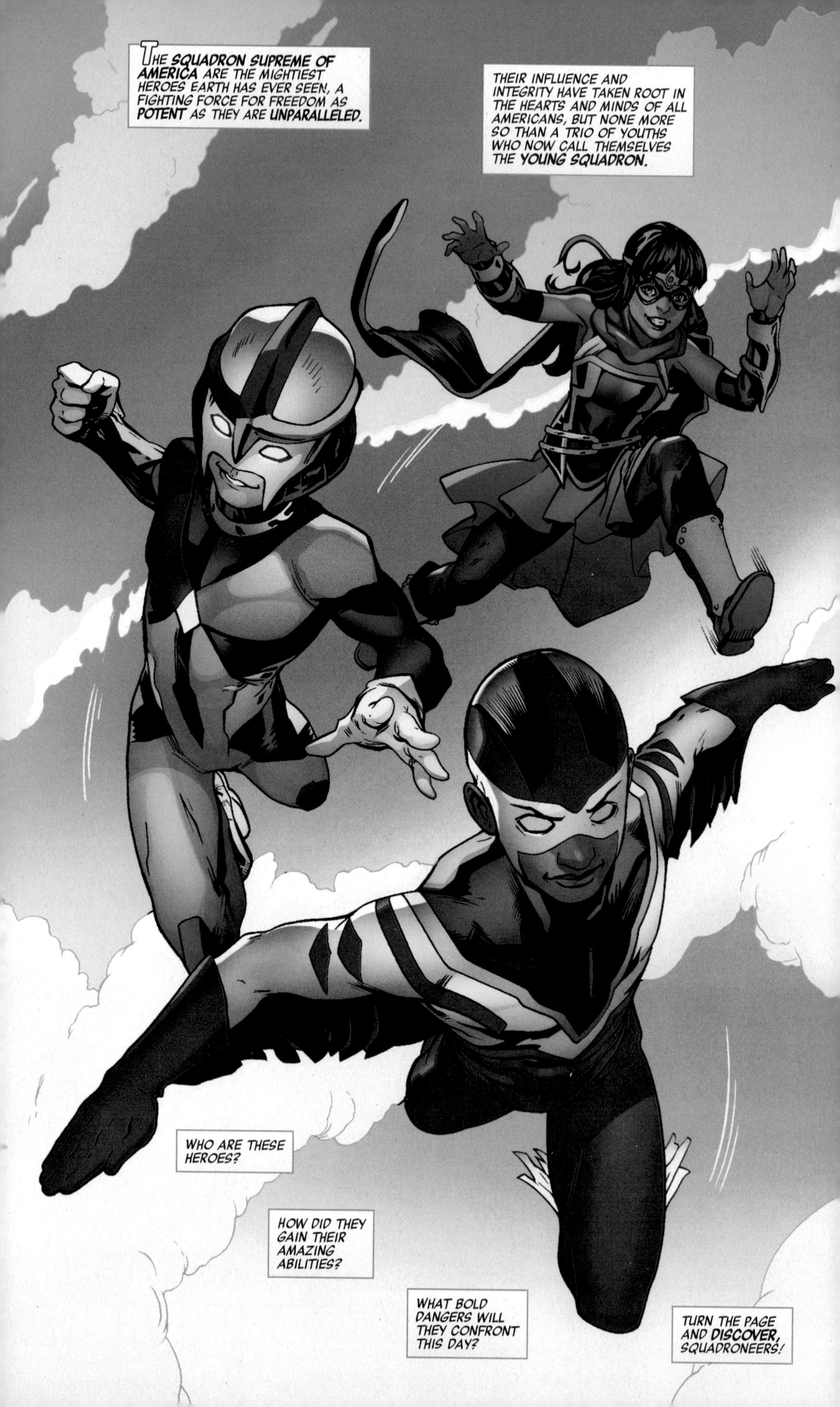
THE SQUADRON SUPREME OF AMERICA ARE THE MIGHTIEST HEROES EARTH HAS EVER SEEN, A FIGHTING FORCE FOR FREEDOM AS POTENT AS THEY ARE UNPARALLELED.
THEIR INFLUENCE AND INTEGRITY HAVE TAKEN ROOT IN THE HEARTS AND MINDS OF ALL AMERICANS, BUT NONE MORE SO THAN A TRIO OF YOUTHS WHO NOW CALL THEMSELVES THE YOUNG SQUADRON.
WHO ARE THESE HEROES?
HOW DID THEY GAIN THEIR AMAZING ABILITIES?
WHAT BOLD DANGERS WILL THEY CONFRONT THIS DAY?
TURN THE PAGE AND DISCOVER, SQUADRONEERS!

In a world in which the Avengers never existed, the Squadron Supreme
of America are and have always been Earth's Mightiest Heroes!

YOUNG
SQUADRON

"TRUTH AT ALL COSTS"

JIM **ZUB** WRITER

STEVEN **CUMMINGS** ARTIST

ERICK **ARCINIEGA** COLOR ARTIST

VC's CLAYTON **COWLES** LETTERER

KARL **KERSCHL** COVER ARTIST

TAKASHI **OKAZAKI** & FELIPE **SOBREIRO** VARIANT COVER ARTISTS

JAY **BOWEN** GRAPHIC DESIGN

MARTIN **BIRO** ASSISTANT EDITOR

ALANNA **SMITH** EDITOR

TOM **BREVOORT** EXECUTIVE EDITOR

C.B. **CEBULSKI** EDITOR IN CHIEF

HEROES
REBORN

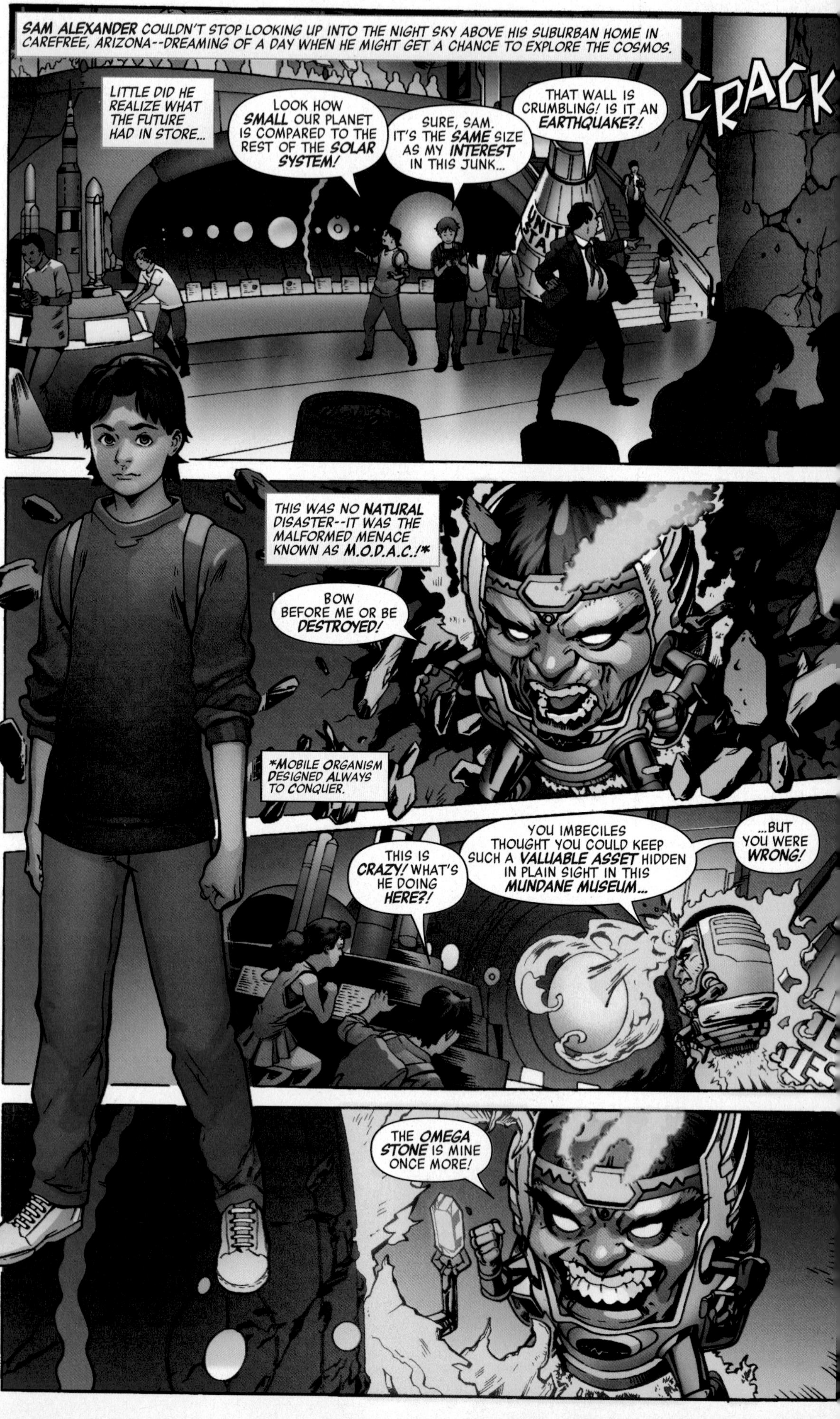
SAM ALEXANDER COULDN'T STOP LOOKING UP INTO THE NIGHT SKY ABOVE HIS SUBURBAN HOME IN CAREFREE, ARIZONA--DREAMING OF A DAY WHEN HE MIGHT GET A CHANCE TO EXPLORE THE COSMOS.
LITTLE DID HE REALIZE WHAT THE FUTURE HAD IN STORE...
LOOK HOW SMALL OUR PLANET IS COMPARED TO THE REST OF THE SOLAR SYSTEM!
SURE, SAM. IT'S THE SAME SIZE AS MY INTEREST IN THIS JUNK...
THAT WALL IS CRUMBLING! IS IT AN EARTHQUAKE?!
CRACK
THIS WAS NO NATURAL DISASTER--IT WAS THE MALFORMED MENACE KNOWN AS M.O.D.A.C.!*
BOW BEFORE ME OR BE DESTROYED!
*MOBILE ORGANISM DESIGNED ALWAYS TO CONQUER.
THIS IS CRAZY! WHAT'S HE DOING HERE?!
YOU IMBECILES THOUGHT YOU COULD KEEP SUCH A VALUABLE ASSET HIDDEN IN PLAIN SIGHT IN THIS MUNDANE MUSEUM...
...BUT YOU WERE WRONG!
THE OMEGA STONE IS MINE ONCE MORE!

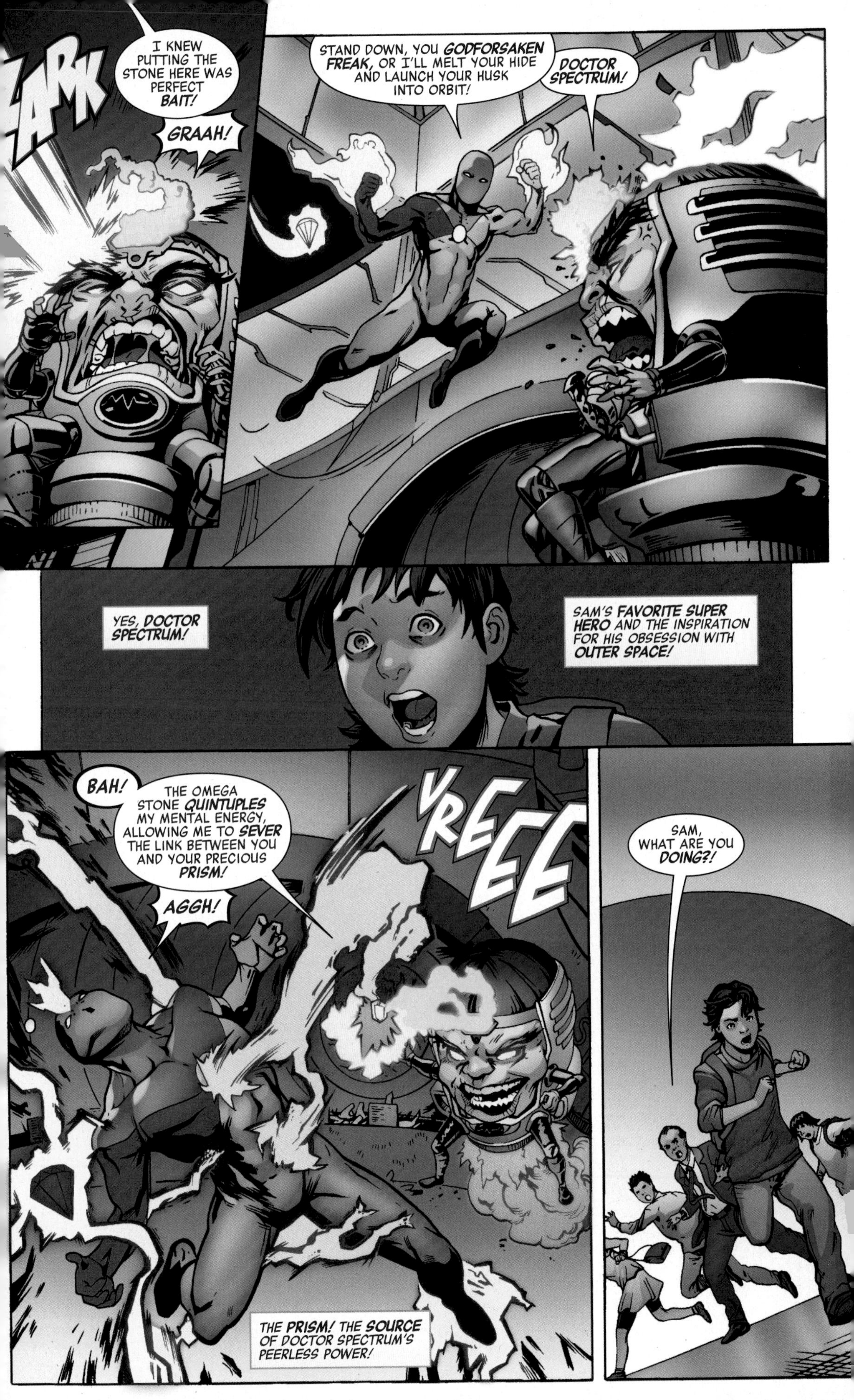
ZARK
I KNEW PUTTING THE STONE HERE WAS PERFECT BAIT!
GRAAH!
STAND DOWN, YOU GODFORSAKEN FREAK, OR I'LL MELT YOUR HIDE AND LAUNCH YOUR HUSK INTO ORBIT!
DOCTOR SPECTRUM!
YES, DOCTOR SPECTRUM!
SAM'S FAVORITE SUPER HERO AND THE INSPIRATION FOR HIS OBSESSION WITH OUTER SPACE!
BAH!
THE OMEGA STONE QUINTUPLES MY MENTAL ENERGY, ALLOWING ME TO SEVER THE LINK BETWEEN YOU AND YOUR PRECIOUS PRISM!
AGGH!
VREEEE
THE PRISM! THE SOURCE OF DOCTOR SPECTRUM'S PEERLESS POWER!
SAM, WHAT ARE YOU DOING?!

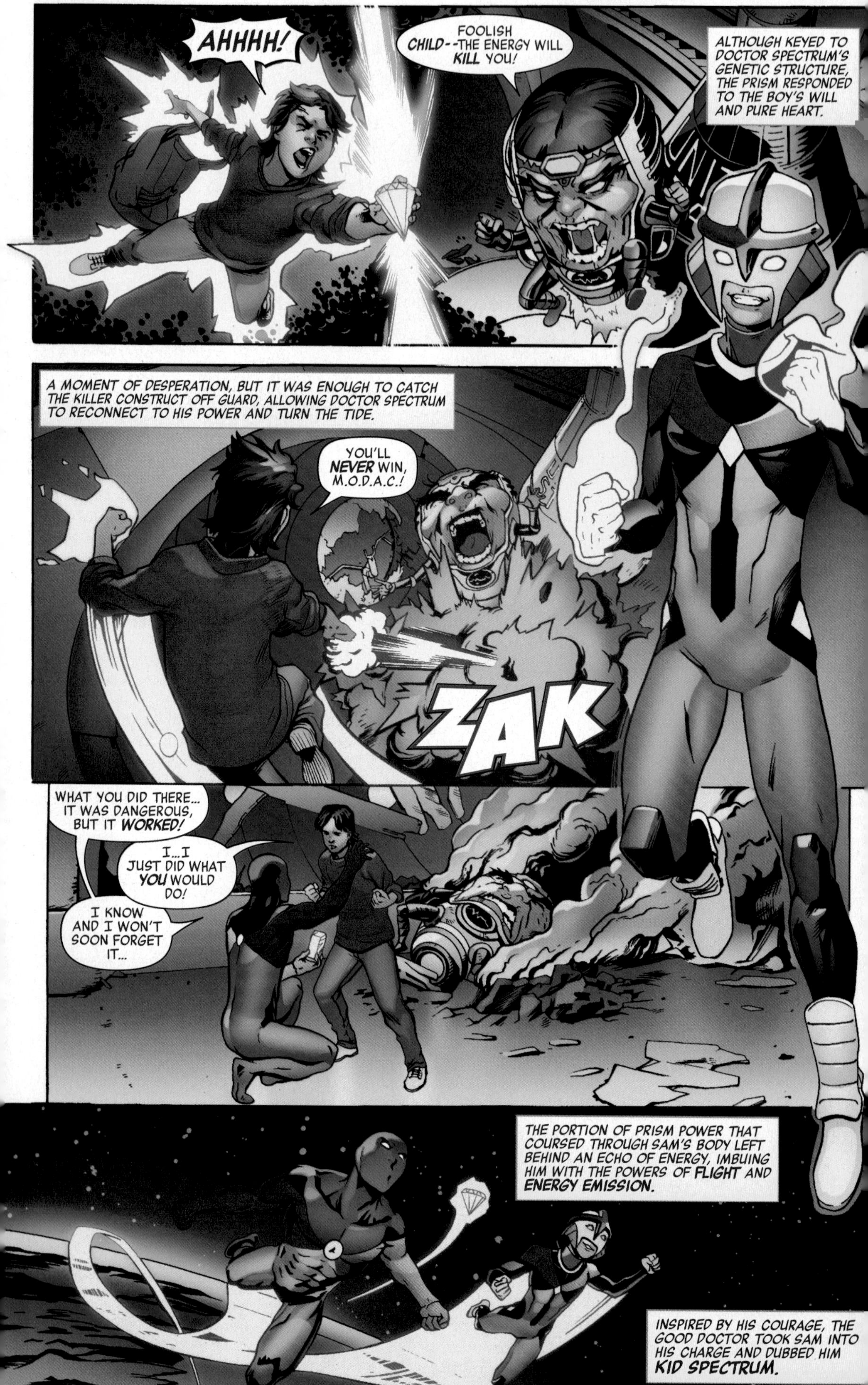
AHHHH!
FOOLISH CHILD--THE ENERGY WILL KILL YOU!
ALTHOUGH KEYED TO DOCTOR SPECTRUM'S GENETIC STRUCTURE, THE PRISM RESPONDED TO THE BOY'S WILL AND PURE HEART.
A MOMENT OF DESPERATION, BUT IT WAS ENOUGH TO CATCH THE KILLER CONSTRUCT OFF GUARD, ALLOWING DOCTOR SPECTRUM TO RECONNECT TO HIS POWER AND TURN THE TIDE.
YOU'LL NEVER WIN, M.O.D.A.C.!
ZAK
WHAT YOU DID THERE... IT WAS DANGEROUS, BUT IT WORKED!
I...I JUST DID WHAT YOU WOULD DO!
I KNOW AND I WON'T SOON FORGET IT...
THE PORTION OF PRISM POWER THAT COURSED THROUGH SAM'S BODY LEFT BEHIND AN ECHO OF ENERGY, IMBUING HIM WITH THE POWERS OF FLIGHT AND ENERGY EMISSION.
INSPIRED BY HIS COURAGE, THE GOOD DOCTOR TOOK SAM INTO HIS CHARGE AND DUBBED HIM KID SPECTRUM.

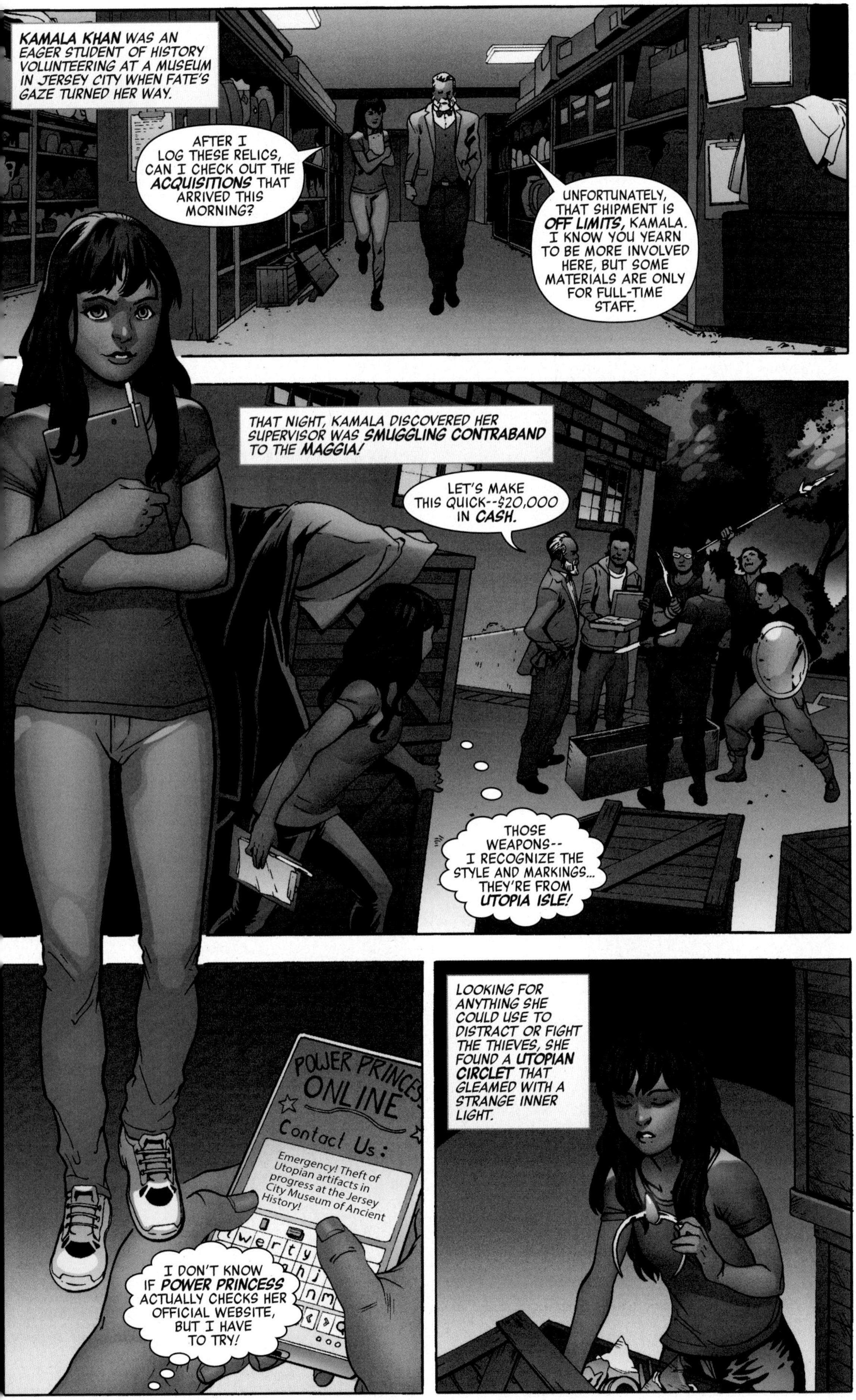
KAMALA KHAN WAS AN EAGER STUDENT OF HISTORY VOLUNTEERING AT A MUSEUM IN JERSEY CITY WHEN FATE'S GAZE TURNED HER WAY.
AFTER I LOG THESE RELICS, CAN I CHECK OUT THE ACQUISITIONS THAT ARRIVED THIS MORNING?
UNFORTUNATELY, THAT SHIPMENT IS OFF LIMITS, KAMALA. I KNOW YOU YEARN TO BE MORE INVOLVED HERE, BUT SOME MATERIALS ARE ONLY FOR FULL-TIME STAFF.
THAT NIGHT, KAMALA DISCOVERED HER SUPERVISOR WAS SMUGGLING CONTRABAND TO THE MAGGIA!
LET'S MAKE THIS QUICK--$20,000 IN CASH.
THOSE WEAPONS-- I RECOGNIZE THE STYLE AND MARKINGS... THEY'RE FROM UTOPIA ISLE!
POWER PRINCESS ONLINE
Contact Us:
Emergency! Theft of Utopian artifacts in progress at the Jersey City Museum of Ancient History!
I DON'T KNOW IF POWER PRINCESS ACTUALLY CHECKS HER OFFICIAL WEBSITE, BUT I HAVE TO TRY!
LOOKING FOR ANYTHING SHE COULD USE TO DISTRACT OR FIGHT THE THIEVES, SHE FOUND A UTOPIAN CIRCLET THAT GLEAMED WITH A STRANGE INNER LIGHT.

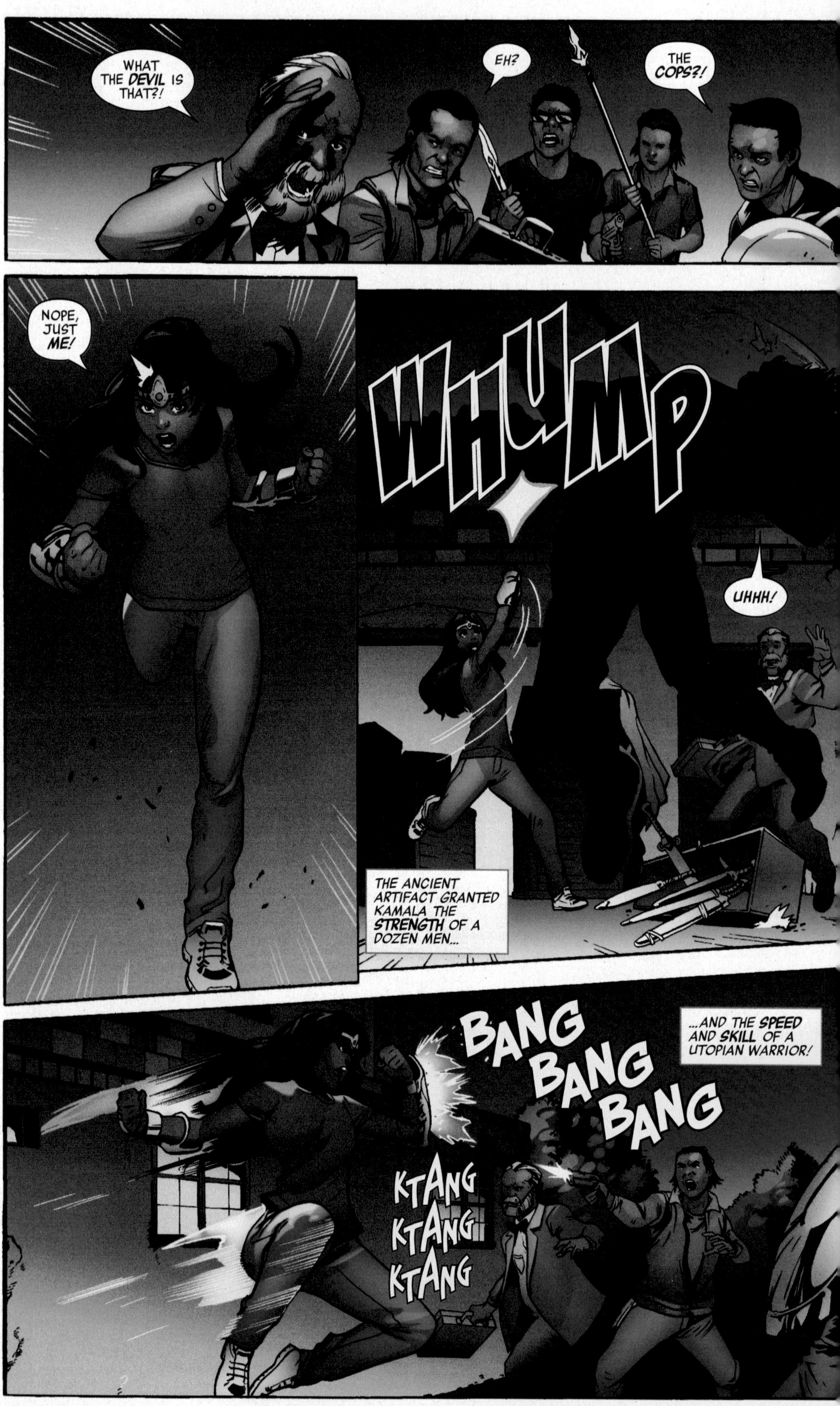
WHAT THE DEVIL IS THAT?!
EH?
THE COPS?!
NOPE, JUST ME!
WHUMP
UHHH!
THE ANCIENT ARTIFACT GRANTED KAMALA THE STRENGTH OF A DOZEN MEN...
...AND THE SPEED AND SKILL OF A UTOPIAN WARRIOR!
BANG BANG BANG
KTANG KTANG KTANG

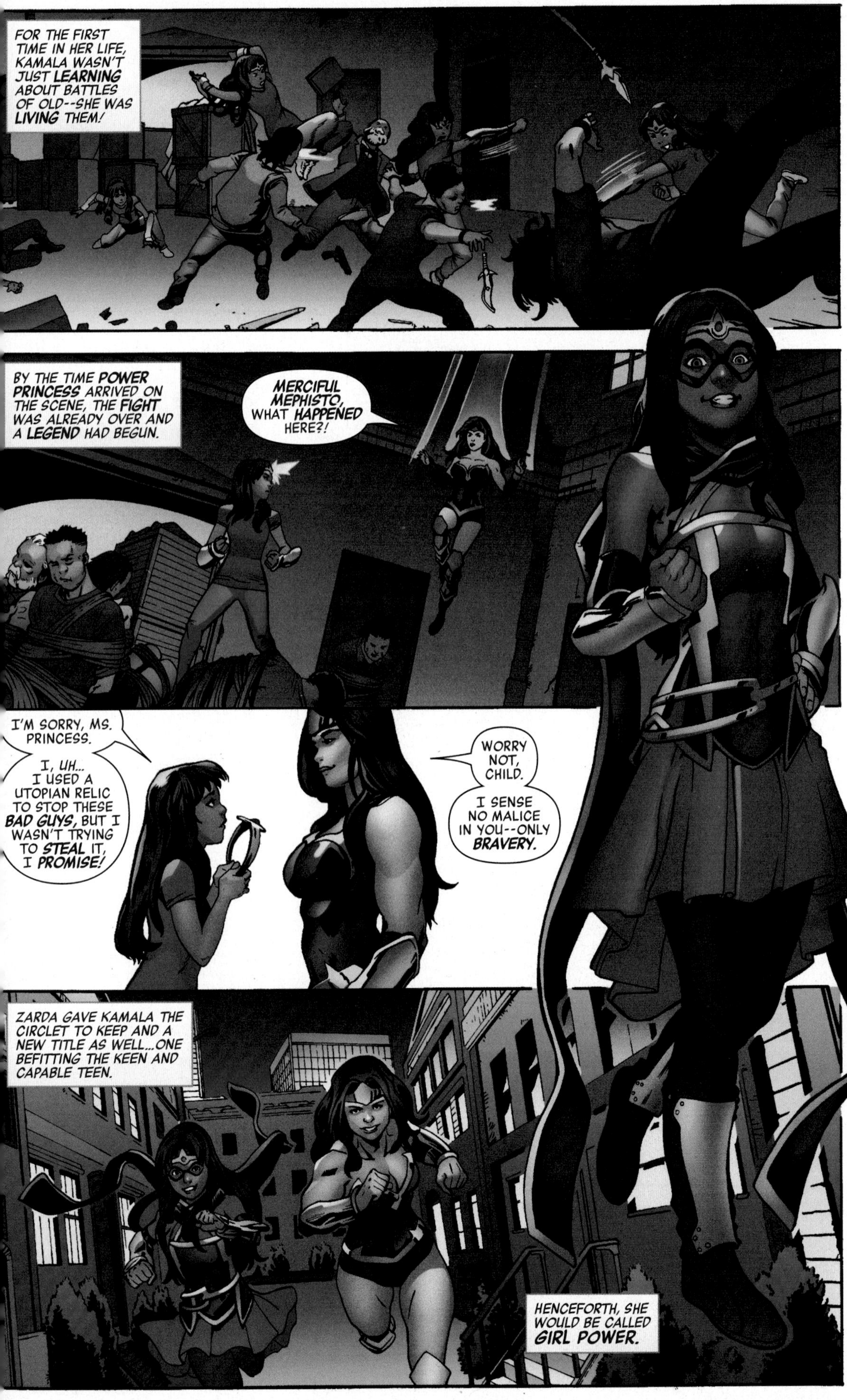
FOR THE FIRST TIME IN HER LIFE, KAMALA WASN'T JUST LEARNING ABOUT BATTLES OF OLD--SHE WAS LIVING THEM!
BY THE TIME POWER PRINCESS ARRIVED ON THE SCENE, THE FIGHT WAS ALREADY OVER AND A LEGEND HAD BEGUN.
MERCIFUL MEPHISTO, WHAT HAPPENED HERE?!
I'M SORRY, MS. PRINCESS.
I, UH... I USED A UTOPIAN RELIC TO STOP THESE BAD GUYS, BUT I WASN'T TRYING TO STEAL IT, I PROMISE!
WORRY NOT, CHILD.
I SENSE NO MALICE IN YOU--ONLY BRAVERY.
ZARDA GAVE KAMALA THE CIRCLET TO KEEP AND A NEW TITLE AS WELL...ONE BEFITTING THE KEEN AND CAPABLE TEEN.
HENCEFORTH, SHE WOULD BE CALLED GIRL POWER.

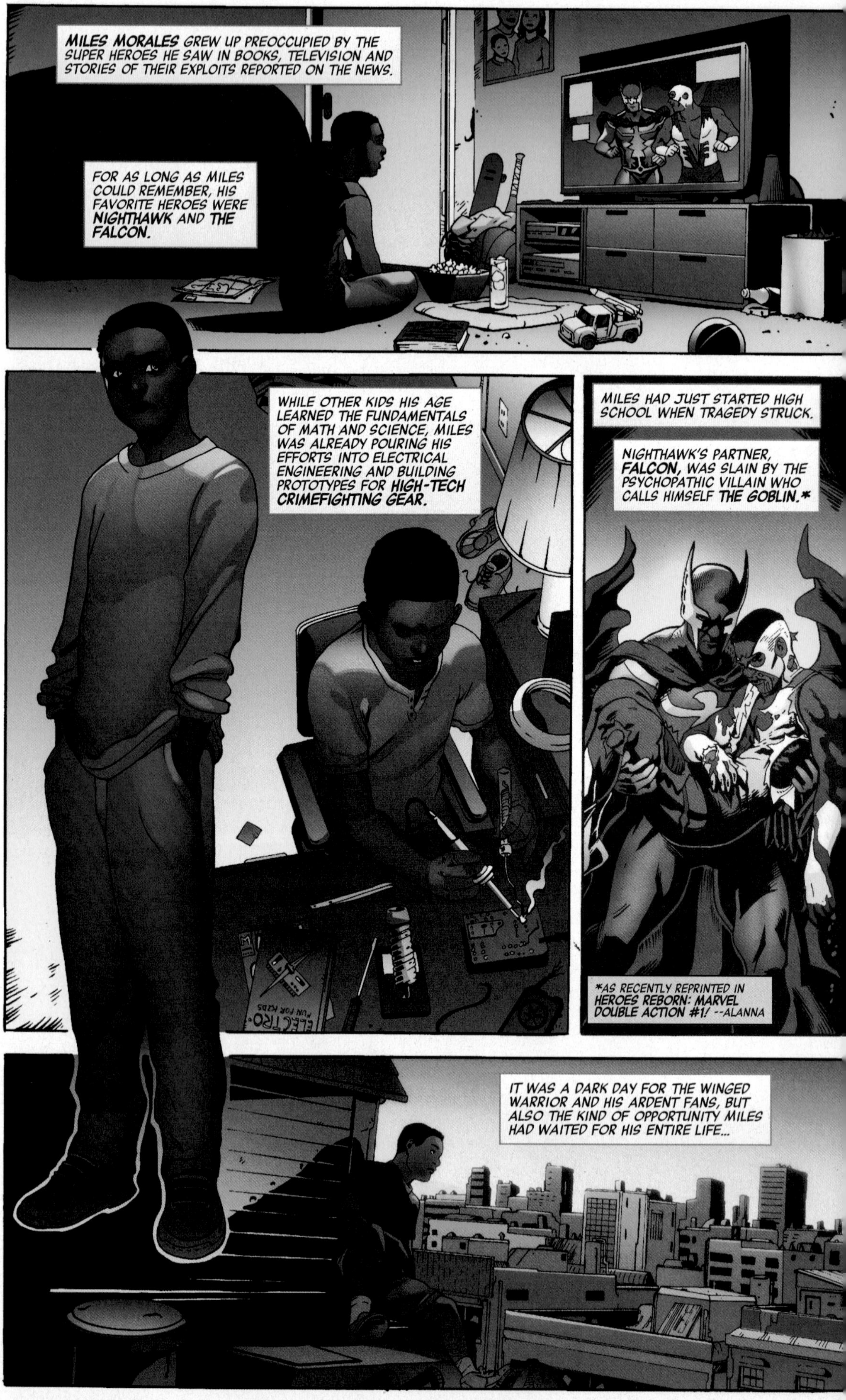
MILES MORALES GREW UP PREOCCUPIED BY THE SUPER HEROES HE SAW IN BOOKS, TELEVISION AND STORIES OF THEIR EXPLOITS REPORTED ON THE NEWS.
FOR AS LONG AS MILES COULD REMEMBER, HIS FAVORITE HEROES WERE NIGHTHAWK AND THE FALCON.
WHILE OTHER KIDS HIS AGE LEARNED THE FUNDAMENTALS OF MATH AND SCIENCE, MILES WAS ALREADY POURING HIS EFFORTS INTO ELECTRICAL ENGINEERING AND BUILDING PROTOTYPES FOR HIGH-TECH CRIMEFIGHTING GEAR.
ELECTRO FUN FOR KIDS
MILES HAD JUST STARTED HIGH SCHOOL WHEN TRAGEDY STRUCK.
NIGHTHAWK'S PARTNER, FALCON, WAS SLAIN BY THE PSYCHOPATHIC VILLAIN WHO CALLS HIMSELF THE GOBLIN.*
*AS RECENTLY REPRINTED IN HEROES REBORN: MARVEL DOUBLE ACTION #1! --ALANNA
IT WAS A DARK DAY FOR THE WINGED WARRIOR AND HIS ARDENT FANS, BUT ALSO THE KIND OF OPPORTUNITY MILES HAD WAITED FOR HIS ENTIRE LIFE...

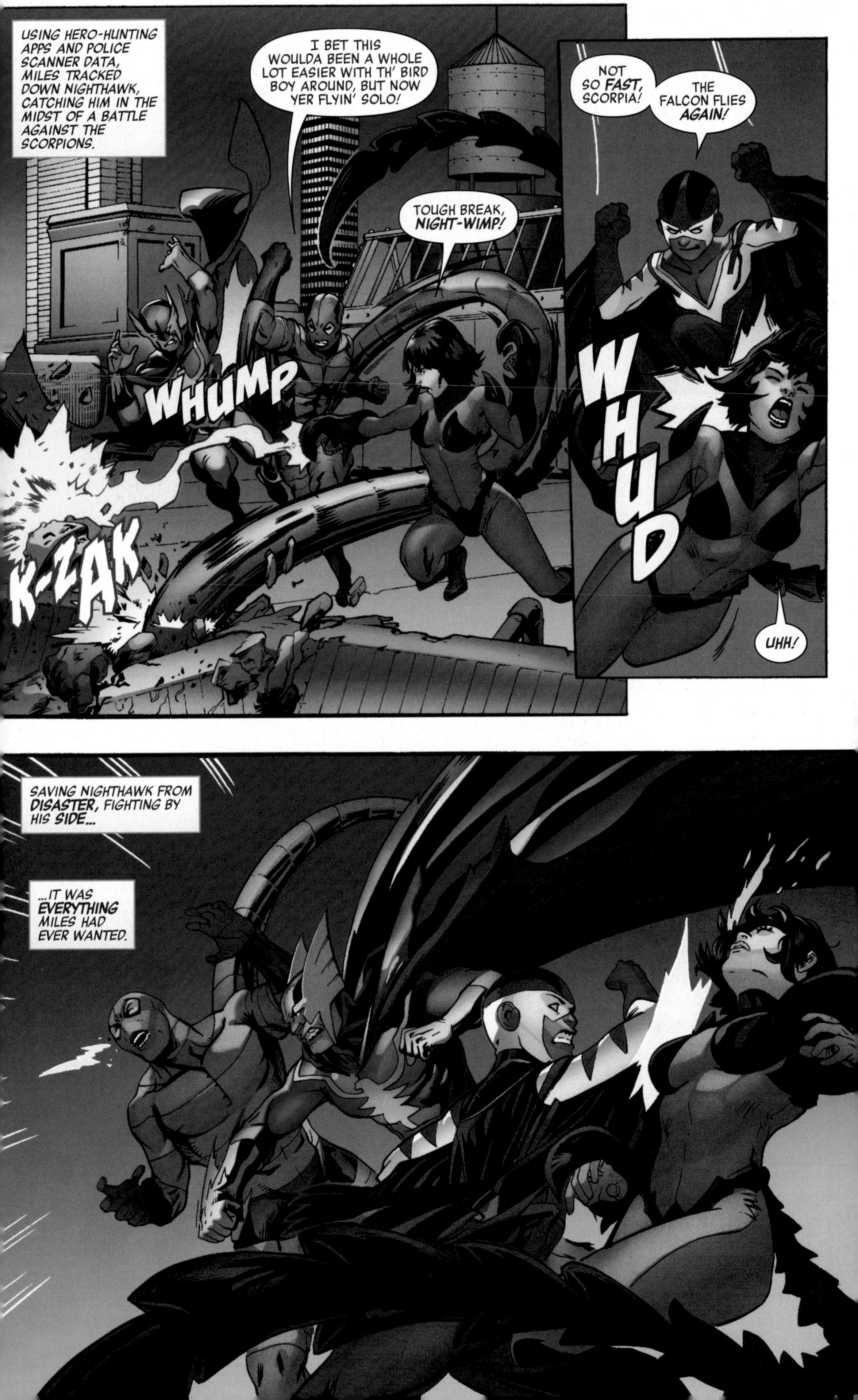
USING HERO-HUNTING APPS AND POLICE SCANNER DATA, MILES TRACKED DOWN NIGHTHAWK, CATCHING HIM IN THE MIDST OF A BATTLE AGAINST THE SCORPIONS.
I BET THIS WOULDA BEEN A WHOLE LOT EASIER WITH TH' BIRD BOY AROUND, BUT NOW YER FLYIN' SOLO!
TOUGH BREAK, NIGHT-WIMP!
WHUMP
K-ZAK
NOT SO FAST, SCORPIA!
THE FALCON FLIES AGAIN!
WHUD
UHH!
SAVING NIGHTHAWK FROM DISASTER, FIGHTING BY HIS SIDE...
...IT WAS EVERYTHING MILES HAD EVER WANTED.

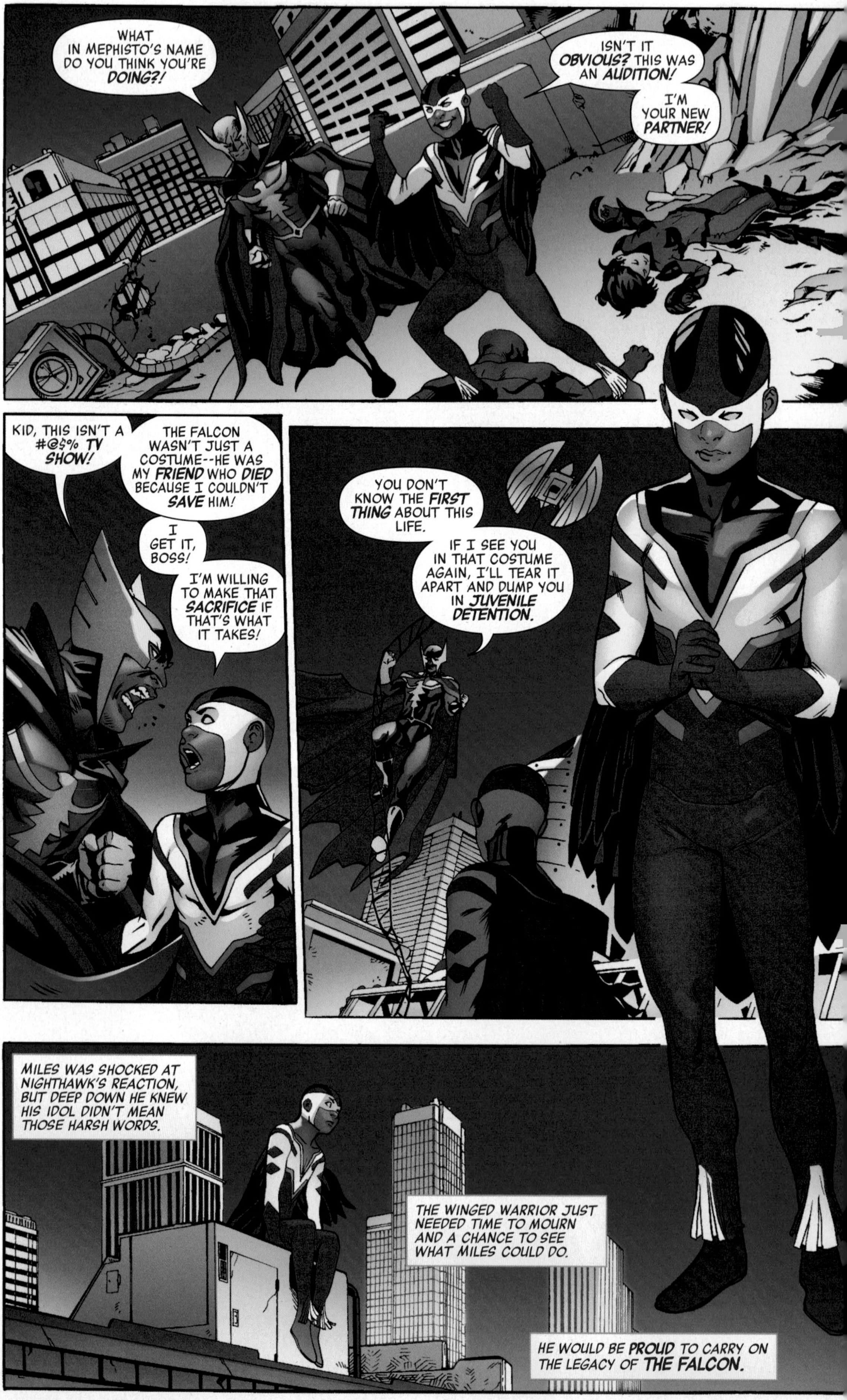
WHAT IN MEPHISTO'S NAME DO YOU THINK YOU'RE DOING?!
ISN'T IT OBVIOUS? THIS WAS AN AUDITION!
I'M YOUR NEW PARTNER!
KID, THIS ISN'T A #@$% TV SHOW!
THE FALCON WASN'T JUST A COSTUME--HE WAS MY FRIEND WHO DIED BECAUSE I COULDN'T SAVE HIM!
I GET IT, BOSS!
I'M WILLING TO MAKE THAT SACRIFICE IF THAT'S WHAT IT TAKES!
YOU DON'T KNOW THE FIRST THING ABOUT THIS LIFE.
IF I SEE YOU IN THAT COSTUME AGAIN, I'LL TEAR IT APART AND DUMP YOU IN JUVENILE DETENTION.
MILES WAS SHOCKED AT NIGHTHAWK'S REACTION, BUT DEEP DOWN HE KNEW HIS IDOL DIDN'T MEAN THOSE HARSH WORDS.
THE WINGED WARRIOR JUST NEEDED TIME TO MOURN AND A CHANCE TO SEE WHAT MILES COULD DO.
HE WOULD BE PROUD TO CARRY ON THE LEGACY OF THE FALCON.

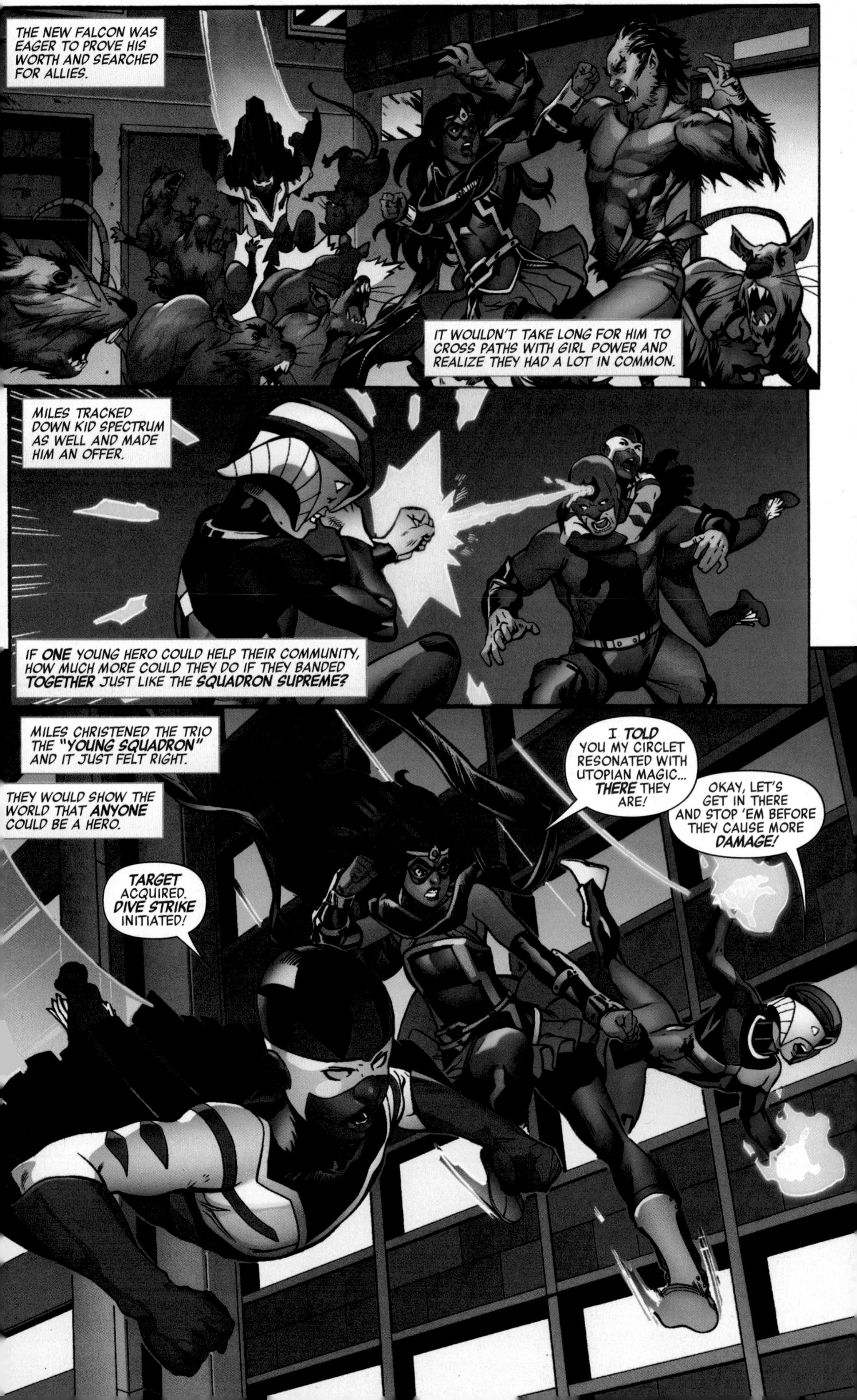
THE NEW FALCON WAS EAGER TO PROVE HIS WORTH AND SEARCHED FOR ALLIES.
IT WOULDN'T TAKE LONG FOR HIM TO CROSS PATHS WITH GIRL POWER AND REALIZE THEY HAD A LOT IN COMMON.
MILES TRACKED DOWN KID SPECTRUM AS WELL AND MADE HIM AN OFFER.
IF ONE YOUNG HERO COULD HELP THEIR COMMUNITY, HOW MUCH MORE COULD THEY DO IF THEY BANDED TOGETHER JUST LIKE THE SQUADRON SUPREME?
MILES CHRISTENED THE TRIO THE "YOUNG SQUADRON" AND IT JUST FELT RIGHT.
THEY WOULD SHOW THE WORLD THAT ANYONE COULD BE A HERO.
I TOLD YOU MY CIRCLET RESONATED WITH UTOPIAN MAGIC... THERE THEY ARE!
OKAY, LET'S GET IN THERE AND STOP 'EM BEFORE THEY CAUSE MORE DAMAGE!
TARGET ACQUIRED. DIVE STRIKE INITIATED!

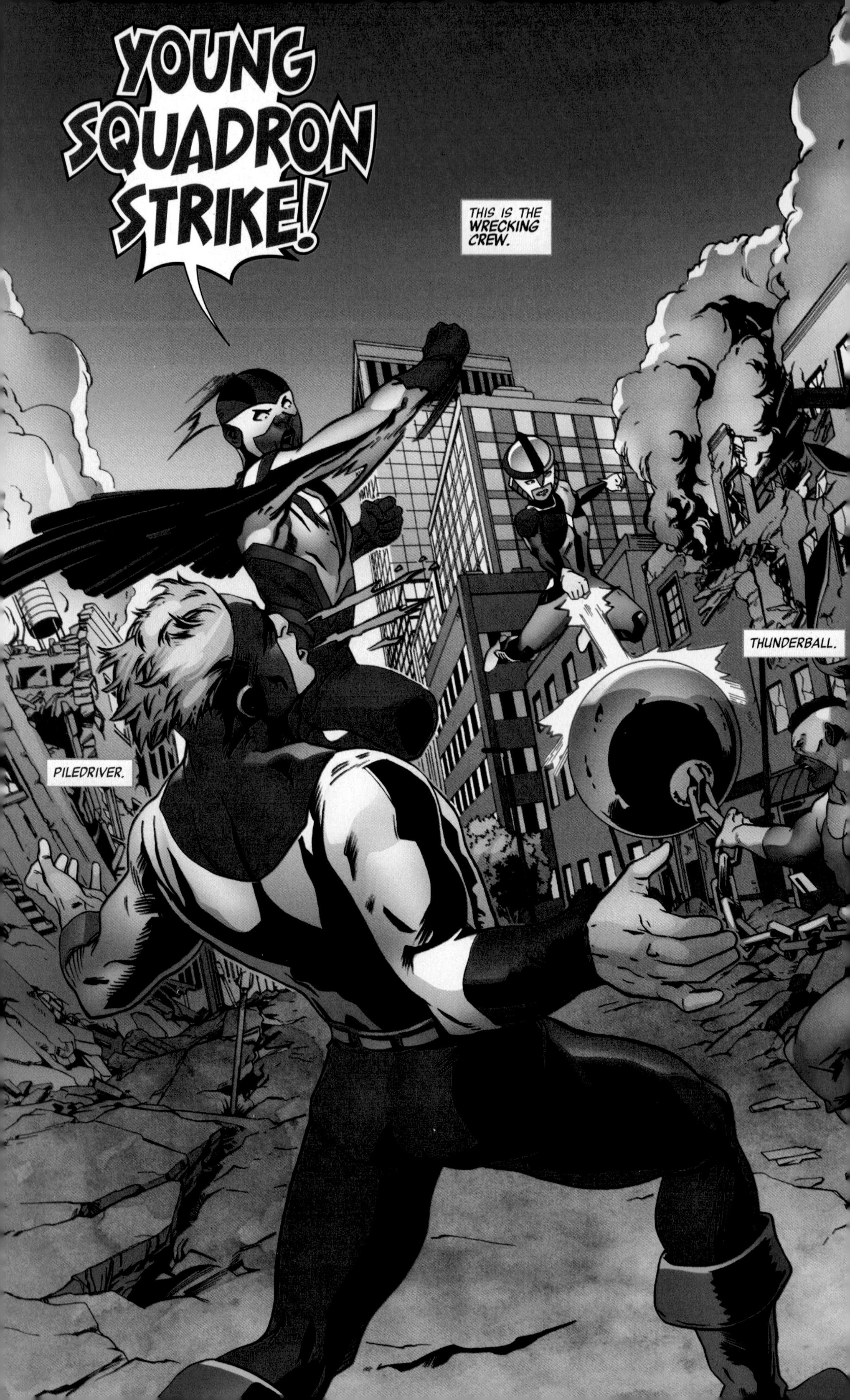
YOUNG SQUADRON STRIKE!
THIS IS THE WRECKING CREW.
THUNDERBALL.
PILEDRIVER.

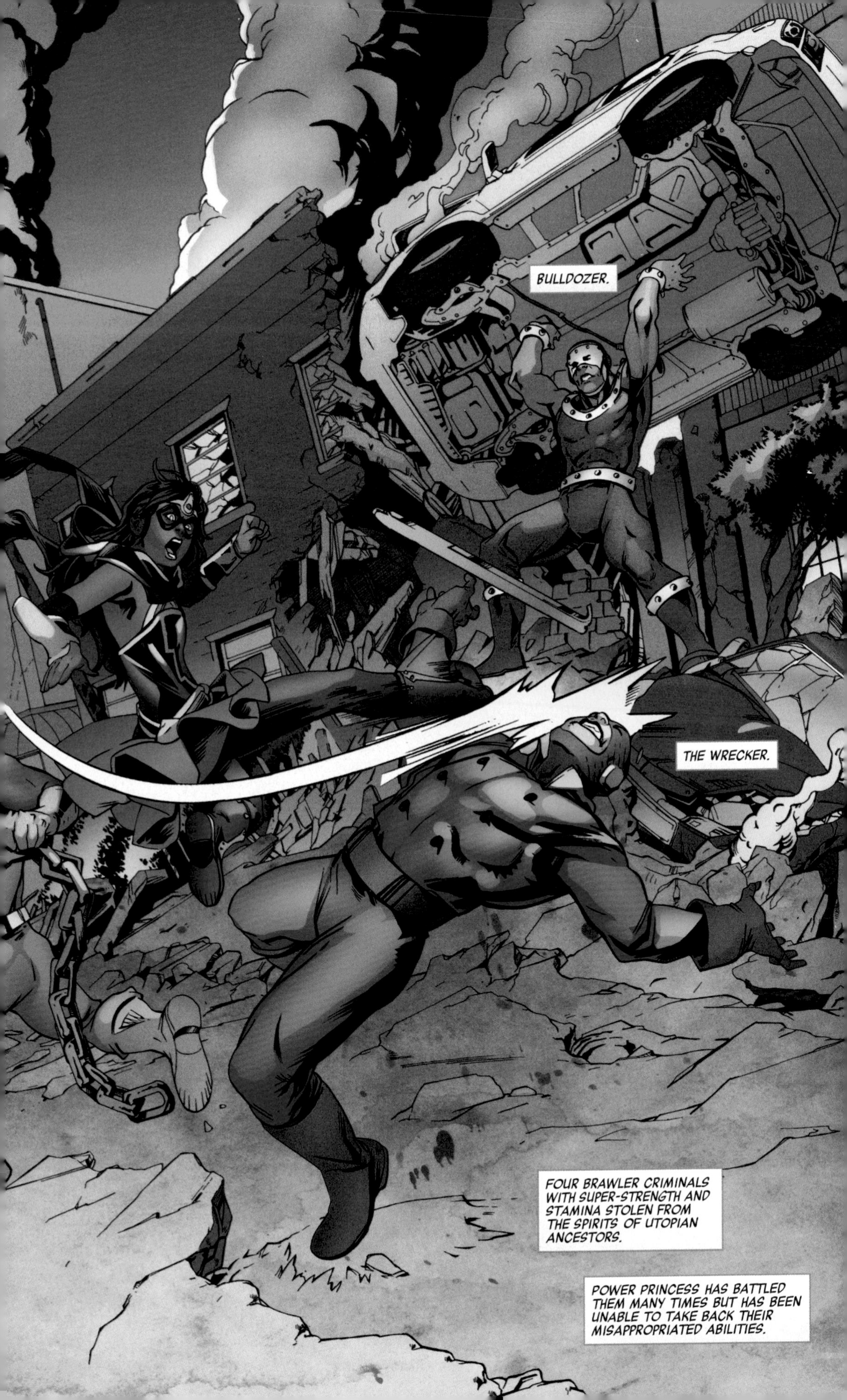
BULLDOZER.
THE WRECKER.
FOUR BRAWLER CRIMINALS WITH SUPER-STRENGTH AND STAMINA STOLEN FROM THE SPIRITS OF UTOPIAN ANCESTORS.
POWER PRINCESS HAS BATTLED THEM MANY TIMES BUT HAS BEEN UNABLE TO TAKE BACK THEIR MISAPPROPRIATED ABILITIES.

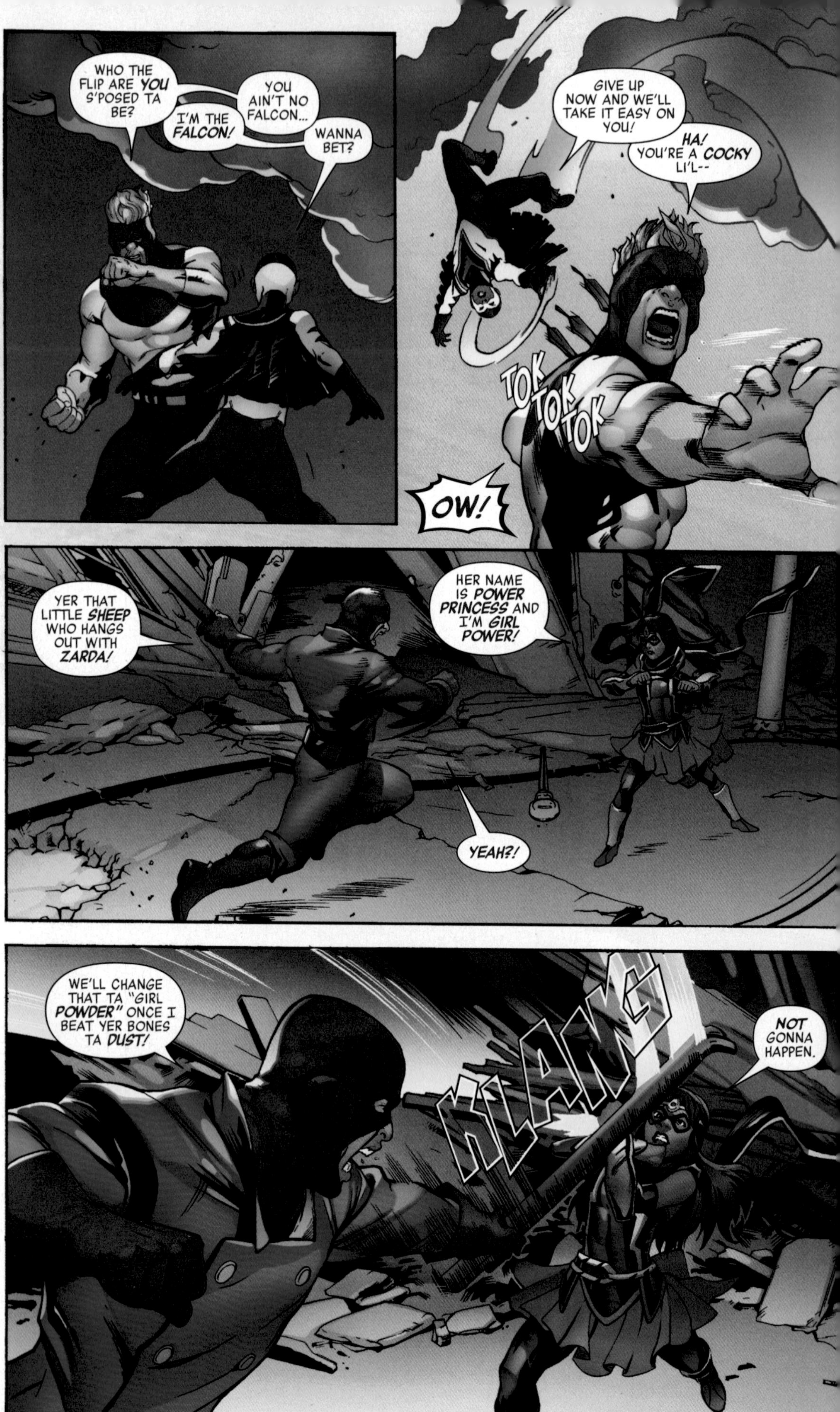
WHO THE FLIP ARE YOU S'POSED TA BE?
I'M THE FALCON!
YOU AIN'T NO FALCON...
WANNA BET?
GIVE UP NOW AND WE'LL TAKE IT EASY ON YOU!
HA! YOU'RE A COCKY LI'L--
TOK TOK TOK
OW!
YER THAT LITTLE SHEEP WHO HANGS OUT WITH ZARDA!
HER NAME IS POWER PRINCESS AND I'M GIRL POWER!
YEAH?!
WE'LL CHANGE THAT TA "GIRL POWDER" ONCE I BEAT YER BONES TA DUST!
KLANG
NOT GONNA HAPPEN.

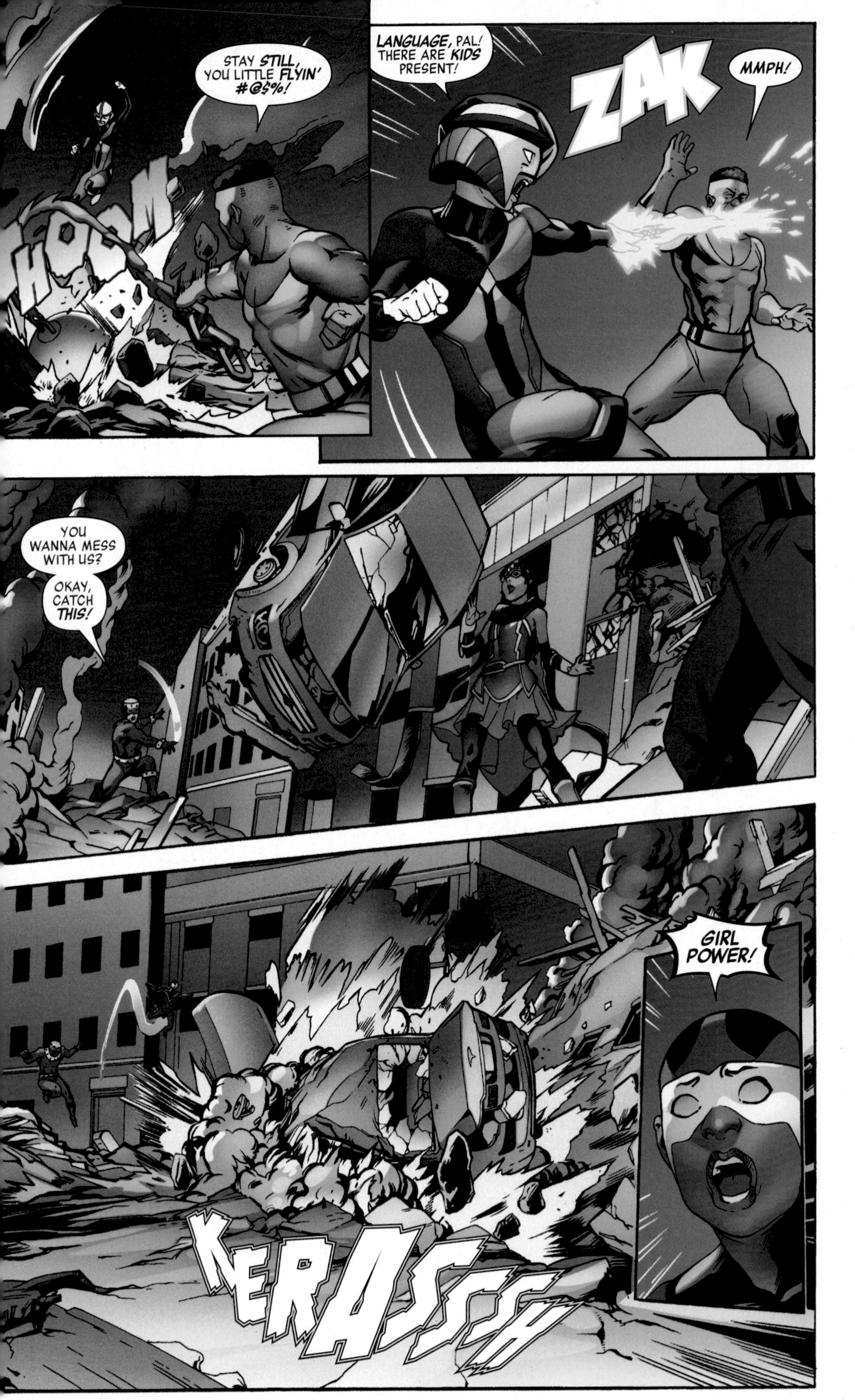
STAY STILL, YOU LITTLE FLYIN' #@$%!
WHOOM
LANGUAGE, PAL! THERE ARE KIDS PRESENT!
ZAK
MMPH!
YOU WANNA MESS WITH US?
OKAY, CATCH THIS!
GIRL POWER!
KERASSH

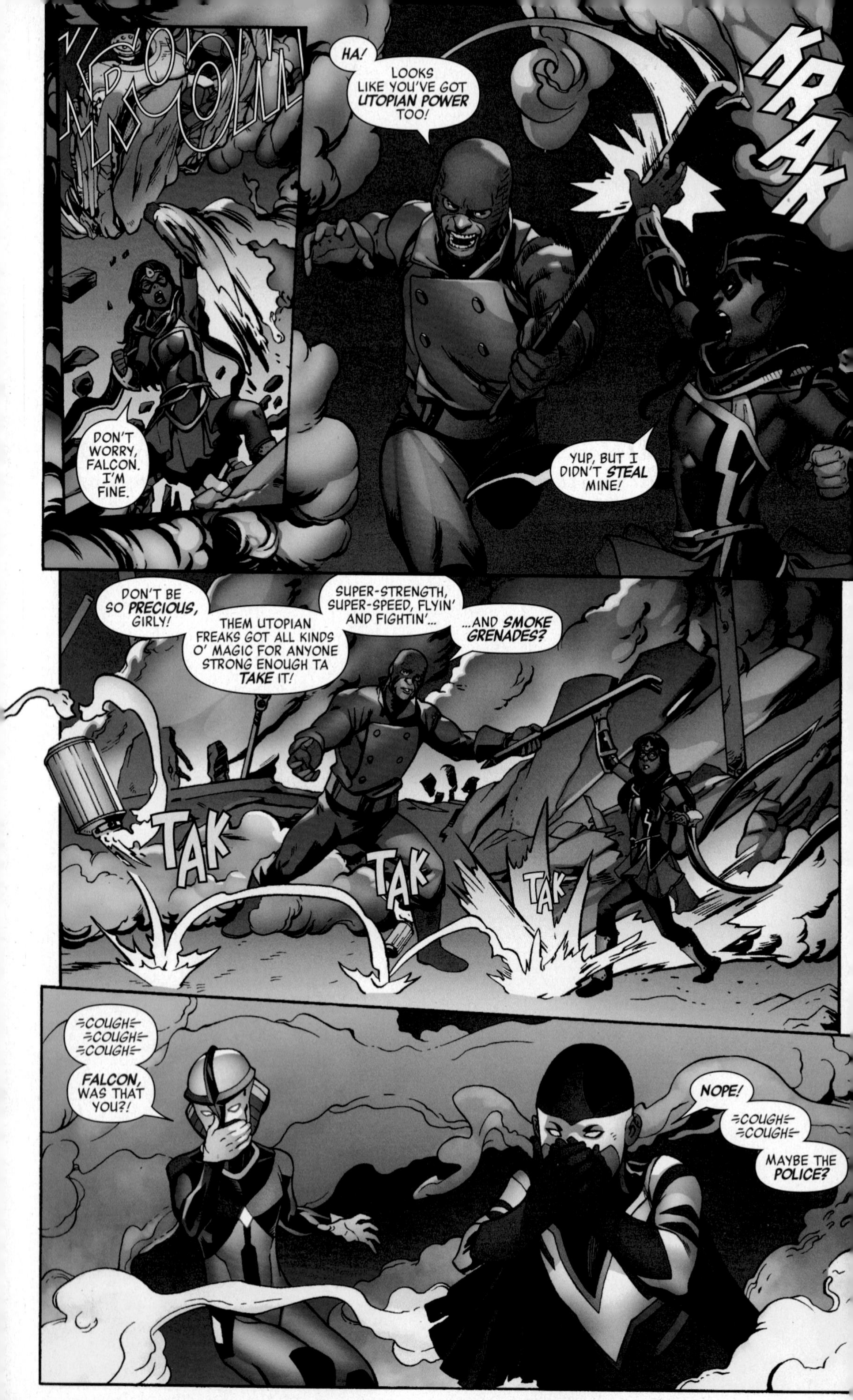
KRA-KOOM
HA!
LOOKS LIKE YOU'VE GOT UTOPIAN POWER TOO!
KRAK
DON'T WORRY, FALCON. I'M FINE.
YUP, BUT I DIDN'T STEAL MINE!
DON'T BE SO PRECIOUS, GIRLY!
THEM UTOPIAN FREAKS GOT ALL KINDS O' MAGIC FOR ANYONE STRONG ENOUGH TA TAKE IT!
SUPER-STRENGTH, SUPER-SPEED, FLYIN' AND FIGHTIN'...
...AND SMOKE GRENADES?
TAK
TAK
TAK
=COUGH= =COUGH= =COUGH=
FALCON, WAS THAT YOU?!
NOPE!
=COUGH= =COUGH=
MAYBE THE POLICE?

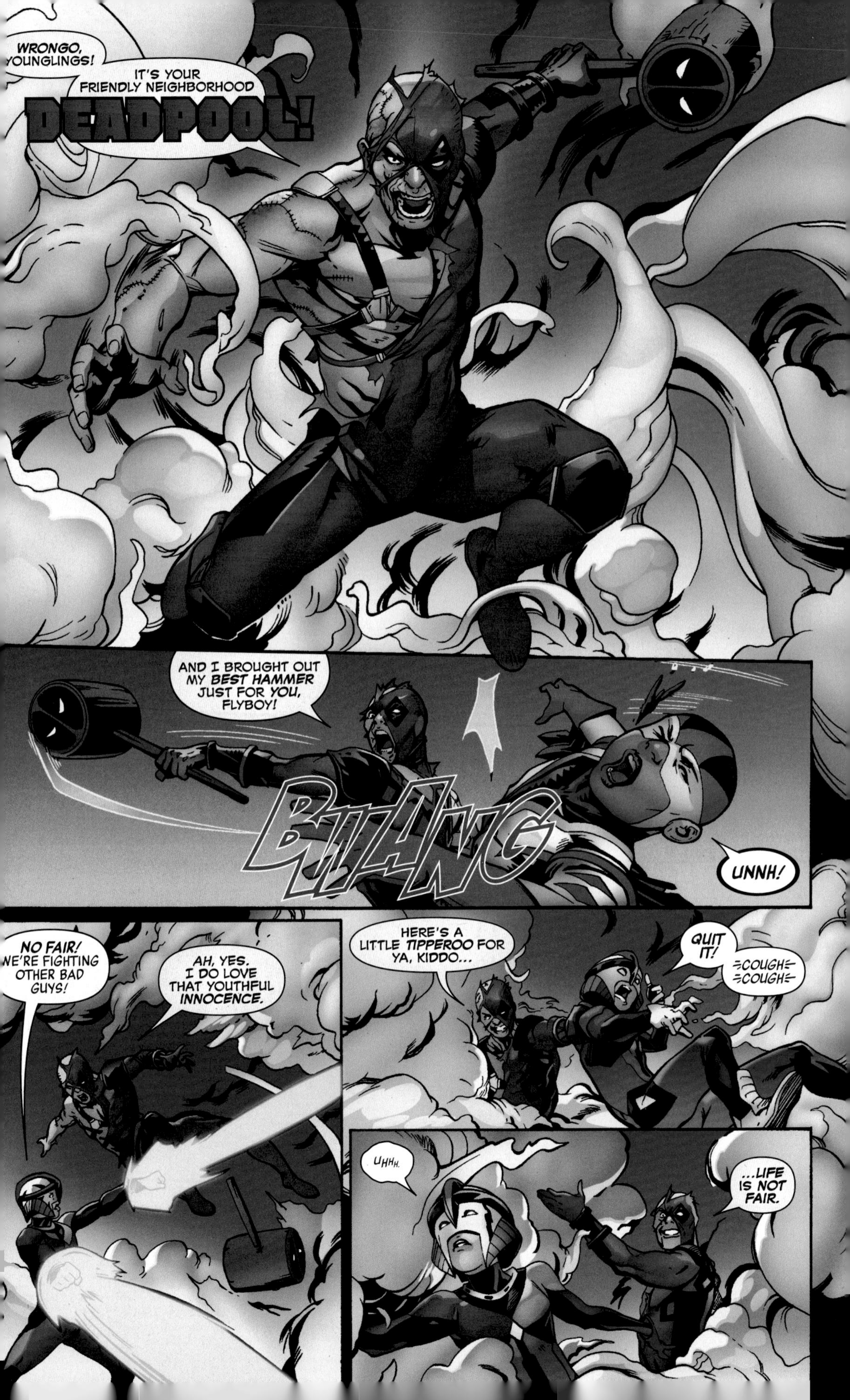

WRONGO, YOUNGLINGS!
IT'S YOUR FRIENDLY NEIGHBORHOOD DEADPOOL!
AND I BROUGHT OUT MY BEST HAMMER JUST FOR YOU, FLYBOY!
BTANG
UNNH!
NO FAIR! WE'RE FIGHTING OTHER BAD GUYS!
AH, YES. I DO LOVE THAT YOUTHFUL INNOCENCE.
HERE'S A LITTLE TIPPEROO FOR YA, KIDDO...
QUIT IT!
=COUGH= =COUGH=
UHHH.
...LIFE IS NOT FAIR.

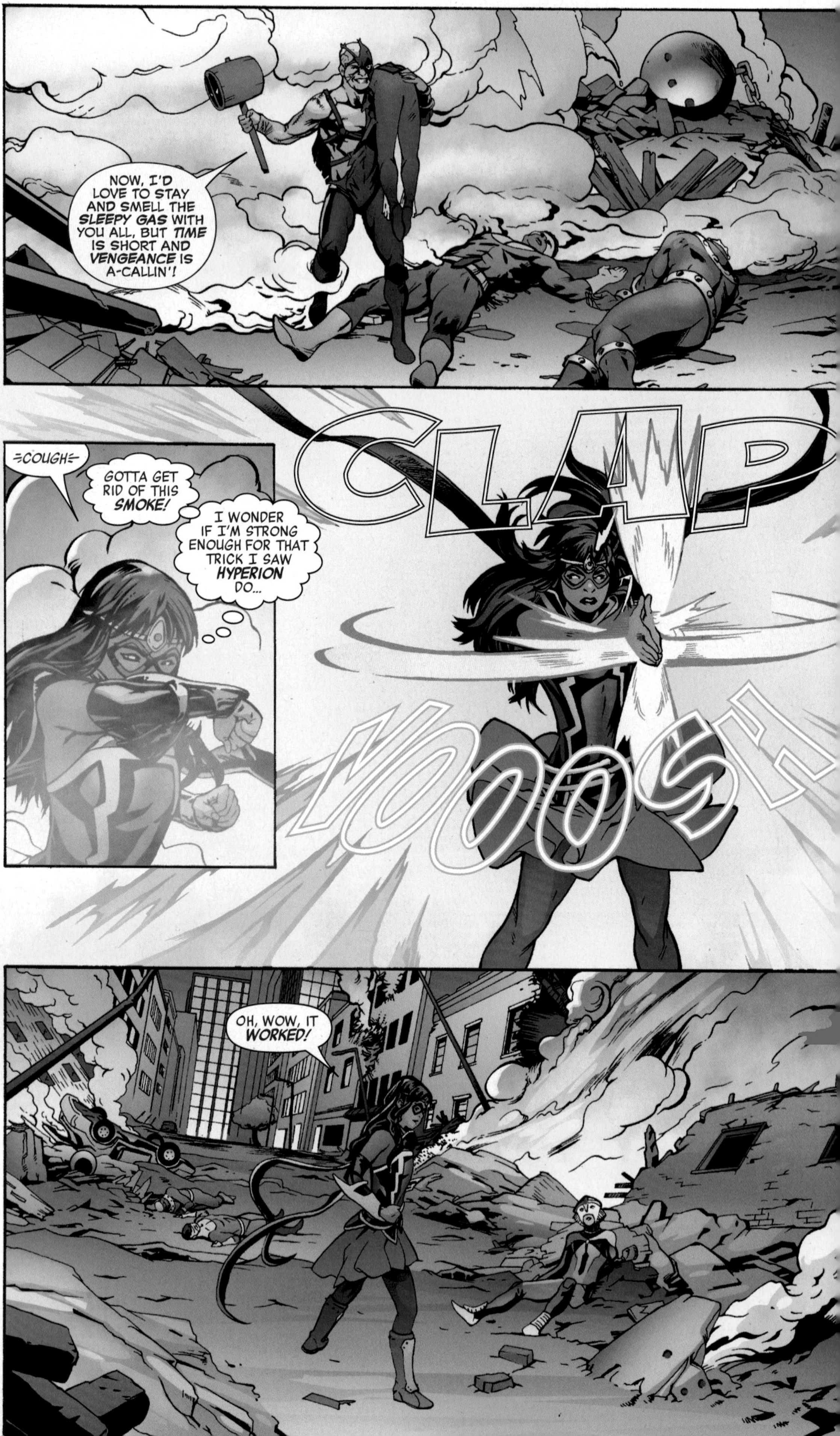

NOW, I'D LOVE TO STAY AND SMELL THE SLEEPY GAS WITH YOU ALL, BUT TIME IS SHORT AND VENGEANCE IS A-CALLIN'!
=COUGH=
GOTTA GET RID OF THIS SMOKE!
I WONDER IF I'M STRONG ENOUGH FOR THAT TRICK I SAW HYPERION DO...
CLAP
WOOOSH
OH, WOW, IT WORKED!

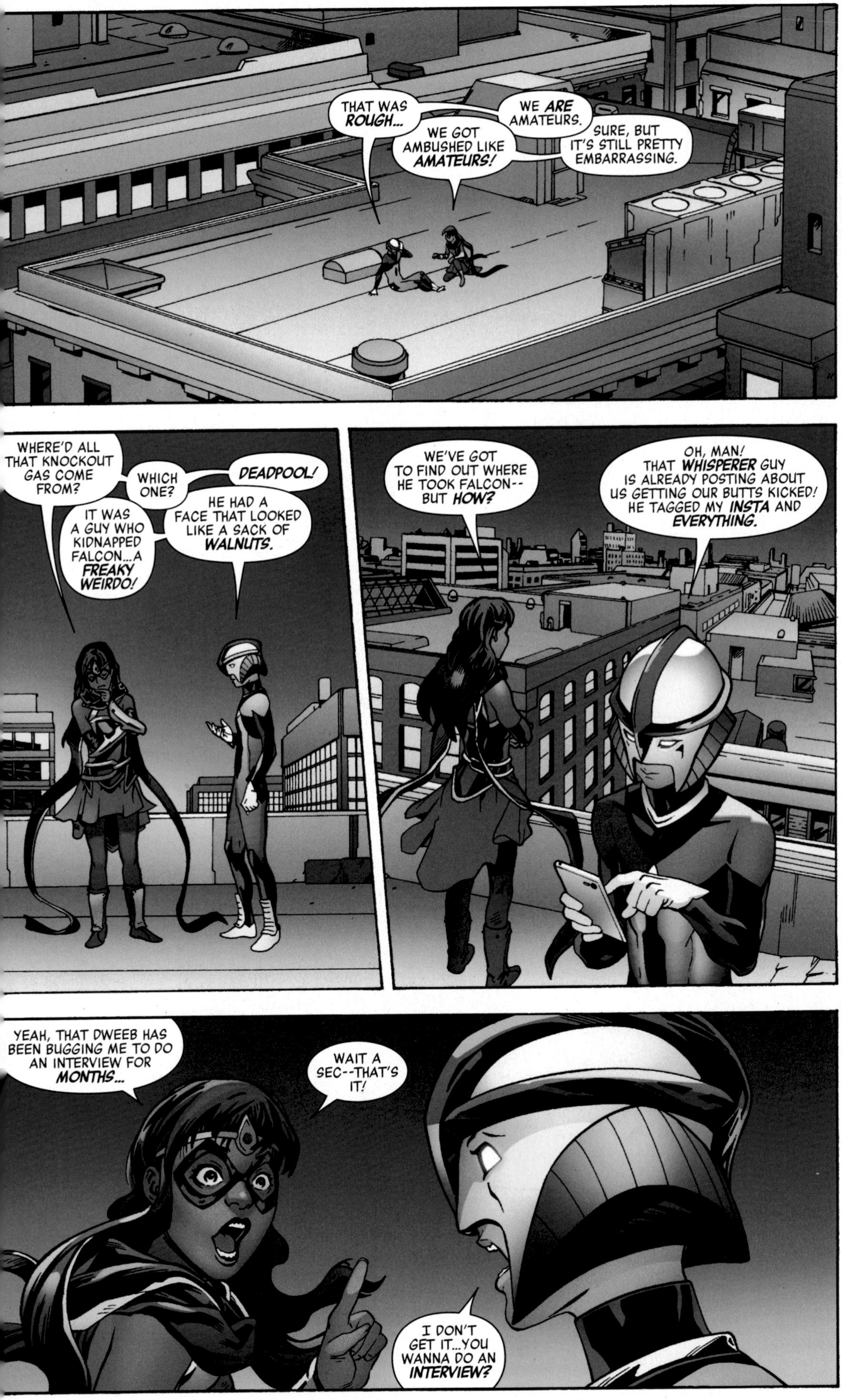
THAT WAS ROUGH...
WE GOT AMBUSHED LIKE AMATEURS!
WE ARE AMATEURS.
SURE, BUT IT'S STILL PRETTY EMBARRASSING.
WHERE'D ALL THAT KNOCKOUT GAS COME FROM?
WHICH ONE?
DEADPOOL!
IT WAS A GUY WHO KIDNAPPED FALCON...A FREAKY WEIRDO!
HE HAD A FACE THAT LOOKED LIKE A SACK OF WALNUTS.
WE'VE GOT TO FIND OUT WHERE HE TOOK FALCON--BUT HOW?
OH, MAN! THAT WHISPERER GUY IS ALREADY POSTING ABOUT US GETTING OUR BUTTS KICKED! HE TAGGED MY INSTA AND EVERYTHING.
YEAH, THAT DWEEB HAS BEEN BUGGING ME TO DO AN INTERVIEW FOR MONTHS...
WAIT A SEC--THAT'S IT!
I DON'T GET IT...YOU WANNA DO AN INTERVIEW?

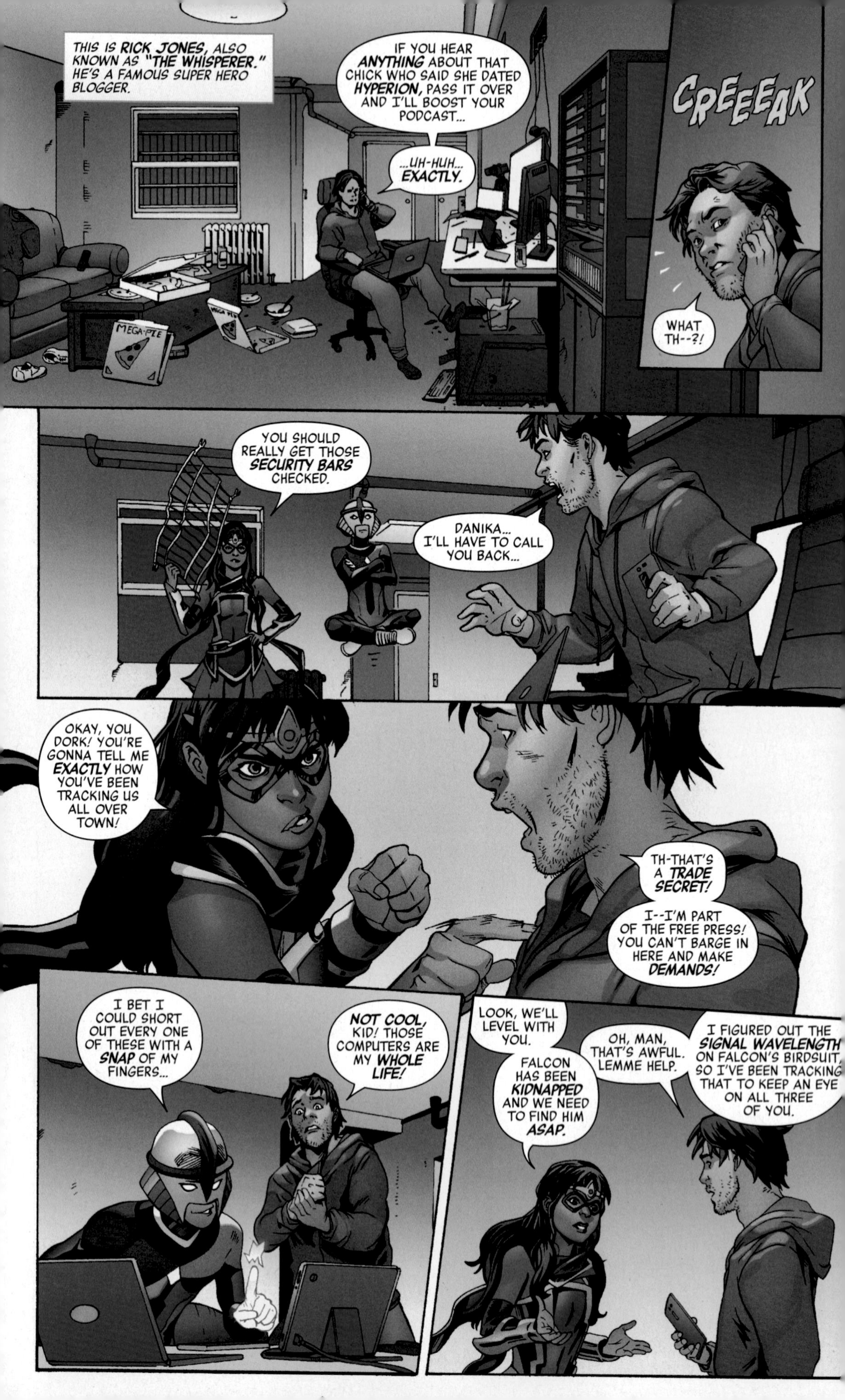

THIS IS RICK JONES, ALSO KNOWN AS "THE WHISPERER." HE'S A FAMOUS SUPER HERO BLOGGER.
IF YOU HEAR ANYTHING ABOUT THAT CHICK WHO SAID SHE DATED HYPERION, PASS IT OVER AND I'LL BOOST YOUR PODCAST...
...UH-HUH... EXACTLY.
CREEEAK
WHAT TH--?!
YOU SHOULD REALLY GET THOSE SECURITY BARS CHECKED.
DANIKA... I'LL HAVE TO CALL YOU BACK...
OKAY, YOU DORK! YOU'RE GONNA TELL ME EXACTLY HOW YOU'VE BEEN TRACKING US ALL OVER TOWN!
TH-THAT'S A TRADE SECRET!
I--I'M PART OF THE FREE PRESS! YOU CAN'T BARGE IN HERE AND MAKE DEMANDS!
I BET I COULD SHORT OUT EVERY ONE OF THESE WITH A SNAP OF MY FINGERS...
NOT COOL, KID! THOSE COMPUTERS ARE MY WHOLE LIFE!
LOOK, WE'LL LEVEL WITH YOU.
FALCON HAS BEEN KIDNAPPED AND WE NEED TO FIND HIM ASAP.
OH, MAN, THAT'S AWFUL. LEMME HELP.
I FIGURED OUT THE SIGNAL WAVELENGTH ON FALCON'S BIRDSUIT, SO I'VE BEEN TRACKING THAT TO KEEP AN EYE ON ALL THREE OF YOU.

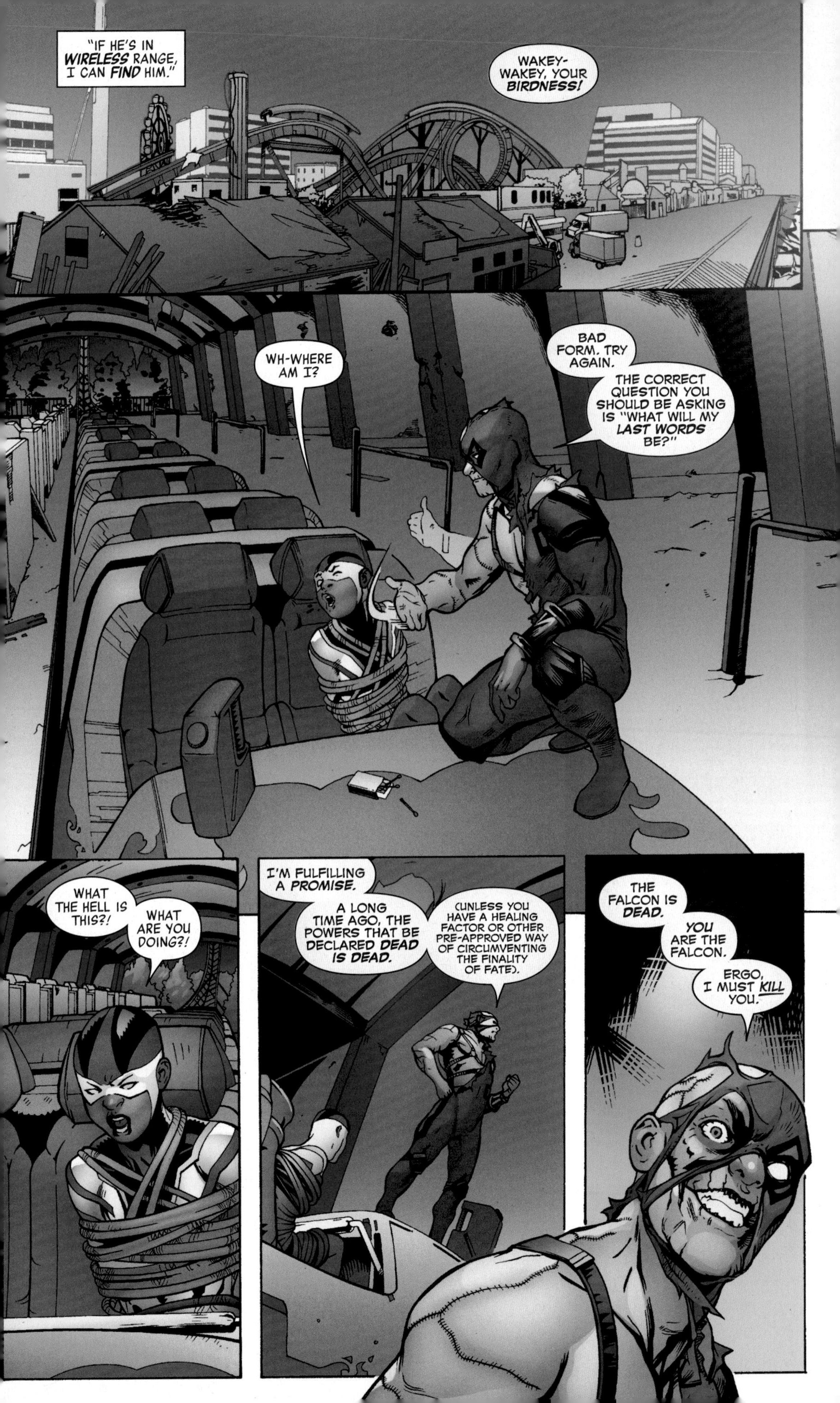
"IF HE'S IN WIRELESS RANGE, I CAN FIND HIM."
WAKEY-WAKEY, YOUR BIRDNESS!
WH-WHERE AM I?
BAD FORM. TRY AGAIN.
THE CORRECT QUESTION YOU SHOULD BE ASKING IS "WHAT WILL MY LAST WORDS BE?"
WHAT THE HELL IS THIS?!
WHAT ARE YOU DOING?!
I'M FULFILLING A PROMISE.
A LONG TIME AGO, THE POWERS THAT BE DECLARED DEAD IS DEAD.
(UNLESS YOU HAVE A HEALING FACTOR OR OTHER PRE-APPROVED WAY OF CIRCUMVENTING THE FINALITY OF FATE).
THE FALCON IS DEAD.
YOU ARE THE FALCON.
ERGO, I MUST KILL YOU.

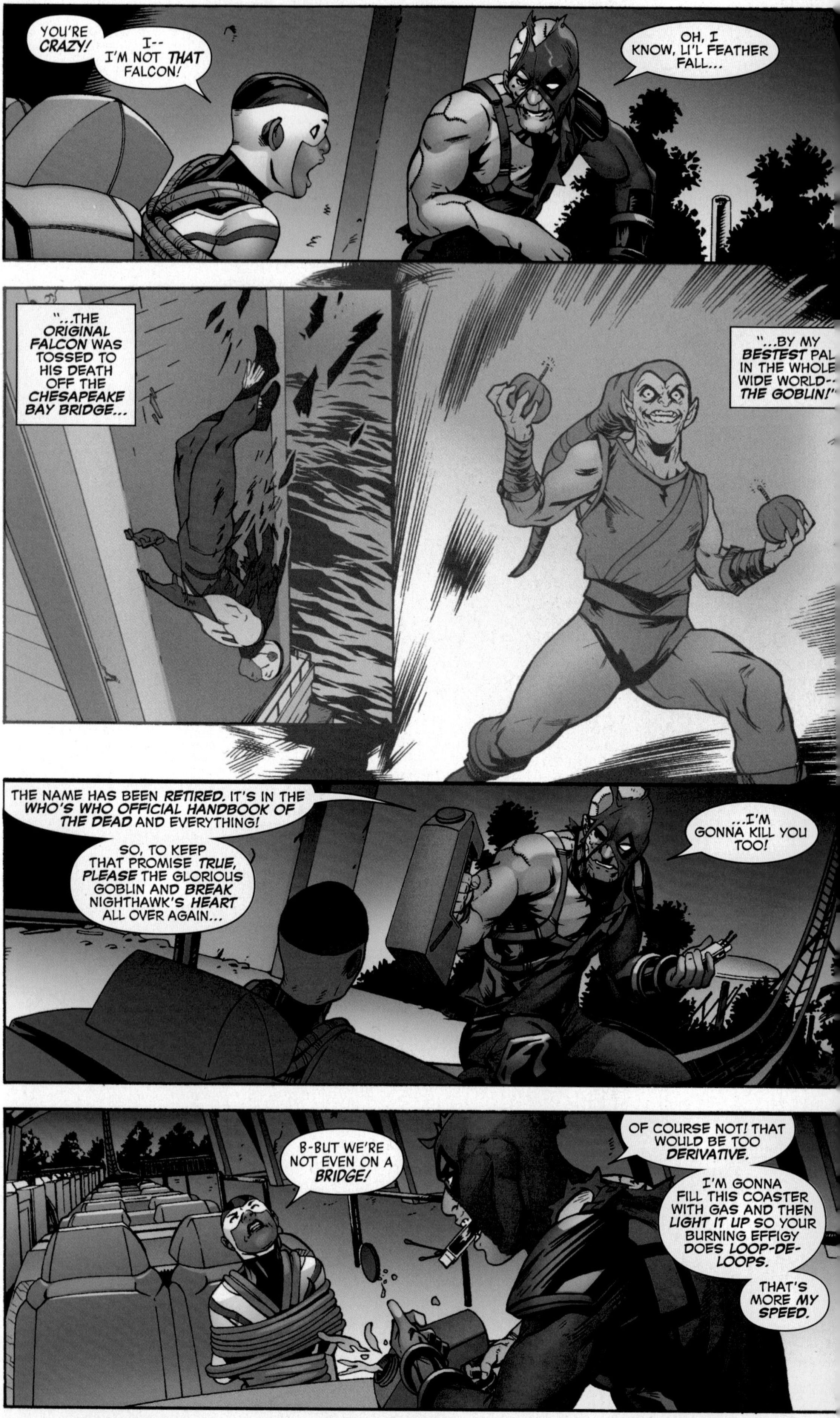
YOU'RE CRAZY!
I-- I'M NOT THAT FALCON!
OH, I KNOW, LI'L FEATHER FALL...
"...THE ORIGINAL FALCON WAS TOSSED TO HIS DEATH OFF THE CHESAPEAKE BAY BRIDGE...
"...BY MY BESTEST PAL IN THE WHOLE WIDE WORLD-- THE GOBLIN!"
THE NAME HAS BEEN RETIRED. IT'S IN THE WHO'S WHO OFFICIAL HANDBOOK OF THE DEAD AND EVERYTHING!
SO, TO KEEP THAT PROMISE TRUE, PLEASE THE GLORIOUS GOBLIN AND BREAK NIGHTHAWK'S HEART ALL OVER AGAIN...
...I'M GONNA KILL YOU TOO!
B-BUT WE'RE NOT EVEN ON A BRIDGE!
OF COURSE NOT! THAT WOULD BE TOO DERIVATIVE.
I'M GONNA FILL THIS COASTER WITH GAS AND THEN LIGHT IT UP SO YOUR BURNING EFFIGY DOES LOOP-DE-LOOPS.
THAT'S MORE MY SPEED.

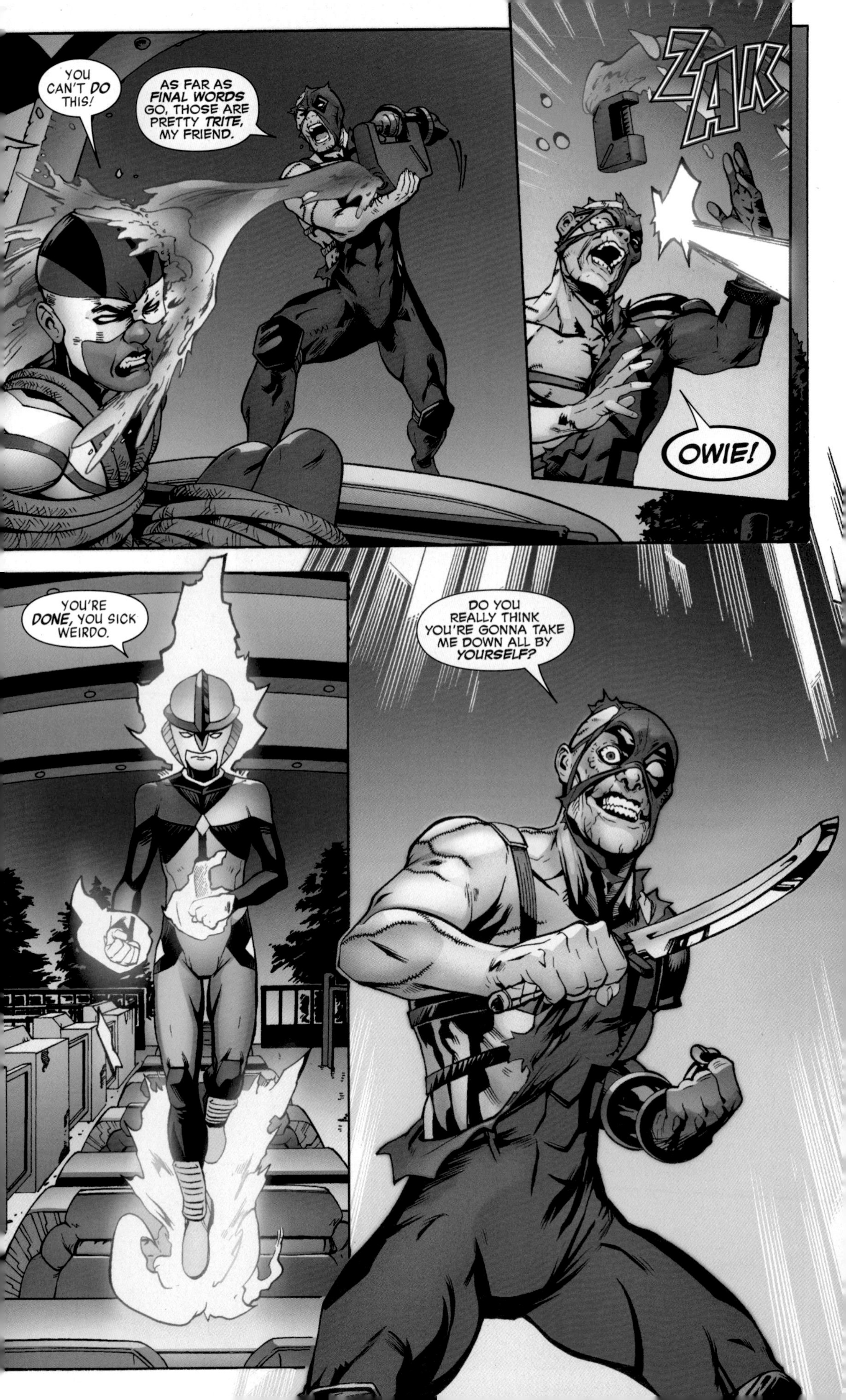
YOU CAN'T DO THIS!
AS FAR AS FINAL WORDS GO, THOSE ARE PRETTY TRITE, MY FRIEND.
ZAK
OWIE!
YOU'RE DONE, YOU SICK WEIRDO.
DO YOU REALLY THINK YOU'RE GONNA TAKE ME DOWN ALL BY YOURSELF?

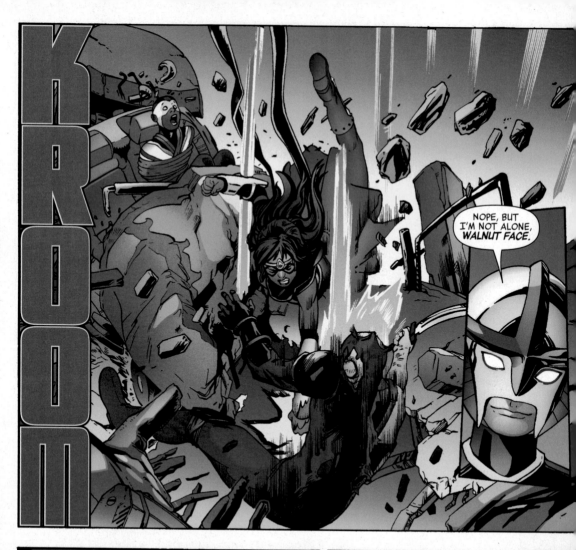

KROOOM

NOPE, BUT I'M NOT ALONE, *WALNUT FACE.*

SAM!

HEY! YOU TOLD ME WE'RE SUPPOSED TO USE *CODENAMES* NO MATTER WHAT!

CAREFUL, I'M FLAMMABLE!

I CAN VAPORIZE THE GAS AND YOUR ROPES AT THE SAME TIME.

THANKS. I... I THOUGHT I WAS GONNA DIE!

WELL, YOU DIDN'T, SO START THINKING OF AN APPROPRIATE REWARD FOR KAMALA AND ME AFTER WE KICK THIS GUY'S *BUTT.*

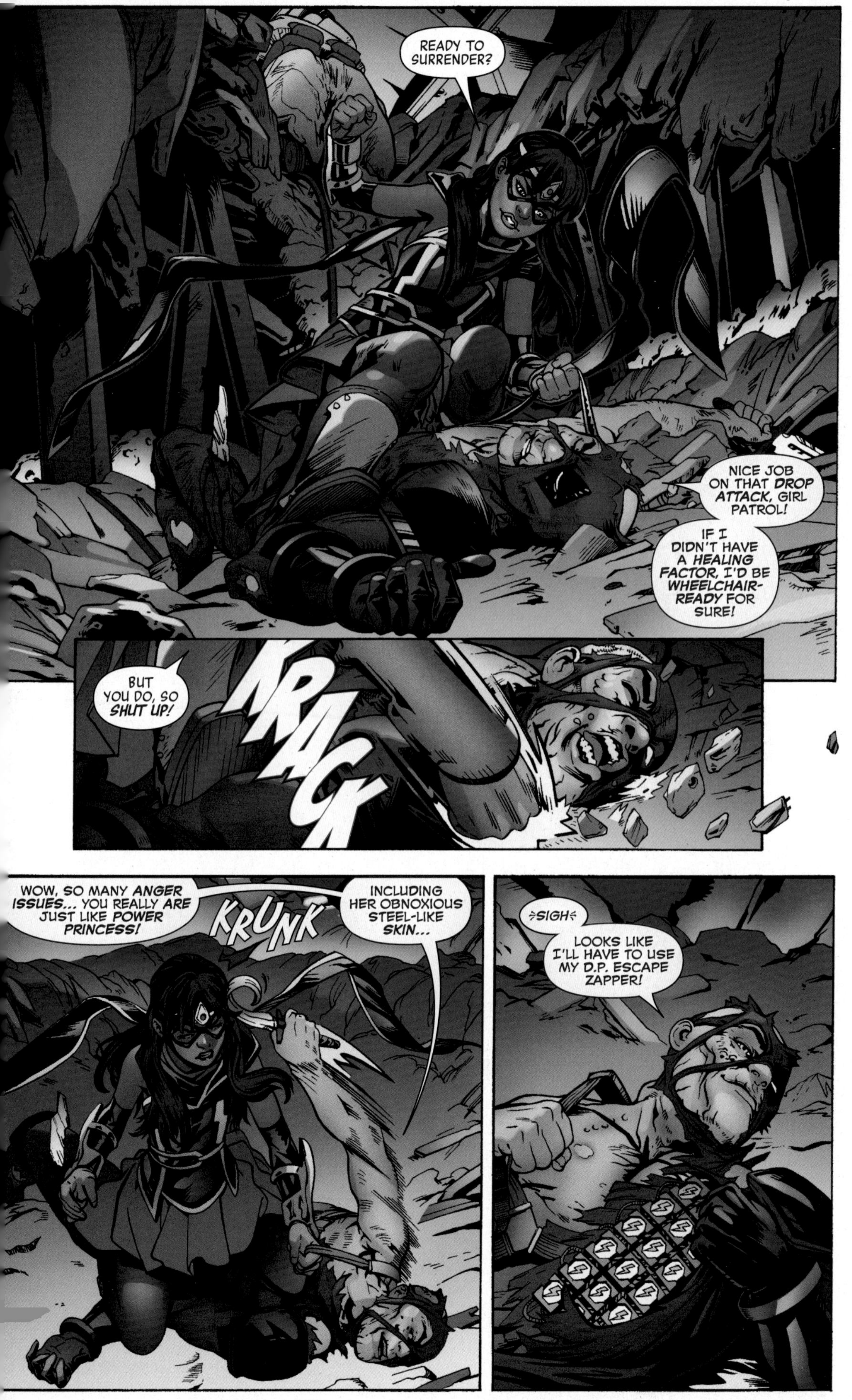
READY TO SURRENDER?
NICE JOB ON THAT DROP ATTACK, GIRL PATROL!
IF I DIDN'T HAVE A HEALING FACTOR, I'D BE WHEELCHAIR-READY FOR SURE!
BUT YOU DO, SO SHUT UP!
KRACK
WOW, SO MANY ANGER ISSUES... YOU REALLY ARE JUST LIKE POWER PRINCESS!
INCLUDING HER OBNOXIOUS STEEL-LIKE SKIN...
KRUNK
SIGH
LOOKS LIKE I'LL HAVE TO USE MY D.P. ESCAPE ZAPPER!

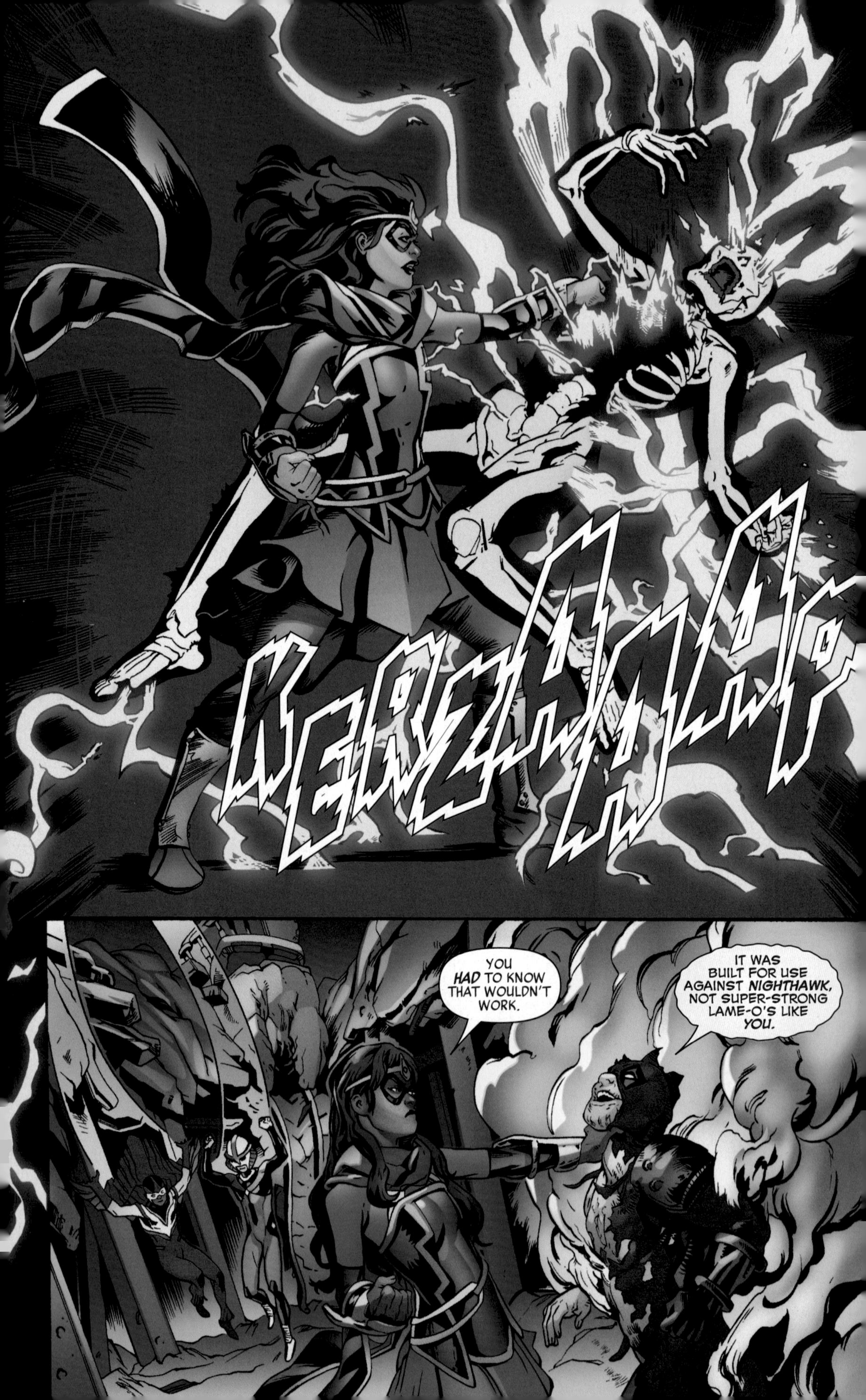
YOU *HAD* TO KNOW THAT WOULDN'T WORK.
IT WAS BUILT FOR USE AGAINST *NIGHTHAWK,* NOT SUPER-STRONG LAME-O'S LIKE *YOU.*

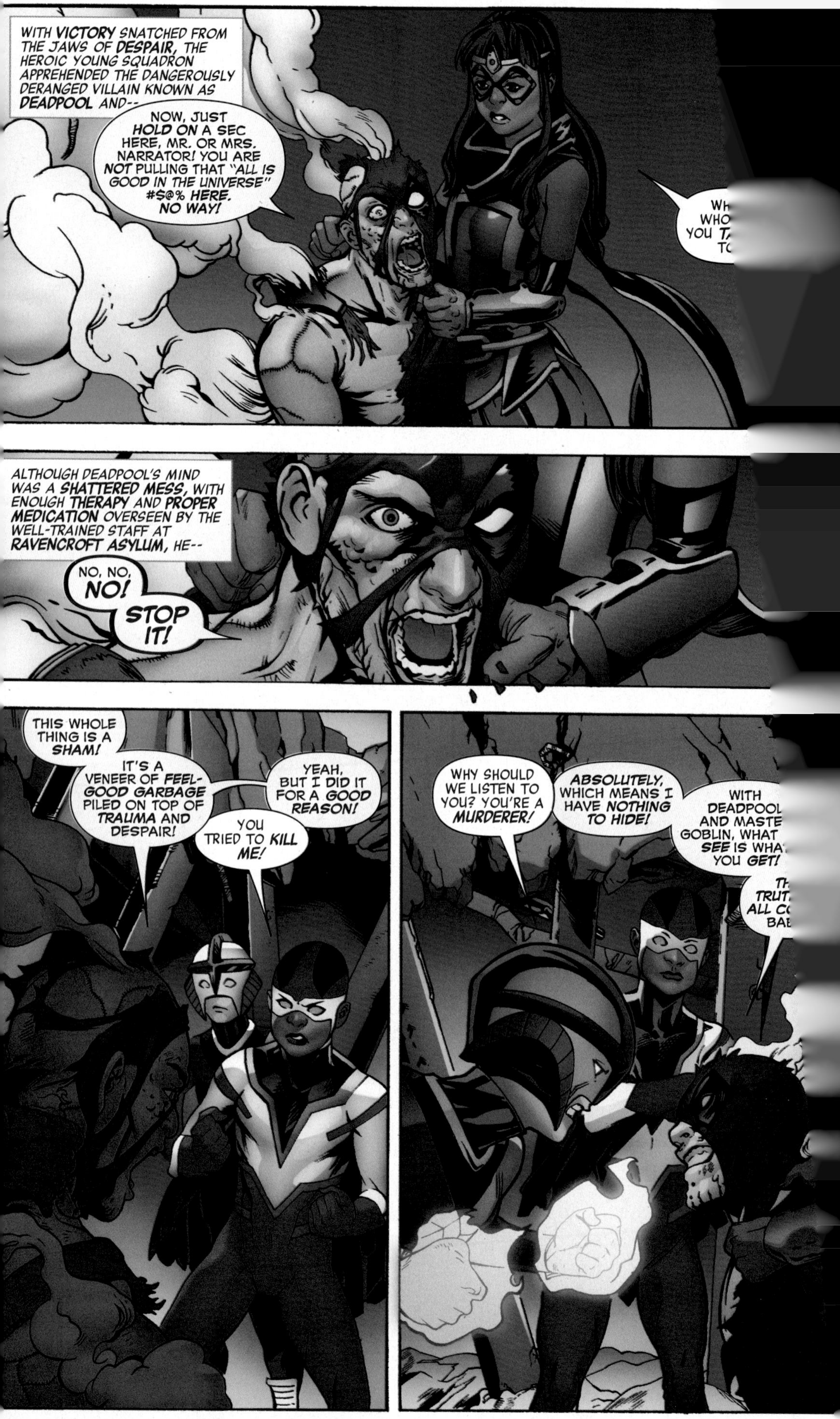
WITH VICTORY SNATCHED FROM THE JAWS OF DESPAIR, THE HEROIC YOUNG SQUADRON APPREHENDED THE DANGEROUSLY DERANGED VILLAIN KNOWN AS DEADPOOL AND--
NOW, JUST HOLD ON A SEC HERE, MR. OR MRS. NARRATOR! YOU ARE NOT PULLING THAT "ALL IS GOOD IN THE UNIVERSE" #$@% HERE. NO WAY!
WH WHO YOU TA TO
ALTHOUGH DEADPOOL'S MIND WAS A SHATTERED MESS, WITH ENOUGH THERAPY AND PROPER MEDICATION OVERSEEN BY THE WELL-TRAINED STAFF AT RAVENCROFT ASYLUM, HE--
NO, NO, NO!
STOP IT!
THIS WHOLE THING IS A SHAM!
IT'S A VENEER OF FEEL-GOOD GARBAGE PILED ON TOP OF TRAUMA AND DESPAIR!
YEAH, BUT I DID IT FOR A GOOD REASON!
YOU TRIED TO KILL ME!
WHY SHOULD WE LISTEN TO YOU? YOU'RE A MURDERER!
ABSOLUTELY, WHICH MEANS I HAVE NOTHING TO HIDE!
WITH DEADPOOL AND MASTE GOBLIN, WHAT SEE IS WHA YOU GET!
TH TRUT ALL C BA

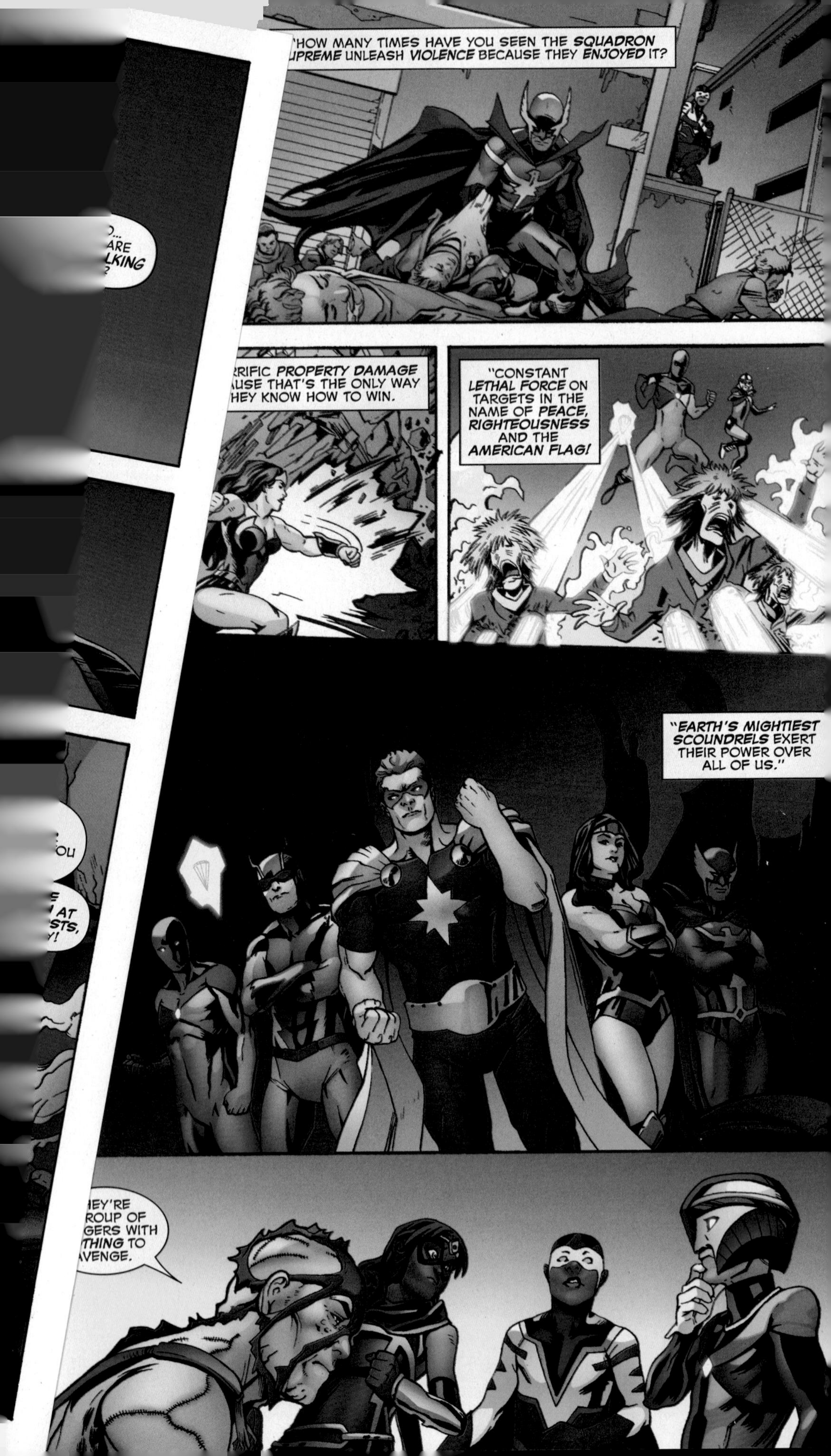

"HOW MANY TIMES HAVE YOU SEEN THE SQUADRON SUPREME UNLEASH VIOLENCE BECAUSE THEY ENJOYED IT?
RRIFIC PROPERTY DAMAGE AUSE THAT'S THE ONLY WAY HEY KNOW HOW TO WIN.
"CONSTANT LETHAL FORCE ON TARGETS IN THE NAME OF PEACE, RIGHTEOUSNESS AND THE AMERICAN FLAG!
"EARTH'S MIGHTIEST SCOUNDRELS EXERT THEIR POWER OVER ALL OF US."
HEY'RE ROUP OF GERS WITH THING TO AVENGE.

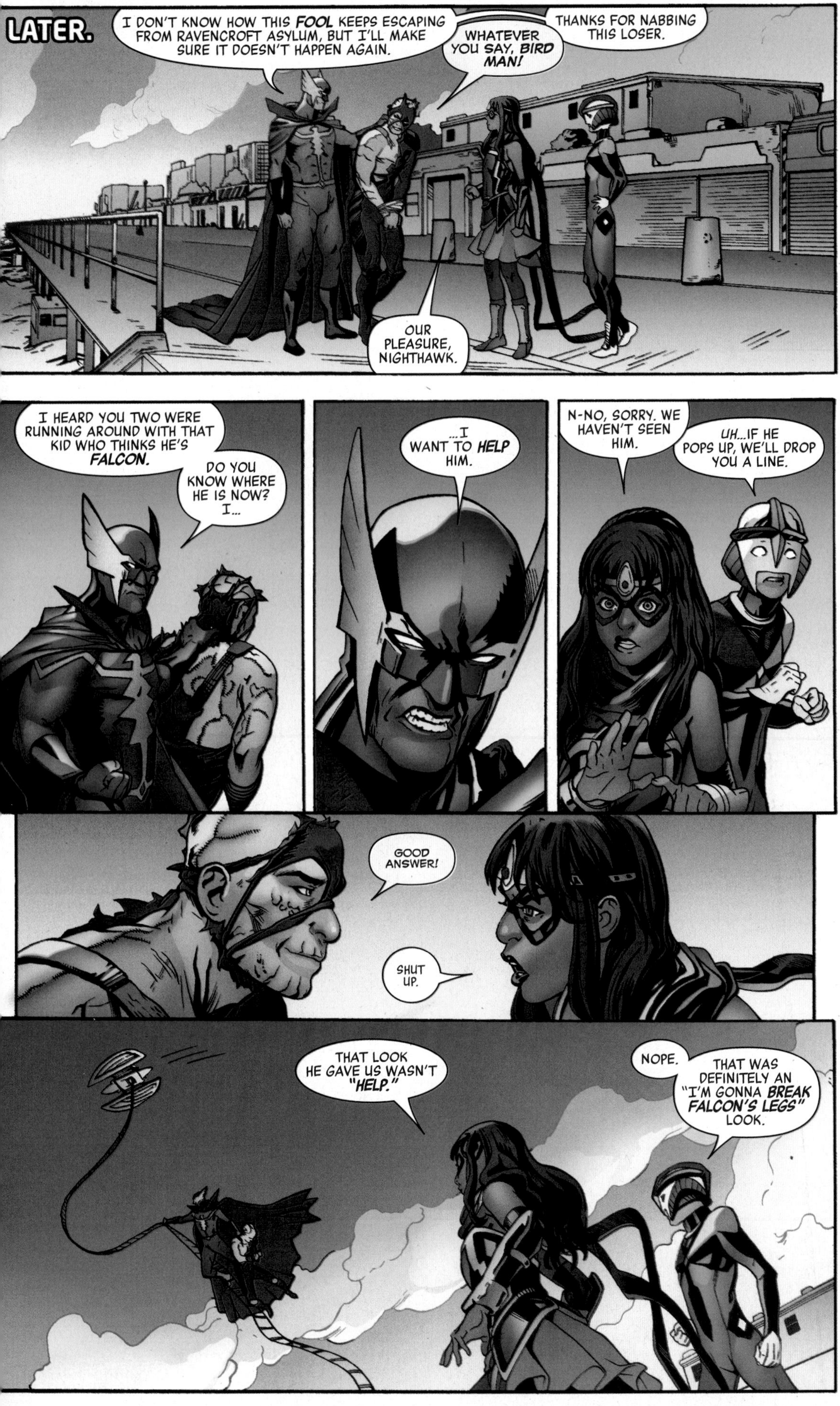
LATER.
I DON'T KNOW HOW THIS FOOL KEEPS ESCAPING FROM RAVENCROFT ASYLUM, BUT I'LL MAKE SURE IT DOESN'T HAPPEN AGAIN.
WHATEVER YOU SAY, BIRD MAN!
THANKS FOR NABBING THIS LOSER.
OUR PLEASURE, NIGHTHAWK.
I HEARD YOU TWO WERE RUNNING AROUND WITH THAT KID WHO THINKS HE'S FALCON.
DO YOU KNOW WHERE HE IS NOW? I...
...I WANT TO HELP HIM.
N-NO, SORRY. WE HAVEN'T SEEN HIM.
UH...IF HE POPS UP, WE'LL DROP YOU A LINE.
GOOD ANSWER!
SHUT UP.
THAT LOOK HE GAVE US WASN'T "HELP."
NOPE.
THAT WAS DEFINITELY AN "I'M GONNA BREAK FALCON'S LEGS" LOOK.

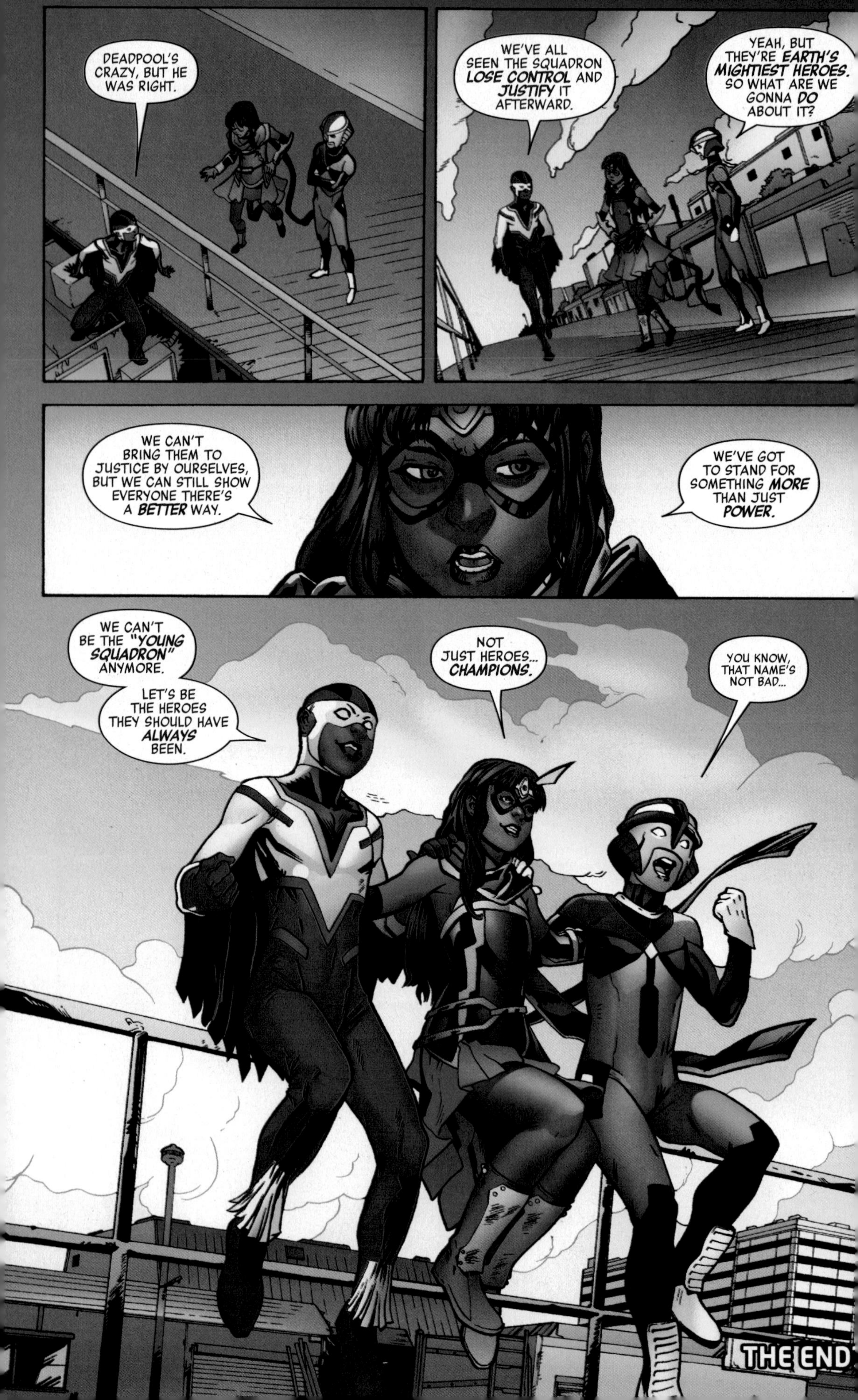
DEADPOOL'S CRAZY, BUT HE WAS RIGHT.
WE'VE ALL SEEN THE SQUADRON LOSE CONTROL AND JUSTIFY IT AFTERWARD.
YEAH, BUT THEY'RE EARTH'S MIGHTIEST HEROES. SO WHAT ARE WE GONNA DO ABOUT IT?
WE CAN'T BRING THEM TO JUSTICE BY OURSELVES, BUT WE CAN STILL SHOW EVERYONE THERE'S A BETTER WAY.
WE'VE GOT TO STAND FOR SOMETHING MORE THAN JUST POWER.
WE CAN'T BE THE "YOUNG SQUADRON" ANYMORE.
LET'S BE THE HEROES THEY SHOULD HAVE ALWAYS BEEN.
NOT JUST HEROES... CHAMPIONS.
YOU KNOW, THAT NAME'S NOT BAD...
THE END

Nº 1

"LONDON FALLING"

SIEGE
SOCIETY

In a world in which the Avengers never existed, the Squadron Supreme of America are and have always been Earth's Mightiest Heroes!

SIEGE
SOCIETY

The Squadron Supreme have been split by a Civil War that pitted Hyperion against Nighthawk and forced the rest to pick sides. The war is now over, but the Squadron are still divided.

CODY ZIGLAR WRITER

PACO MEDINA ARTIST

PETE PANTAZIS COLORIST

VC's **JOE SABINO** LETTERER

KEN LASHLEY & BRIAN **REBER** COVER ARTISTS

MARCELO **FERREIRA** & MORRY **HOLLOWELL** VARIANT COVER ARTISTS

JAY BOWEN GRAPHIC DESIGN

LINDSEY COHICK ASSISTANT EDITOR

RALPH MACCHIO CONSULTING EDITOR

NICK LOWE EXECUTIVE EDITOR

C.B. CEBULSKI EDITOR IN CHIEF

HEROES
REBORN

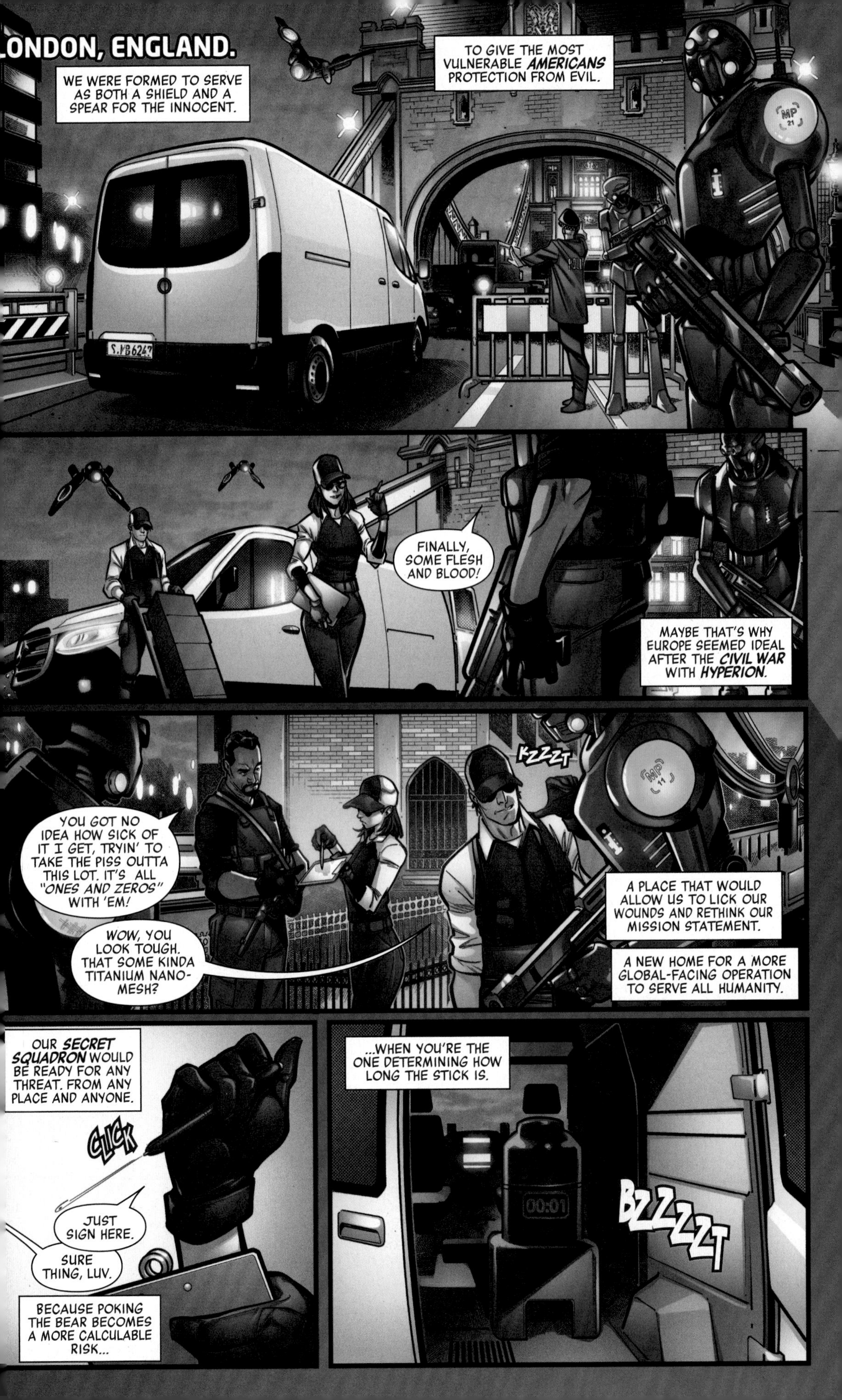
LONDON, ENGLAND.
WE WERE FORMED TO SERVE AS BOTH A SHIELD AND A SPEAR FOR THE INNOCENT.
TO GIVE THE MOST VULNERABLE AMERICANS PROTECTION FROM EVIL.
FINALLY, SOME FLESH AND BLOOD!
MAYBE THAT'S WHY EUROPE SEEMED IDEAL AFTER THE CIVIL WAR WITH HYPERION.
YOU GOT NO IDEA HOW SICK OF IT I GET, TRYIN' TO TAKE THE PISS OUTTA THIS LOT. IT'S ALL "ONES AND ZEROS" WITH 'EM!
WOW, YOU LOOK TOUGH. THAT SOME KINDA TITANIUM NANO-MESH?
KZZZT
A PLACE THAT WOULD ALLOW US TO LICK OUR WOUNDS AND RETHINK OUR MISSION STATEMENT.
A NEW HOME FOR A MORE GLOBAL-FACING OPERATION TO SERVE ALL HUMANITY.
OUR SECRET SQUADRON WOULD BE READY FOR ANY THREAT. FROM ANY PLACE AND ANYONE.
CLICK
JUST SIGN HERE.
SURE THING, LUV.
BECAUSE POKING THE BEAR BECOMES A MORE CALCULABLE RISK...
...WHEN YOU'RE THE ONE DETERMINING HOW LONG THE STICK IS.
00:01
BZZZZT

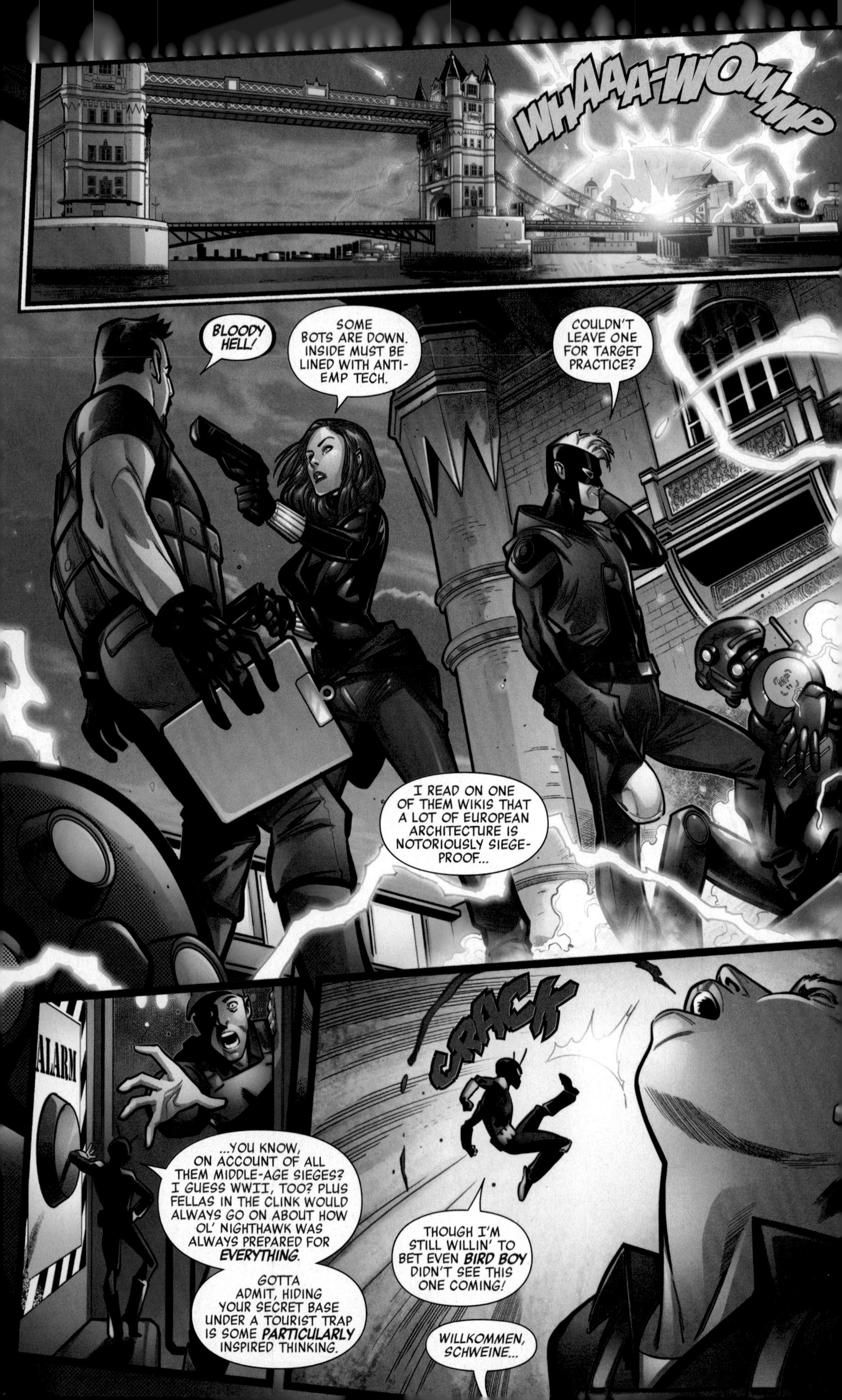
WHAAA-WOMMP
BLOODY HELL!
SOME BOTS ARE DOWN. INSIDE MUST BE LINED WITH ANTI-EMP TECH.
COULDN'T LEAVE ONE FOR TARGET PRACTICE?
I READ ON ONE OF THEM WIKIS THAT A LOT OF EUROPEAN ARCHITECTURE IS NOTORIOUSLY SIEGE-PROOF...
ALARM
CRACK
...YOU KNOW, ON ACCOUNT OF ALL THEM MIDDLE-AGE SIEGES? I GUESS WWII, TOO? PLUS FELLAS IN THE CLINK WOULD ALWAYS GO ON ABOUT HOW OL' NIGHTHAWK WAS ALWAYS PREPARED FOR EVERYTHING.
GOTTA ADMIT, HIDING YOUR SECRET BASE UNDER A TOURIST TRAP IS SOME PARTICULARLY INSPIRED THINKING.
THOUGH I'M STILL WILLIN' TO BET EVEN BIRD BOY DIDN'T SEE THIS ONE COMING!
WILLKOMMEN, SCHWEINE...

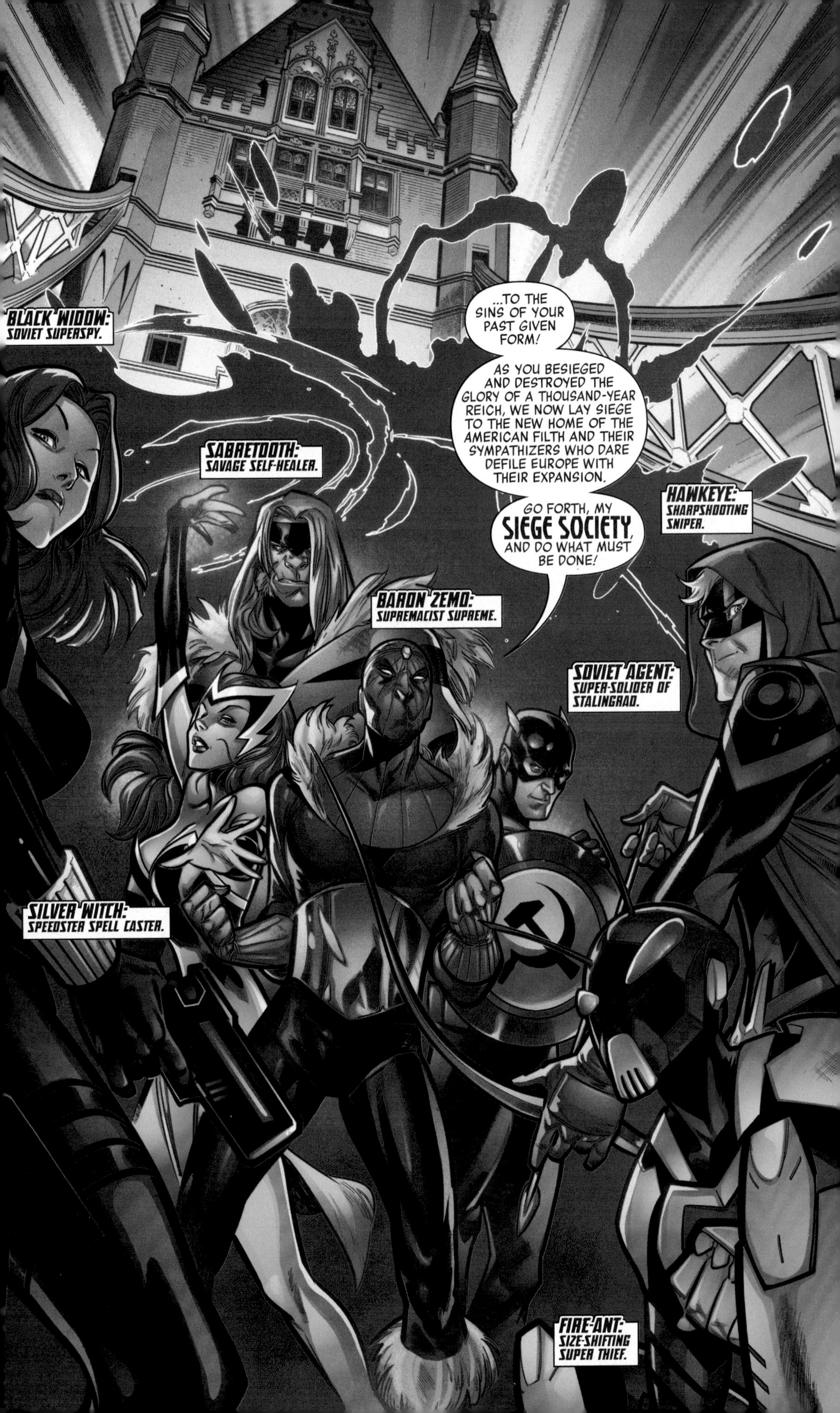
BLACK WIDOW: SOVIET SUPERSPY.
...TO THE SINS OF YOUR PAST GIVEN FORM!
AS YOU BESIEGED AND DESTROYED THE GLORY OF A THOUSAND-YEAR REICH, WE NOW LAY SIEGE TO THE NEW HOME OF THE AMERICAN FILTH AND THEIR SYMPATHIZERS WHO DARE DEFILE EUROPE WITH THEIR EXPANSION.
GO FORTH, MY SIEGE SOCIETY, AND DO WHAT MUST BE DONE!
SABRETOOTH: SAVAGE SELF-HEALER.
HAWKEYE: SHARPSHOOTING SNIPER.
BARON ZEMO: SUPREMACIST SUPREME.
SOVIET AGENT: SUPER-SOLIDER OF STALINGRAD.
SILVER WITCH: SPEEDSTER SPELL CASTER.
FIRE-ANT: SIZE-SHIFTING SUPER THIEF.

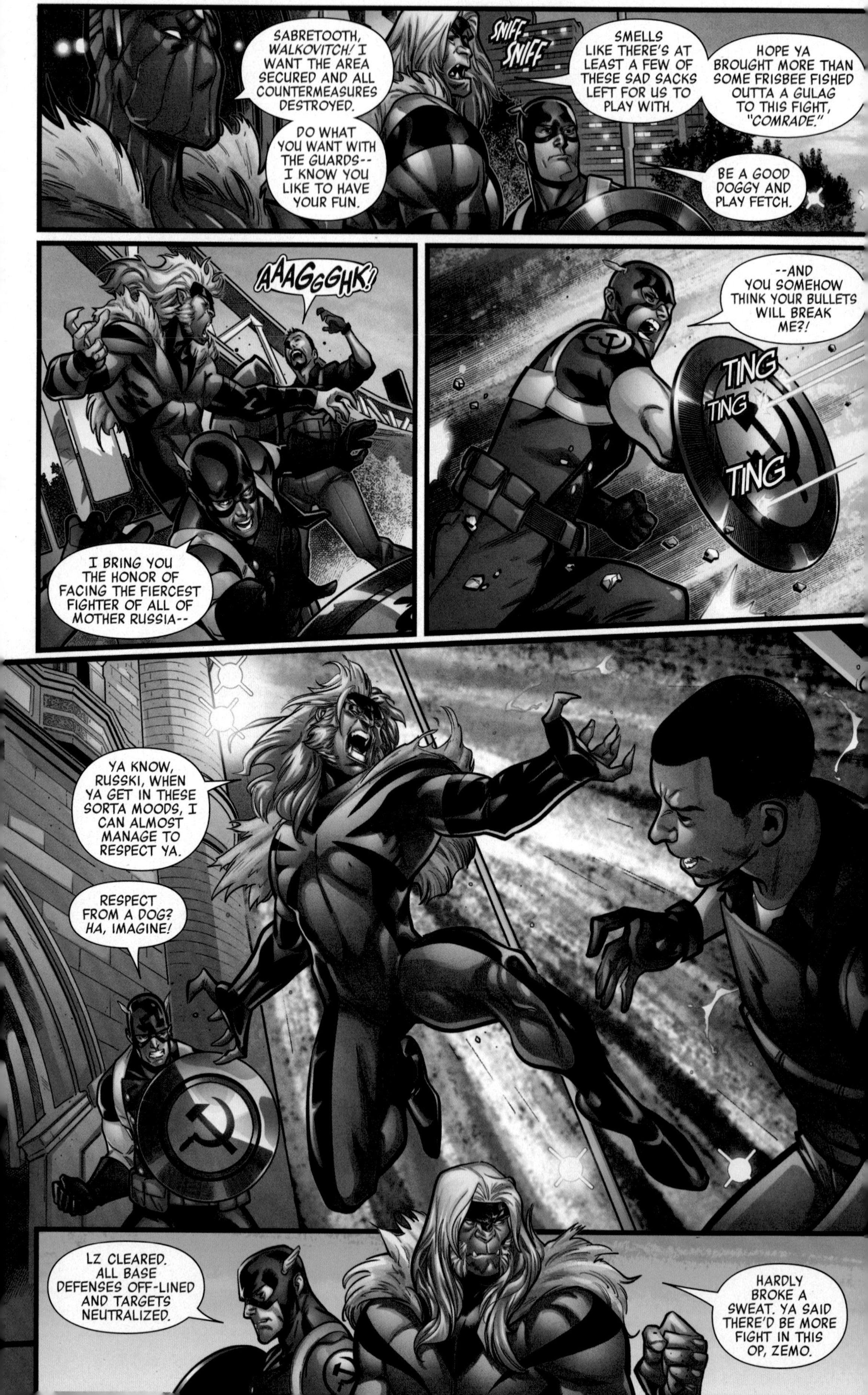
SABRETOOTH, WALKOVITCH! I WANT THE AREA SECURED AND ALL COUNTERMEASURES DESTROYED.
DO WHAT YOU WANT WITH THE GUARDS-- I KNOW YOU LIKE TO HAVE YOUR FUN.
SNIFF SNIFF
SMELLS LIKE THERE'S AT LEAST A FEW OF THESE SAD SACKS LEFT FOR US TO PLAY WITH.
HOPE YA BROUGHT MORE THAN SOME FRISBEE FISHED OUTTA A GULAG TO THIS FIGHT, "COMRADE."
BE A GOOD DOGGY AND PLAY FETCH.
AAAGGGHK!
I BRING YOU THE HONOR OF FACING THE FIERCEST FIGHTER OF ALL OF MOTHER RUSSIA--
--AND YOU SOMEHOW THINK YOUR BULLETS WILL BREAK ME?!
TING
TING
TING
YA KNOW, RUSSKI, WHEN YA GET IN THESE SORTA MOODS, I CAN ALMOST MANAGE TO RESPECT YA.
RESPECT FROM A DOG? HA, IMAGINE!
LZ CLEARED. ALL BASE DEFENSES OFF-LINED AND TARGETS NEUTRALIZED.
HARDLY BROKE A SWEAT. YA SAID THERE'D BE MORE FIGHT IN THIS OP, ZEMO.

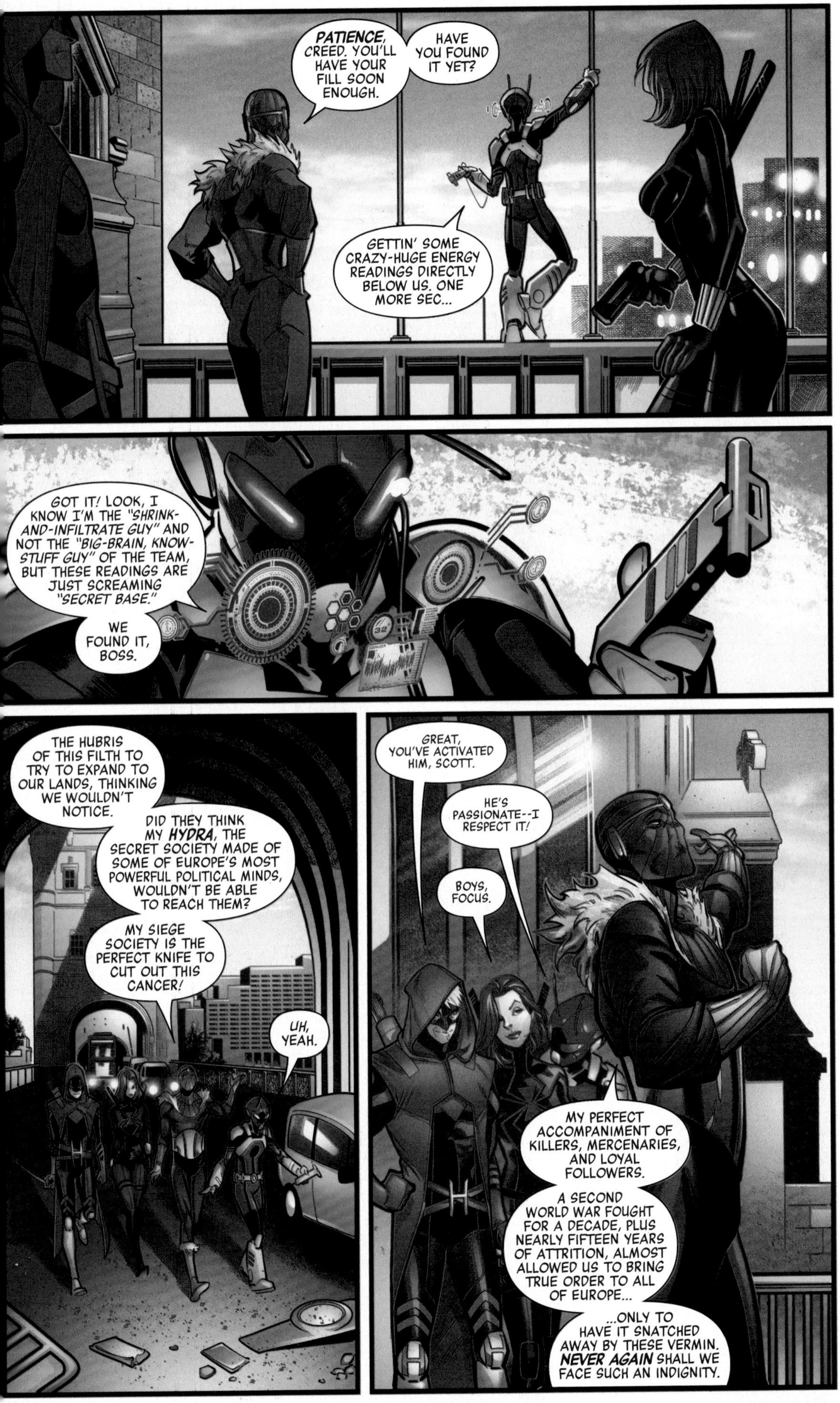
PATIENCE, CREED. YOU'LL HAVE YOUR FILL SOON ENOUGH.
HAVE YOU FOUND IT YET?
GETTIN' SOME CRAZY-HUGE ENERGY READINGS DIRECTLY BELOW US. ONE MORE SEC...
GOT IT! LOOK, I KNOW I'M THE "SHRINK-AND-INFILTRATE GUY" AND NOT THE "BIG-BRAIN, KNOW-STUFF GUY" OF THE TEAM, BUT THESE READINGS ARE JUST SCREAMING "SECRET BASE."
WE FOUND IT, BOSS.
THE HUBRIS OF THIS FILTH TO TRY TO EXPAND TO OUR LANDS, THINKING WE WOULDN'T NOTICE.
DID THEY THINK MY HYDRA, THE SECRET SOCIETY MADE OF SOME OF EUROPE'S MOST POWERFUL POLITICAL MINDS, WOULDN'T BE ABLE TO REACH THEM?
MY SIEGE SOCIETY IS THE PERFECT KNIFE TO CUT OUT THIS CANCER!
UH, YEAH.
GREAT, YOU'VE ACTIVATED HIM, SCOTT.
HE'S PASSIONATE--I RESPECT IT!
BOYS, FOCUS.
MY PERFECT ACCOMPANIMENT OF KILLERS, MERCENARIES, AND LOYAL FOLLOWERS.
A SECOND WORLD WAR FOUGHT FOR A DECADE, PLUS NEARLY FIFTEEN YEARS OF ATTRITION, ALMOST ALLOWED US TO BRING TRUE ORDER TO ALL OF EUROPE...
...ONLY TO HAVE IT SNATCHED AWAY BY THESE VERMIN. NEVER AGAIN SHALL WE FACE SUCH AN INDIGNITY.

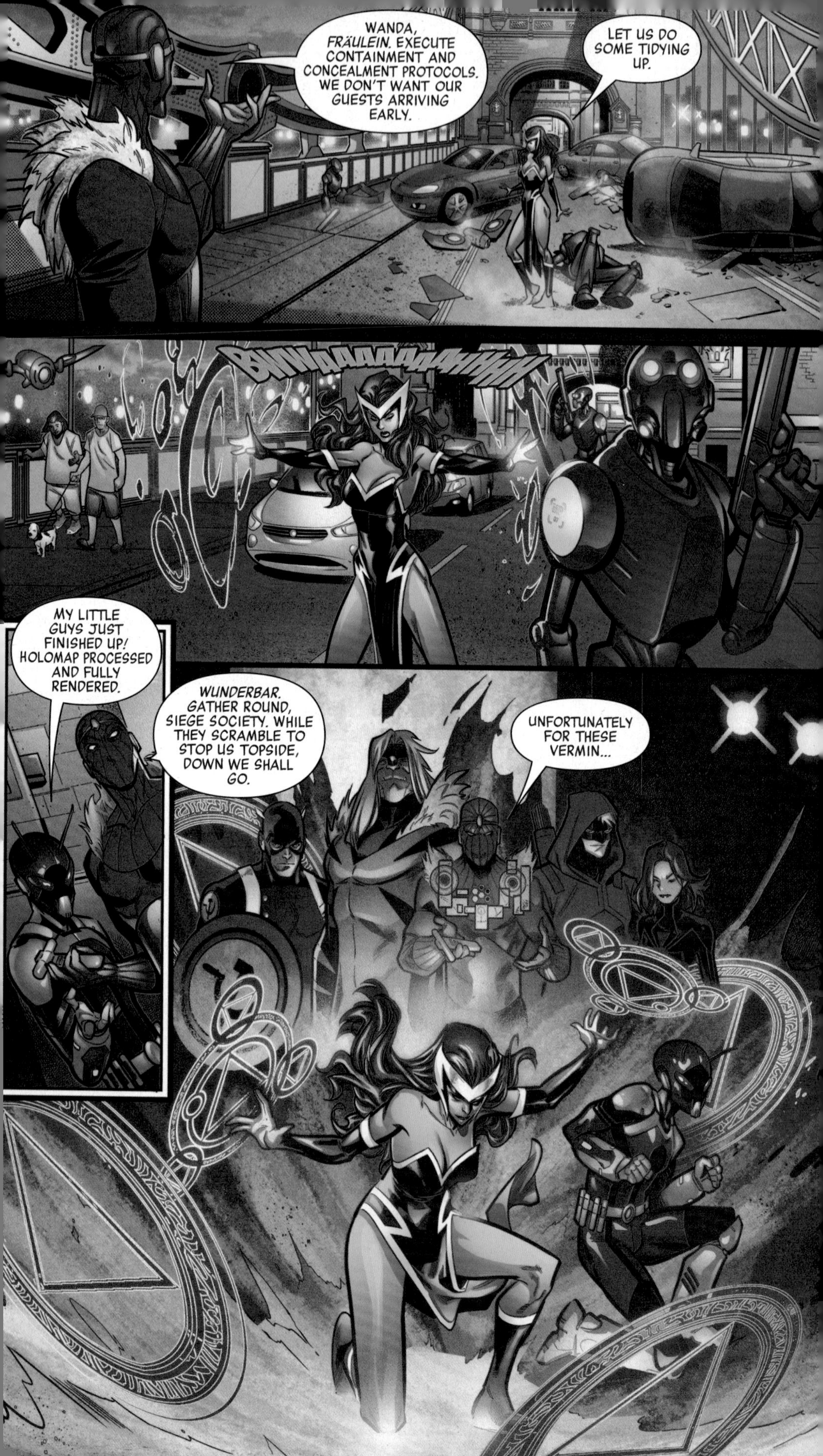
WANDA, FRÄULEIN. EXECUTE CONTAINMENT AND CONCEALMENT PROTOCOLS. WE DON'T WANT OUR GUESTS ARRIVING EARLY.
LET US DO SOME TIDYING UP.
BWWAAAAAAMMM
MY LITTLE GUYS JUST FINISHED UP! HOLOMAP PROCESSED AND FULLY RENDERED.
WUNDERBAR. GATHER ROUND, SIEGE SOCIETY. WHILE THEY SCRAMBLE TO STOP US TOPSIDE, DOWN WE SHALL GO.
UNFORTUNATELY FOR THESE VERMIN...

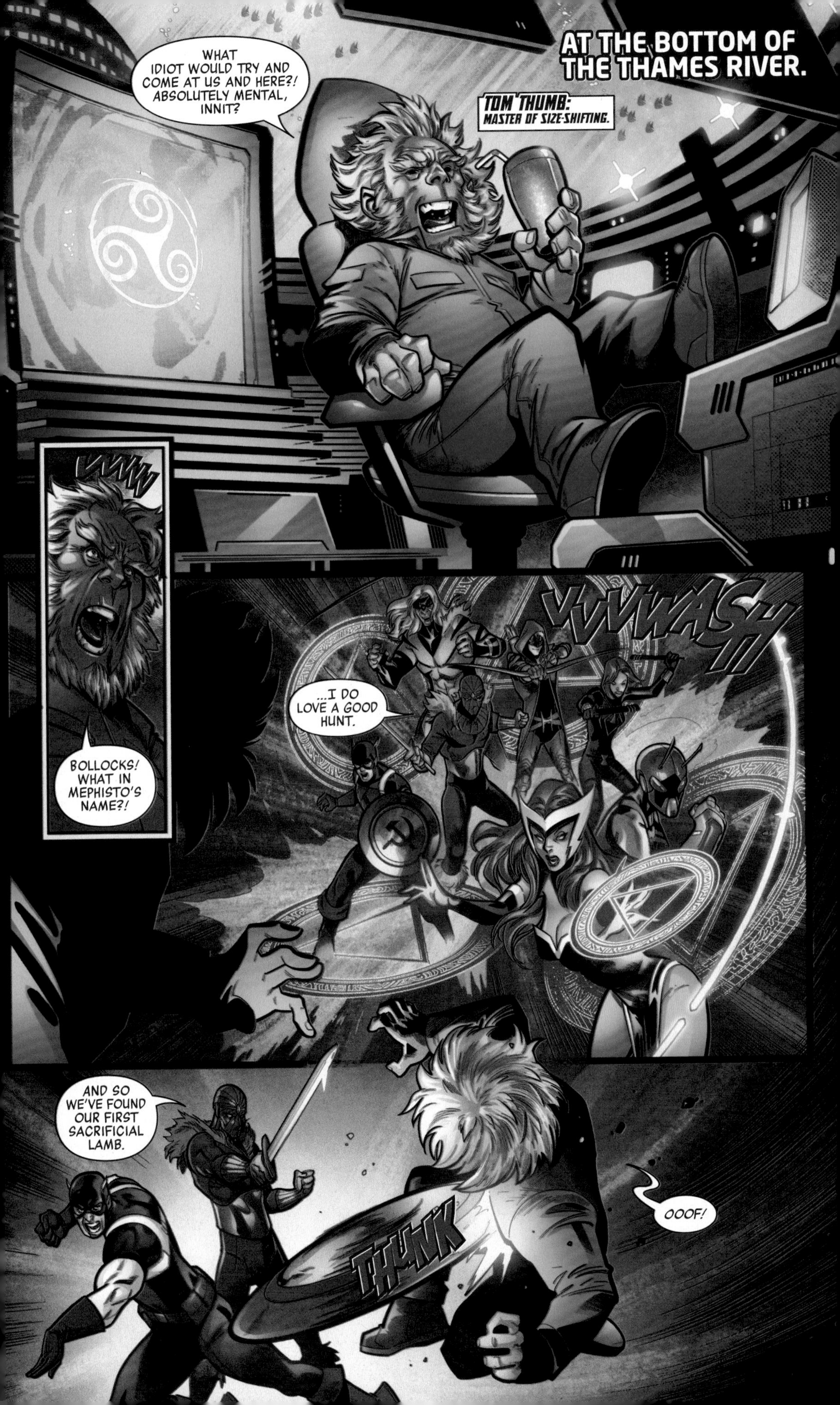
AT THE BOTTOM OF THE THAMES RIVER.
WHAT IDIOT WOULD TRY AND COME AT US AND HERE?! ABSOLUTELY MENTAL, INNIT?
TOM THUMB: MASTER OF SIZE-SHIFTING.
VVVVWASH
...I DO LOVE A GOOD HUNT.
BOLLOCKS! WHAT IN MEPHISTO'S NAME?!
AND SO WE'VE FOUND OUR FIRST SACRIFICIAL LAMB.
THUNK
OOOF!

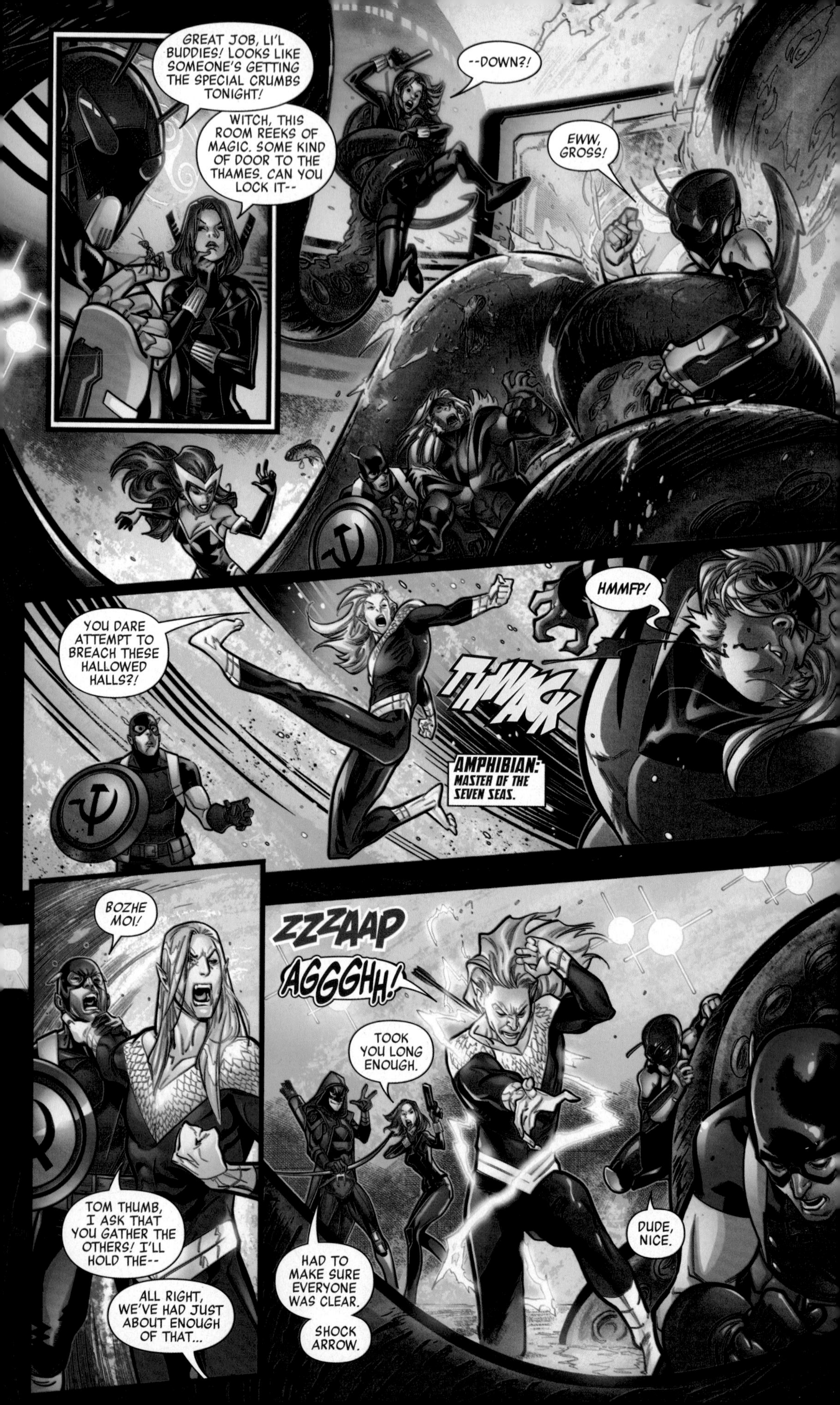
GREAT JOB, LI'L BUDDIES! LOOKS LIKE SOMEONE'S GETTING THE SPECIAL CRUMBS TONIGHT!
WITCH, THIS ROOM REEKS OF MAGIC. SOME KIND OF DOOR TO THE THAMES. CAN YOU LOCK IT--
--DOWN?!
EWW, GROSS!
YOU DARE ATTEMPT TO BREACH THESE HALLOWED HALLS?!
THWACK
HMMFP!
AMPHIBIAN: MASTER OF THE SEVEN SEAS.
BOZHE MOI!
ZZZAAP
AGGGHH!
TOOK YOU LONG ENOUGH.
TOM THUMB, I ASK THAT YOU GATHER THE OTHERS! I'LL HOLD THE--
ALL RIGHT, WE'VE HAD JUST ABOUT ENOUGH OF THAT...
HAD TO MAKE SURE EVERYONE WAS CLEAR.
SHOCK ARROW.
DUDE, NICE.

I WAS MISTAKEN. IT APPEARS *THIS* ONE SEEKS THE GLORY OF BEING THE FIRST TO DIE.

I APPLAUD YOUR EFFORTS, FISCH MANN. KNOW THAT THERE IS MUCH HONOR IN YOUR BRAVERY...

RRRrAAAAGGGGHHHHH!

ZZZZAAAATTTT

...AND I NOW HONOR THAT BRAVERY WITH A SWIFT DEATH!

SLICE

LEVEL 2

A-AMPHIBIAN!

WE GOT A RUNNER!

COME ON, BUDDY, WE CAN WORK THIS OUT. TINY MAN TO TINY MAN!

LANG, FOCUS.

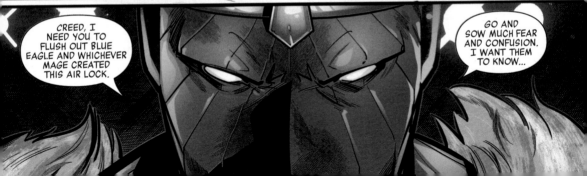

CREED, I NEED YOU TO FLUSH OUT BLUE EAGLE AND WHICHEVER MAGE CREATED THIS AIR LOCK.

GO AND SOW MUCH FEAR AND CONFUSION. I WANT THEM TO KNOW...

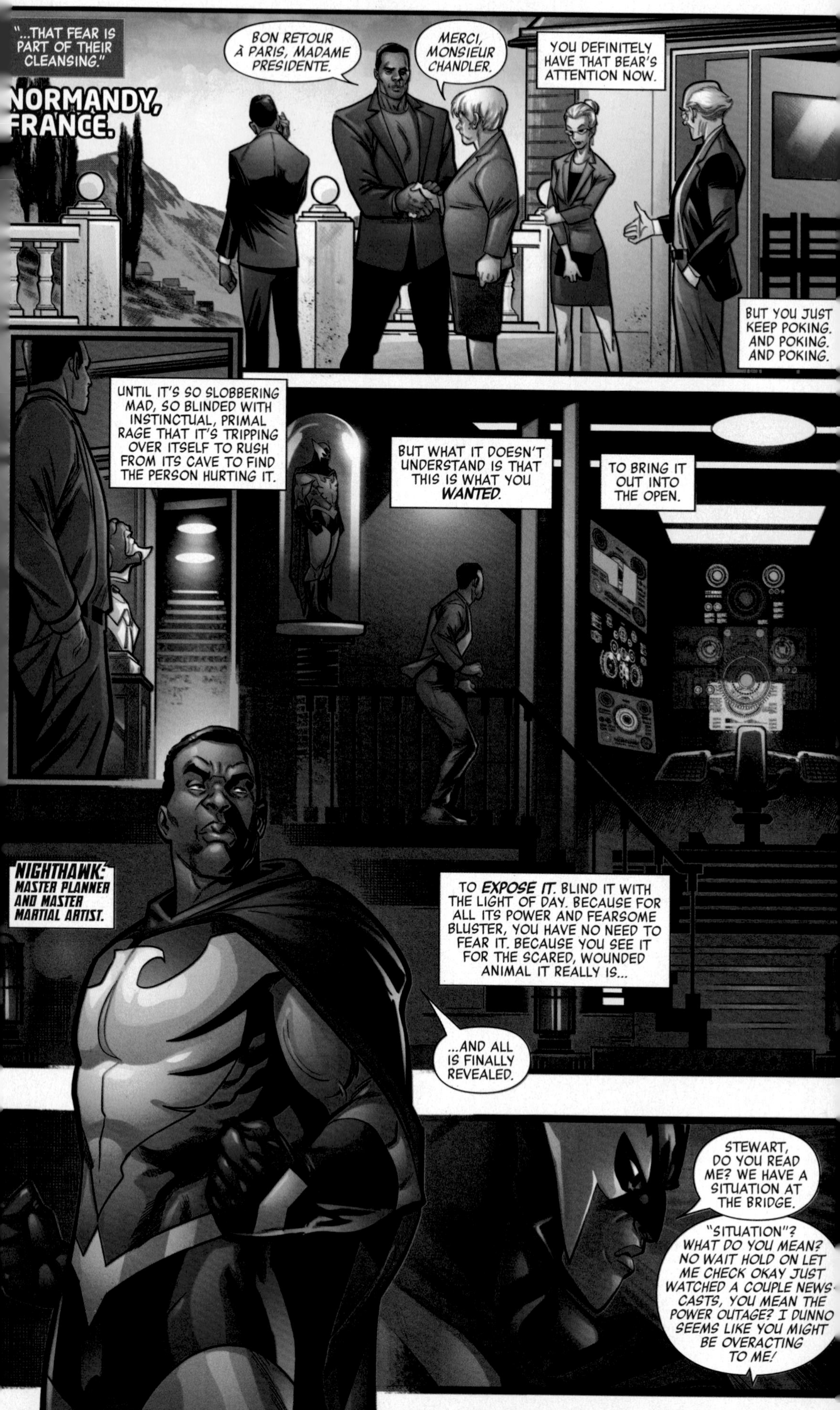
"...THAT FEAR IS PART OF THEIR CLEANSING."
NORMANDY, FRANCE.
BON RETOUR À PARIS, MADAME PRESIDENTE.
MERCI, MONSIEUR CHANDLER.
YOU DEFINITELY HAVE THAT BEAR'S ATTENTION NOW.
BUT YOU JUST KEEP POKING. AND POKING. AND POKING.
UNTIL IT'S SO SLOBBERING MAD, SO BLINDED WITH INSTINCTUAL, PRIMAL RAGE THAT IT'S TRIPPING OVER ITSELF TO RUSH FROM ITS CAVE TO FIND THE PERSON HURTING IT.
BUT WHAT IT DOESN'T UNDERSTAND IS THAT THIS IS WHAT YOU WANTED.
TO BRING IT OUT INTO THE OPEN.
NIGHTHAWK: MASTER PLANNER AND MASTER MARTIAL ARTIST.
TO EXPOSE IT. BLIND IT WITH THE LIGHT OF DAY. BECAUSE FOR ALL ITS POWER AND FEARSOME BLUSTER, YOU HAVE NO NEED TO FEAR IT. BECAUSE YOU SEE IT FOR THE SCARED, WOUNDED ANIMAL IT REALLY IS...
...AND ALL IS FINALLY REVEALED.
STEWART, DO YOU READ ME? WE HAVE A SITUATION AT THE BRIDGE.
"SITUATION"? WHAT DO YOU MEAN? NO WAIT HOLD ON LET ME CHECK OKAY JUST WATCHED A COUPLE NEWSCASTS, YOU MEAN THE POWER OUTAGE? I DUNNO SEEMS LIKE YOU MIGHT BE OVERACTING TO ME!

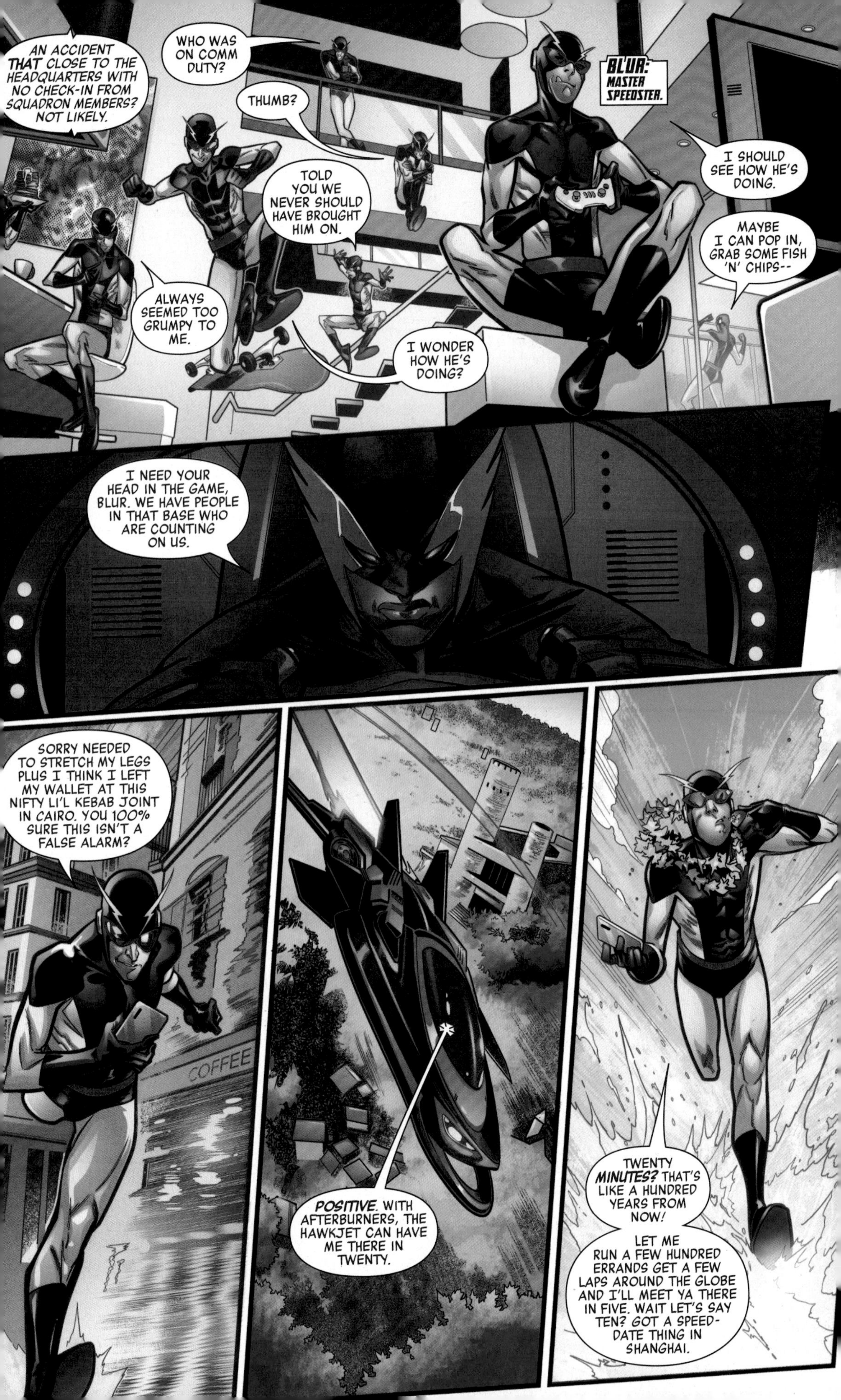
AN ACCIDENT THAT CLOSE TO THE HEADQUARTERS WITH NO CHECK-IN FROM SQUADRON MEMBERS? NOT LIKELY.
WHO WAS ON COMM DUTY?
THUMB?
BLUR: MASTER SPEEDSTER.
I SHOULD SEE HOW HE'S DOING.
TOLD YOU WE NEVER SHOULD HAVE BROUGHT HIM ON.
MAYBE I CAN POP IN, GRAB SOME FISH 'N' CHIPS--
ALWAYS SEEMED TOO GRUMPY TO ME.
I WONDER HOW HE'S DOING?
I NEED YOUR HEAD IN THE GAME, BLUR. WE HAVE PEOPLE IN THAT BASE WHO ARE COUNTING ON US.
SORRY NEEDED TO STRETCH MY LEGS PLUS I THINK I LEFT MY WALLET AT THIS NIFTY LI'L KEBAB JOINT IN CAIRO. YOU 100% SURE THIS ISN'T A FALSE ALARM?
COFFEE
POSITIVE. WITH AFTERBURNERS, THE HAWKJET CAN HAVE ME THERE IN TWENTY.
TWENTY MINUTES? THAT'S LIKE A HUNDRED YEARS FROM NOW!
LET ME RUN A FEW HUNDRED ERRANDS GET A FEW LAPS AROUND THE GLOBE AND I'LL MEET YA THERE IN FIVE. WAIT LET'S SAY TEN? GOT A SPEED-DATE THING IN SHANGHAI.

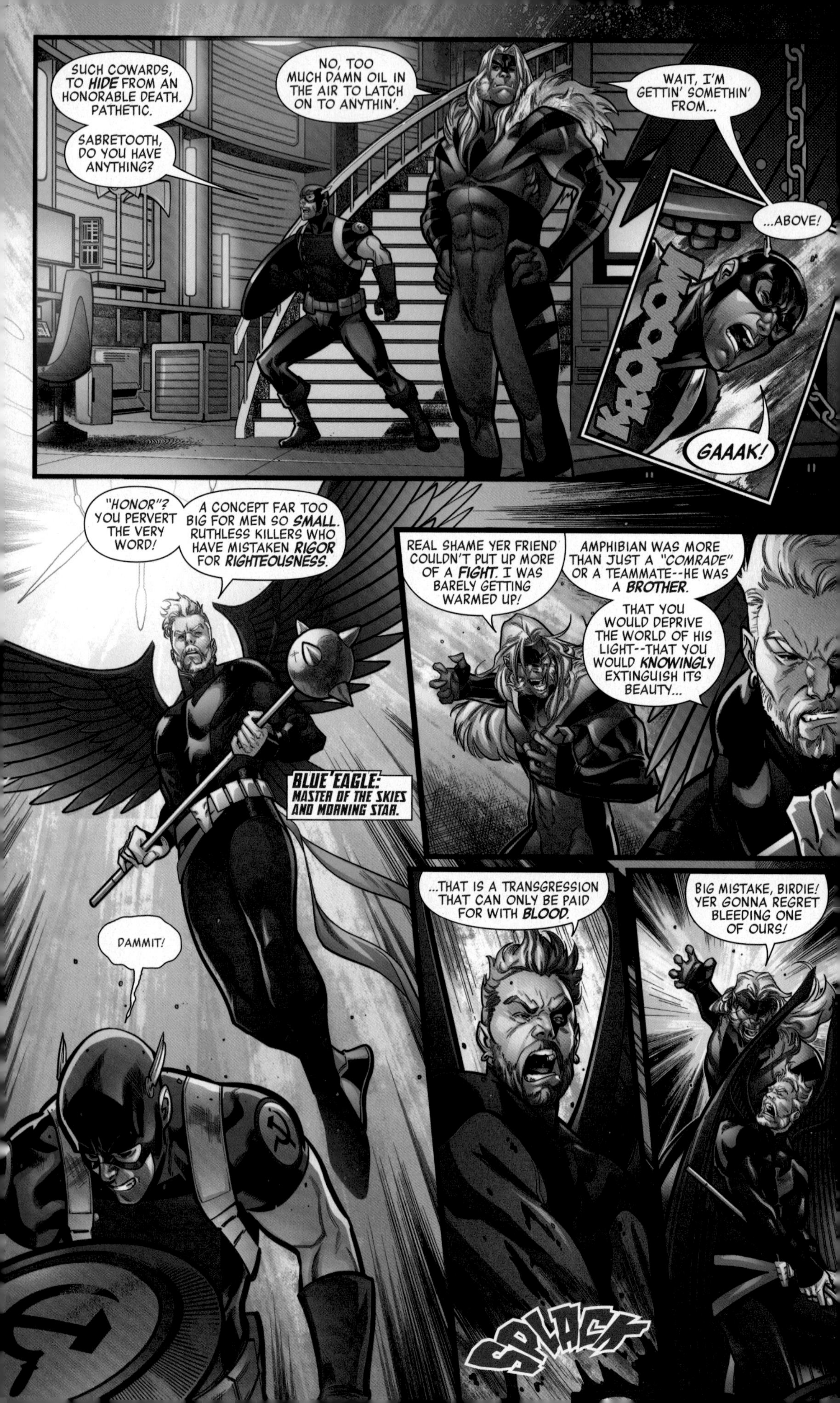
SUCH COWARDS, TO HIDE FROM AN HONORABLE DEATH. PATHETIC.
SABRETOOTH, DO YOU HAVE ANYTHING?
NO, TOO MUCH DAMN OIL IN THE AIR TO LATCH ON TO ANYTHIN'.
WAIT, I'M GETTIN' SOMETHIN' FROM...
...ABOVE!
KROOOM
GAAAK!
"HONOR"? YOU PERVERT THE VERY WORD!
A CONCEPT FAR TOO BIG FOR MEN SO SMALL. RUTHLESS KILLERS WHO HAVE MISTAKEN RIGOR FOR RIGHTEOUSNESS.
BLUE EAGLE: MASTER OF THE SKIES AND MORNING STAR.
DAMMIT!
REAL SHAME YER FRIEND COULDN'T PUT UP MORE OF A FIGHT. I WAS BARELY GETTING WARMED UP!
AMPHIBIAN WAS MORE THAN JUST A "COMRADE" OR A TEAMMATE--HE WAS A BROTHER.
THAT YOU WOULD DEPRIVE THE WORLD OF HIS LIGHT--THAT YOU WOULD KNOWINGLY EXTINGUISH ITS BEAUTY...
...THAT IS A TRANSGRESSION THAT CAN ONLY BE PAID FOR WITH BLOOD.
BIG MISTAKE, BIRDIE! YER GONNA REGRET BLEEDING ONE OF OURS!
SPLACK

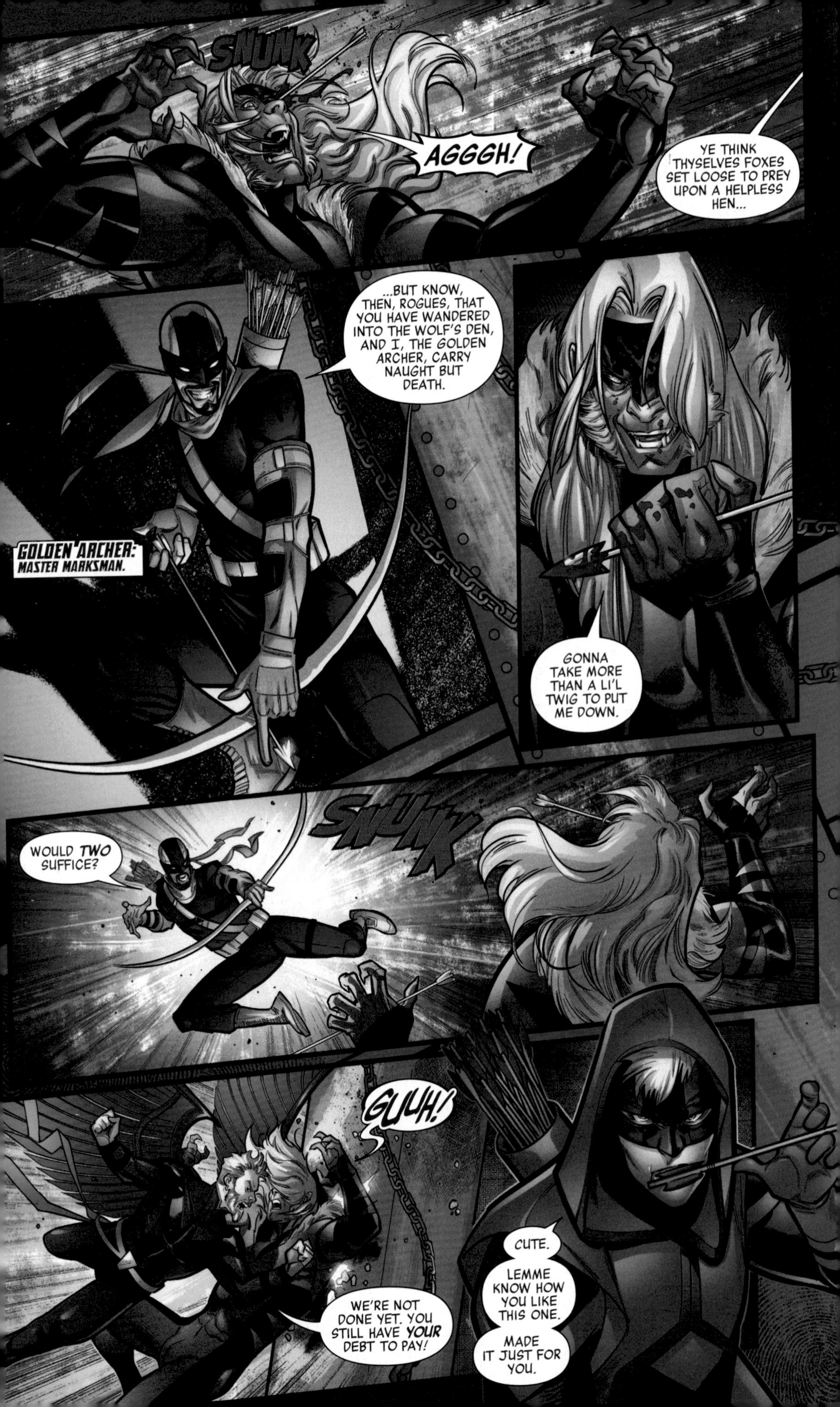
SNUNK
AGGGH!
YE THINK THYSELVES FOXES SET LOOSE TO PREY UPON A HELPLESS HEN...
...BUT KNOW, THEN, ROGUES, THAT YOU HAVE WANDERED INTO THE WOLF'S DEN, AND I, THE GOLDEN ARCHER, CARRY NAUGHT BUT DEATH.
GOLDEN ARCHER: MASTER MARKSMAN.
GONNA TAKE MORE THAN A LI'L TWIG TO PUT ME DOWN.
WOULD TWO SUFFICE?
SNUNK
GUUH!
WE'RE NOT DONE YET. YOU STILL HAVE YOUR DEBT TO PAY!
CUTE.
LEMME KNOW HOW YOU LIKE THIS ONE.
MADE IT JUST FOR YOU.

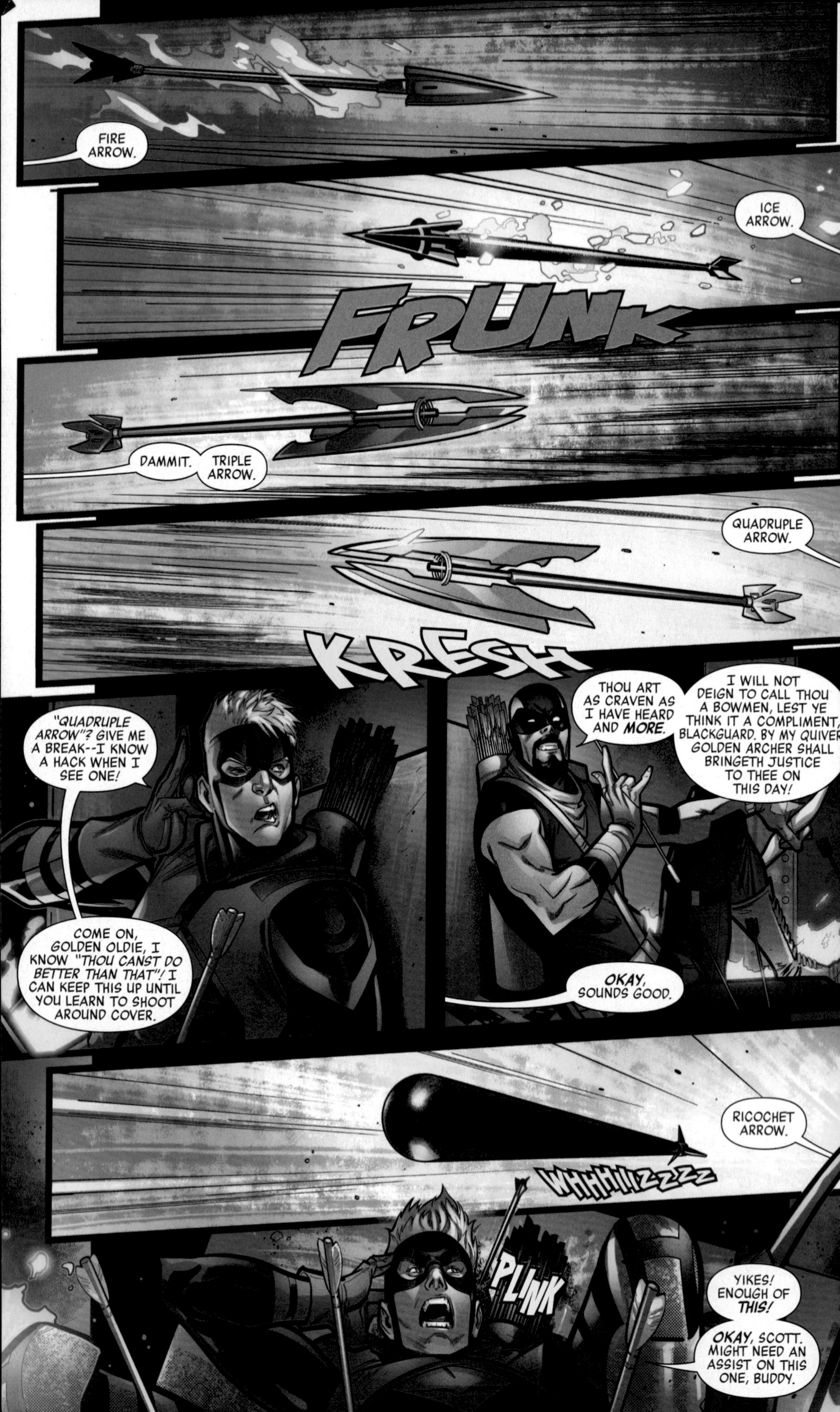
FIRE ARROW.
ICE ARROW.
FRUNK
DAMMIT.
TRIPLE ARROW.
QUADRUPLE ARROW.
KRESH
"QUADRUPLE ARROW"? GIVE ME A BREAK--I KNOW A HACK WHEN I SEE ONE!
THOU ART AS CRAVEN AS I HAVE HEARD AND MORE.
I WILL NOT DEIGN TO CALL THOU A BOWMEN, LEST YE THINK IT A COMPLIMENT, BLACKGUARD. BY MY QUIVER GOLDEN ARCHER SHALL BRINGETH JUSTICE TO THEE ON THIS DAY!
COME ON, GOLDEN OLDIE, I KNOW "THOU CANST DO BETTER THAN THAT"! I CAN KEEP THIS UP UNTIL YOU LEARN TO SHOOT AROUND COVER.
OKAY, SOUNDS GOOD.
RICOCHET ARROW.
WHHHIIIZZZZ
PLINK
YIKES! ENOUGH OF THIS!
OKAY, SCOTT. MIGHT NEED AN ASSIST ON THIS ONE, BUDDY.

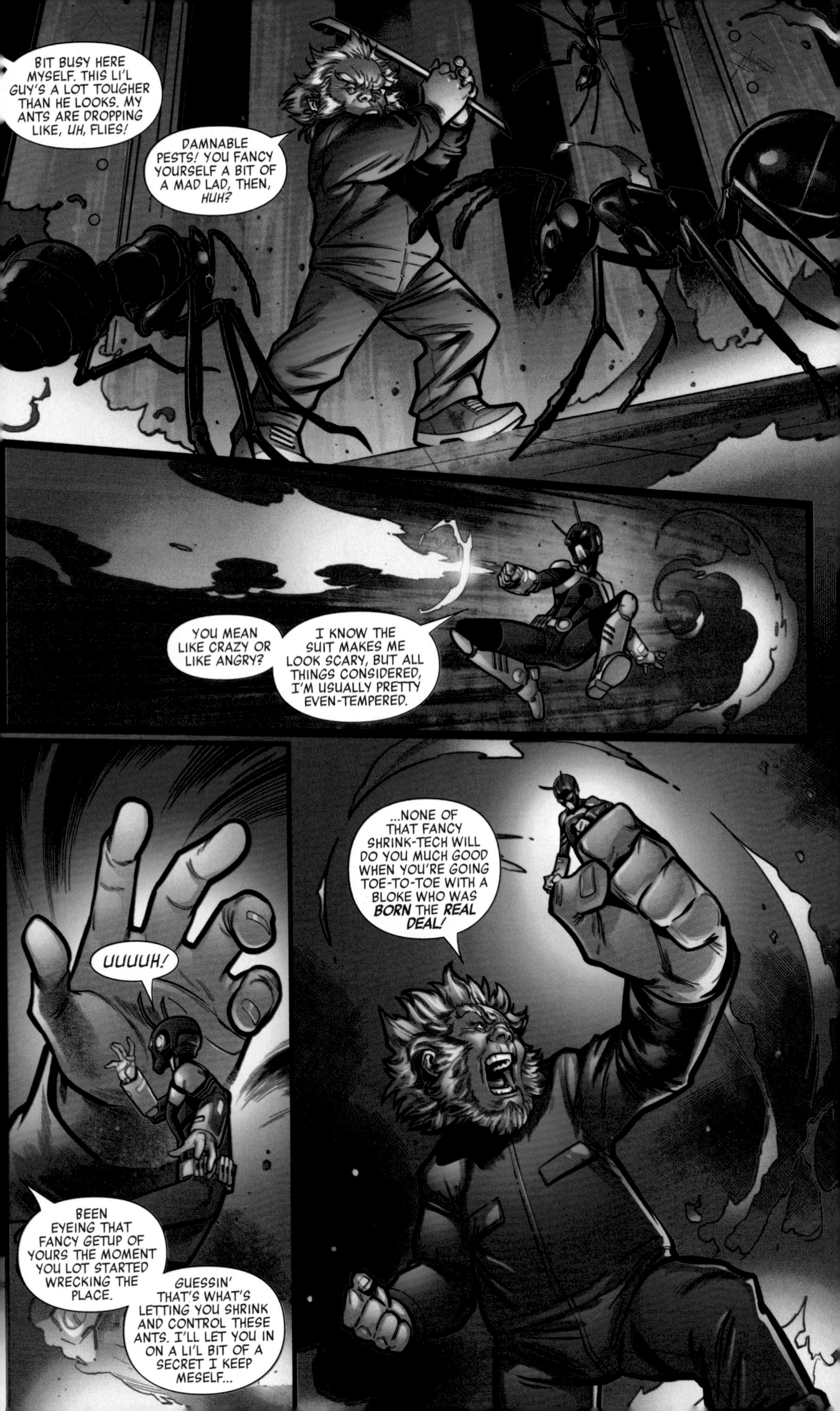

BIT BUSY HERE MYSELF. THIS LI'L GUY'S A LOT TOUGHER THAN HE LOOKS. MY ANTS ARE DROPPING LIKE, *UH,* FLIES!
DAMNABLE PESTS! YOU FANCY YOURSELF A BIT OF A MAD LAD, THEN, *HUH?*
YOU MEAN LIKE CRAZY OR LIKE ANGRY?
I KNOW THE SUIT MAKES ME LOOK SCARY, BUT ALL THINGS CONSIDERED, I'M USUALLY PRETTY EVEN-TEMPERED.
UUUUH!
BEEN EYEING THAT FANCY GETUP OF YOURS THE MOMENT YOU LOT STARTED WRECKING THE PLACE.
GUESSIN' THAT'S WHAT'S LETTING YOU SHRINK AND CONTROL THESE ANTS. I'LL LET YOU IN ON A LI'L BIT OF A SECRET I KEEP MESELF...
...NONE OF THAT FANCY SHRINK-TECH WILL DO YOU MUCH GOOD WHEN YOU'RE GOING TOE-TO-TOE WITH A BLOKE WHO WAS ***BORN*** THE ***REAL DEAL!***

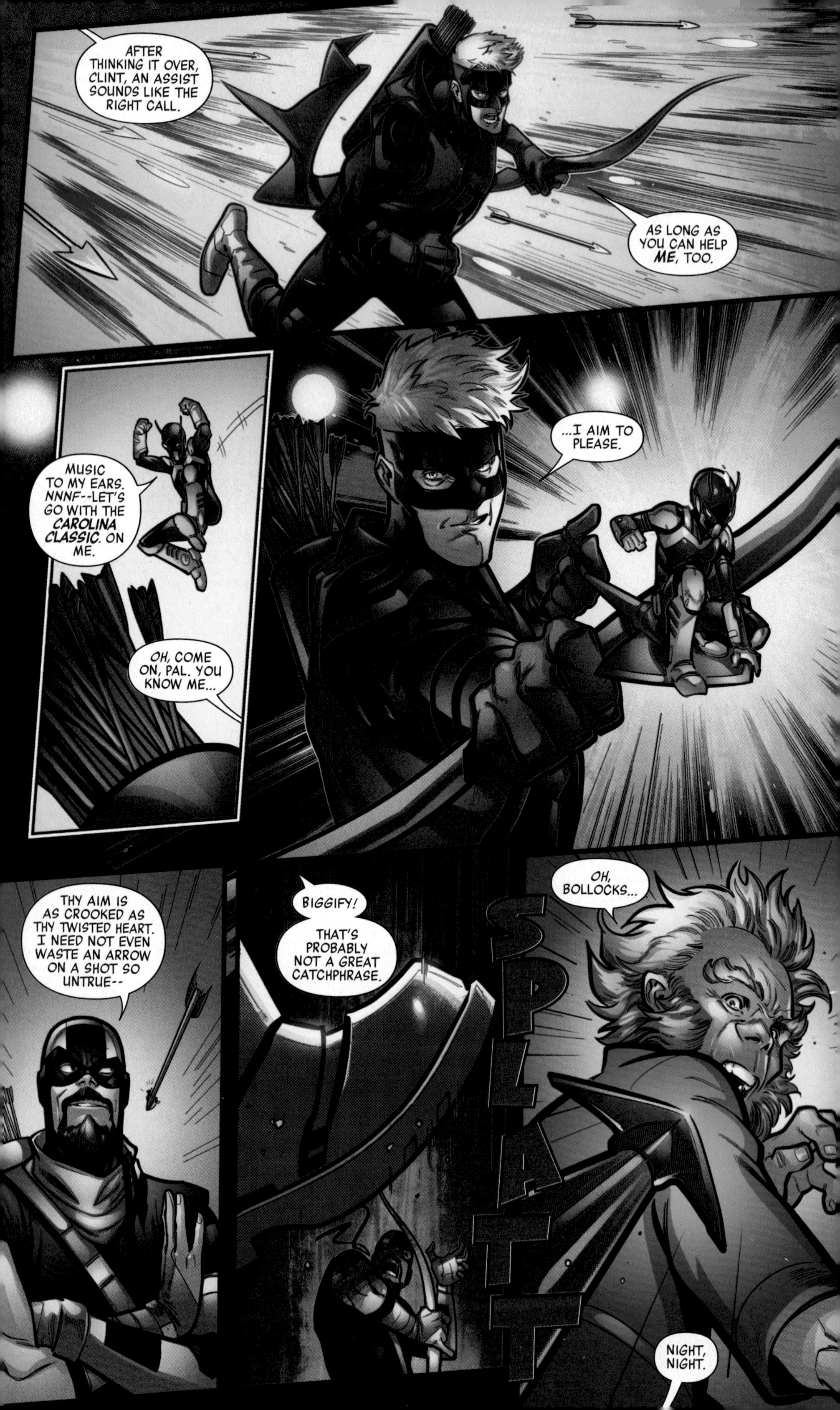
AFTER THINKING IT OVER, CLINT, AN ASSIST SOUNDS LIKE THE RIGHT CALL.
AS LONG AS YOU CAN HELP ME, TOO.
MUSIC TO MY EARS. NNNF--LET'S GO WITH THE CAROLINA CLASSIC. ON ME.
OH, COME ON, PAL. YOU KNOW ME...
...I AIM TO PLEASE.
THY AIM IS AS CROOKED AS THY TWISTED HEART. I NEED NOT EVEN WASTE AN ARROW ON A SHOT SO UNTRUE--
BIGGIFY!
THAT'S PROBABLY NOT A GREAT CATCHPHRASE.
OH, BOLLOCKS...
SPLAT
NIGHT, NIGHT.

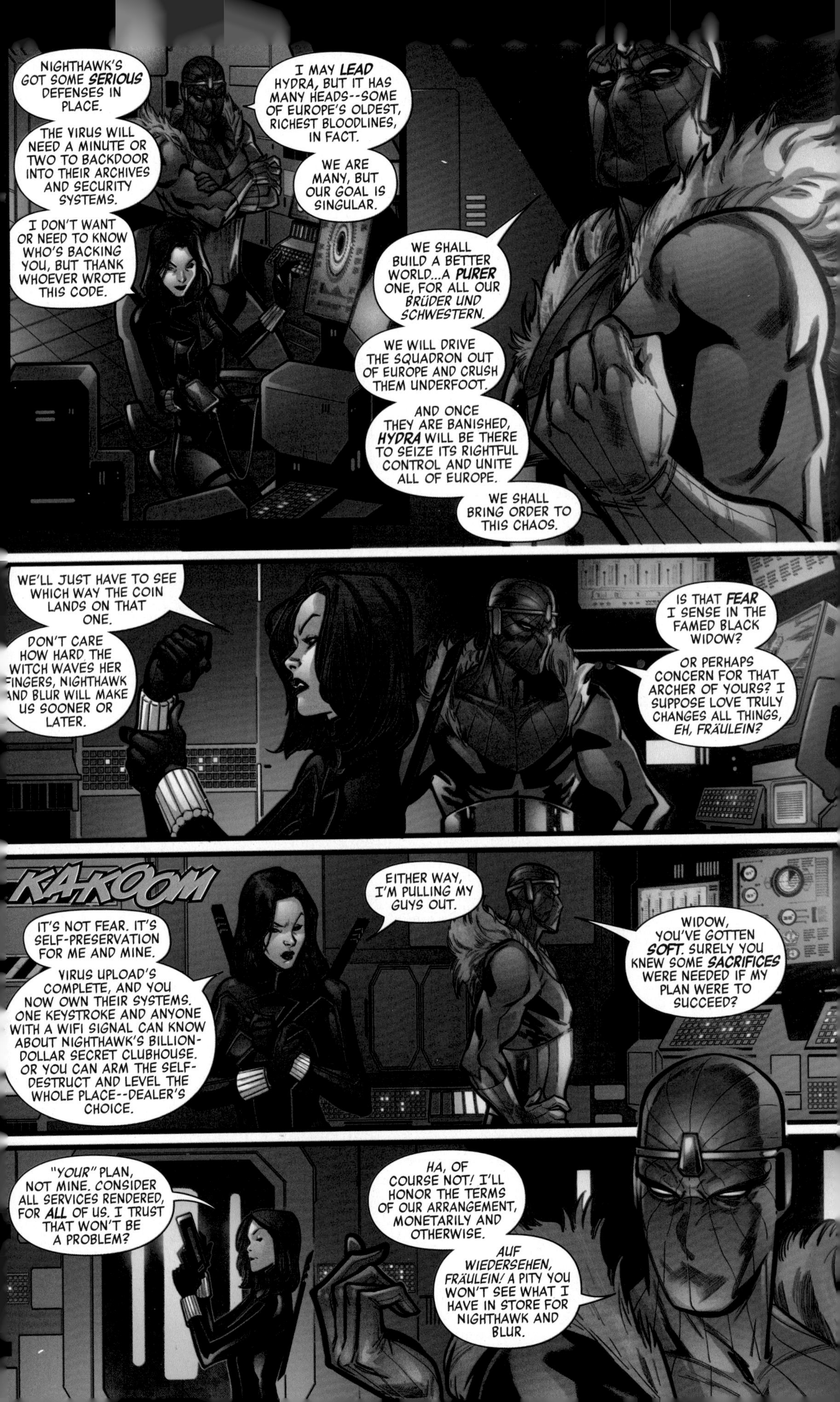
NIGHTHAWK'S GOT SOME SERIOUS DEFENSES IN PLACE.
THE VIRUS WILL NEED A MINUTE OR TWO TO BACKDOOR INTO THEIR ARCHIVES AND SECURITY SYSTEMS.
I DON'T WANT OR NEED TO KNOW WHO'S BACKING YOU, BUT THANK WHOEVER WROTE THIS CODE.
I MAY LEAD HYDRA, BUT IT HAS MANY HEADS--SOME OF EUROPE'S OLDEST, RICHEST BLOODLINES, IN FACT.
WE ARE MANY, BUT OUR GOAL IS SINGULAR.
WE SHALL BUILD A BETTER WORLD...A PURER ONE, FOR ALL OUR BRÜDER UND SCHWESTERN.
WE WILL DRIVE THE SQUADRON OUT OF EUROPE AND CRUSH THEM UNDERFOOT.
AND ONCE THEY ARE BANISHED, HYDRA WILL BE THERE TO SEIZE ITS RIGHTFUL CONTROL AND UNITE ALL OF EUROPE.
WE SHALL BRING ORDER TO THIS CHAOS.
WE'LL JUST HAVE TO SEE WHICH WAY THE COIN LANDS ON THAT ONE.
DON'T CARE HOW HARD THE WITCH WAVES HER FINGERS, NIGHTHAWK AND BLUR WILL MAKE US SOONER OR LATER.
IS THAT FEAR I SENSE IN THE FAMED BLACK WIDOW?
OR PERHAPS CONCERN FOR THAT ARCHER OF YOURS? I SUPPOSE LOVE TRULY CHANGES ALL THINGS, EH, FRÄULEIN?
KA-KOOM
IT'S NOT FEAR. IT'S SELF-PRESERVATION FOR ME AND MINE.
VIRUS UPLOAD'S COMPLETE, AND YOU NOW OWN THEIR SYSTEMS. ONE KEYSTROKE AND ANYONE WITH A WIFI SIGNAL CAN KNOW ABOUT NIGHTHAWK'S BILLION-DOLLAR SECRET CLUBHOUSE. OR YOU CAN ARM THE SELF-DESTRUCT AND LEVEL THE WHOLE PLACE--DEALER'S CHOICE.
EITHER WAY, I'M PULLING MY GUYS OUT.
WIDOW, YOU'VE GOTTEN SOFT. SURELY YOU KNEW SOME SACRIFICES WERE NEEDED IF MY PLAN WERE TO SUCCEED?
"YOUR" PLAN, NOT MINE. CONSIDER ALL SERVICES RENDERED, FOR ALL OF US. I TRUST THAT WON'T BE A PROBLEM?
HA, OF COURSE NOT! I'LL HONOR THE TERMS OF OUR ARRANGEMENT, MONETARILY AND OTHERWISE.
AUF WIEDERSEHEN, FRÄULEIN! A PITY YOU WON'T SEE WHAT I HAVE IN STORE FOR NIGHTHAWK AND BLUR.

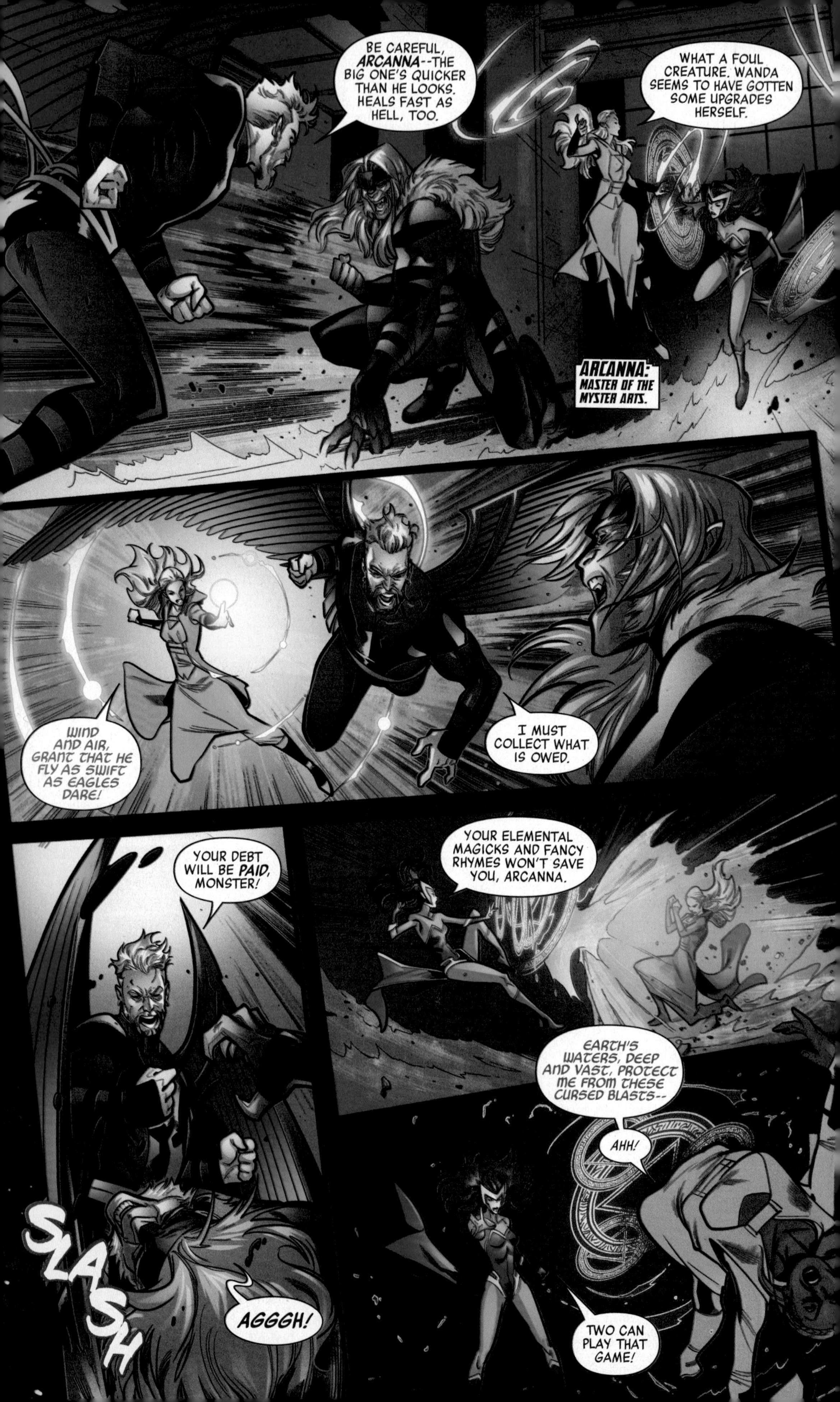

BE CAREFUL, ARCANNA--THE BIG ONE'S QUICKER THAN HE LOOKS. HEALS FAST AS HELL, TOO.
WHAT A FOUL CREATURE. WANDA SEEMS TO HAVE GOTTEN SOME UPGRADES HERSELF.
ARCANNA: MASTER OF THE MYSTER ARTS.
WIND AND AIR, GRANT THAT HE FLY AS SWIFT AS EAGLES DARE!
I MUST COLLECT WHAT IS OWED.
YOUR DEBT WILL BE PAID, MONSTER!
SLASH
AGGGH!
YOUR ELEMENTAL MAGICKS AND FANCY RHYMES WON'T SAVE YOU, ARCANNA.
EARTH'S WATERS, DEEP AND VAST, PROTECT ME FROM THESE CURSED BLASTS--
AHH!
TWO CAN PLAY THAT GAME!

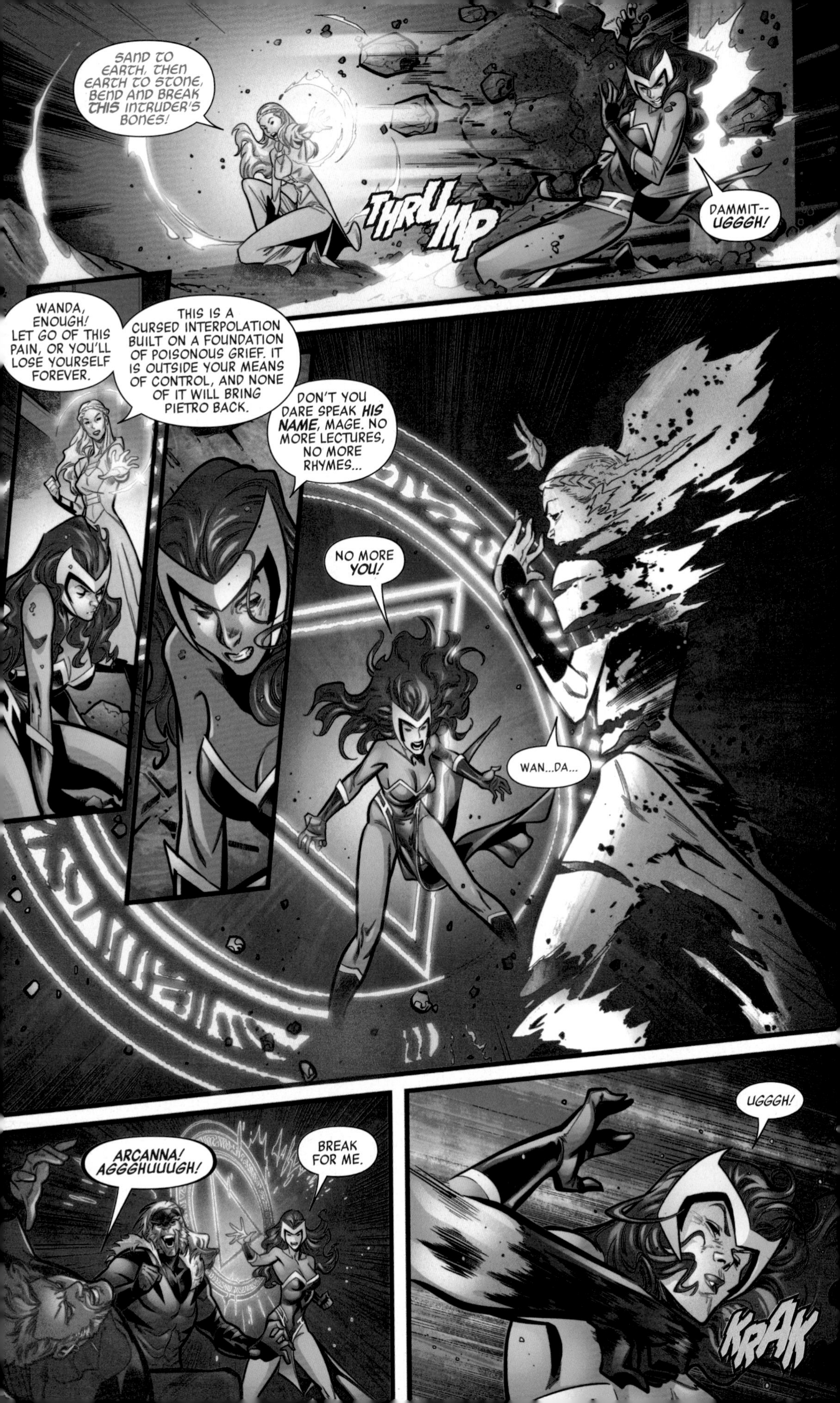
SAND TO EARTH, THEN EARTH TO STONE, BEND AND BREAK THIS INTRUDER'S BONES!
THRUMP
DAMMIT-- UGGGH!
WANDA, ENOUGH! LET GO OF THIS PAIN, OR YOU'LL LOSE YOURSELF FOREVER.
THIS IS A CURSED INTERPOLATION BUILT ON A FOUNDATION OF POISONOUS GRIEF. IT IS OUTSIDE YOUR MEANS OF CONTROL, AND NONE OF IT WILL BRING PIETRO BACK.
DON'T YOU DARE SPEAK HIS NAME, MAGE. NO MORE LECTURES, NO MORE RHYMES...
NO MORE YOU!
WAN...DA...
ARCANNA! AGGGHUUUGH!
BREAK FOR ME.
UGGGH!
KRAK

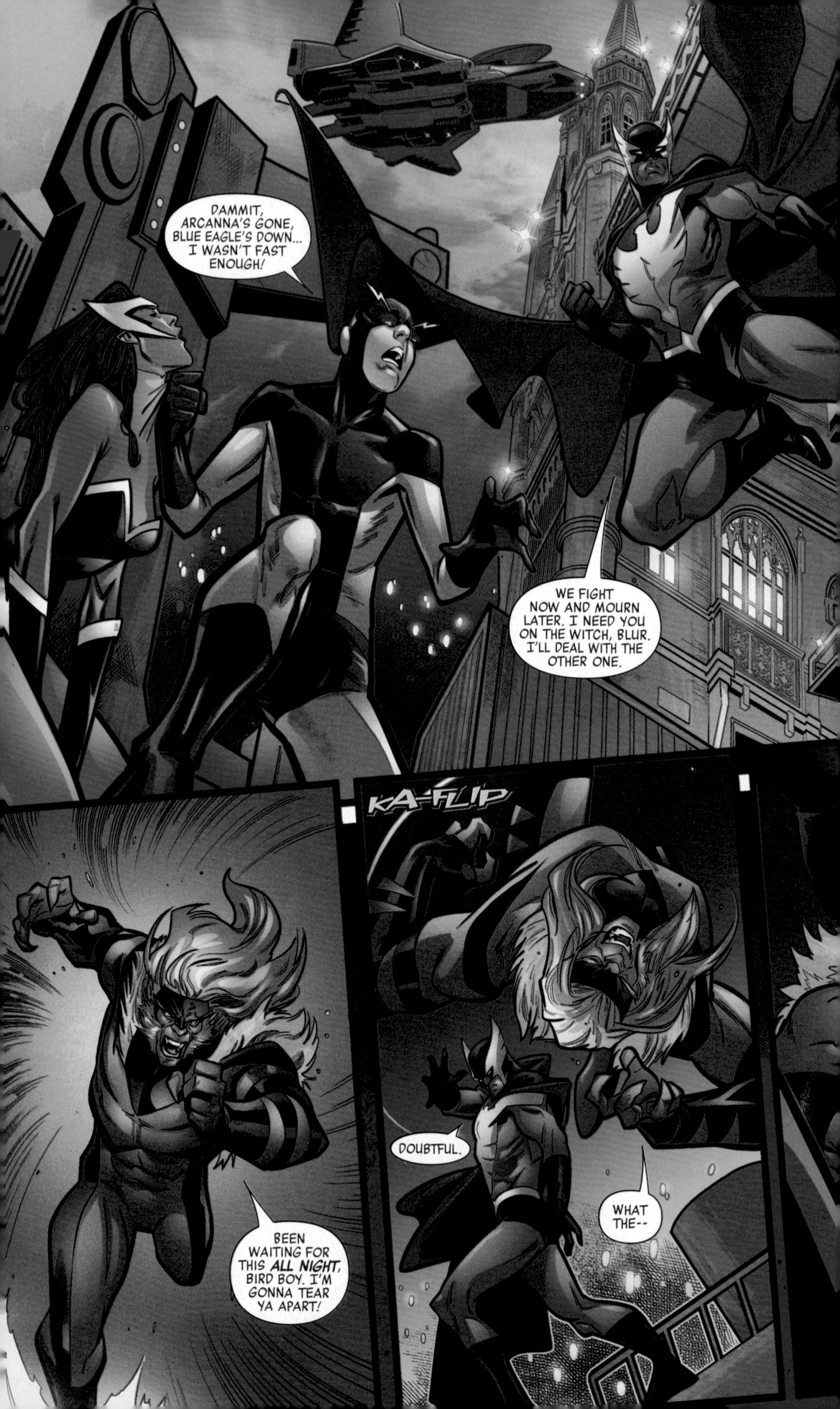
DAMMIT, ARCANNA'S GONE, BLUE EAGLE'S DOWN... I WASN'T FAST ENOUGH!
WE FIGHT NOW AND MOURN LATER. I NEED YOU ON THE WITCH, BLUR. I'LL DEAL WITH THE OTHER ONE.
BEEN WAITING FOR THIS ALL NIGHT, BIRD BOY. I'M GONNA TEAR YA APART!
KA-FLIP
DOUBTFUL.
WHAT THE--

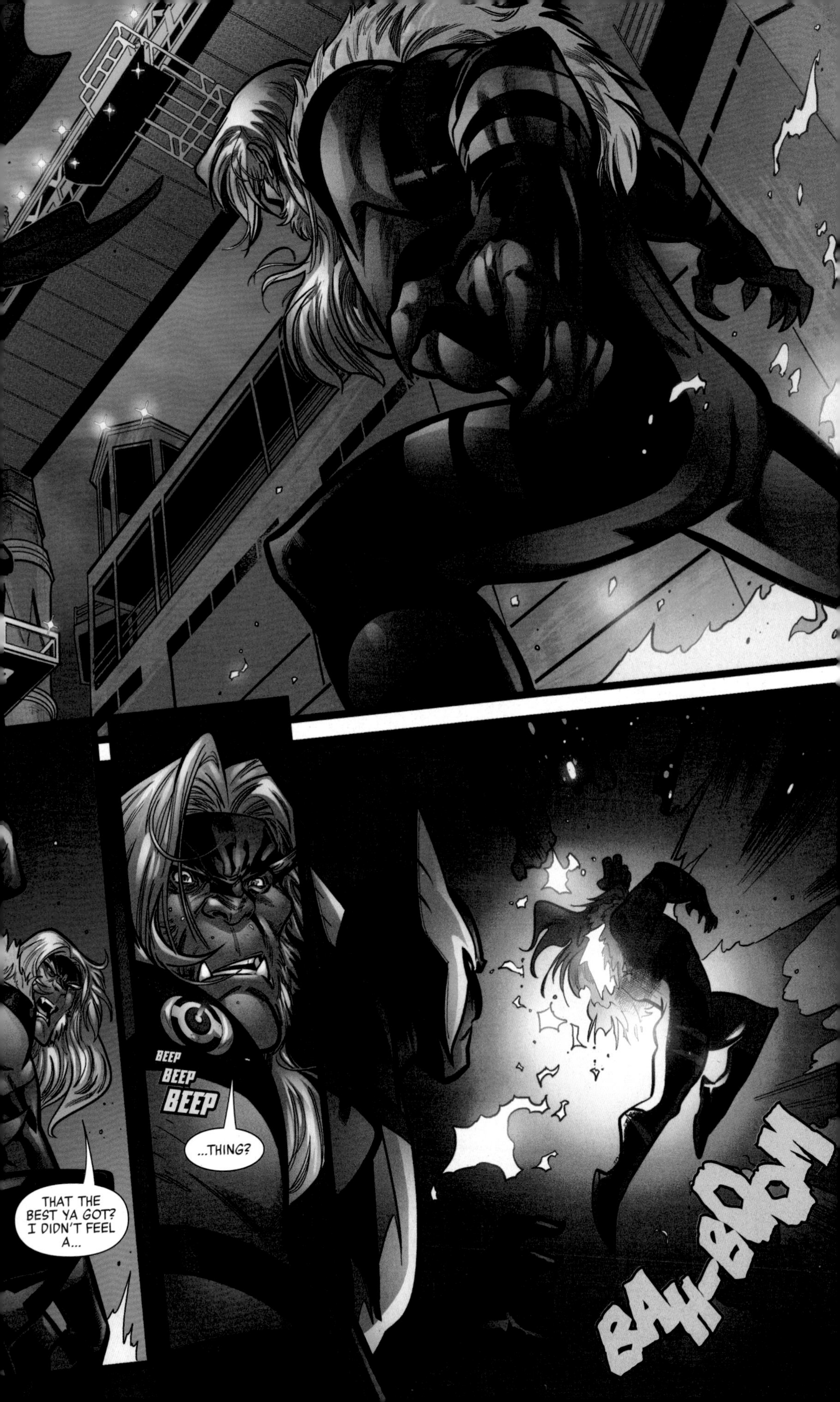
THAT THE BEST YA GOT? I DIDN'T FEEL A...
BEEP
BEEP
BEEP
...THING?
BAH-BOOM

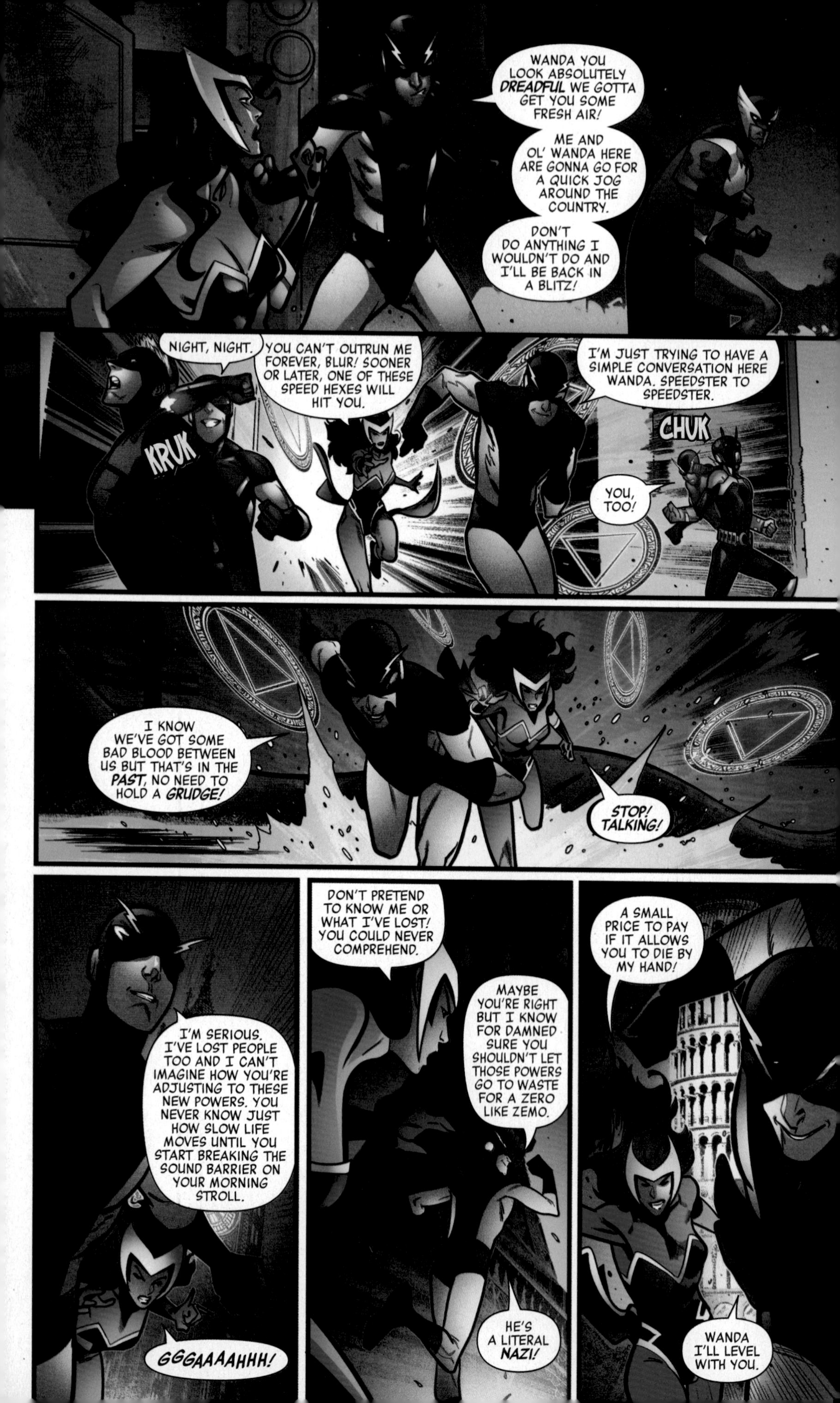
WANDA YOU LOOK ABSOLUTELY DREADFUL WE GOTTA GET YOU SOME FRESH AIR!
ME AND OL' WANDA HERE ARE GONNA GO FOR A QUICK JOG AROUND THE COUNTRY.
DON'T DO ANYTHING I WOULDN'T DO AND I'LL BE BACK IN A BLITZ!
NIGHT, NIGHT.
KRUK
YOU CAN'T OUTRUN ME FOREVER, BLUR! SOONER OR LATER, ONE OF THESE SPEED HEXES WILL HIT YOU.
I'M JUST TRYING TO HAVE A SIMPLE CONVERSATION HERE WANDA. SPEEDSTER TO SPEEDSTER.
CHUK
YOU, TOO!
I KNOW WE'VE GOT SOME BAD BLOOD BETWEEN US BUT THAT'S IN THE PAST, NO NEED TO HOLD A GRUDGE!
STOP! TALKING!
I'M SERIOUS. I'VE LOST PEOPLE TOO AND I CAN'T IMAGINE HOW YOU'RE ADJUSTING TO THESE NEW POWERS. YOU NEVER KNOW JUST HOW SLOW LIFE MOVES UNTIL YOU START BREAKING THE SOUND BARRIER ON YOUR MORNING STROLL.
GGGAAAAHHH!
DON'T PRETEND TO KNOW ME OR WHAT I'VE LOST! YOU COULD NEVER COMPREHEND.
MAYBE YOU'RE RIGHT BUT I KNOW FOR DAMNED SURE YOU SHOULDN'T LET THOSE POWERS GO TO WASTE FOR A ZERO LIKE ZEMO.
HE'S A LITERAL NAZI!
A SMALL PRICE TO PAY IF IT ALLOWS YOU TO DIE BY MY HAND!
WANDA I'LL LEVEL WITH YOU.

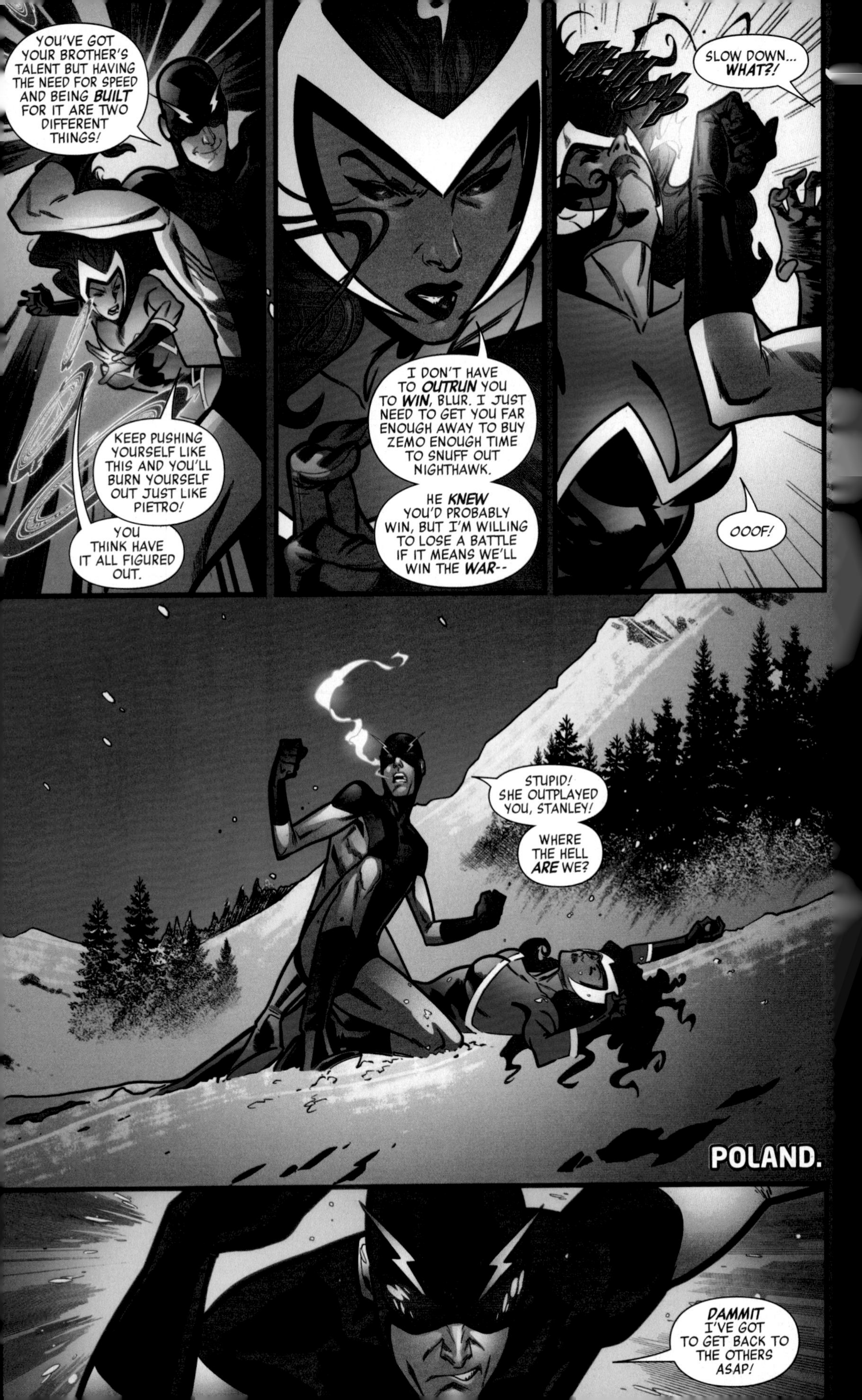
YOU'VE GOT YOUR BROTHER'S TALENT BUT HAVING THE NEED FOR SPEED AND BEING BUILT FOR IT ARE TWO DIFFERENT THINGS!
KEEP PUSHING YOURSELF LIKE THIS AND YOU'LL BURN YOURSELF OUT JUST LIKE PIETRO!
YOU THINK HAVE IT ALL FIGURED OUT.
I DON'T HAVE TO OUTRUN YOU TO WIN, BLUR. I JUST NEED TO GET YOU FAR ENOUGH AWAY TO BUY ZEMO ENOUGH TIME TO SNUFF OUT NIGHTHAWK.
HE KNEW YOU'D PROBABLY WIN, BUT I'M WILLING TO LOSE A BATTLE IF IT MEANS WE'LL WIN THE WAR--
SLOW DOWN... WHAT?!
OOOF!
STUPID! SHE OUTPLAYED YOU, STANLEY!
WHERE THE HELL ARE WE?
POLAND.
DAMMIT I'VE GOT TO GET BACK TO THE OTHERS ASAP!

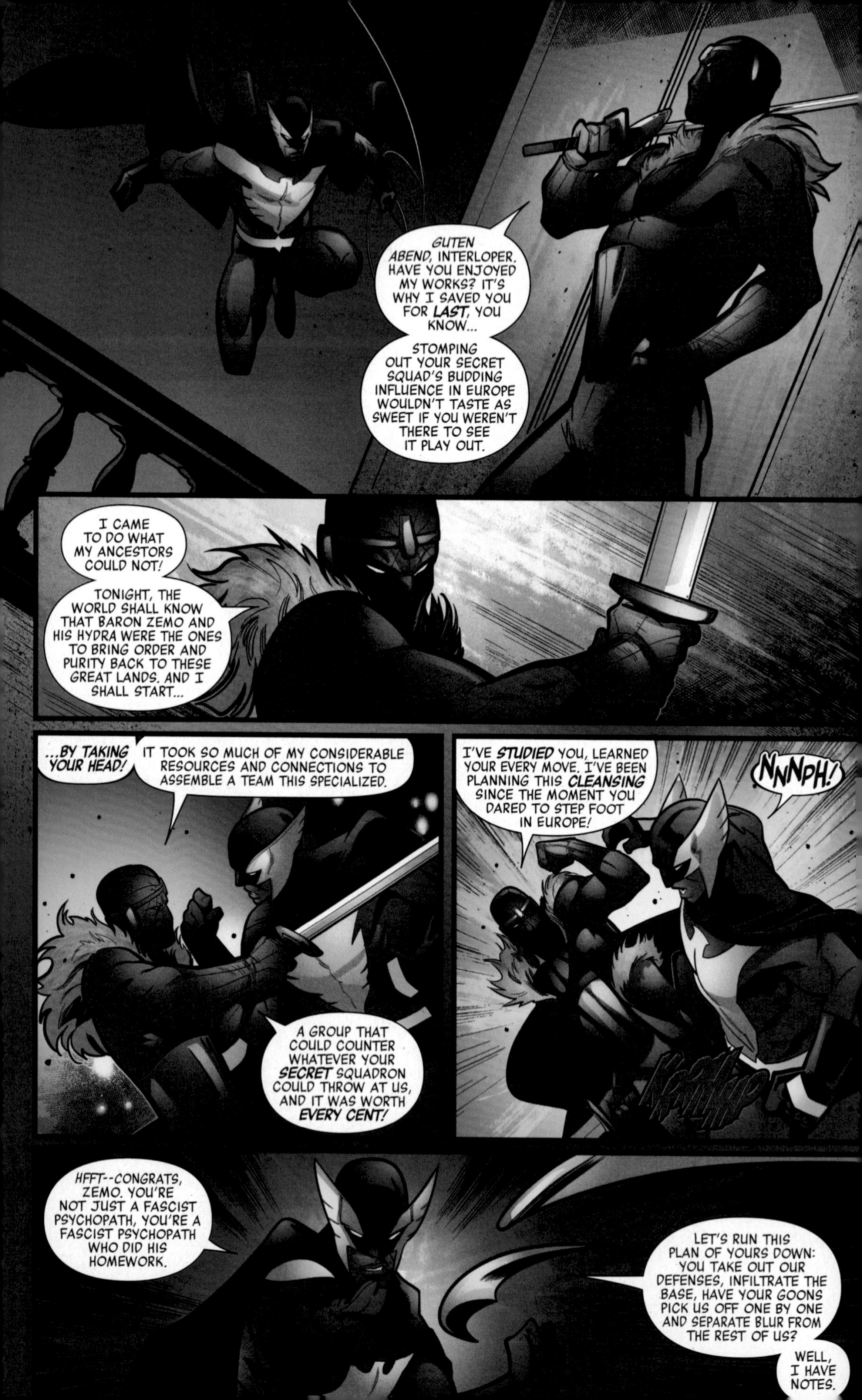
GUTEN ABEND, INTERLOPER. HAVE YOU ENJOYED MY WORKS? IT'S WHY I SAVED YOU FOR LAST, YOU KNOW...
STOMPING OUT YOUR SECRET SQUAD'S BUDDING INFLUENCE IN EUROPE WOULDN'T TASTE AS SWEET IF YOU WEREN'T THERE TO SEE IT PLAY OUT.
I CAME TO DO WHAT MY ANCESTORS COULD NOT!
TONIGHT, THE WORLD SHALL KNOW THAT BARON ZEMO AND HIS HYDRA WERE THE ONES TO BRING ORDER AND PURITY BACK TO THESE GREAT LANDS. AND I SHALL START...
...BY TAKING YOUR HEAD!
IT TOOK SO MUCH OF MY CONSIDERABLE RESOURCES AND CONNECTIONS TO ASSEMBLE A TEAM THIS SPECIALIZED.
A GROUP THAT COULD COUNTER WHATEVER YOUR SECRET SQUADRON COULD THROW AT US, AND IT WAS WORTH EVERY CENT!
I'VE STUDIED YOU, LEARNED YOUR EVERY MOVE. I'VE BEEN PLANNING THIS CLEANSING SINCE THE MOMENT YOU DARED TO STEP FOOT IN EUROPE!
NNNPH!
HFFT--CONGRATS, ZEMO. YOU'RE NOT JUST A FASCIST PSYCHOPATH, YOU'RE A FASCIST PSYCHOPATH WHO DID HIS HOMEWORK.
LET'S RUN THIS PLAN OF YOURS DOWN: YOU TAKE OUT OUR DEFENSES, INFILTRATE THE BASE, HAVE YOUR GOONS PICK US OFF ONE BY ONE AND SEPARATE BLUR FROM THE REST OF US?
WELL, I HAVE NOTES.

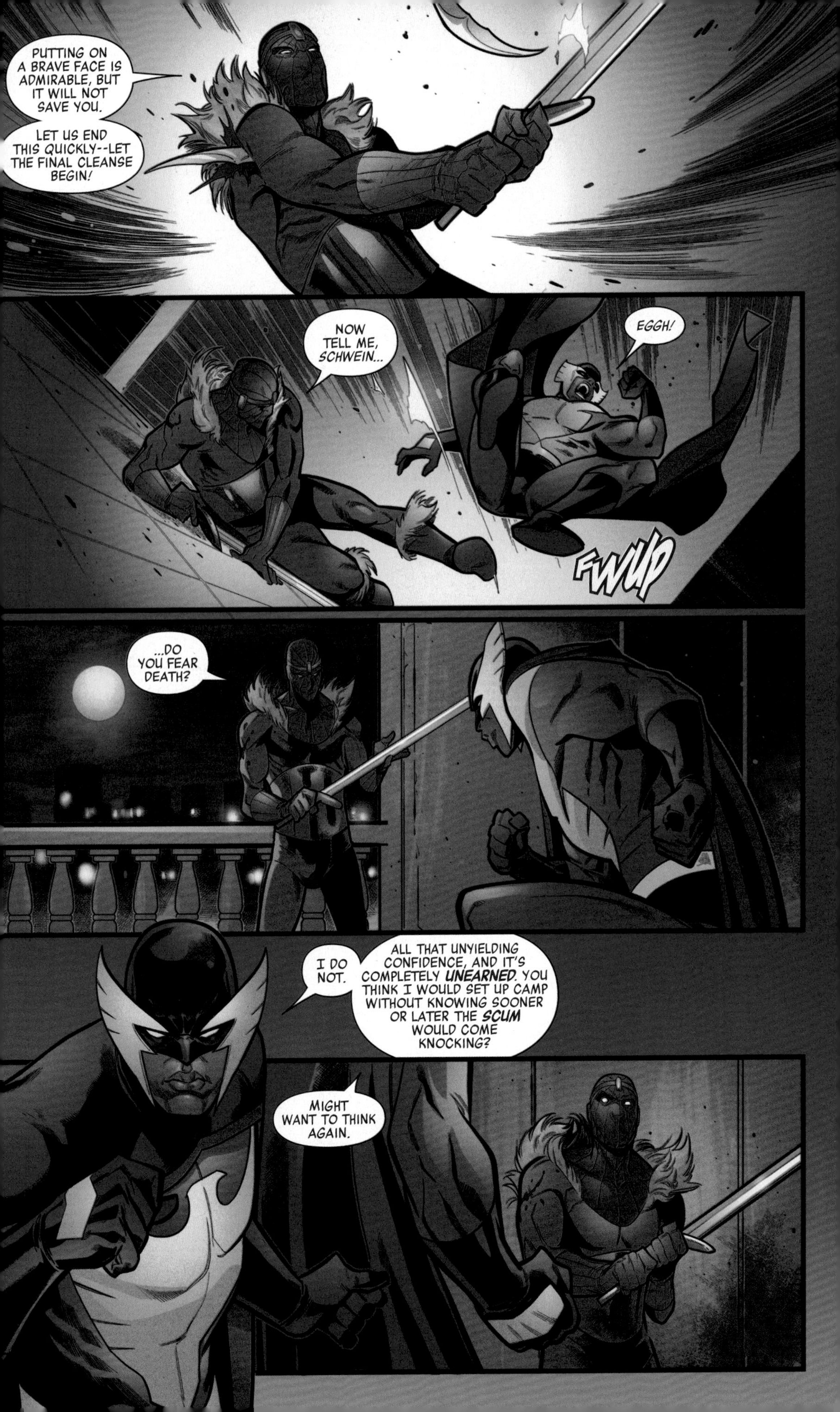
PUTTING ON A BRAVE FACE IS ADMIRABLE, BUT IT WILL NOT SAVE YOU.
LET US END THIS QUICKLY--LET THE FINAL CLEANSE BEGIN!
NOW TELL ME, SCHWEIN...
EGGH!
FWUP
...DO YOU FEAR DEATH?
I DO NOT.
ALL THAT UNYIELDING CONFIDENCE, AND IT'S COMPLETELY UNEARNED. YOU THINK I WOULD SET UP CAMP WITHOUT KNOWING SOONER OR LATER THE SCUM WOULD COME KNOCKING?
MIGHT WANT TO THINK AGAIN.

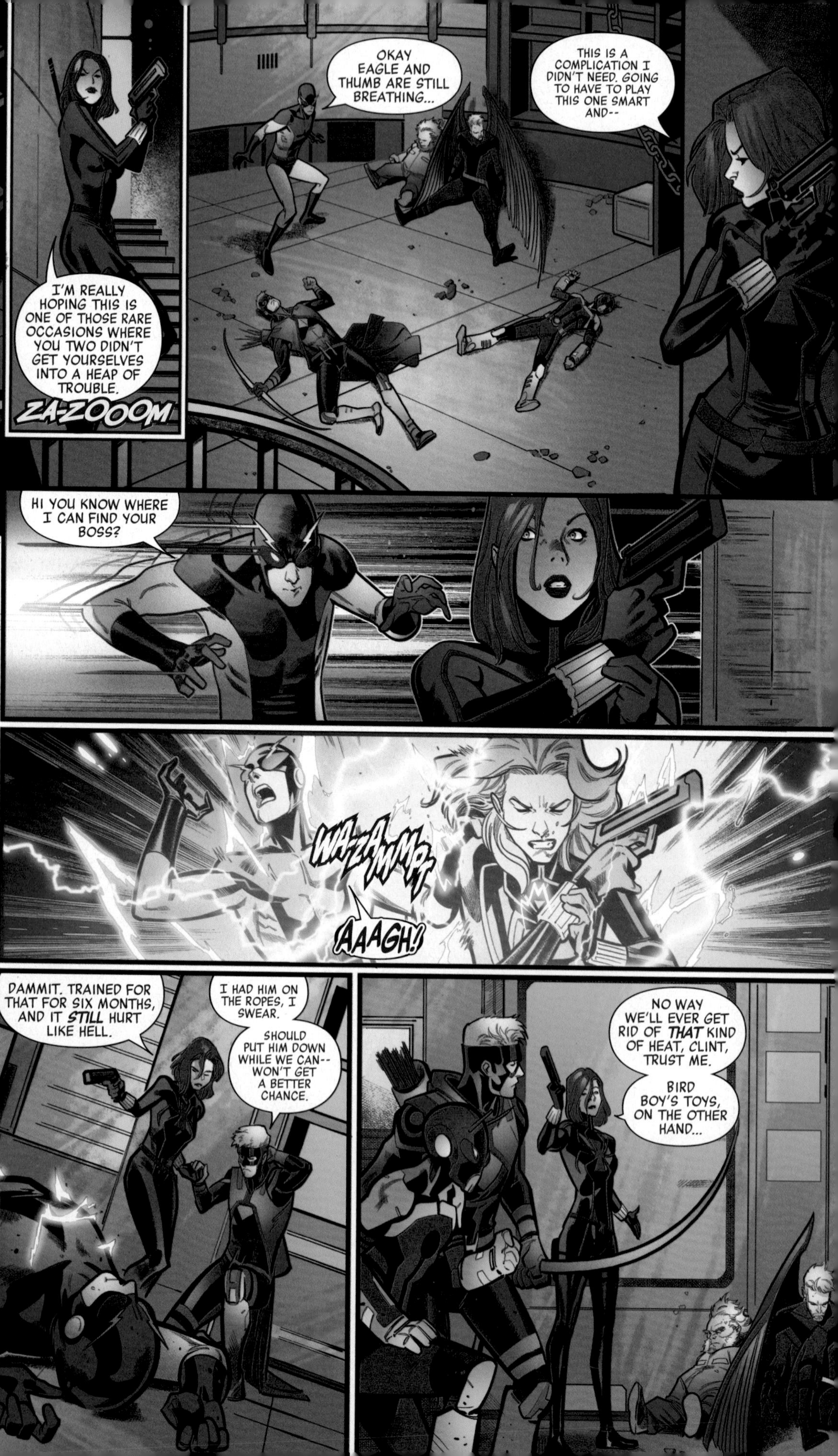
I'M REALLY HOPING THIS IS ONE OF THOSE RARE OCCASIONS WHERE YOU TWO DIDN'T GET YOURSELVES INTO A HEAP OF TROUBLE.
ZA-ZOOOM
OKAY EAGLE AND THUMB ARE STILL BREATHING...
THIS IS A COMPLICATION I DIDN'T NEED. GOING TO HAVE TO PLAY THIS ONE SMART AND--
HI YOU KNOW WHERE I CAN FIND YOUR BOSS?
WA-ZAMMMP!
AAAGH!
DAMMIT. TRAINED FOR THAT FOR SIX MONTHS, AND IT STILL HURT LIKE HELL.
I HAD HIM ON THE ROPES, I SWEAR.
SHOULD PUT HIM DOWN WHILE WE CAN-- WON'T GET A BETTER CHANCE.
NO WAY WE'LL EVER GET RID OF THAT KIND OF HEAT, CLINT, TRUST ME.
BIRD BOY'S TOYS, ON THE OTHER HAND...

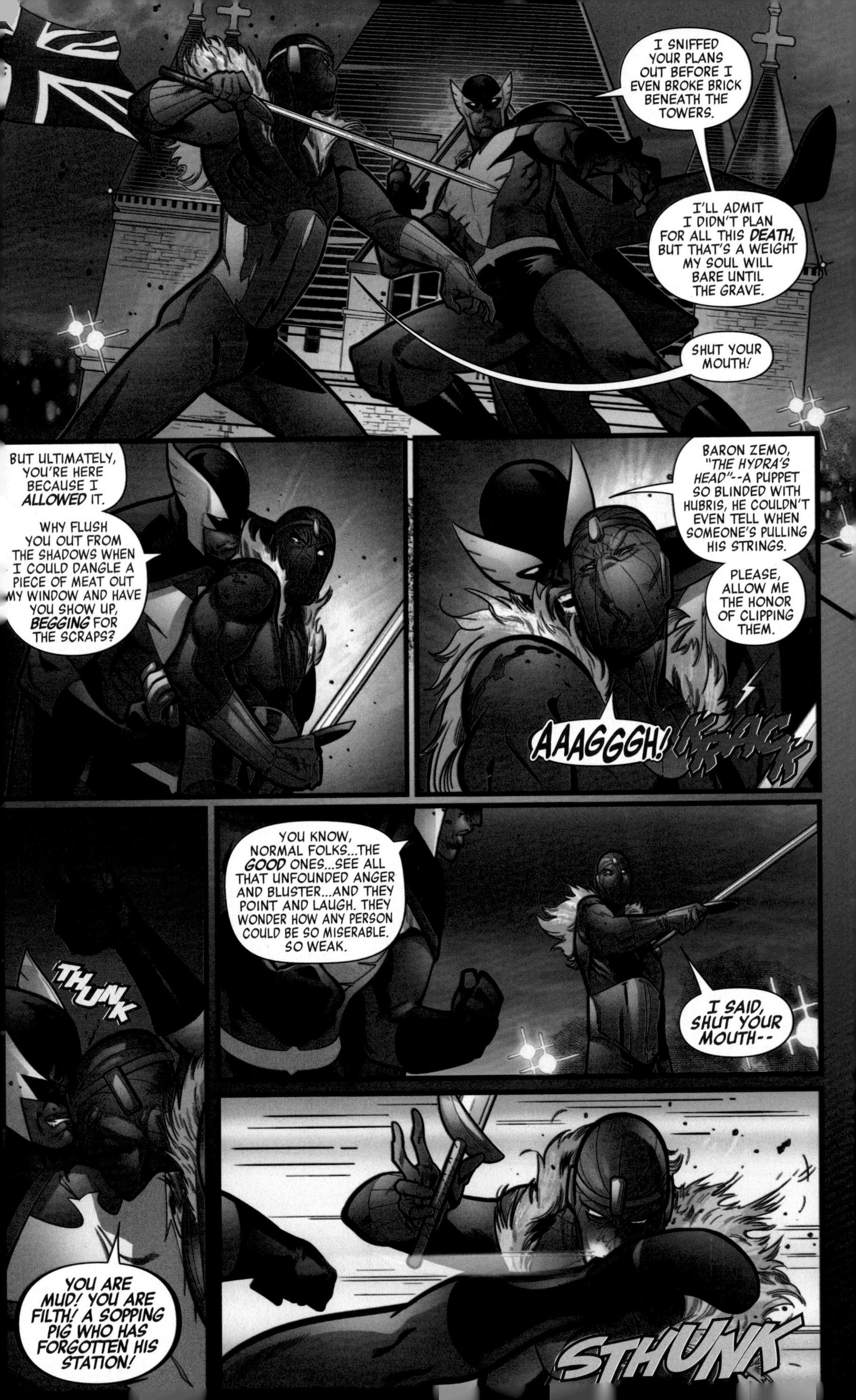
I SNIFFED YOUR PLANS OUT BEFORE I EVEN BROKE BRICK BENEATH THE TOWERS.
I'LL ADMIT I DIDN'T PLAN FOR ALL THIS DEATH, BUT THAT'S A WEIGHT MY SOUL WILL BARE UNTIL THE GRAVE.
SHUT YOUR MOUTH!
BUT ULTIMATELY, YOU'RE HERE BECAUSE I ALLOWED IT.
WHY FLUSH YOU OUT FROM THE SHADOWS WHEN I COULD DANGLE A PIECE OF MEAT OUT MY WINDOW AND HAVE YOU SHOW UP, BEGGING FOR THE SCRAPS?
BARON ZEMO, "THE HYDRA'S HEAD"--A PUPPET SO BLINDED WITH HUBRIS, HE COULDN'T EVEN TELL WHEN SOMEONE'S PULLING HIS STRINGS.
PLEASE, ALLOW ME THE HONOR OF CLIPPING THEM.
AAAGGGH!
KRACK
YOU KNOW, NORMAL FOLKS...THE GOOD ONES...SEE ALL THAT UNFOUNDED ANGER AND BLUSTER...AND THEY POINT AND LAUGH. THEY WONDER HOW ANY PERSON COULD BE SO MISERABLE. SO WEAK.
I SAID, SHUT YOUR MOUTH--
THUNK
YOU ARE MUD! YOU ARE FILTH! A SOPPING PIG WHO HAS FORGOTTEN HIS STATION!
STHUNK

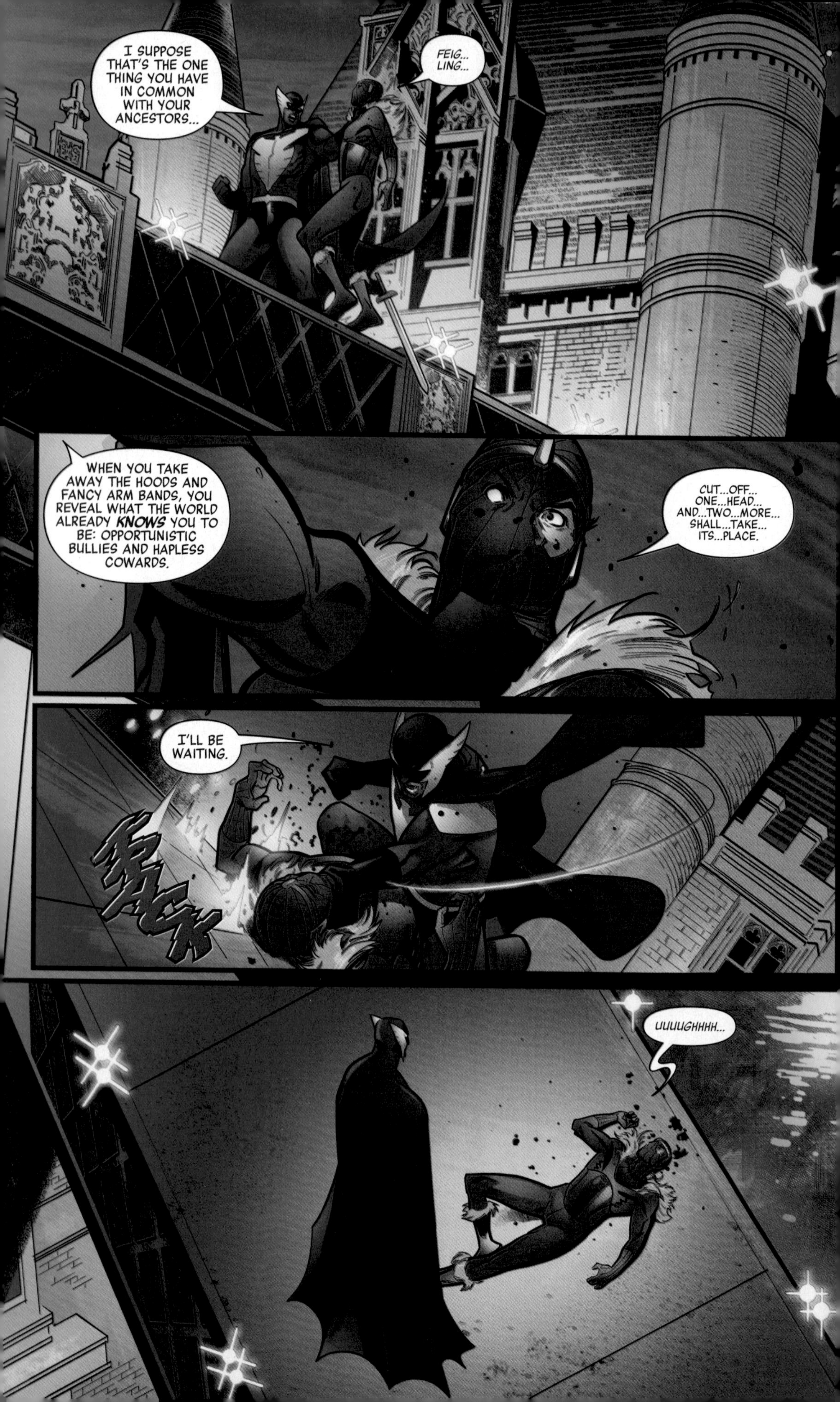
I SUPPOSE THAT'S THE ONE THING YOU HAVE IN COMMON WITH YOUR ANCESTORS...
FEIG... LING...
WHEN YOU TAKE AWAY THE HOODS AND FANCY ARM BANDS, YOU REVEAL WHAT THE WORLD ALREADY **KNOWS** YOU TO BE: OPPORTUNISTIC BULLIES AND HAPLESS COWARDS.
CUT...OFF... ONE...HEAD... AND...TWO...MORE... SHALL...TAKE... ITS...PLACE.
I'LL BE WAITING.
UUUUGHHHH...

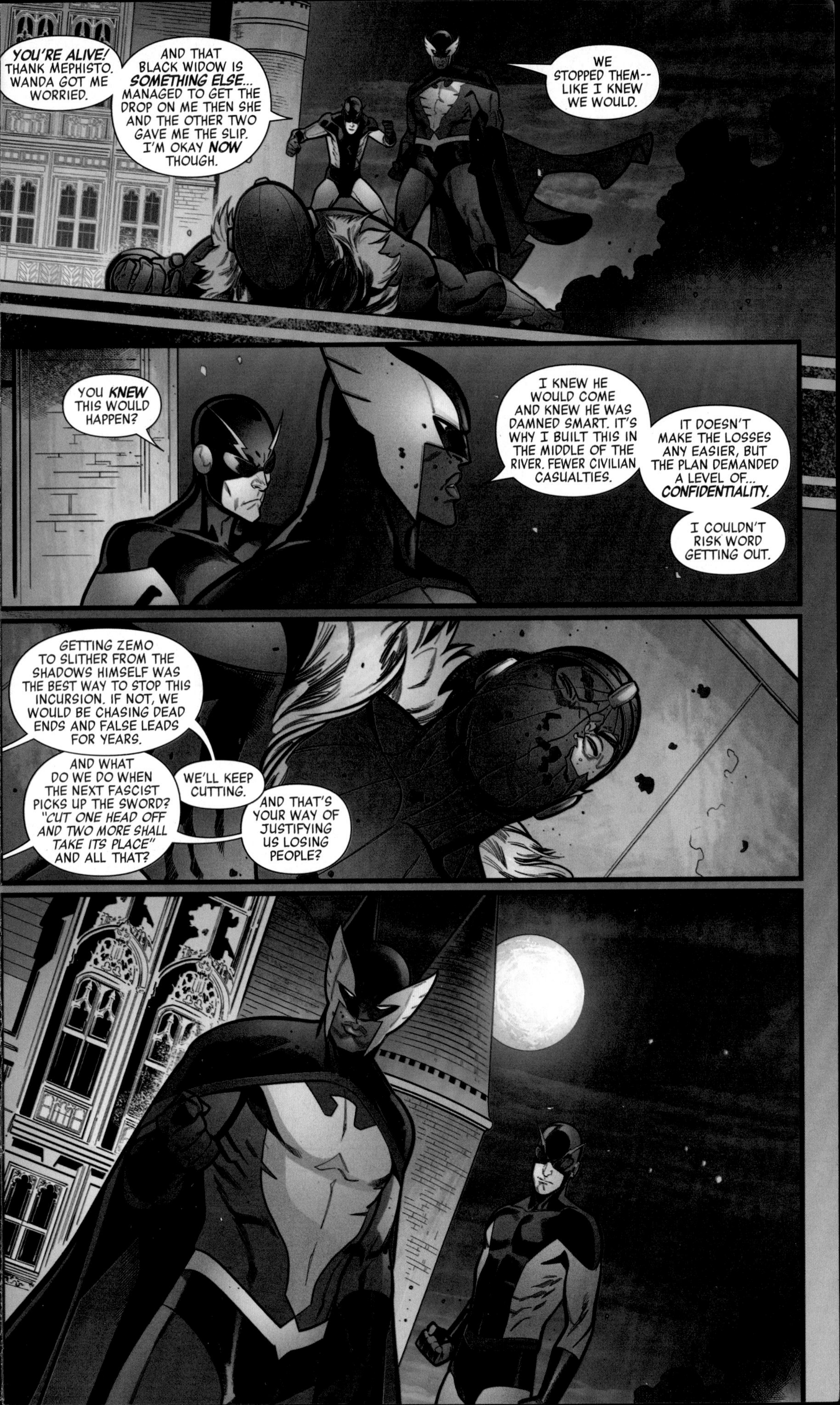

YOU'RE ALIVE! THANK MEPHISTO. WANDA GOT ME WORRIED.
AND THAT BLACK WIDOW IS SOMETHING ELSE... MANAGED TO GET THE DROP ON ME THEN SHE AND THE OTHER TWO GAVE ME THE SLIP. I'M OKAY NOW THOUGH.
WE STOPPED THEM-- LIKE I KNEW WE WOULD.
YOU KNEW THIS WOULD HAPPEN?
I KNEW HE WOULD COME AND KNEW HE WAS DAMNED SMART. IT'S WHY I BUILT THIS IN THE MIDDLE OF THE RIVER. FEWER CIVILIAN CASUALTIES.
IT DOESN'T MAKE THE LOSSES ANY EASIER, BUT THE PLAN DEMANDED A LEVEL OF... CONFIDENTIALITY.
I COULDN'T RISK WORD GETTING OUT.
GETTING ZEMO TO SLITHER FROM THE SHADOWS HIMSELF WAS THE BEST WAY TO STOP THIS INCURSION. IF NOT, WE WOULD BE CHASING DEAD ENDS AND FALSE LEADS FOR YEARS.
AND WHAT DO WE DO WHEN THE NEXT FASCIST PICKS UP THE SWORD? "CUT ONE HEAD OFF AND TWO MORE SHALL TAKE ITS PLACE" AND ALL THAT?
WE'LL KEEP CUTTING.
AND THAT'S YOUR WAY OF JUSTIFYING US LOSING PEOPLE?

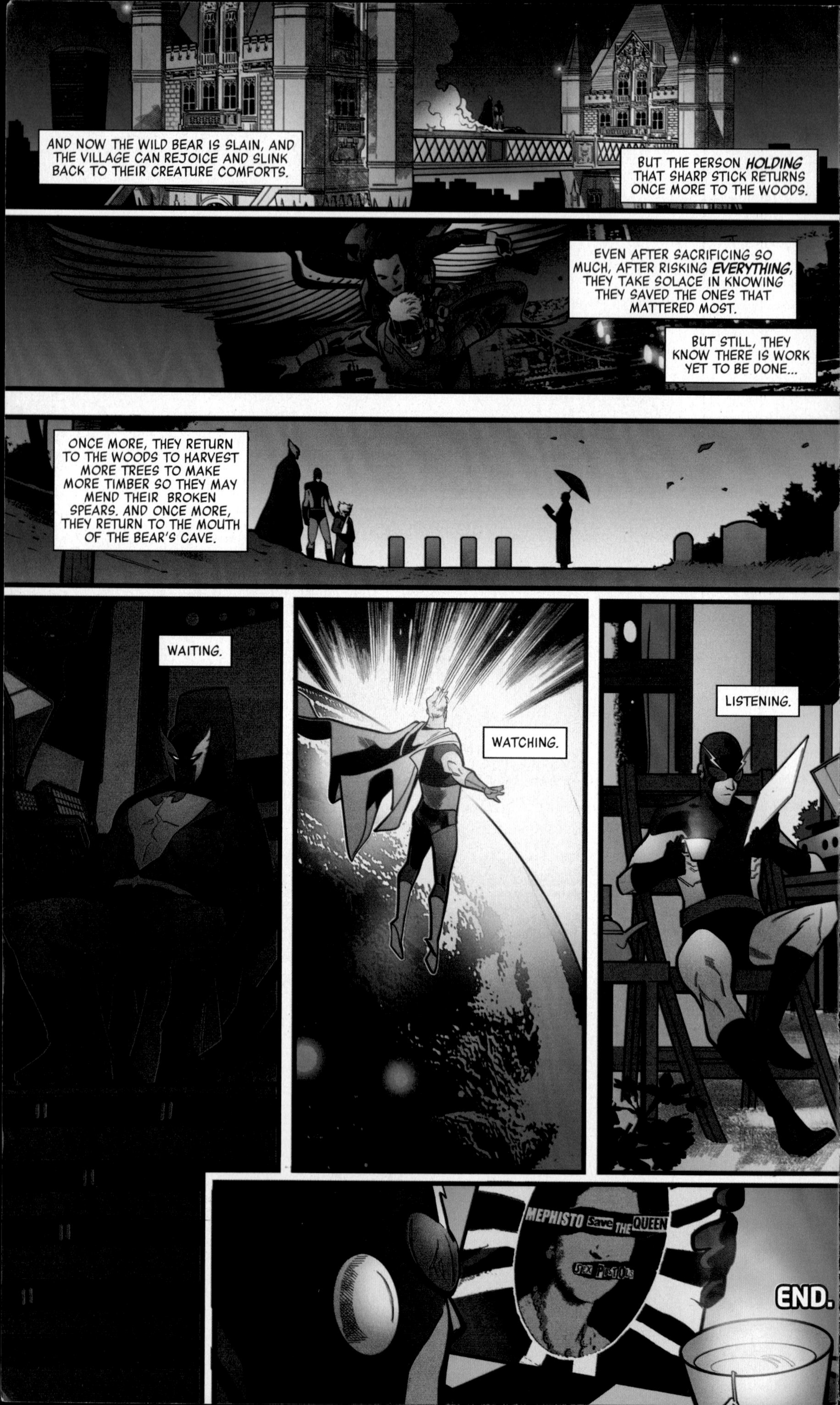

AND NOW THE WILD BEAR IS SLAIN, AND THE VILLAGE CAN REJOICE AND SLINK BACK TO THEIR CREATURE COMFORTS.
BUT THE PERSON HOLDING THAT SHARP STICK RETURNS ONCE MORE TO THE WOODS.
EVEN AFTER SACRIFICING SO MUCH, AFTER RISKING EVERYTHING, THEY TAKE SOLACE IN KNOWING THEY SAVED THE ONES THAT MATTERED MOST.
BUT STILL, THEY KNOW THERE IS WORK YET TO BE DONE...
ONCE MORE, THEY RETURN TO THE WOODS TO HARVEST MORE TREES TO MAKE MORE TIMBER SO THEY MAY MEND THEIR BROKEN SPEARS. AND ONCE MORE, THEY RETURN TO THE MOUTH OF THE BEAR'S CAVE.
WAITING.
WATCHING.
LISTENING.
MEPHISTO Save THE QUEEN
SEX PISTOLS
END.

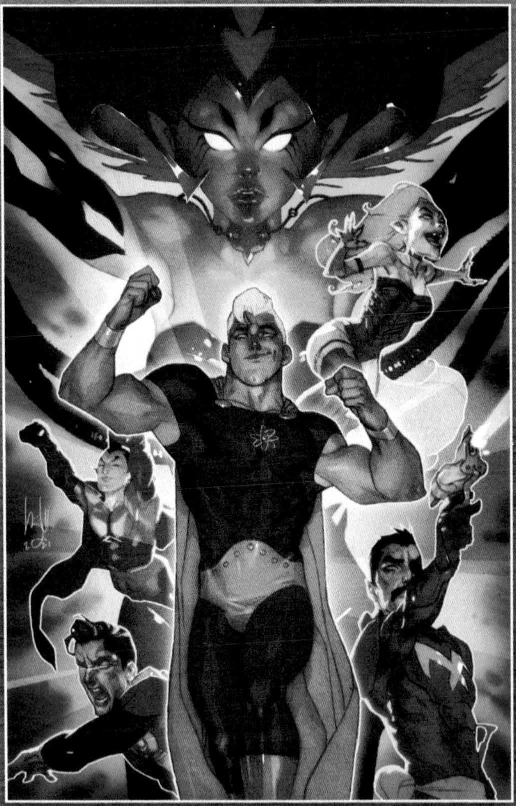

BEN **CALDWELL**

HEROES REBORN: HYPERION & THE IMPERIAL GUARD Nº1 VARIANT

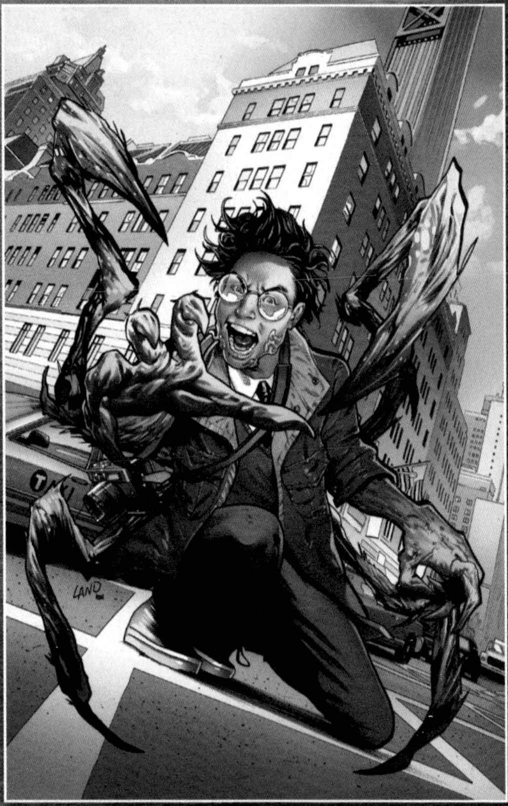

GREG **LAND** & FRANK **D'ARMATA**

HEROES REBORN: PETER PARKER, THE AMAZING SHUTTERBUG Nº1 VARIANT

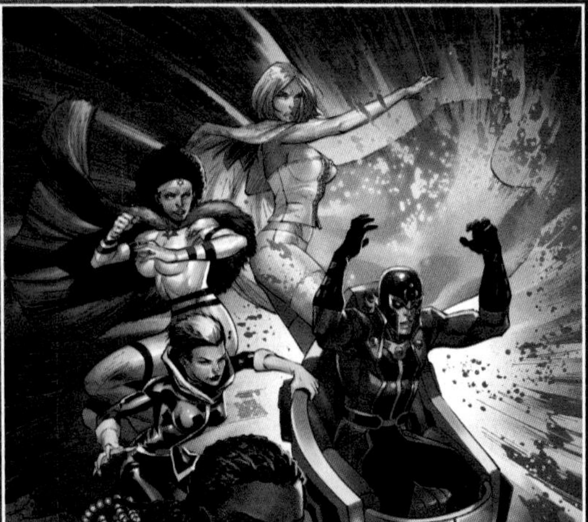

RYAN **BENJAMIN** & RAIN **BEREDO**

HEROES REBORN: MAGNETO & THE MUTANT FORCE Nº1 VARIANT

BERNARD CHANG & MARCELO MAIOLO
HEROES REBORN: MAGNETO & THE MUTANT FORCE Nº1
VARIANT

TAKASHI OKAZAKI & FELIPE SOBREIRO
HEROES REBORN: YOUNG SQUADRON Nº1 VARIANT

MARCELO FERREIRA & MORRY HOLLOWELL
HEROES REBORN: SIEGE SOCIETY Nº1 VARIANT